Luce Irigaray: Teaching

Also by Luce Irigaray and available from Continuum:

Democracy Begins Between Two
The Ethics of Sexual Difference
Luce Irigaray: Key Writings
Thinking the Difference
To Speak is Never Neutral
The Way of Love
Sharing the World
Conversations

Luce Irigaray: Teaching

Edited by Luce Irigaray with Mary Green

continuum

Continuum International Publishing Group
The Tower Building
11 York Road
London
SE1 7NX
www.continuumbooks.com

80 Maiden Lane,
Suite 704
New York
NY 10038

British Library Cataloguing-in-Publication Data
A catalogue record for this book is available from the British Library.

ISBN: HB: 1-8470-6067-6
          978-1-8470-6067-9

          PB: 1-8470-6068-4
          978-1-8470-6068-6

Library of Congress Cataloging-in-Publication Data
A catalog record for this book is available from the Library of Congress.

Typeset by BookEns Ltd, Royston, Herts.
Printed and bound in Great Britain by Cromwell Press Ltd, Trowbridge, Wiltshire.

To pay homage to each one
especially to Karen Burke

Contents

Introduction

Luce Irigaray

In 2004, the University of Nottingham offered me a post of special professor for three years, the first initiator of this offer being Professor Bernard McGuirk. I accepted with gratitude and proposed to take on this responsibility by holding an international seminar for people doing their PhD on my work. This suggestion was agreed to by the university. I thus began to organize such a seminar, that I continue to hold each year.

The framework of the seminar is this: fifteen researchers doing their PhD on my work stay a week on the campus of the university. The timetable includes a presentation by each one of the aspect of their PhD which most focuses on my work, the discussion of this presentation by the group, my own comments and answers to the questions asked by each one, and also sessions devoted to an explanation of some key-words or key-thoughts of my work chosen by the participants. During the period of the seminar, I give a public talk, which in some years takes place on the occasion of a conference on my work. The participants in the seminar pay their travel costs, but, at least until now, they receive hospitality from the universities at my own request. The seminar has been welcomed by the University of Nottingham during the first three years and by the University of Liverpool during the fourth year. It has been followed by a conference on my work, in June 2006 at the University of Nottingham and in June 2007 at the University of Liverpool.

This volume gathers together essays by the participants in the seminar at the University of Nottingham in May 2004, May 2005 and June 2006, and essays by Laine Harrington, Gillian Howie and Helen Fielding, who teach or pass on my thought through their texts, and who gave a talk during the conference *In All the World We Are Always Only Two*, which ends these seminars. The book also includes three talks that I gave during the seminar at the University of Nottingham and an 'Afterword' by Michael Worton who introduced the conference and with whom I am collaborating since a few years ago.

Why have I proposed to organize a seminar devoted to researchers who are doing their PhD on my work? There are different reasons. I was deprived of my post of teaching at the University of Vincennes (France) after the publication of *Speculum*, and although I kept my post of researcher at the Centre National de la Recherche Scientifique Française, I did not have the opportunity to teach my thinking. This represents a personal frustration but also causes harm to thought itself. This is passed on in a really incomplete and partial way and, in addition, I am seldom able to take advantage of questions asked by researchers. Nevertheless, it is not primarily for myself that I decided to hold the seminar. I have learned through my own experience that to pursue research in solitude is a difficult task, and I imagine that even today many people feel lonely when doing their PhD on my work. I thus want to provide them with some comfort and help, not only through my own presence and teaching but also by allowing them to meet other researchers doing their PhD on my work. Our times are really difficult, notably because of the lack or the poverty of human relationships. The seminar I hold is not only an opportunity for intellectual research, it is also a place where being with the other(s) plays an important part. I think that all the participants in the seminar have appreciated this aspect of the week spent together. Many of them remain in contact and continue to communicate somehow or other. My intention, while working on this book, was to maintain such relationships even though, for various reasons, the participants could not all have a part in the volume.

Whoever will glance through the book will understand another of my aims in organizing the seminar. Participants come from different regions of the world, they belong to different cultures, traditions and fields of research. The essays have been put together according to five domains: healing, art, the maternal order, spirituality and religion, philosophy. In each of these thematic parts, diverse domains, approaches and methods are represented. Furthermore the contributors come from different regions of the USA, from Canada, from Spain, from Southern Africa, from New Zealand, from Ireland and, of course, from various universities in the UK; in the seminar, people of other countries took part who do not figure in the book: Korea, Vietnam, Australia, Ceylon, Italy, Latvia, etc. If it is not the theme of the seminar, this is, however, a training course in multiculturalism for all, including myself. In a week, we receive instruction in ethnology, literature, spiritual traditions, art and wisdom of various peoples and cultures; we become more familiar with authors, creators or customs and therapies from Southern Africa, New Zealand, UK, Germany, Chile, France, China, Korea, USA, Italy, the Nordic countries ... Beyond all these teachings, we learn to live together, to respect one another and to share in difference: during the time devoted to the work, and during meals, walks, drinks in the bar, personal meetings. It is difficult to describe the atmosphere that results from all of that: it is intense, living and loving, fruitful and joyful, in spite of tiredness and minor problems coming from those who might not fully appreciate or understand the intention of the seminar and the opportunity that is offered to them.

Being and sharing together with respect to all our differences is not the least of my intentions in organizing the seminar. I consider this aspect as essential as intellectual teaching. My way of thinking does not go without a way of living. It is never only theoretical in a traditional sense: it presupposes a manner of dealing with oneself, with nature and the world, with the other and others, with thought and culture. People who come to the seminar only with the aim of becoming more competent, of accumulating knowledge, of receiving a certificate are not the best candidates, because they do not engage in the meeting with their whole presence and run the risk of both being disappointed and disappointing others. The ones who most benefit from the seminar are those who live it as an experience which concerns their whole being. These people succeed in writing their PhD, and further discover new possibilities and horizons in their own journey. I am really happy when I hear what positive change happens in the existence of a person who has participated in the seminar, beyond courage and joy in pursuing their research. I offer my availability for a sharing of knowledge, experiences, and also lives.

On the occasion of the publication of this book, I would like to thank again the University of Nottingham which welcomed my seminar during three years and the conference which ended it. I thank all the people who helped me to organize the seminar, the conference and the sojourn of the participants. I thank all those who participated in the seminar, especially the contributors to this volume, for their confidence and for their work. I feel a real gratitude towards Mary Green for her faithful collaboration in preparing the volume for publication. Hearty thanks also to Angelika Dickmann for her help to complete the book within the allotted time, and to the editorial staff of Continuum, especially to Sarah Campbell, for supporting this project on teaching.

November 2007

Part I

Healing Through Gaining Silence and Self-Affection

Chapter 1

Reborn from Silence and Touch: Gender Violence in Southern Africa

Jessica Murray

Universities of York, United Kingdom and Stellenbosch, South Africa

Rivers begin in the sky. Rivers begin with our tears. Grandmother's cry follows me everywhere. I touch my tongue. It is heavy like stone. I know nothing of rivers.
Grandmother is a river. I am not Grandmother . . . Grandmother is a river. The river is inside her body. The river is held in her mouth, held in her body. (Yvonne Vera, *Under the Tongue*, p. 2)

Searching for One's Own Voice

In her novel *Under the Tongue,* Yvonne Vera, a Zimbabwean author, tells the story of Zhizha, a young girl who has fallen silent after being raped by her father. It is my contention that Vera is creating a new discourse that is uniquely able to voice the female experience of gender violence. Her style of writing is particularly important as it facilitates an intimacy between Vera's characters and the readers who are confronted with the extent of the abuse suffered by the characters. Her style, indeed, prevents the alienation and distance that might result from the exposition of a mere litany of horrors. The strategies that Vera utilizes in her development of an alternative discourse are myriad. They include the deconstruction of traditional binary oppositions that pervade language; the incorporation of orality; the fusion of poetry and prose; a consistent focus on the space that a community of women can provide for healing; and the suggestion of a specifically female relationship with nature. This particular female interaction with nature helps to empower women instead of perpetuating the relegation of women to the subordinate sphere in the culture/nature binary, which justifies their secular denigration.

The theories of Luce Irigaray have been particularly enriching in reading Vera's subversion of conventional language. Vera's texts display a determination to liberate women from their confinement to the body while simultaneously refusing to disavow the female body. In this regard her work can be considered as bringing into play applications of the Irigarayan imperative to 'guard and keep our bodies and at the same time make them emerge from silence and subjugation' ('The Bodily Encounter with the Mother', in *The Irigaray Reader*, p. 42). Vera's reclamation of the power of the female body is signalled in her titular emphasis on the tongue and developed throughout the novel by Zhizha's negotiation with the materiality of her own body, as well as with the bodies of her grandmother and mother, as part of the process of healing.

Vera's writing meets with the problems inherent in voicing the female experience in a man-made language pervaded by masculine systems of representation and metaphors. Her attempt to subvert these systems aims to destabilize language and discourse as such, rather than substituting a female-centred discourse for a male-centred discourse. Thus she works towards a deconstruction of binary oppositions where one term is privileged at the expense of another. Irigaray's thought has been instrumental in my understanding of the way in which Vera uses language to bring about fundamental changes on both a social and symbolic level. Vera's texts can most fruitfully be read through the Irigarayan theoretical advice that encourages women to

> find, find anew, invent the words, the sentences that speak the most archaic and most contemporary relationship with the body of the mother, with our bodies, the sentences that translate the bond between her body, ours, and that of our daughters. (op. cit., p. 43)

Vera suggests that images of water and laughter can bring about such a reconnection with the body of the mother.

Remembrance of the Body: Water and Laughter

In *Under the Tongue*, Zhizha's trauma is compounded by the separation from her mother, after she was sent to prison for killing the husband who raped Zhizha, their daughter. Zhizha's reconnection with the body of the mother is thus mainly facilitated by her maternal grandmother. In Vera's creation of an alternative discourse, she places great emphasis both on the maternal body, represented in this novel by the body of the grandmother, and on water, in particular embodied in the river. In her discussion of the imagery utilized by female poets, Suskin Ostriker identifies water as one commonly used image. However, 'rather than supporting traditional interpretations of woman as desired and dreaded other', she says that these images are used in ways that 'resist [conventional] meanings and imply alternatives' (*Stealing the Language*, p. 108). Vera employs images such as those of nature and female bonding, but she hollows out their conventional, disempowering meanings to reappropriate them for women and, in their newness, they explode onto the pages of her prose.

The association between the grandmother and the river is repeated throughout the novel to striking effect. The river – which waits inside Grandmother 'to be remembered' – is posited as a healing space where Zhizha, who is at this moment unable to speak, will gain access to alternative forms of speaking

(*Under the Tongue*, p. 2). The river that Grandmother keeps within her also contains the 'forgotten songs' that she will teach Zhizha. These 'forgotten songs', which are associated with the maternal body, suggest a way of speaking that has been suppressed along with the female body, but which can be excavated and appropriated by women in their efforts to speak. This language lies in the grandmother's body and Zhizha can enter it because the 'body remembers' (Irigaray, *This Sex Which Is Not One*, p. 214).

Vera's concern with developing alternative ways of speaking for women is also evident in the manner through which Zhizha communicates with her grandmother. Although she does not speak, as her tongue 'is heavy like stone' (*Under the Tongue*, p. 3), she does laugh. Her silence, laughter and gestures allow her to speak, even after her 'cry [was] stolen' (ibid.) when her father raped her. When she touches her grandmother and when she 'rest[s] [her] face along her face' (op. cit., p. 2) she manages to laugh. It is significant that this mode of expressing herself takes place amidst repeated references to the river within her grandmother. The notion of fluidity, and the capacity of that fluidity to foster intimacy, is articulated by Irigaray in her seminal essay 'When our Lips Speak Together':

> How can I speak to you? You remain in flux, never congealing or solidifying. What will make that current flow into words? It is multiple, devoid of causes, meanings, simple qualities. Yet it cannot be decomposed. These movements cannot be described as the passage from a beginning to an end. These rivers flow into no single, definitive sea. These streams are without fixed banks, this body without fixed boundaries. (*This Sex Which Is Not One*, p. 215)

The rejection of 'hardness' and the 'love of fluidity' (ibid.) that Irigaray encourages are evident in both the style and the content of Vera's writing. The language that Vera uses offers an alternative to patriarchal discourse by celebrating a linguistic status which is 'open-ended, anarchic [and] irreducibly multiple' (Marianne DeKoven, *A Different Language*, p. xiii). There is, in other words, no attempt to force meaning into any 'single, definitive sea' (*This Sex Which Is Not One*, p. 215).

A good example of Vera's celebration of fluidity and multiplicity can be found in her treatment of the image of the river. The patriarchal tendency to equate the female with nature and to reserve culture as the domain of men is appropriated and subverted in a complex, multidimensional way. The grandmother is associated with the river. However, there is no simplistic veneration of nature as 'a comfort in a troubling world or the special province of women' (Carolyn Martin Shaw, 'Turning her back on the moon', *Africa Today*, 51:2, p. 39). This is clearly signalled in the novel by the assertion that 'rivers begin with our tears' (*Under the Tongue*, p. 2). In this passage, the river is connected with weeping, but it is also the place to which Zhizha needs to return in order to 'find her [grandmother] again' (ibid.) and thus have access to the female space where healing will take place. Here, 'nature reflects [the] world through its contradictions and antagonisms' (Martin Shaw, op. cit., p. 39). Instead of appropriating nature for the ideological support of a gendered viewpoint, Vera assents to a discourse in which, as Irigaray suggests, 'the use of words, silences, rhythms tends to disclose nature rather than control it' (*Everyday Prayers*, p. 30).

Although I argue in favour of Vera's acknowledgement of the impossibility of pinning nature down to some singular meaning, I register the fact that she does use a heavily metaphorized language to give voice to nature. When Vera states, for instance, that 'Grandmother is a river' (*Under the Tongue*, p. 2), she runs the risk of still falling into the trap of bifurcating experience into categories of sensible/mental or body/mind. I agree with Irigaray that, when telling nature, we can only do it justice when we accept that 'words will be all the more appropriate if they remain living matter, as nature itself. To speak about nature, it would be better to avoid metaphors and allegories which assimilate it to our world' (*Everyday Prayers*, p. 35). The difficulty of this challenge cannot be overestimated. While Vera's contribution to the development of a new way of speaking is important, much work and innovation are still needed because, as Irigaray puts it, 'we are still lacking words for this speaking in which we commune with nature: within us and outside us, enriching our being with everything it gives us to live through' (op. cit., p.36).

Once one acknowledges the need for a new way of speaking, Vera's reclamation of the power of silence becomes all the more important, for it is in stillness that the process of 'listening to what it [nature] really is' (op. cit., p. 35) can take place. In this regard, we must pay closer attention to Grandmother's statement that 'we cannot fear our silence, our desire, our release' (*Under the Tongue*, p. 2). Penny Ludicke emphasizes that Vera 'reverses the usual colonial legacy of silence which is imposed on the colonised and on women in particular, and allows the [...] Zimbabwean women to improvise a "speech" in order to communicate their experiences' ('Writing from the Inside-out, Reading from the Outside-in', in *Contemporary African Fiction*, p. 67). It is important to note that Vera does not do this by simply appropriating for women the speech that has so often been denied to them. Rather, she understands silence in a different way, so that it is no longer associated with disempowerment and voicelessness. Once again, I turn to Irigaray's words to explore the different dimensions that silence can have. She writes:

> initial, or gained, silence safeguards things and the other in their withdrawal – their integrity, their virginity. It lets them be before any monstration, any appearing: left to their will, their growth. The veil of mystery, which then shields them, shelters them in their innocence. It is different from that veil which re-covers them because of their submission [...] to a language that has always already veiled them. (*The Way of Love*, p. 32)

Reborn from Silence

Although Zhizha's silence is initially induced by trauma, it comes to give her a space where she can heal and find herself again. Thus, while Zhizha 'long[s] to defeat the silence' (*Under the Tongue*, p. 5), there is also a recognition that silence can serve positive ends. Grandmother is still dealing with the loss of her baby Tonderayi, and Zhizha reflects that she must 'keep [her own] silence to protect her [grandmother's] trembling voice and her shaking hands' (op. cit., p. 59). At different moments of the novel, which represent different stages in Zhizha's healing process, she longs to either defeat or maintain her silence. There is no sense of contradiction when Zhizha asserts that 'under the tongue is a healing silence' (op. cit., p. 41). The potential value of keeping silent and of speaking is acknowledged.

The rehabilitation of silence is a project that Vera has incorporated into her work from her first novel, *Nehanda*. In a scene depicting a group of women who are present at the birth of the eponymous character, Vatete is described as the 'most important of human presences in the room' and she is 'as silent as the shadow which climbed the wall behind her back' (*Nehanda*, p. 5). Vera offers no specific reason for Vatete's silence. In the next two paragraphs, she states, in two short emphatic sentences, that Vatete's 'arms were surprisingly strong' and that 'Vatete was highly respected' (op. cit., p. 6). The passage thus suggests that silence and strength can coexist. In this way, Vera offers her alternative to the traditional equation of silence and disempowerment. It is even possible for silence to reflect a more profound strength and understanding. George Steiner asserts that 'the truth needs no longer suffer the impurities and fragmentation that speech necessarily entails' (*Language and Silence*, p. 12).

In addition to recognizing the potential power of silence, Vera also leaves open the possibility that silence can constitute a way of speaking that does not involve words. A central part of Vera's work is what Irigaray refers to as:

> a search for gestures, including gestures in language – such as keeping silent, listening, praising, choosing words and syntax which favour dialogue, using living language, a language of touch – which would lead us to closeness while preserving the duality of subjects meeting together. (Part I, Philosophy, 'Introduction', in *Key Writings*, p. 6).

The development of such an alternative way of speaking is located by Vera within the space of a community of women. It is in this context that Zhizha states that she 'long[s] for the silence of mothers and grandmothers, their promises of a blissful remembrance' (*Under the Tongue*, p. 61). This silence, to be sure, does not signify a lack of communication. On the contrary, Zhizha notes that 'Grandmother looks closely at mother and her looking is her speaking of the things they understand between each other, which they speak and speak, in their silence' (op. cit., p. 30).

A great deal is thus 'said' even though there is 'not a word from Grandmother' (ibid.). These women also communicate through a 'language of touch' (Irigaray, Part I, Philosophy, 'Introduction', in *Key Writings*, p. 6). It is after 'Grandmother touches [Zhizha's] forehead with her tongue' that Zhizha is able to 'find the word Grandmother has given to [her]' (*Under the Tongue*, p. 53). Vera then utilizes the tongue's capacity for touch as much as its capacity for speech. This ability to communicate in alternative ways seems to flow from the female body and the connection between women's bodies that originates from the sharing of fluids in the womb. Grandmother's power to speak to her daughter and granddaughter through touch and silence is described by Vera as 'say[ing] the things women say when they have met each other in water' (op. cit., p. 30). Another crucial aspect of silence is that it allows for listening to take place. Zhizha repeats the phrase 'I listen' throughout the novel, and this enables these women to become unified in listening while also preserving a space in which they can hear nature speak, including themselves as nature, as Irigaray writes ('Before and Beyond Any Word', in *Key Writings*, p. 140).

A Healing Touch

In her novel *The Stone Virgins*, Vera offers examples of different types of touch and illustrates the capacity of the appropriative touch to destroy and of the reciprocal touch to heal. It is in the relationship between the sisters Nonceba and Thenjiwe that Vera most closely approximates Irigaray's notion of a 'touch that does not resolve itself into touched or toucher, and thereby eludes an appropriative grasp,' as Alexandra Winter writes ('Touching Skin', p. 6). Irigaray utilizes the image of two palms resting against one another to explain an alternative kind of touch:

> With no object or subject. With no passive or active, or even middle-passive. A sort of fourth mode? Neither active, nor passive, nor middle-passive. Always more passive than the passive. And nevertheless active. The hands joined, palms together, fingers outstretched, constitute a very particular touching. A gesture often reserved for women (at least in the West) and which evokes, doubles, the *touching of the lips* silently applied upon one another. A touching more intimate than that of one hand taking hold of the other. A phenomenology of the passage between the interior and exterior. (*An Ethics of Sexual Difference*, pp. 134–5; italics in original)

Vera's representation of the relationship between the sisters can most fruitfully be read in terms of this Irigarayan approach and, although Vera writes from an African context, her work reserves such a kind of touch for female relationships. Between the sisters, 'the gesture of the one who caresses has nothing to do with ensnarement, possession or submission of the freedom of the other' that Irigaray notes in the texts of male Western philosophers about sexual relations, especially about the caress (cf. *To Be Two*, p. 26). Nonceba is so much a part of Thenjiwe, that she feels as if her sister 'had already been holding her hand quietly and forever' (*The Stone Virgins*, p. 42). Since they have always been holding hands, there is no taking of the hand of the one by the other, and the quietness of the connection excludes any sense of grasping. There is no need for one to claim the other because, in their relationship, boundaries are at once dissolved and kept by love and intimacy. The 'caress between women is here represented as a mutual giving of and respect for borders, even as it dissimulates this boundary' (Winter, 'Touching Skin', p. 7). Although Thenjiwe recognizes that they are different, she regards 'her sister [as] nearer to her than her own shadow' (*The Stone Virgins*, p. 42). And while Cephas, her male partner, 'encircle[s]' her with his 'cool breath' (op. cit., p. 33), Nonceba's breath is 'her own breath flowing into her body' (op. cit., p. 42).

Vera seems to be postulating a specific kind of connection that exists among women and that renders hierarchies and boundaries irrelevant. Thenjiwe's description of her relationship with her sister 'Nonceba who, though different, is also she, Thenjiwe' (ibid.) most closely resembles Irigaray's notion of a caress that

> is an awakening to intersubjectivity, to a touching between us which is neither passive nor active; it is an awakening of gestures, of perceptions which are at the same time acts, intentions, emotions. This does not mean that they are ambiguous, but rather, that they are attentive to the person who touches and the one who is touched, to the two subjects who touch each other. (*To Be Two*, p. 25)

In Vera's other texts this particularly female relationship and non-appropriative way of touching the other also function as a healing act. In *Under the Tongue*, the hands of the father play a central role in Zhizha's rape:

> Father holds my breathing in his palm. His palm is wide and widening, grooved and wet. Then he lifts a heavy arm and touches the edge of the moon, in my sleep. I shout through fingers so strong, so hard, his fingers saying in their buried touch Zhizha . . . Zhizha. (*Under the Tongue*, p. 4)

These hard and heavy hands attempt to stifle Zhizha's cry during the rape. In the relationship with her mother and grandmother, however, Vera explores the capacity of the reciprocal touch to return Zhizha's voice to her. Zhizha, Grandmother and Runyararo experience a bond where their personal borders become so porous that their identities 'flow' into one another like a 'river' (op. cit., p. 82, p. 22). The following description reveals the gentleness and absence of appropriation in Grandmother's touch:

> Grandmother's song enters into my growing and finds parts of me hidden and alone, full of the forgotten things of the earth. She moves nearer to me and touches me with her shadow. The shadow falls from her mouth, falls from deep inside her dream. I am swallowed by the shadow which grows from Grandmother and bends deep into the earth, lifting me from the ground, raising me high. It is warm inside the shadow. It is warm like sleep. I meet the sky in that warm place and the sky is inside Grandmother and it is filled with voiceless stars. The stars fall like rain from Grandmother's waiting arms which fold slowly over my shoulders like something heavy, sorrowful. (op. cit., p. 41)

The shadow allows for the most subtle and gentle touching of the vulnerable child. The shadow, which is present only as an absence of light, challenges conventional notions of the toucher and the touched, and of active and passive, as it renders the one who touches as an ephemeral presence that is less present and less of a concrete subject than the one that is being touched. It is, in Irigaray's words, 'more passive than the passive. And nonetheless active' (*An Ethics of Sexual Difference*, p. 135). Or, to articulate it in a different way, the shadow is the epitome of absence. And yet it is present. This healing touch is reminiscent of Irigaray's description of being caressed by air in *To Be Two*: 'The air which touches: invisible presence. Love's return everywhere. In this infinite being touched, the wound vanishes. The first and last resource envelops me: clouds or angels, down or soft arms, smiles or words for children' (p. 2).

The Weaving of Women's Genealogy

Throughout Vera's work, great emphasis is placed on the fact that 'there is a genealogy of women within our family: on our mother's side we have mothers, grandmothers and great-grandmothers, and also daughters' ('The Bodily Encounter with the Mother', in *The Irigaray Reader*, p. 44). As depicted by Vera, women who have been violated all turn to mothers, grandmothers, daughters and sisters to heal. These relations with the mother do not, however, remain only in the realm of nature. It is important to underline this, because it is necessary to acknowledge the cultural dimension of our female genealogy to liberate the mother–daughter relation from being reduced to the depreciated status of being mere nature (Irigaray's teaching for students doing their PhD on her work at the University of Nottingham, seminar May 2005). Women must, according to Irigaray, 'struggle to obtain the recognition of a culture of their own, of a symbolic order in the feminine, of a respect not only for their physical but also their intellectual or spiritual status' (Part V, Politics, 'Introduction', in *Key Writings*, p. 197).

It is with these considerations in mind that I want to read the mat weaving of Zhizha's mother, Runyararo. Some critics, for example Jessica Hemmings, have tended to analyse Runyararo's creative work as an attempt to gain 'a sense of balance and control' in the face of the 'unevenness that will haunt the disrupted family unit' ('The Voice of Cloth', in *Sign and Taboo*, p. 58). While I do not dismiss such readings, I argue for a wider interpretation from Irigaray's perspective on the need to reclaim cultural achievements in the female genealogy. Although it is unlikely that Runyararo's mats impact on the greater historical scheme of things, they do represent a creative cultural activity that is valued and passed down among generations of women. When Runyararo's mats are mentioned, Vera emphasizes that, thanks to their weaving, Runyararo comes to occupy a status of creator of cultural artefacts. The process of creating mats evokes the skill and dedication that are needed for the creation of a work of art:

Her left arm waited patiently while her right hand caught the thread underneath her left arm, under the mat, and she pulled it to a tightness that spread over the entire length of her left arm, and she felt the stretching along her shoulder and held the thread tighter still so that her fingers pressed hard again along *the cloth she had created*. (*Under the Tongue*, p. 68; emphasis added)

Later in the novel, Runyararo refers to the mats as 'something precious' that 'she had created' (op. cit., p. 92). In the context of Vera's work, it is also important to note that the mother of Runyararo 'had taught her to sew mats' (op. cit., p. 68). By passing down the technique of mat weaving, these women can be seen to develop a strategy for connecting to a female genealogy that goes beyond a simple natural sharing with the mother. Even while Runyararo is in prison, the novel continues to assert her presence by describing her mat weaving. In a socio-cultural context that tries to destroy the power of the mother, in this case through imprisonment, the mat weaving serves as a reminder that women like Zhizha 'already have a history' ('The Bodily Encounter with the Mother', in *The Irigaray Reader*, p. 44). Irigaray stresses the need for us to 'try to situate ourselves within this female genealogy so as to conquer and keep our identity' (ibid.). Vera's work ensures that Zhizha's positioning in this genealogy takes place on both a natural and a cultural level. The first is facilitated through the connection between women's bodies that is represented by the river, and the second through the inter-generational cultural transmission of mat weaving skills.

Conclusion: The Meaning and Importance of Female Virginity

Vera's recovery of language and culture is of crucial importance if her ultimate goal is to stop perpetuating a society that permits the violation of women. It is necessary to realize that the literal, physical abuse of women is made possible by the symbolic and figurative oppression of the female, and that any attempt to eradicate the former without addressing the latter will be doomed to end in failure. This inextricably intertwined nature of real or literal and symbolic or figurative abuse is clearly acknowledged in Vera's writing on the incestuous rape of Zhizha. Irigaray's profound recognition of the ways in which material and symbolic abuse interact makes the use of her theory for reading Vera's work extremely illuminating. Irigaray's articulation of how this interaction operates in the case of incest is of particular importance here:

Men who do not respect women's genealogy, who consider children, and virgin girls in particular, to be their property are uncivil. Ethnologists theorize that this way of using girls is the basis of culture [...] This is symbolic incest, but real incest also exists, and to a much greater extent than is known. ('Civil Rights and Responsibilities for the Two Sexes', in *Key Writings*, p. 205)

Irigaray claims that 'the right to virginity should be part of girls' civil identity as a right to respect for their physical and moral integrity' (op. cit., p. 206). I am following Irigaray and using the term 'virginity' to refer to more than the physical intactness of the hymen; that is, as including the 'existence of a spiritual interiority' ('The Redemption of Women', in *Key Writings*, p. 152). When Zhizha initially stops speaking after the rape, she is displaying the silence of an abused child, which constitutes a paralysis of speaking rather than a real silence. As I hope to have shown in the foregoing discussion, her silence develops from this imposed paralysis to an active returning to her own interiority in order to heal. In a reclamation of herself and of her virginity, the touching of the two lips that is maintained by her silence becomes a healing activity to counter the pain that was caused by the enforced parting of the vaginal lips by the father. It is through this silence that she is able to cultivate the stillness that is needed to hear the rivers that connect her to the bodies of her mother and grandmother, and it is this connection that ultimately enables her to return home: to herself, within herself.

Chapter 2

Virginal Thresholds

Christine Labuski

University of Texas at Austin, USA

On a warm Sunday afternoon in mid-October of 2005, I received a phone call from Daphne. Daphne was a woman that I met the previous spring, during a year of ethnographic fieldwork among women with persistent genital pain. Women with this pain, labelled *vulvar vestibulitis syndrome* (VVS) by physicians and medical researchers, are usually unable to engage in sexual intercourse or to tolerate any kind of touch to the opening of their vagina (the *vulvar vestibule*). Daphne and I met at the clinic where I conducted my research, and we became particularly close. During the approximately six months that I worked with her, I attended the majority of her clinical appointments, which included a handful of consultations with her physician, and about fifteen sessions with a physical therapist that specialized in genital pain. In addition to these more formal events, Daphne and I stole moments for coffee or lunch and, on a few occasions, spent a few leisurely hours shopping together. All of these activities gave us the opportunity to get to know each other better; we often used them to explore the many facets of vulvar pain and female sexuality in which we were entangled, always mixing broad cultural insights with our own personal anecdotes. In October, I was finished with fieldwork and I was just beginning to write about Daphne and the other women that I met through the clinic. I was living in another part of the country and so, instead of inviting me out for coffee, Daphne was calling my cellphone with some very big news: over the weekend, she had engaged in painless intercourse with her boyfriend for the first time. And, although we giggled at the aspects of her experience that had been 'anticlimactic', there was no question that for Daphne, and for me, this was a celebratory phone call.

Significantly, Daphne's first painless intercourse was also her first intercourse of any kind – she was a virgin, in the anatomical sense, when we met that spring. Unlike many of the women that I met at the clinic, Daphne became aware of her vulvar pain before she attempted to engage in sexual intercourse. This earlier awareness is one piece of Daphne's story that distinguishes her from many other diagnosed women. The majority of women with symptoms of VVS 'discover' their pain during their initial attempt/s at sexual intercourse; their struggle to confront their pain is then compounded by a complex set of emotional reactions on the part of their husband or partner. Daphne, on the other hand, encountered her pain while she was engaged in an active emotional recovery from sexually abusive experiences in her past. This discovery, although unpleasant for Daphne, gave her an opportunity to understand and begin to heal from her pain outside of any investment in making intercourse more tolerable. In other words, she was able to confront her genitals in and of themselves, before and away from any connection that they would eventually have with the genitals of an other.

I would like to use this essay to explore Daphne's experience, and to discuss how and why it differs from that of so many other women in the United States, whether or not they suffer the symptoms of VVS. To do so, I will engage with Luce Irigaray's (re)conceptualization of virginity, and I will argue that Daphne's painless 'loss' of virginity was fundamentally enabled and informed by her cultivation of the kind of spiritual virginity that Irigaray describes. This virginity, which Irigaray suggests could 'correspond to a female becoming' ('The Redemption of Women', in *Key Writings*, p. 152), is most explicitly articulated in her later work, for example, *Key Writings* and *The Way of Love*. Careful attention to earlier writings, however, reveals that it is both a foundational component and a natural evolution of the theory of sexuate difference that she has developed over 35 years. Sexuate difference, according to Irigaray, must be accompanied by the recognition of an irreducible and horizontal transcendence of, and from, him or her who is other, and its existence 'calls for a different discourse, a different logic' (*The Way of Love*, p. 9). Theorizing this most fundamental of sexuate difference requires 'the constitution of [...] a place, always becoming, [...] for a relation between subjective and objective where the one could never assume nor integrate the other because the one and the other are two' (ibid.).

A full apprehension of sexuate difference is inextricably linked with a radical re-examination of the most intimate aspects of heterosexual relationships. Indeed, thinking this difference sometimes feels like the only productive place from which to analyse heterosexual dynamics in the United States, and/or the only theoretical space from which to develop meaningful interventions, both cultural and individual. This perspective, which I also describe as a radical heterosexuality, is strikingly useful in explaining the strategic choices of couples whose sexual activity is thwarted by the vulvar pain of VVS. The sexual repertoire of these couples is embedded within a masculinized sexuality, one that defines sex as vaginal penetration by a penis. For a variety of reasons – physiological, relational, and emotional – the pain of VVS makes this activity virtually impossible. Stripped of the ability to engage in what they perceive to be 'real' sex, couples are forced to alter their most basic understandings of what it is that men and women can physically do together. Behavioural changes, however, stem from an enormous range of coexisting organizing principles, and many of the couples that I met during my fieldwork adapted to their 'different' sexual situations without substantially altering the masculinist discourse(s) in which they were enmeshed. Indeed, what drove the search for treatment for many couples was nothing more than the desire to engage in the kind of sex that counts as real.

In Daphne's case, however, her desire for this culturally sanctioned sexuality was supplanted by her cultivation of a sexuality in the feminine. For her, this included an attention to her self, to the integrity of both her spirit and her flesh. Importantly, it also included the support of others. For Irigaray, this kind of shared self-care needs a '*virgin space*' ('Spiritual Tasks for Our Age', in *Key Writings*, p. 175; italics in original). As we will see, it is the development of this space that allows Daphne, at least partially, to transcend the masculinist sexualities that are available to her in the US, and to begin to engender a radical heterosexuality that is based in difference.

Returning to Herself

In the twenty-first century United States, under the influences of both Judaeo-Christian and scientific belief systems, the idea of virginity is first and foremost a material matter. In many places, a widespread use of menstrual tampons has displaced the vaginal hymen from its role of virginal arbiter, but the parameters of virginity are still defined by the act of penile–vaginal intercourse. Discursively, abstention from that act remains consonant with moral and physical purity. Developed countries like the United States do not attach political or legal ramifications to the loss of anatomical sexual purity, and many would argue that few religious or cultural sanctions exist. With an increasing presence of fundamentalist Christians in the US, however – a presence that is reflected at all three levels of government – virginity has (re)surfaced in popular and political discourses. This is particularly apparent in 'abstinence-based' school health curricula that teach teenagers to 'just say no' to sexual intercourse, rather than promoting the use of condoms to prevent both unintended pregnancies and the spread of sexually transmitted infections.

Varying levels of religious sanctions are used to convince young women who are taught from these curricula, or who attend Christian churches promoting the 'new' virginity, to remain sexually pure. 'Waiting', that is, for marriage, is symbolically linked with greater personal integrity and with the promise of a more wholesome and lasting love relationship. Confining sex to a legal marriage – and to procreation – also lays important political groundwork for Christian-informed efforts to limit contraception access, outlaw abortion, and ban gay marriages and adoptions. This promotion of physical chastity, however, leaves the body itself unexplored. Young women strive to be good (Christian) girls with their bodies, but are left to do so with a set of rules that absent their flesh and do little to 'safeguard their [...] integrity' (Irigaray, Part V, Politics, 'Introduction', in *Key Writings*, p. 197). Significantly, 'just say no' campaigns also use socio-biological explanations of sexual difference to fortify their efforts. Young women and men are taught that it is hormonally and neurologically natural for men to sexually pursue women, and equally so for women to be selective about bestowing their most precious gift. Not surprisingly, female desire is entirely absent from these discussions.

For Irigaray, the myth and preservation of anatomical virginity hold no such promise, religious or otherwise. In Chapter 10 of *Elemental Passions* – the 'fire' component of her elemental quaternary – she says:

> Exchange between men is sealed by the gift of a virgin. And the rite of breaking and entering, of raping and stealing the hymen, represents a denial of what was always already offered: exchange within women [...] But, without the prerequisite openness, without those lips, always leaving a passage from inside to outside, from outside to inside, and staying in between as well, the place of exchange would not be secure. It is the closed-open lips of the woman which make it practical for them. (p. 64)

Much of *Elemental Passions* – and of Irigaray's work in general – deals with the openness and fluidity of the female body, particularly as it opposes the firm and rigorous body of the male. 'What terrifies you?', Irigaray asks her imagined male interlocutor, to which she immediately suggests, 'That lack of closure' (op. cit., p. 71). This need for closure, she later suggests, is a pre-emptive strike that attempts to deny the very existence of the female. In a later essay, 'The Female Gender', she says of masculinized language forms: 'This must all be closed and complete. Perhaps so that the feminine cannot be added on?' (*Sexes and Genealogies*, p. 114). Like Irigaray's earlier works, *Elemental Passions* is a plea, an angry plea that will no longer tolerate a masculine-usurped heterosexuality. Irigaray analyses the sexual relationship(s) between men and women with words that are acutely personal in their conviction. With an honesty and a clarity that are often missing from more explicit accounts of contemporary heterosexual dynamics, Irigaray articulates the emotional and intellectual situation of a woman that is all-too-aware of what is sexually (im)possible in a masculinized world:

> Each time you separated me from myself, power flowed out of me. [...] Leaving myself far behind, I would espouse your penetration. [...] I had not begun to exist. I was nothing but your sheath, your other side, your inverse [...]. You filled me with your emptiness. You filled me up with your lacks. (*Elemental Passions*, pp. 60–1)

If these words strike a chord with the reader, if they hurt in their unblinking candour, it may be related to women's inability, thus far, to significantly disrupt this dynamic. The masculine-dominated sexual relationships in which many women not only find themselves, but are also often complicit, are a cultural product, a product of the discourses in which all of our daily practices and sexual behaviours are unquestioningly entrenched. Many feminists have suggested that heterosexuality in itself cannot escape this discursive ubiquity, and they argue that lesbian or non-committed relationships with men are the only ways that women can maintain political or spiritual autonomy in their sexual lives. Irigaray, however, insists that we take a different path. For her, women need to create feminine and female spaces that are in proximity to, although different from, those occupied by men.

Irigaray's use of the term 'proximity' is worth examining, because it consists of far more than a being-near. Proximity involves an approach towards, but this approach 'is possible only in the recognition of the irreducible difference between the one and the other' (Irigaray, *The Way of Love*, p. 153). As with virginity, this later concept of Irigaray's is both foundation and product of her thinking about sexuate difference, and the possibilities that this difference opens up for (heterosexual) relationships. 'To approach', she says, 'implies [...] becoming aware of the diversity of our worlds and creating paths which, with respect for this diversity, allow holding dialogues' (op. cit., p. 68). For Irigaray, then, neither separatism nor enmeshment are the answer. Rather, proximity is dependent on the existence of a separate and feminine space, one that is irreducible to that of men. Our hopes for a sexual integrity can therefore be fuelled by returning to, and engendering, a world in the feminine.

Irigaray suggests that this return is, at least in part, a practice that can be socially cultivated. 'In our tradition', she says,

> women perhaps miss the experience of discovering and living our initiation into sexuality *together* [...] For women, th[e] initiation into sexuality is a solitary event, even when it is observed. [...] Women [...] rarely initiate one another into their developing roles as women [...] Of their sexual needs and desires they speak almost not at all. [...] Women exchange bits and pieces of games that have already been played. They rarely invent new games, games *of their own*. (*Sexes and Genealogies*, pp. 180–1; italics in original)

Recuperating Virginity

In the spring of 2005, Daphne *was inventing a game of her own*, and it was based on one fundamental and unbending rule: she was a 26-year-old survivor of childhood sexual abuse and she wanted to heal her damaged relationship with her genitals and her sexuality. Daphne was still a virgin at this time, and she told me, in a subsequent interview, about some of the negative associations with sex that came from her religious background. She had, however, psychologically coped with many of these, and had a relationship with her virginity characterized more by 'just not yet', than by 'just say no'. It is this 'not yet' that makes it possible to analyse Daphne's decision using Irigaray's thought about virginity, because Daphne's 'not yet' took full account of her flesh and its sexual desires – it was not a question of abstention as a set of behaviours, what Irigaray calls 'secular alienation or privations' in her essay 'The Redemption of Women' (*Key Writings*, p. 163). In other words, instead of holding back from something, that is, sexual intercourse, Daphne held herself in place. As she committed herself to recovering from sexual abuse – through psychotherapy, journaling, bodywork and reconfigured relationships with her family – Daphne continually returned to herself and to her own self-care measures. Her choice to wait, and her relationship to this choice, flowed from her ability to be with and for

herself first. Indeed, she had already ended more than one relationship with
a man that could not accept her decision. In recalling Irigaray's lament from
Elemental Passions (pp. 7–8), we can see that Daphne was engaged in a struggle
to exist, unwilling to espouse the penetration of the other until she could be
sure that she would not leave herself behind.

Like many other women with vulvar pain, Daphne had a tremendous opportunity to be with herself during genital physical therapy sessions. This experience was key in developing the spiritual virginity under consideration here.
Physical therapy, in the case of VVS, is intended to provide the patient with a
better understanding of, and greater control over, the pelvic floor and its mus-
culature. Vestibular pain is almost always superficial, that is, at the level of the
skin, but it eventually becomes deeper as the muscles become involved. With
the approach of a potentially painful stimulant – a tampon, a penis, or a gynaecological instrument – women with VVS learn to 'pull in' their vaginal and pelvic floor muscles, not unlike the action that an animal with a tail makes when
it is afraid or ashamed, using muscular strength in the service of physical and
emotional protection. Ultimately, however, this strategy proves maladaptive, as
the once superficial, acute and localized vestibular pain becomes one that is
deep, diffuse and lingering in the large muscles of the pelvic floor. Physical
therapy, done by a trained and empathetic provider, teaches a woman with
VVS, and the consequent pelvic floor *myalgia*, to both undo, and to gain greater
control over, this compensatory pain.

Daphne's physical therapist understood pelvic floor pain in the context of
a body and a life out of balance. Her treatment approach encompassed long-
term restorative practices, such as proper breathing and emotional resilience,
and it did not dwell on the still poorly understood medical explanation(s) for
VVS. Her goals for Daphne, then, were specific enough to help her vaginal
muscles, but broad enough to include her general coping skills and life orientation. In describing her use of biofeedback, the therapist told Daphne, 'We're
going to look at how you *do life*. That's what biofeedback means.' In these sessions, which began – always began – with the breath, Daphne was encouraged
to explore what she was made of and to play with how to use it. Although the
technical goal was for her to painlessly tolerate vestibular touch and vaginal
penetration, her therapy ultimately provided her with much more. Through
working with her breath at almost every session, Daphne learned to cultivate
a reservoir of strength and stability to which she could return again and again.
In later sessions, Daphne described using her breathing techniques to emotionally stabilize herself in a wide variety of situations, and it became easier for
her to imagine that this could eventually include a sexual one. It was in these
moments, when she understood that her sexual experiences could, at least partially, be controlled by *herself* and her non-genital body – her diaphragmatic
breath, for example – that Daphne began to craft new sexual 'moves', moves
that Irigaray suggests 'have still to be invented' by most women (*Sexes and
Genealogies*, p. 179).

Irigaray describes an experience such as Daphne's in terms of fidelity to, and
affection towards, oneself. She explicitly links such 'auto-affection' with the

capability for a woman to reach a virginity of her own, and which corresponds to an aspect of female transcendence. In her essay 'The Age of the Breath', in *Key Writings*, she says:

> To remain faithful to herself, to turn back to herself, within herself, to be born again free, animated by her own breath, her own words, her own gestures, this corresponds to the most decisive conquest for women. And to speak of woman's liberation, women's liberation, without such a course, such autonomy, is not possible. (p. 166)

Importantly, this turning back to herself is not only a solitary endeavour. In 'A Future Horizon for Art?', Irigaray revisits the issue of women's sociality and writes that 'the paradigm of their *She*', that is, 'the place where they reach and sustain their transcendence' could result from 'affirming the value of virginity for themselves and between women, in particular between mother and daughter' (*Key Writings*, p. 108; italics in original). In my mind, this place of *She* marks the uniqueness of Irigaray's vision, because *She* allows for the simultaneity of self-affection and a being with the other. For Irigaray, it is the couple – that is, a relationship between two differently sexuate identities – that 'represents the basic social unit' (*Sexes and Genealogies*, p. 153); other women, therefore, occupy a space that is not the same as that of the other man. A woman's return and fidelity to herself includes – but is not defined by – a return to these other women.

In the treatment room, this place of *She* was continuously secured as the therapist and I both bore witness and helped to engender Daphne's own becoming. It was explicitly present on the day that Daphne chose to insert her own finger into her vagina for the first time, finally confronting the place in her that allows for both openness and closure, the place that 'goes on touching itself indefinitely, from the inside' (*Elemental Passions*, p. 15). The therapist and I asked if we should step out; Daphne replied that she needed us there, 'emotionally'. I argue that in this instance, not only did we collectively usher in a part of Daphne's sexual becoming, or initiation, but that the therapist and I contributed to her having access to virgin space as well. In Irigaray's terms, in 'affirming the value of [this] virginity [...] between women', we came to 'the paradigm of [our] *She*, the place where [we would] reach and sustain [our] transcendence' ('A Future Horizon for Art?', in *Key Writings*, p. 108; italics in original).

Daphne's touching of herself in this instance cannot be underestimated. When Daphne came to the physician's office for the first time, she narrated a knowledge of her genital body that was both alien and intimately traumatized: 'I'm not used to how it feels to be touched there. I haven't done much at all. Since the abuse. Even myself. I couldn't even look for a long time. *Until I had to.*' Daphne 'had to', in her understanding, get used to how it felt to touch herself when she decided to investigate the source of her pain. She did not identify a need, or an ability, to do so until she perceived that something was amiss, that something was wrong with her body. Initially, Daphne touched her vulva only to facilitate a better visual examination – her external genitalia had become red-dened, a normal consequence of VVS, and she looked at herself with a mirror several times a day in order to monitor this skin change. During her first few medical evaluations, her physician and I were both somewhat concerned about these self-examinations, in that they seemed to reiterate a dis-eased relation-ship with the mirror. This was complicated, however, by our respective experi-ences with feminism and the feminist health movement that emerged in the US during the late 1960s. Women in this movement located power in the mirror and in genital self-visualization, and they reclaimed both as productive tools with which to confront the male-dominated institution of gynaecological medi-cine. Influenced by this movement, Daphne's physician and I could together attest to how the regular use of a mirror could substantially increase a woman's physical comfort with her genital body. Nonetheless, our unease existed, and we struggled with how we could support Daphne's genital awareness yet steer her away from a purely pathologized relationship to her (symptomatic) vulva.

In her essay 'Divine women', Irigaray eloquently describes some of the seeds of our discomfort, by reminding us of the cultural context in which women live with their reflected image. 'The mirror', after all,

> almost always serves to reduce us to a pure exteriority [...] We look at our-selves in the mirror to *please someone*, rarely to interrogate the state of our body or our spirit, rarely for ourselves and in search of our own becoming. [...] the mirror is a frozen – and polemical – weapon to keep us apart. (*Sexes and Genealogies*, p. 65; italics in original)

When I met Daphne in the spring of 2005, her use of the mirror ran the risks to which Irigaray alludes. The vulvar awareness that she brought to her first clinic visit – applauded by her physician and I in the abstract – was nevertheless created and sustained in a state of exteriority that wanted for deeper bodily integration. I suggest that this exteriority was all that was available to Daphne at this stage of her becoming, however. Until she came to the clinic, Daphne was coping with her symptoms alone; looking at her labia offered her some sense of control over a body that had suddenly become chaotic. Additionally, Daphne's experiences of sexual abuse had significantly disrupted her relationship with her genitals – she had not wanted to visually (re)encounter the site from which earlier sexual expectations had been so selfishly stolen.

The feminist health movement also influenced Daphne's physical therapist, in that she, too, supplied a mirror to interested patients. Indeed, Daphne's even-tual self-penetration with her finger was done with the guidance of a mirror. I hint, however, that a distinct mechanism had come into place since Daphne's first visit with her physician, and in regards to her self-examination. That is, in using a mirror to guide her finger's own penetration, Daphne extended her genital integration beyond the visual. Because of this, her relationship to her vulva was no longer constituted by image alone; in fact it was now the touching that guided the looking, instead of the other way around. Irigaray's analysis of the link between the visual and the tactile, as articulated in *Elemental Passions*, makes room for this very possibility. In her view, looking is engendered by the act of self-touch: 'If I can make contact with myself in the touching myself again and again of my night then I can bear my body being visible as well' (*Elemental Passions*, p. 44). Done for herself, and in 'a relation of dialogue with [her] own gender' ('The Redemption of Women', in *Key Writings*, p. 153), Daphne's self-penetration both initiates and reveals a virginity that is always available to her. Discovered by her, it is a part of her sexuality that can neither be taken away by, nor given to, an other or Other.

Fulfilling Her Humanity

Not long after I met Daphne, in May of 2005 to be precise, I met Luce Irigaray. I was fortunate to participate in a week-long seminar with twelve other graduate students, all of whom were using Irigaray's work in their dissertations – an engagement with her work at PhD level was the main criterion for inclusion in the seminar. It is impossible to convey with writing what took place between us that week, although we struggled to do so while we were there, as it felt that important. In coming together during the seminar, taking meals afterwards in the dining hall, walking the grounds of the University of Nottingham, and even drinking a little beer and wine in the pubs of our respective dormitories, we developed an intimacy with both Luce and her work, a working familiarity that could never come from texts alone, not even with the closest of readings, nor the most sophisticated analyses. Some of us came to the seminar with a limited purview of her written work; I, for example, was familiar only with *Speculum* and *This Sex Which Is Not One*. Prior to and during our meetings, Luce prevailed upon us to read her work more broadly, explaining that we came dangerously close to misrepresenting her if we did not do so. In May, I intellectually understood and agreed with her point. Six months later, I have had the pleasure of more fully engaging with the texts discussed in this essay and, although I remain committed to and profoundly moved by the crystalline fury of her first two seminal texts, I can say with certainty that they do not adequately represent the full theoretical importance of Luce Irigaray.

I chose to examine the concept of virginity for this essay because it best illuminates the progression in my own thinking since my trip to Nottingham. Virginity was on my mind during my fieldwork at the vulvar clinic, since all of the patients that I met with VVS told me that they had delayed the practice of penetrative intercourse until they were married. This was a striking and surprising reality to me; I practised as a gynaecological clinician in the field of women's health care for almost twenty years, and had not previously encountered this intriguing group of patients. My analysis of virginity, however, had stopped at its anatomical definition, at the holding *back* that I describe on page 17. It was during the seminar that I came to appreciate the holding *in* aspects of Irigaray's interpretation of virginity. This conceptual shift provided me with a new set of trajectories through which to analyse the patients that I continued to encounter throughout the summer. This essay could not have been written without that shift.

Most memorable to me was the afternoon when Luce Irigaray described the relation between virginity and the sacred syllable *om*. This resonant sound is sometimes uttered at the beginning of a yoga or meditation practice in order to collectively reach an intentional union with the divine. When uttered, the sound *om* gradually moves the lips from an open to a closed position. Their closing in this instance signifies that which remains interior, mysterious, 'and not yet manifested' (*Sexes and Genealogies*, pp. 100–1), that which somehow would correspond to an 'indeterminate absolute that determines us none-theless' ('Spiritual Tasks for Our Age', in *Key Writings*, p. 172). In the case of female sexuality, we could recall women's two sets of contiguous lips, and also relate this linguistic pronunciation *om* to a genital real. Such a parallel allows us to imagine Daphne's 'just not yet' as an intentional preservation of a divine mystery. More importantly, it allows us to imagine that this preservation can be maintained during sexual intercourse with a male other.

Indeed, it is also in relationship(s) that Irigaray explicitly imagines the culti-vation of virginity:

> Keeping one's virginity means not losing oneself in the attraction for the other, nor letting oneself be ruled by the other [...] It is to give oneself a feminine mind or soul, an internal dwelling, which is not only physical but also spiritual: linked to breath, to speech, to the mind. ('The Redemption of Women', in *Key Writings*, p. 161)

Daphne, as I have demonstrated, came to inhabit the figure of Luce Irigaray's virgin, and she did so through these very channels – her breath, her speech and her mind. How she preserved *this* virginity, even when she engaged in the kind of sexual intercourse that ultimately disrupted her vaginal hymen, is the crux of what I have put forth in this essay. This is largely because, in the context of *vulvar vestibulitis syndrome* (VVS), Daphne's pain-free sexual experience is noth-ing short of miraculous. This pain is so poorly understood by mainstream medi-cine that women who suffer its symptoms must often chart their own courses of health and well-being. However, masculinized medical science pervades our cultural discourse to such an extent that few women find 'cures' that are not somehow dependent upon its technologies. At present, these include surgery, topical anaesthetics, and pharmaceuticals, none of which are completely alle-viating. Daphne's virgin-space, initiated in her desire to heal from a sexually abusive past, and sustained in a therapeutic dialogue within the horizon of a *She*, gave her a resilience that remains independent of technology and any male other. I suggest that Daphne 'lost' her (anatomical) virginity without pain because she both became and stayed a virgin.

Daphne's next developmental tasks will involve preservation and differen-tiation. Having transcended the externally imposed, and physiologically limit-ing, definitions of her sexual status, Daphne has become again divine in her virginity. Irigaray, however, cautions that 'woman is divine from birth. But to remain divine, she must preserve her autonomy and virginity [...] and preserve her integrity [...] [by] protecting her own interiority' (Part IV, Spirituality and

Religion, 'Introduction', in *Key Writings*, pp. 146–7). Consonant with an understanding of the two, the work towards our becoming divine must also be done in relating with the other. Autonomy and interiority would reside between and behind the closed lips of the *om*, present and lingering during an intentional union with the other. The *om*, as a spiritual invocation, meets the other in the manner in which Irigaray encourages women to extend their welcome(s). Uttered collectively, the *om* means the importance of a universal belonging. But yoga practice does not stop at this utterance: each person returns to their own body, regulating and being responsible for their own postures and their own breath. Each practitioner, collectively cloaked in an *om* which transcends its particularity, remains differentiated from the group. Irigaray, in *The Way of Love*, describes this as a 'singularity', and suggests that its cultivation

> requires an attention to each moment in order to distinguish what belongs to one's birth, growth, consciousness, and what belongs to the world [...] in which the subject lives. [...] to merge into a universal described as 'human' is often preferred to stopping to analyze the difference between oneself and the other. (pp. 119–20)

I end with this quotation from *The Way of Love* because it invokes the most recent of Irigaray's theoretical threads. The final essay in the Spirituality and Religion section of her *Key Writings* is entitled 'Fulfilling Our Humanity'. On the first page, Irigaray says:

> To pursue human becoming to its divine fulfillment, such seems the spiritual task most adapted to our age. Not simply to submit to already-established truths, dogmas, and rites, but to search for the way of a human flourishing still to come. (p. 186)

On the Saturday when our seminar ended, participants sat and talked with each other in between goodbyes to departing friends and individual meetings with Luce Irigaray. It was a difficult day, because we knew that we could not take our 'culture in the feminine' back to our respective homes. As I said earlier, when I came to Nottingham, I was most familiar with the work of a younger and angrier writer. As I have also said, I continue to be moved by the words of this writer, as I believe that they still hold enormous relevance in the contemporary US. With a more fully informed approach to the rest of Irigaray's work, facilitated by our seminar conversations, I perceive a wider horizon than I had before, one that includes the whole of humanity. In speaking to the spiritual needs and tasks for all of us, for 'our age', Luce Irigaray is not leaving her quest for the acknowledgement of sexuate difference behind. Rather, she is taking its theoretical and practical significance – that of an acknowledgement of the irreducible differences between us – through another natural progression. In so doing, Luce Irigaray is helping us to imagine a new world.

Chapter 3

'The Power to Love Without Desiring to Possess': Feminine Becoming Through Silence in the Texts of Antonia White

Sherah Wells

University of Warwick, United Kingdom

> Difference, alone, allows intimacy.
> To kiss you, there is the threshold of the shared:
> Pure proximity
> That nothing brings under control.
> Touch that is strange to something other than itself.
> Ecstasy from the time
> To be built again after such an opening
> Where I arrive at you,
> Finding and losing myself
> In this inappropriable
> Nearness,
> As much birth as mourning.
> Access to the other
> Who I shall never be,
> Who will never be me.
>
> (Luce Irigaray, *Everyday Prayers*, 28 October, p. 74)

Introduction: Preparing a Place of Proximity

On 6 October 1935, Antonia White wrote the following prayer in her diary: 'If I prayed today . . . I would say . . . Take away from me the desire to be loved and admired and give me instead the power to love without desiring to possess' (*Antonia White: Diaries 1926–1957*, p. 59).[1] At this point in her life, White, aged 36, had already suffered a severe mental breakdown and was fast approaching the precipice of another. She was married to her third husband, had two children, and three years earlier had published what was to be her most famous novel, *Frost in May*. For the remaining 45 years of her life, White subjected herself to a continuous self-analysis which she painstakingly recorded in three more novels, short stories, 40 notebooks comprising her diaries, and an unfinished autobiography. In these texts, White most often concerned herself with constructing and confirming her own subjectivity. In my opinion, White's fiction and non-fiction must be read in conjunction. Each text, from the very small number of 'purely' fictional passages in her novels to the most introspective moments in her diaries calls into question the very nature of fiction, but it is only by reading the *œuvre* as a whole that White's internal struggle becomes apparent.

At times for White, existence itself appeared to be an illusory concept, and her only method for confirming it was to write herself into existence. As an adult she wrote most freely in her diaries, filling notebooks when she was unable to complete a chapter of her novels. She writes on 27 August 1938 that 'They [her diaries] are still a sign of distrust of myself: I look at them when I feel confused or lose my sense of identity. They are like a photograph of myself to which I refer' (*Diaries 1926–1957*, p. 149). Each of the protagonists White created were interpretations of herself. She was christened Eirene Botting but adopted the name and, arguably, assumed the identity of Antonia White with her first published text. The protagonists of White's texts are also arguably constructions of herself. They are called Nanda Grey, Clara Batchelor, and Julian Tye.

On 6 January 1935, when pondering the novel which is to follow *Frost in May*, White says 'I am sick to death of E[irene] and her convent education' (op. cit., p. 35). White's discussion of herself from what one might call an external viewpoint illustrates the many layers of her subjectivity which lend themselves well to a study of the construction of subjectivity and the boundaries of the psyche. Of course, the scope of this article and the scholarship of its author do not allow for a psychoanalytic or medical diagnosis of White's particular psychosis. The statement White herself makes on 6 October 1935 may provide a clue to the cultural implications of her psychosis and the way in which it calls into question the credibility of autobiographical fiction if it is read in the context of the work of Luce Irigaray.

Psychosis occurs when the boundaries which delineate the subjectivity of an individual are overwhelmed, and they dissolve. White expresses her fear of this dissolution through her desire to engage in non-possessive relationships. Written seventy years ago, White's prayer makes a direct appeal to the contemporary philosophy of Irigaray. This philosophy exposes the false nature of intimacy in Western culture when one subject is appropriated by another subject, and intimacy then falls into sameness. Irigaray's philosophy and poetry sustain that 'Difference, alone, allows intimacy' (*Everyday Prayers*, p. 74), and, therefore, difference must be preserved in a relationship so that two subjects, the feminine and the masculine, may exist. White, like many women in the first half of the twentieth century, often perceived herself as an object to be loved and admired. If she positioned herself as a loving subject, her desire was to consume or possess that which she loved. As one who was loved, she allowed herself to be consumed. According to Irigaray, though, both of these positions are masculine and result in the elimination of the feminine subject.

Conventional models of the self in Western culture subscribe to Freudian theories of subjectivity which state that woman only exists starting from the lack or absence of male sexuate values (Freud, 'Femininity', in *New Introductory Lectures in Psychoanalysis*, pp. 145–69). This 'economy of the same', according to Irigaray, results in the existence of only one subject, the masculine subject (*This Sex Which Is Not One*, p. 74). While Irigaray's early work critically responds to Freud's theories on female sexuality (cf., for example, *The Irigaray Reader*), her more recent work focuses on outlining a path for constructing a culture of two subjects. In her proposed culture of two subjects, love cannot arouse a desire to possess the other or to make the other the same as oneself. The other is to be respected whether it exists internally or as an external subject. This conception of love is an integral part of my study of White's work: it is her struggle with internal and external others and the struggle to establish the boundaries of her subjectivity that she narrates in her work.

In the world of two subjects, the most basic social unit is not an individual subject, but a relation between two subjects, between whom an irreducible dif-ference remains.[2] This difference creates and maintains a space between the two subjects that cannot be collapsed into sameness, allowing for an intimacy that only exists when each subject recognizes and respects that irreducible dif-ference (Irigaray, *Between East and West*, p. 129; and 'Towards a Divine in the Feminine'). 'The way of love' to which I allude, as Irigaray describes it in her book of the same name, involves the continuous traversing by two subjects of this irreducible difference between them. She claims that 'To approach the other, for two different subjects, does not mean to live in the neighborhood of one another [...] To approach implies rather becoming aware of the diversity of our worlds and creating paths which with respect for this diversity, allow hold-ing dialogues' (*The Way of Love*, p. 68). In this way Irigaray reconstructs bounda-ries of intimacy which presuppose a space between the two subjects. Intimacy then partly amounts to the journey between two subjects who will never occupy precisely the same space. This sort of intimacy or proximity between two sub-jects ensures that one will never appropriate the other.[3]

What White's work shows is that without the inappropriable space between two different subjects, which guarantees proximity and intimacy, one subject can be transformed into an object, thereby obliterating its subjectivity, as could also hap-pen in the fusion between two subjects. Psychosis, as it is depicted in White's litera-ture, can result from this. In order to stave off psychosis, female subjectivity requires the realization of a becoming of her own. Before woman may enter into a relation-ship with a sexually different subject, she must take charge of her own becoming, a process which involves the cultivation of interiority through a return to the self. Once this interiority has begun to be established, only then is it possible to aim towards a full feminine becoming. There are many ways to accomplish this. White's work lends itself well to a study of this nature because through her texts it is possi-ble to find the initial germs of a 'feminine becoming', which are then stamped out by patriarchal culture. I have chosen to explore silence as a place and guarantee of the 'not yet manifest' in feminine becoming (Irigaray, 'Towards a Divine in the Feminine'), and as it ought to exist in the inappropriable space between two sub-jects in the texts of Antonia White, in which silence is a prominent theme. These texts can help to illustrate the importance of silence in feminine becoming.

The Space Where Silence Takes Place: White's Struggle to Define Her Subjectivity

Silence.[4] When it is analysed within the 'economy of the same', it is often considered as a weapon of oppression, imposed upon the weak. Perhaps for this reason, contemporary feminists, wishing to express themselves and assert their power as individuals, feel they must speak in order to establish their subjectivity. For them, to be silent is to acquiesce, to submit to the confines of patriarchy. Then, man and woman engage in a constant struggle, each hoping that his or her voice will be heard above the other, resulting ultimately in the conquest or appropriation of one voice. Such a need to speak at the expense of another individual does not open the path to a culture of two subjects, according to Irigaray. Instead, the culture corresponding to one subject is often defined by 'appropriation' in both 'our manner of reasoning, our manner of loving' (Irigaray, Part I, Philosophy, 'Introduction', in *Key Writings*, p. 5). It is in this culture that feminism fears silence as a 'paralysis of speech' (Irigaray, in seminar, May 2005). If, however, as Irigaray suggests, 'the other's flesh is enjoyed as the discovery of an intimacy more intimate to one than oneself, as a mystery that invites each one to dwell, without dissolving, in order to keep both the other and oneself', then silence is not paralysing but necessary for maintaining the distance between oneself and the other (*Everyday Prayers*, p. 39). Silence in this case is not the absence of a voice; it is the possibility of a speech which makes communication possible. This in-finite moment of possibility may be likened to the continuous journey in approaching the other in Irigaray's 'way of love'.

In *I Love to You*, Irigaray develops the notion of silence as a space which allows sharing between two subjects. Not only must this space be irreducible, it must also be unknowable. The potential must rest in its unknowable nature, the 'not yet manifest', so that as Irigaray states, 'No longer is it a matter of listening to a message in terms of a content that has already been coded by society or language' (*I Love to You*, p. 116). Silence then exists as the space between two subjects which is necessary both for love and for becoming. In *To Be Two*, this silence is revealed to be, according to Irigaray, the basis for love. She states that 'to love each other between us, woman and man, women and men, requires the protection of a space, a place of silence' (*To Be Two*, p. 62). If this space is not maintained, as is demonstrated in White's texts, what results is not love but madness.

As White's fiction and diaries attest, the fear of losing her identity existed in almost every relationship into which she entered. In order to understand her attempts to construct her subjectivity and cultivate her interiority, it is important to note the way in which White's identity was formed in relation to other subjects in her texts. This article will examine two heterosexual relationships portrayed by White in her texts. The first, with Clive Heron, may be described as an intersubjective relationship, in the Irigarayan sense, which encourages Clara's feminine becoming. The second, between Clara and Richard Crayshaw, facilitates the dissolution of Clara's interiority which initiates her psychosis.

Clive Heron appears as Clara's second husband in *The Sugar House* (1952), *Beyond the Glass* (1954), and White's unfinished works 'Clara IV' and 'Julian

Tye'.[5] It is possible to interpret Clara and Clive's relationship as a representation of the non-possessive exchange for which White longs. Julian, an older version of Clara, and Clive are praised for being the 'perfect example of a modern marriage', and Julian says 'Their life together was a kind of art: it involved suppressions and exclusions but it had its reward for Julian in an extraordinary delight that she knew she would never find with any other human being' (*As Once in May*, p. 92). These 'suppressions and exclusions' may be interpreted as an attempt to maintain the irreducible difference which Irigaray claims is necessary for a relationship between two subjects.

In *Beyond the Glass*, prior to their marriage, Clive lectures Clara on the dangers of owning objects. He says: 'Once you own things you're a slave to them' (p. 90). This theory is applied to his and Clara's marriage as White depicts it in 'Clara IV' and 'Julian Tye'.[6] Isabel Batchelor, Clara's mother, notices that their marriage is different to typical patriarchal marriages. As the wife of a devout Catholic, Isabel 'secretly envied Clara for being so wonderfully free, for having all the advantages of marriage and none of the disadvantages, [but] she sometimes wondered how any husband, as obviously devoted as Clive, could be so-so *unpossessive*' (*As Once in May*, p. 26; emphasis in original). Clive and Clara respect each other's differences and maintain a distance between their individual subjectivities, even though they are married. Their marriage challenges the traditional narrative of the romance plot in which characters merge their subjectivities. Because of this, Clara depends on Clive to draw her away from her insanity, unlike her relationship with Richard Crayshaw, which seems to facilitate her psychosis.

Richard's love poses the greatest threat to Clara's subjectivity because she happily fuses her identity with his and allows herself to be appropriated by him. The scene in which Clara and Richard meet aptly illustrates this process of fusion and appropriation. Clara and Clive attend a party hosted by Richard's sister, Nell Crayshaw. Richard plays a 'game' with Clara in which he launches an attack on her consciousness:

> She felt that someone was trying to attract her attention. [...] She did her best to ignore this plucking at her attention but it continued with a gentle, teasing persistence. [...] She spoke silently to the unseen intruder: 'Stop it. I don't *want* to be disturbed.' It was almost as if she heard the reply. 'I know you don't. All right. See if you *can* stop me.' [...] 'You may as well give in. My will's stronger than yours.' (*Beyond the Glass*, p. 127; italics in original)

Richard injects himself into Clara's mind without her consent, although she takes up his game of telepathy readily enough. They never make plans to meet. Instead, he wills her to the correct destination at the appropriate time (op. cit., p. 142).

This overwhelming form of affection stands in stark contrast to the necessary space that always remains between Clive and Clara, which Clara describes at the party:

> Clara noticed how precisely he [Clive] timed each step, as if he were dancing himself, so that he slid slowly and deftly through the shifting crowd, neither

jostling nor being jostled [...] He was like a ghost; moving imperceptibly and intangible in his own dimension. It would be impossible to imagine Clive deliberately impinging on her mind as the unknown man had done. (op. cit., p. 129)

Clara becomes so absorbed with the prospect of marriage to Richard and sharing her life with him that she allows her own interiority to dissolve completely. The merging or fusing of the subjectivities of Richard and Clara is most clearly demonstrated in their shared telepathy. As Kylie Valentine notes, 'It is not the over-exercising of her capacity for telepathy that drives Clara mad, but the exaggerated receptivity and passivity that this capacity actually is' (*Psychoanalysis, Psychiatry, and Modernist Literature*, p. 183). This sense of familiarity reflected in her 'exaggerated receptivity and passivity' with another human being is intoxicating for Clara, but it causes her to lose her own boundaries and the sense that she and Richard are two separate identities.

According to Irigaray, this way of loving is not unusual in Western culture:

We have been accustomed to reduce the other to ours or ourselves [...] Our manner of reasoning, our manner of loving is often an appropriation, either through a lack of differentiation, a fusion, or through a transformation into an object [...] We act in this way especially towards others who are closest to us, forgetting that they are other, different from us. (Part I, Philosophy, 'Introduction', in *Key Writings*, p. 5)

Richard is the first to notice that their invasion of each other's boundaries is having a detrimental effect on Clara's identity. He tells her: 'I look at you sometimes and it's as if you are melting away. Sometimes when we're together . . . even when I have you in my arms . . . it's almost as if you suddenly weren't there' (*Beyond the Glass*, p. 154). Clara is unaware that this is happening. White depicts Clara's loss of identity as physical disturbances which coincide with symptoms of her madness. Clara receives only 'one flash of recognition' which she records in her black notebook, the first of many diaries: 'I begin to feel there must be a space between us however one we are. We are like two spinning planets magnetized in harmony. But it is essential each keep to its own orbit and not be drawn into the other's' (op. cit., p. 176). White's portrayal of Clara's desire to keep a space between Richard and herself gestures towards White's own plea to love without desiring to possess, outlined earlier, and Irigaray's assertion that an irreducible difference must be kept between two subjects, even in love.

The competing demands of White's need to construct her identity through her writing and the expectations of patriarchal society are manifested throughout her texts by a fracturing of the protagonist's subjectivity. This reaches its climax in White's fourth autobiographical novel, *Beyond the Glass,* when Clara's subjectivity becomes so fractured that she suffers from psychosis and is committed to Nazareth Royal Hospital, a psychiatric institution in London, for nine months, a time during which her subjectivity is reborn. Within the asylum, Clara must delineate the boundaries of her subjectivity through a cultivation

of her interiority. She must separate herself from the other patients in order
to try to identify who she is. This becomes most visible when 'gradually she
became aware of certain changes. The most remarkable was that, whenever she
was fully awake, she was always the same person. That person was called Clara'
(op. cit., p. 229). The novel ends with Clara released from Nazareth, but no
longer engaged to marry Richard. Instead, she holds a set of rosary beads in
her hand, and it is the weight of these against her palm, and not a possessive
and invasive relationship with a man, which binds her to reality.

Irigaray's proposition of respecting the other as other, without attempting to
possess her/him, contributes to ensuring that the whole of one's own subjectivity remains intact. In psychosis, that integrity disintegrates when the individual's subjectivity is overwhelmed by external stimuli, which ultimately conquer
and possess the subject. Maintaining an 'irreducible difference' between subjects helps to reduce the risk of external stimuli overwhelming each of them.
White's, and consequently Clara's, psychosis may be interpreted as a result of
an inability to love without desiring to possess, a process in part taught by patriarchal culture, notably through the father, and an inability which, according to
Irigaray, is common in individuals in Western culture, particularly through the
reduction of the other to an object.

That Which is Not Yet Manifest: Silence as a Return to the Self

According to Irigaray, silence not only allows communication between two different subjects but also favours a feminine becoming because it allows for a
return to the self.[7] The process of becoming may result in an internal struggle
if external demands attempt to prevent this return. Several factors contribute
to Antonia White's internal struggle, which she externalizes in her writing. The
most prominent of these is Catholicism because it shapes White's perception of
herself and her relationship with other subjects.

White's recurring periods of mental illness, including the first episode which
she describes in *Beyond the Glass*, and their causes tormented her for most of her
life, as did her struggle with her faith. White's family converted to Catholicism
in 1906 when she was seven years old. From that moment until her death in
1980, religion influenced White's perception of herself and her writing. Her
first and most famous novel, *Frost in May* (1933), details White's experiences
as a young girl in a convent school. In the introduction to the Virago Modern
Classics edition of *Beyond the Glass*, Carmen Callil describes the relationship
between White's spirituality and her texts in this way:

As a Catholic her relationship with Catholic belief and practice has always
been intense, a wrestling to live within its spiritual imperatives in a way which
accorded with her own nature, clinging to her faith, as she says, 'by the skin
of my teeth'. The struggle is brilliantly felt in this quartet, permeating everything that happens to Clara, affecting her adolescence, sexuality, her relationships with men. ('Introduction', in *Beyond the Glass*, p. 4)

White's engagement with Catholicism partly explains the internal struggles which are involved in cultivating her feminine becoming and maintaining her subjectivity.

In recent years feminist scholars, such as Jeannette King, Heather Ingman and Paulina Palmer, have sought to expose and undermine the patriarchal ideologies which underpin many religious institutions, including Christianity. Indeed, many critics have emphasized the repressive nature of the convent atmosphere in their readings of White's novels. However, White's treatment of Catholicism and psychosis is by no means this straightforward. In fact, as Julietta Benson notes in her discussion of *Frost in May*, White's text 'forms a *critical engagement* with the semantics of Catholic belief', rather than a simple criticism or rejection of its dogma ('Varieties of "Dis-Belief"', *Journal of Literature and Theology*, 7, p. 284; italics in original). White's complex and challenging engagement with her faith problematizes any value judgements which a critic might be tempted to make regarding her work. In this regard, Irigaray's theories concerning feminine becoming and spiritual virginity are especially useful.

Irigaray therefore does not advocate dismissing Christianity as a possible path for feminists simply because it has been manipulated by patriarchy. Rather, in her view we must open ourselves to new ways of considering the feminine role in religion outside the confines of patriarchy. She invites feminist scholars to consider the foundational elements of Christianity so that by 'Listening to the spirit instead of to the letter, it is possible to reinterpret the great events of Christianity in a feminine perspective and celebrate them as a recognition of feminine qualities' (Part IV, Spirituality and Religion, 'Introduction', in *Key Writings*, p. 146). Clearly this does not resolve all of the conflicts between feminism and Christianity, but it does aid in illuminating the complexity of White's struggle.

Irigaray's theory of spiritual virginity may be linked to her reinterpretation of crucial aspects of Christianity. For example, she reinterprets the Annunciation in this way:

> Woman cannot therefore remain pure nature, even in motherhood. It is as a 'virgin' that she can give birth to a divine child. The word 'virgin' here doesn't signify the presence or absence of a physiological hymen, of course, but the existence of a spiritual interiority of her own, capable of welcoming the word of the other without altering it. Virgin and mother therefore mean: capable of a relationship with the other, in particular with the other gender, respecting the other and oneself. Virgin and mother could correspond to a female becoming, on condition that these words are understood in the spiritual and not just in the material-natural sense. It is with her 'virgin' soul, as much as if not more than with her body, that Mary gives birth to Jesus. The figure that she can represent for us is that of a woman who stays faithful to herself in love, in generation. In this, Mary's virginity surpasses, in divine dignity, motherhood. ('The Redemption of Women', in *Key Writings*, pp. 151–2)

While other theorists limit themselves to highlighting the impossible duality of virgin and mother which is traditionally attributed to Mary, Irigaray reinterprets these concepts outside the confines of patriarchy.[8] Traditional interpretations position Mary as a passive receptacle for God's word. However, Irigaray relates the remarkable quality of the Annunciation to Mary's intersubjective relation with God. According to Irigaray, 'Mary is a virgin because she was able to keep and to cultivate a spiritual relation to breathing, to the soul [...] Conserving her breath virginal, free and available, Mary retains a relation to life, to the soul, to love, particularly divine love, that is neither appropriation nor consumption of the self, nor of the other, nor of God' (*Between East and West*, pp. 78–9). This intersubjective relation could exemplify the perfect exchange whereby the other is respected as other. For White, her time in the convent school allowed her to begin to cultivate her spiritual virginity and to move towards developing intersubjectivity with others.

For Irigaray, constructing spiritual virginity involves cultivating one's own interiority and demarcating the boundaries of selfhood so that a new relationship is possible with the other gender. If these boundaries are not established, there is a danger of fusion and of the loss of individual subjectivity through appropriation or reduction to an object. Antonia White's texts are a manifestation of her fear of losing her self-hood in just such appropriative relationships, as her novels, short stories, diaries and autobiography show. Through an examination of the social community established by the convent in *Frost in May*, it is possible to gain insight into her portrayal of her psychosis and its relationship to her faith.

Frost in May, White's fictionalized account of her experiences at the Convent of the Sacred Heart, referred to as the Convent of the Five Wounds and Lippington school, presents conflicting views on convent education as seen through the eyes of the protagonist, Nanda. When she arrives as an eight year old, the nuns immediately begin to strip her of her familial influences so that 'she felt so immeasurably older, so much unpicked and resewn and made over to a different pattern' (*Frost in May*, p. 36). Many critics today rebel against such unequivocal indoctrination, just as Nanda does as an adolescent. The nuns feel that her greatest weakness is spiritual pride, while Nanda does not wish to rebel against the spirit of Catholicism, only against 'Lippington's methods' (op. cit., p. 157). Because of this, they justify chastising her, even when she is outwardly obedient, because she does not exhibit enough 'natural naughtiness' (op. cit., p. 49).

It is interesting to contrast Nanda's adolescent point of view as depicted by White in *Frost in May* to White's retrospective perspective as an adult in 'A Child of the Five Wounds', in which she says 'It is a great mistake to suppose that children in a school like Lippington are unhappy, or even that their spirits are crushed' (*As Once in May*, p. 155). No matter how one chooses to interpret the convent disciplinary structure, it was extremely influential in forming White's subjectivity. While acknowledging its potential for a negative impact on its students, this article emphasizes the way in which the convent's policy regarding silence aids in cultivating Nanda's interiority.

As White portrays them in *Frost in May*, the convent regulations encourage the students to remain silent, not only during the annual retreat, but also during many daily activities. This is to encourage them to examine themselves and their conscience, and which may be interpreted as a 'return to self'. As discussed above, according to Irigaray, in an intersubjective relationship an irreducible difference between the subjects must exist which can be embodied by air and silence. In order to preserve this irreducible difference, a return to the self is necessary. Silence can be a means of fecund being, particularly in a same-sex environment, in that it helps to once again define the boundaries between the self and an exterior other (Irigaray, 'Towards a Divine in the Feminine').

White's portrayal of this silence and the disciplinary structure at the convent may be interpreted in various ways. What is clear, though, is that Nanda/Clara/White is most comfortable with herself, with her identity, and with her writing talents when she resides at the convent. *Frost in May* is the only novel in which the protagonist is able to freely express herself in a creative manner without the persistent writer's block which plagues future protagonists and their author. Clara's affiliation with the convent continues in the novel *The Lost Traveller* (1950), White's sequel to *Frost in May*, when Clara must return home for her grandfather's funeral. Although she travels with her family to Paget's Fold, their country home, she 'began to long more than ever for the day when she could get back to school. Though the discipline was strict and every minute of her time parcelled out and supervised, she felt free there' (*The Lost Traveller*, p. 44). These external restrictions, which essentially serve to separate her from the other students, give her a sense of freedom because she is able to explore her subjectivity. This is an indication that the convent may be interpreted in White's texts as a positive space for female becoming through the cultivation of a certain interiority.

The interiority which Clara is able to cultivate in the convent is nevertheless depicted by White as a creature growing inside her. It is both alien and familiar to her; its malicious or friendly nature is dependent upon the degree of fragmentation of Clara's subjectivity. When Clara arrives home for her grandfather's funeral, she is uncertain of this 'other' inside herself. She says 'There seemed to be a new creature growing up inside her, something still unformed and skinless that could not bear to be exposed to the light' (op. cit., p. 35). The 'creature' within Clara could be read as a representation of something which occupies the space of what Irigaray calls 'the not yet manifest', a potentiality which would be embodied in this way in the convent atmosphere.

Irigaray relates the existence of this 'not yet manifest' to woman's ability to keep breath inside her. Man needs to employ his breath to construct, to create things which are exterior to him. Woman, on the other hand, is more able to create inside herself: 'She knows that the source of life is in her, that she need not construct it outside of herself. Her breath need not leave her in order to build, to fabricate, to create' (*Between East and West*, p. 85). According to Clara, 'In the enforced silences of the convent day the mysterious creature could breathe and grow' (*The Lost Traveller*, p. 44). Here she is able to nourish the 'other' or 'creature' within herself. This is the reason that the influence of the convent continues to be so strong even after Clara leaves. It is the only place where she is allowed to cultivate her own interiority rather than be forced into relationships which are dictated by the appropriative nature of patriarchy.

Conclusion: Conquering the Beast

In later years, Antonia White referred to her psychosis as 'the beast' inside her which periodically revealed itself. This article proposes that 'the beast' was not a monster hidden in White or her characters, but the result of the dissolution of her 'feminine becoming', if it is contextualized within Irigaray's theory. The silent atmosphere of the convent may be interpreted as a possible representation of the space in which the 'not yet manifest' in Clara's subjectivity could exist. It is when Clara submits to the demands of patriarchal culture that her subjectivity is again alienated and the creature becomes a threatening 'beast'. Read in the context of Irigaray's theory, Clara's recovery from psychosis indicates her restructuring of her subjectivity through a regenerative silence 'which consists not at all in a lack of words, but in an almost tactile retouching of the spiritual in oneself' ('The Age of Breath', in *Key Writings*, p. 167). In the mental asylum, Clara is able to rebuild her interiority and reconnect with the spirituality she was allowed to cultivate in the convent.

In this way, Irigaray's theory may be used to illuminate certain points of White's texts, and in so doing it is possible to see the way in which silence is able to transcend the traditional active/passive dichotomy and become an integral aspect of the processes of feminine becoming and the cultivation of intersubjectivity. According to Irigaray, 'soon love needs differentiation, presence: to hold the other in one's hand, to let the voice of the other flow through one, allowing him, or her to be and to go' (*Everyday Prayers*, p. 39). In order to establish this differentiation, the boundaries of one's own subjectivity need to be clearly defined. This requires a space in which silence be maintained between the two subjects, notably through a return to the self. Only then is it possible to envision a real feminine becoming.

Notes

1 White's diaries were edited and published posthumously by her daughter, Susan Chitty.

2 Irigaray, in seminar at the University of Nottingham, May 2005. See also *I Love to You, To Be Two* and *The Way of Love*.

3 Irigaray commented on this in her seminar at the University of Nottingham, May 2005, and also in her latest books.

4 I developed my position on silence within a culture of two subjects during a conversation with Luce Irigaray and other participants in the seminar with Luce Irigaray, University of Nottingham, May 2005.

5 'Clara IV' and 'Julian Tye' appear in a collection of White's writings entitled *As Once in May: The Early Autobiography of Antonia White and Other Writings*.

6 It is notable that while Clive Heron retains his name in 'Julian Tye', White changes Clara Batchelor's name to Julian Tye.

7 According to Irigaray, a 'return to self' is possible for woman through the perception of two lips touching one another. In this way, woman can experience self-affection, and feel how to keep an irreducible difference between herself and the other, a crucial condition in pursuing her own becoming (cf. 'The Return' and 'Towards a Divine in the Feminine').

8 For a detailed account of the historical evolution of the depiction of the Virgin Mary, see Marina Warner, *Alone of All Her Sex: The Myth and Cult of the Virgin Mary.*

Part II

Dwelling in Oneself and with the Other(s) Through Art

Chapter 4

Music and the Voice of the Other: An Engagement with Irigaray's Thinking and Feminine Artistic Musical Performance

Esther Zaplana

Universidad de Castilla-La Mancha, Spain and University of Newcastle, United Kingdom

> Confident in you,
> Without any doubt,
> I listen to you.
> Greeting your voice,
> Receiving your talk
> As what first occurs,
> Must linger in saying,
> Singing the words
> Like a rustle of leaves,
> A beating of wings,
> A throb of the soul,
> Barely audible
> Still tactile.
>
> (Luce Irigaray, *Everyday Prayers*, 21 April, p. 126)

Poetic writing speaks a suggestive, dislocating language that stretches beyond our imagination, as if to activate the senses and to fill readers with emotion. The mood here evokes sound, a welcoming gesture of listening to the voice and to the musicality of nature, of listening to the tenuous vibration of singing words. Words, Luce Irigaray tells us, may be simple and 'transform little but [...] let be, bringing to mind and conveying what is without modifying it, submitting it to our world. [...] Words that respect sensibility, movement', and engage with the real without the distortion of any constructed reality (*Everyday Prayers*, p. 43).[1] In the poem, the singing words flow rhythmically and remain palpable in the soul, as tangible as the other senses, as compelling as the sounds of nature and life. The voice of the other is embraced and evocatively invited to reside within; the voice that dwells in us is also actively required to be listened to. The airy rhythm or vibration that calls through the poem seems to again transform the words and images into a 'vital energy, [...] binding us in a mysterious intimacy' (op. cit., p. 35).

Irigaray explains in the introduction to her collection of poems, *Everyday Prayers*, that the way to arrive at this intimacy implies reaching 'another subjectivity where friendship with nature prevails over its domination, and being-with over being-above or below' (ibid.). Our culture has, in her view, been constructed without consideration for the duality of subjectivity; it has been erected on the foundations of a lone subject, the masculine, and we have now reached a time in which a cultural transition is under way. Her thinking involves the development of, or working towards, a culture of two, the masculine and the feminine, as well as a dialogic relationship between both. 'Poetic language' represents for Irigaray a way of speaking 'more appropriate to this work than speculative discourse, where, in part, I talk the other's language', so that new horizons can be opened and the dialogue between masculine and feminine cultures preserved. This implies that I, as woman, talk a language in the feminine 'letting the other [as man] hear something of the mystery that I represent for him' (op. cit., p. 47). Poetry and artistic expression take us back to the beginnings of our Western culture, which subsequently has been imbued with a dominant masculine perspective; as such, it underpins the principles and values embodied in the representation and misrepresentation of the feminine. Irigaray's challenge to cultural representation entails a culture in the feminine, that has been repressed or tainted by the masculine subject, and would be able to offer the signs and symbols that avoid misrecognition of feminine subjectivity and, in this way, allows the safeguarding of the two cultures (ibid.).

In my search for the cultural meanings of especially contemporary feminine music and vocal performance, and in a close engagement with Irigaray's thinking, I will attempt in what follows to consider the significance and appropriateness of some of Irigaray's ideas for the interpretation of the singing voice in women's musical performance. The aim is to establish a dialogue or engagement with Irigaray's understanding of cultural difference and representation, and to show its relevance for reading musical and vocal performance by women artists. The approach is not meant to exhaust interpretations of the singing voice of every female artist, but it tries, in a broader sense, to illustrate the pertinence of Irigaray's philosophical thinking – as working towards a culture in the feminine – for the reading of auditory artistic production. This research primarily refers to women artists who are creators of music; although the styles and musical forms of women artists may vary from artist to artist, women as creators of music are already sizeable within an art that has largely presented women only as listeners or interpreters of male musical traditions. But it is becoming more usual to find examples of women vocal performers and musicians that succeed in the fields of popular and avant-garde music, and thus their cultural production presents an interesting body of work.[2]

The interpretative reading of the auditory can involve abstract articulations and persuasive language, and hence Irigaray's work, her open narrative and representations of the feminine create the space for the expression of a new auditory culture: her writing theorizes, yet at the same time it would also seem to *perform* the feminine. Her texts and her own poetic writing seem, in some sense, to operate as enactments of feminine expression. In this sense, women's singing can be seen as an elaboration of an Irigarayan aesthetic and as generating complex nexuses of meanings that evoke representations or performances of the feminine analogous to those in Irigaray's writing. The fluidity in musical or vocal articulation and the modulation of the voice can be associated with these Irigarayan representations, which, in turn, may be taken as underlying a culture rendered in the feminine.

Voice and listening share an equivalent place in music and both are located in the invisible channels of communicative exchange between two cultures: masculine and feminine. In Irigaray's view, artistic expression needs 'to enter into [...] sexuate relationships [...] to cultivate our sensorial perceptions, and give to us a dynamic global unity, thanks to a creative imagination' (Part III, Art, 'Introduction', in *Key Writings*, p. 99). Whilst listening can be understood as an activity of perception and even of consumption, singing the words – led by the voice – is a productive activity that circulates performatively in our culture. 'Thanks to music', Irigaray tells us, 'listening allows a becoming that is more flowing than looking. The scale of tones, of sounds, arouses an elevation of energy which does not end in a definite configuration' ('Before and Beyond Any Word', in *Key Writings*, p. 135). Meaning remains open; the text, in her own words, is 'always open onto a new sense, and onto a future sense, and I would say also onto a potential 'You' [*Tu*], a potential interlocutor' (interview with Elizabeth Hirsh and Gary A. Olson, 'Je-Luce Irigaray'). 'Singing the words' in Irigaray's poem of 21 April may then be understood diaphorically, rather than metaphorically, because it implies an open meaning and a continuum distinct from the transposition-duplication of meaning conveyed by metaphor. A female voice and song can signify differently if they are seen from the perspective of a representational and artistic musical 'language' or idiom (as a mode of expression in music) that is enacted from within Irigaray's understanding of a culture in the feminine.

The voice of the artist, originating in her body, becomes a major creative resource, but her artistic power can also flow through the expressiveness of music and lyrics: through the textual, auditory and visual communications that can all act as cultural signs. Women's artistic performance is not necessarily dependent on meanings that already exist, or at least not in the way that they exist. It is possible that their vocal and musical production integrates a range of musical influences or techniques, some of which are specific to the artist, particularly in the case of avant-garde work; yet such influences are processed through their personal sensibility and hence through their perceptual subjective experience. In this sense, the work of women composers and originators of musical styles can be thought not to have been born out of men's words and models. Women's musical creativity appears in some cases to embody an aspiration to explore an internal world that is then outwardly communicated; in some cases, the vocal sound may take us back to a pre-verbal stage with regard to Western language, a simile for the recuperation of a primal source or power of women's creativity. These aspects can be read in the work of artists who are able to create, or recreate, unique sounds, words and melodies through the development of certain vocal techniques, their music, performance art and/or their use of technology. This is, above all, where Irigaray's thinking becomes relevant, because these women artists could be said to sing the words of the 'other's musical language', that is, the feminine, and articulate a musical/vocal production that can be seen from within the perspective of Irigaray's culture in the feminine. Their cultural production can be viewed in this way as embodying open meanings that subvert or destabilize the cultural hegemonic values and ideals of our world.

The Duality of Subjectivity and 'Intra-subjective' Performance

Irigaray's advocacy of the duality of subjectivities entails considerations of identity and the female imaginary, inasmuch as cultural identifications may be distinct for each sex. This is not only according to Irigaray's way of thinking, but it would then seem possible to conceive of female identity as a product of specific feminine symbolizations, which substantiate the notions of a female imaginary and a female subjectivity.[3] In order for women to develop their creativity, they need a discursive space from which to articulate their voice, a space that is not tainted by dominant discourse. Irigaray points out that both voice and discourse are gendered, although whilst the sounds produced by the vocal organs of men and women rest *a priori* on equivalent value, gender difference, in the case of a specified manner of speaking and of discourse, is marked by unequal value.[4] The perception of a person through his or her voice calls attention to gendered values attached to voice modulation and tone, as well as the discourse embedded in our culture. For this reason, a woman must find a space from which to speak and communicate her own position as a subject in discourse. Yet this discourse must not be subjected to our traditional logic, to *logos*, and should, amongst other things, recuperate a musical quality that has been long lost in Western culture (Irigaray, 'Before and Beyond Any Word', in *Key Writings*, pp. 136–7). Within her model of speech, Irigaray has developed *parler-femme* and investigated the position of a subject of enunciation in the feminine, of the feminine 'I' of enunciation (cf. *This Sex Which Is Not One, To Speak Is Never Neutral* and *I Love to You*). Some women singers often seek to perform from their own subject position in discourse and aim to articulate their female 'I' of enunciation through the artistic performance. A singer communicates in the artistic medium and her performance can generate encounters and subjective identifications amongst the audience.

The recognition of the duality of subjectivities expands the interpretative possibilities of women's artistic production, since it is then possible from this stance to articulate the specificity of the woman's creativity; from that specificity, it also becomes valid to look into the 'intra-subjective' relation that flows from within her self and her artistic performance, the singing product, as it were. The artist's vocality can be interpreted as a way to emphasize her own subject position and her singing delivery as a means to explore and enact a diversity of subject positions during the artistic performance. The case of the female singer/songwriter who composes and writes her own songs can draw attention to her subjectivity, the specificity of her own representation, as well as the 'intra-subjective' relation between her self, her voice, her body, and the singing persona of her artistic performance.

Women vocal performers would seem to stage an interplay that touches upon Irigaray's dialectical strategies. Irigaray offers a definition of the 'I' beyond that of a simple subjectivity which expresses itself: it is not only important to say 'I', but also 'I SHE' in order to keep a dialectic between subjectivity and objectivity. This allows us to foreground the fact that the subject is two – not a unique neuter subject, but two sexuate subjects: 'I SHE' and 'I HE' – and that 'I SHE' can establish a dialogue with 'You SHE', 'I HE', 'You HE' and so on, by way of communications between differently sexuated subjects.[5] Then a woman artist can accede to a different cultural 'I' by constructing a new objectivity that corresponds to an 'I' that is sexed feminine, not an indifferent 'I' or, in fact, a 'he' who dictates the truth. It is thus necessary that a dialectic process between subjectivity and objectivity also remains within the woman as a sexuate, and not unique, subject: 'I SHE'. The woman's artistic 'product' presents an interesting instance of a constructed subject, whereby she can generate her own representation through this double structure. The 'subject' of her singing persona is enacted with the sole purpose of the artistic musical performance.

Following Irigaray, the artist would construct her singing performance in accordance to a sensible 'truth' or reality, based notably on her sensorial perceptions, which may change over time, but which would nonetheless enter into a dialectic process with respect to the 'I' sexed feminine. The artist could not revert to a mere 'I' since she could only interpret her own experience *a posteriori*, by recourse to a dialectic process.[6] Yet she could artistically perform – by means of her singing persona – a fractional narrative of her own experience as product of her subjective and/or perceptual experience. Given that the dialectic movement between subjectivity and objectivity must remain open within the 'I SHE', according to Irigaray, it could never be said that hers is always already the experience of a woman, although the artistic 'product' seems to offer the space for the enactment of a more subjective, though partial, personal experience.

Being with an Other as Performance

Irigaray's conception of two different subjects and of 'being in two' implicates the construction of 'inter-subjectivity' in respect of sexual difference. It requires us to go outside of ourselves in order to enter into relation with an other, and then to return within ourselves, in order to keep our own identity without spreading to infinity or merging with the other. Two separate concentric circles graphically represent a way of expressing difference between the two subjects and their world; each subject would have to come partly outside one's world in order to meet the other in a middle space, and then to return to one's own space so as to enable an economy of infinite entering in relation.[7] In other words, a dialectical interchange is created between inside and outside, whereby going outside and returning inside contribute to the cultivation of movement, through a going and letting go, and this movement furnishes an economy of space and time.[8] Given that one can never be the other, the middle space or possible meeting point in between the two circles – corresponding to the two subjects – is opened by the negative, which limits each of the two subjects, providing them with borders, with a frame that safeguards their identities and their difference.[9]

'Being in two' involves performing, and returning to oneself also forms part of the performance of 'being in two'. Irigarayan thinking makes a distinction between 'acting out' – which implies letting out a repressed feeling, doing something without reflection or mediation – and 'performance', which Irigaray understands as an act that is made more consciously. Her premise implies that one considers culture in a conscious manner. The dialectical interchange, or the coming and going outside and inside ourselves embedded in the conception of two different subjects and of 'being in two', hence becomes a qualitative aspect of the performance; sensory perceptions, voicing and listening can thus join in creating the performance of 'being in two'. Irigaray's approach of 'being in two' as a dialectical exchange primarily refers to the relation between two different subjects, and should not therefore be theorized into a concept that might tentatively be applied outside of the ethics of such a relationship. But her idea of cultivating oneself in a conscious manner can be relevant for the interpretation of women's artistic performance, since this is an intentional and conscious activity that involves, moreover, the emergence and expansion of women's creativity. The artist's subjectivity and identity as they appear in the musical performance can reinscribe the relation of the listeners towards women's artistic and music production.

Artistic Production as Meta-performance

A woman artist, as an individual, may embrace feminine performance in the Irigarayan sense of a subjective relation in being two, whilst her artistic performance is understood more accurately as a meta-performance, as something consciously produced or created.[10] Meta-performance is also understood vis-à-vis the mediation surrounding contemporary artistic production, since the musical 'product' contains performative elements 'frozen' in a recording, and this is ready to be repeated and consumed. Technologically mediated images and sounds and their repetition generate responsiveness from the listeners through identificatory mechanisms with the musical work, and thus the listeners' receptiveness of that artistic work can bring the music to life. At the time of interpreting women's musical and vocal production, Irigaray's flowing and open representations, which have been recovered to increase sensory perceptions and energy, may be evoked.[11] Women artists utilize existing music codes and/or create their own, in a way that would seem to reappropriate and transform music into a dissident, even subversive, musical sound that reflects their perceptual experience. They may opt for a vocal performance that mimics suffering or madness, for example, with the purpose of revealing that which 'was meant to remain hidden' (Irigaray, *je, tu, nous*, p. 108). In this way, they would appear to retain a sense of openness to build up a self-representation of their own that connects with Irigaray's argument that art is 'to create another reality, by transforming the real that we are, that we live' (Part III, Art, 'Introduction', in *Key Writings*, p. 98).

For Irigaray, the 'musical universe as such' has 'to speak [...] the whole body, the whole self' and it is 'to the universe of the flesh – my flesh and that of the other – that we have to listen first to compose a work of music' ('Before and Beyond Any Word', in *Key Writings*, p. 136). Since women's bodies enter female subjectivity, it is possible that 'listening to the flesh' becomes closely connected with women's musical production. Artistic meta-performance would not correspond *stricto sensu* to the musicality of the relation of 'being in two', although it can positively tally with Irigaray's cultural sexual difference. Women artists' meta-performance could be associated, in an Irigarayan sense, with the capacity to think about life and the real perception of our world. This means that women become creative and challenge the signifiers until now connected with the feminine; this requires women to find other gestures, other words to say, and to avow their identity, body and subjectivity. Reading artistic production by women from an Irigarayan perspective can help reclaim the 'musical language' of the other that is, with respect to Western culture, the feminine musical language.

Sexual difference can constitute, in Irigaray's view, the horizon of more fecund worlds than previously allowed for. The fecundity is not only envisaged with a literal sense, but as the 'production of a new age of thought, art, poetry and language: the creation of a new *poetics*' (*An Ethics of Sexual Difference*, p. 7; italics in original). A first gesture that can bring autonomy for each subject is to move from exteriority to interiority, and to develop interiority through the cultivation of multifaceted sensitivity, which emphasizes the significance of self-affection, breathing, listening and silence (cf. Irigaray, 'Before and Beyond Any Word', in *Key Writings*, pp. 137–9). Interacting with the world through increased sensorial perceptions can make a dialectical exchange or a dialogue in difference possible without losing oneself. If the interchange is to be positive, this type of performance – understood each time as a performance – is a way of *jouissance*, and the relation to the other, and/or to nature, may also be taken as the discovery of enjoyment. One significant means to preserve ourselves in enjoyment is the artistic process. This can be a major way for women to keep the rhythm of the dialectical interactions of coming and going outside and inside themselves.

It seems possible to integrate some of these ideas into the interpretation of auditory artistic expression. The sensations that are generated when the performer sings and the audience listens to the voice may suggest a manner for women to develop their culture, as well as feelings of *jouissance* transmitted from the performer to the listener. Artistic expression in our epoch is usually mediated by technology, and thus a direct interaction with the artist and an immediate response from the audience become extremely difficult, except perhaps in the case of live performance. Even live performance can only offer the singer a collective encounter with the audience, and a collective identification, therefore, of the listeners with *jouissance*. The exchange may nonetheless operate both ways, since the *jouissance* generated in the process of listening to a singing voice also happens through the multiple technological and communication channels. The recorded song loses its spontaneity, but it can recreate melodies and rhythms that the listener experiences as a means of accessing energy and enjoyment. Albeit mediated, a certain degree of response from audiences to the female artist's work can take place via the constructive utilization of these channels, and thus women's production, worked on again through a feminine lens, still brings about artistic cultural transformation. What is important is that women's artistic production becomes audible and visible at levels previously unknown. Their work can be relevant to other women, but also to men, given that they will be able to reach out to many subjectivities and thus their creative expression can be felt to inspire their listeners.

Conclusion

Women's artistic performance can engage with Irigaray's thinking of art, which suggests a less linear and more flowing, fluctuating and perceptive mode of expression associated with the feminine. Attached to this understanding is the establishment of a dialogic and open-ended relational model with the 'other' and his/her 'others'. As we have seen, women artists' 'singing', and more generally the 'voice', can be articulated both around 'intra-subjective' performance and the duality of subjectivity: artistic production, meta-performance, and being with the other as performance. The discussion of these aspects vis-à-vis feminine artistic performance takes into account difference and the experience of woman with respect to her own subjectivity and her perceptual experience, particularly at the time of articulating women's musical creativity and singing performance. This suggests that women's musical work can be read as the production of an aesthetic activity, which is more open and challenges the boundaries of the masculine. It then enables the development of another culture with respect to Western tradition, a culture which is less dichotomous, more dual at the level of subjectivities, more multiple and inclusive.

Western culture's dichotomies, according to Irigaray, result from man's necessity 'to differentiate himself from mother and/as nature, and to master them by means of techniques, beginning with the one which organizes language itself' ('Before and Beyond Any Word', in *Key Writings*, p. 136). She writes that 'in the masculine Western tradition [...] a set of logical rules claims to control the whole of culture. Then art, including musical art, becomes a secondary domain with regard to logical requirements', and too often 'art itself has become a technique at the service [...] of man' (op. cit., pp. 136–7). Irigaray advocates the recuperation of music that, in our culture, 'loses its function of enlivening and making the whole body subtle', as it 'abandons its role of mediation between nature and humans, between humans themselves and between humans and gods – a media-tion in love and in the access to the divine' (op. cit., p. 137). Her thought there-fore encourages the cultivation of a poetic language, related to music, as a form of expression, faithful to our maternal-natural-material belonging, and not yet encumbered by traditional masculine logic.[12] Some women's artistic perform-ance and creativity, their voice and singing, seem to be close to Irigaray's per-spective with respect to a culture of perceptions, as is the modulation of songs according to the body, the heart, the breath, the touch and silence. Poetry and music as expressions of creativity should emerge from the whole of the living world, as 'from a silent background', and invite everyone to communicate, start-ing from their whole being, and from the breath and the energy of the universe (cf. op. cit., pp. 140–1). For a 'transformation of energy' to take place, it is nec-essary to listen to music in a way 'both active and passive', in the sense that one has to 'welcome what is perceived and to let it act' (op. cit., p. 135). Women's musical and vocal performance could be viewed and listened to as if they would arise from a whole, where music connects with the living universe and allows a becoming through breathing, silence, touching and expressivity.

Notes

1 Irigaray understands that men have tried to go outside the relation with the mater-nal-natural-material belonging by forgetting that which gives and renews life, that which they have received with the body. This goes with their staying in sameness among men, which implies a production by assimilation, and through the mediation, of the female or females (cf. *An Ethics of Sexual Difference*, pp. 85–6). According to Irigaray 'the human species is made up of two different beings and Beings which each enter into relation with the real in a specific way' (*The Way of Love*, p. 110). The feminine human subject has his-torically been prevented 'from attaining its own Being [...]. The return of the masculine subject to himself as well as the constitution of the world realized by him are from then on perverted – they do not get to the bottom of the reality of the real and carry out a becoming of oneself and of the world upon incomplete and unreal bases' (ibid.). Our Western culture has not yet elaborated a relation with the real that takes into account sexuate identity; we lack a cultivation of our sexuate identity as real. The real existing is at least three: 'a real corresponding to the masculine subject, a real corresponding to the feminine subject, and a real corresponding to their relation. These three reals thus each correspond to a world but these three worlds are in interaction [...], but their relation 'cannot be founded exclusively upon a relation to the same, to a single Same, to which each part should become appropriate. [...] It is a work of putting into relation – with oneself, with the world, with the other in the respect of their difference, and also with a common universe – that manifests this real and that elaborates it' (op. cit., p. 111).
2 Examples of these artists are, among others, Meredith Monk, Joan La Barbara, Laurie Anderson, Diamanda Galás, Tori Amos, Susan Deyhim, Björk and Fátima Miranda.
3 Irigaray's elaboration of the existence of female subjectivity takes account of further considerations, which are covered in her earlier works. One of them is the entry of the sexed body into the definition of subjectivity and culture (cf. *Speculum*). Margaret Whitford also examines and clarifies some of the complexities of female subjectivity and the female imaginary in Irigaray's work (in *Luce Irigaray: Philosophy in the Feminine*).

4 Notes, seminar held by Luce Irigaray for students doing their PhD on her work at the University of Nottingham, 16–21 May 2005.

5 Irigaray maintains that the '*I* is another [...] sometimes attributed to the unconscious, can be understood in a different way. *I* is never simply *mine* in that it belongs to a gender. Therefore, I am not the whole: I am man or woman. And I am not simply a subject, I belong to a gender. I am objectively limited by this belonging' (*I Love to You*, p. 106; italics in original). She also writes that 'women and men must therefore be recognized as representatives or as incarnations of human gender. They have to be valorized for the sake of the becoming of their sexed *I*, for the relations between them and for the constitution of a spiritual dialectic of these relations' (op. cit., p. 108).

6 On this point, Irigaray believes that 'the purely narrative, autobiographical "I" or the "I" that expresses only affect, risks being an "I" that collapses back into a role traditionally granted to woman: an "I" of pathos, that the woman also uses in her place, the home'. Thus, she cannot affirm her own experience alone since 'this is something I know only after the fact, by means of discussion, and so on. I can't affirm that this is always already the experience of a woman. It must be a dialectic between subjectivity and objectivity' (in Hirsh and Olson, 'Je-Luce Irigaray').

7 Irigaray's later works focus on the existence of two different subjects and on how to establish an ethical, political and, fundamentally, philosophical relationship between them, without one being subjugated to the other. She is interested in constructing a dialogue between two different subjects that respects difference between sexuate identities and permits the interpretation and, further, the construction, of the world from two gender perspectives (cf. *I Love to You* and *To Be Two*).

8 According to Irigaray, in our tradition, 'the feminine is experienced as space, but often with connotations of the abyss and night [...], while the masculine is experienced as time' (*An Ethics of Sexual Difference*, p. 7). The relation between space and time must remain dialectic: space must be turned into time and time into space, and thus the interchange expands the scope elaborated by Western culture's reductionistic model of consistently turning space into time (op. cit., pp. 7–9). Temporal and spatial representations of the female voice and body by women artists are significant for the interpretation of musical performance.

9 Note here that 'negativity' as providing borders for each one implies a meeting space between the two subjects, that is opened by their difference. This negative involves that a person is never a mere subjectivity, but is objectively limited by belonging to a gender. It establishes the irreducibility between both subjects. Since one can never become the other, a necessary return to oneself occurs. Irigaray explains that, 'contrary to Hegel, the negative at work here does not serve to integrate the outside in a unique subjectivity – thus, in a way, the "you" in the "I" – in the search for a unique Absolute. I depart from Hegel and use the dialectical process in a different manner: now it is in the service of intersubjectivity. The task and the finality are no longer to reach a unique Absolute, that is, to succeed in projecting, to the infinite, the aspirations or the intentions of a unique subject – and of those who are the same as him – onto a supposedly objective totality. Rather the negative is used to maintain the duality of subjectivities, and a space between them, which belongs neither to the one nor to the other, and which allows them to meet together.' The negative for Hegel serves 'to reduce the all to a one – a One', whereas for Irigaray 'it is used to maintain the two' (Part I, Philosophy, 'Introduction', in *Key Writings*, p. 3).

10 Irigaray's reflections on performance speak of presence and the relational quality of 'being in two', which, in her opinion, always requires performing, and turning back to oneself as being also part of the performance of being in two. She points out that

any discussion on artistic performance could be a question of meta-performance (notes, seminar held by Luce Irigaray at the University of Nottingham).

11 Note here that 'flowing' is meant as smooth, continuous, not rigid or abrupt. 'Fluid' may perhaps be used in the sense of 'flowing', although the important point in Irigaray's work is that textual meaning is open, not closed off. The feminine is not meant as spreading and losing women's energy, given that the borders, the limits are kept and thus energy cannot leak out.

12 Irigaray's poetic language 'seeks to preserve and promote [...] a becoming, which does not divide itself from nature' and where 'the use of words, silences, rhythms tends to disclose nature rather than control it'. She understands poetic writing as an 'open-ended telling' left to 'its own multiple germination and to the multiple ways in which it can be heard' (cf. *Everyday Prayers*, p. 30).

Chapter 5

'But What if the Object Started to Speak?': The Representation of Female Consciousness On-Screen

Lucy Bolton

Queen Mary, University of London, United Kingdom

Luce Irigaray's analysis of the way in which patriarchy represents women, also describes the traditional portrayal of women in classical cinema. Irigaray calls for a movement away from a masculine logic of representation and for the creation of a feminine subjectivity, which can exist and flourish in a culture of inter-subjectivity between men and women. In this article, I will demonstrate how the writings of Irigaray can be used to inform and inspire both film criticism and film-making practice with an evocatively visual language of morphological figurality, gesture, colour and touch. I will take an overarching approach to Irigaray's work, drawing upon aspects from across the range of her thought: from the recourse to the speculum and the tactic of mimesis, to the need to return to oneself and the creation of a culture of two. I propose the construction of an approach to film that initiates a visual language of feminine subjectivity, which has implications for the representation of individuality and of relationships. This article will thus engage with the notions and ideas of Irigaray in relation to Jane Campion's film, *In the Cut* (2003). It is my contention that this film offers a subtle yet radical representation of feminine consciousness and social relationships, between women and women, and men and men, and between men and women, which becomes explicable and coherent when analysed in Irigarayan terms.

Icon, Idol, Fetish

The objectification of women in film, and the way in which female spectators relate to these objectified women, has been a major preoccupation of feminist film theory, in particular since Laura Mulvey's groundbreaking article on visual pleasure and 'the gaze' in 1975 (cf. 'Visual pleasure and narrative cinema').[1] Mulvey dissects the relation of woman on-screen to the male director/camera/spectator by analysing the way in which 'the look' brought to bear upon the on-screen female was constructed: woman was the signifier of sexual difference, with man being the subject and maker of meaning. For Mulvey, woman on-screen is either a frame-freezing spectacle or a fetishized object.

The fetishization and/or punishment of women on-screen is such a common feature of mainstream cinema that many of Mulvey's points remain apt today. Women on-screen frequently function in relation to the male hero, enabling him to demonstrate bravery, resourcefulness and virility. For Irigaray, in masculine discourse such as that of Freud 'the feminine is defined as the necessary complement to the operation of male sexuality, and, more often, as a negative image that provides male sexuality with an unfailingly phallic self-representation' (*This Sex Which Is Not One*, p. 70). This certainly seems to be an apt description of women in mainstream cinema, although clearly this is not to say that all films portray women in such a way. There are many films that feature women in lead roles, with female-centred or female-focused narratives, which concern women's experiences and choices. However, it is still rare to find a film in which a woman's subjectivity is the driving force propelling the narrative. Even if the female character is central, it is unusual for the audience to be invited to share her point of view, to be concerned with her thoughts, observations, reactions and concerns, or to bear witness to her journey of self-discovery. There are usually other driving forces which rob women of their subjectivity; for example, the way in which a narrative may be built around the investigation and demystification of a female character by a male, as in *Marnie* (dir. Alfred Hitchcock, 1964). I would argue that this robbery extends to the majority of women in film, both contemporary and classical.

Irigaray's analysis of the problem of the lack of a true sexual difference in Western society informs acutely our understanding of the reasons why feminine consciousness has failed to be represented on-screen in any meaningful way or at all:

> this fault, this deficiency, this 'hole', inevitably affords woman too few figurations, images, or representations by which to represent herself. It is not that she lacks some 'master signifier' or that none is imposed upon her, but rather that access to a signifying economy, to the coining of signifiers, is difficult or even impossible for her because she remains an outsider, herself [a] subject to their norms. She borrows signifiers but cannot make her mark, or re-mark upon them. (*Speculum*, p. 71)

The idea that women lack a feminine symbolic provides a reason for the paucity of female cinematic imagery outside of the phallocratic treatments first exposed by Mulvey. Irigaray shows that the necessary and inevitable consequence of such lack is: 'a latent but not actual psychosis, for want of a practical signifying system' (ibid.). It could perhaps be said that if there is a collective malaise of women in film, it is as a result of the lack of a specifically feminine symbolic enabling the creation and preservation of female subjectivity.

In the Cut, however, engages with feminine subjectivity in ways which are both fresh and subtle. The film is driven by the subjective contemplations and motivations of the lead character, Frannie, and allows space for her subjective feminine consciousness to be explored and expressed throughout the whole film. The strategies of Irigaray enable us to locate such spaces on-screen, and suggest imagery and action that may constitute the expression of subjectivity within this space.

The analysis by Irigaray of the way in which 'woman needs to accede to a love of self' which 'might perhaps be compared to the *icon* insofar as that differs from the *idol* and the *fetish*' (*An Ethics of Sexual Difference*, p. 60; italics in original), echoes Mulvey's explanation of the representation of women in film as fetishized spectacle. For Irigaray, the icon 'irradiates the invisible', its gaze being 'beyond our usual perceptions' (ibid.). The idol, however, 'attracts the gaze but blinds it with a brilliance that bars access to the invisible' (op. cit., pp. 60–1). Furthermore, the fetish 'would have us believe in a valuable mystery or mysterious value; it would set up or destroy in seduction the power of the invisible' (op. cit., p. 61). Mulvey's examples of the showgirl Marilyn Monroe in *The River of No Return* (dir. Otto Preminger, 1954) and of Marlene Dietrich as Joseph von Sternberg's fetishized image (*Visual and Other Pleasures*, pp. 20–3), exemplify Irigaray's idol and fetish respectively: the dazzling brilliance of the images attracts the gaze of the spectator but prohibits an engagement with the on-screen woman which is beyond superficial appearance. It is the irradiation of the invisible, enabling a perception beyond the usual, which *In the Cut* attempts to create.

'But What if the Object Started to Speak?'[2]

Hypothesizing a sea change that could challenge conventional objectification in masculine discourse, Irigaray suggests strategies which women might employ to create a new way of becoming and being. The language and style of Irigaray's writing is sometimes evocatively visual in my opinion. Her use of morphological figurality, gestures, fluids and a maternal divine, all present very physical and even visual possibilities. These processes are deployed in order to encourage and inspire the setting up of a new feminine symbolic and imaginary by accessing a woman's conscious interiority and enabling her to represent herself in a new way. So, this idea of 'getting inside' the woman is not about a physical phallic penetration, which could only lead to further subjective annihilation or objectification. It is about a psychological concern with entering a realm of feminine subjectivity. The answer to the problem of the transformation of women into objects, according to Irigaray, is not to reclaim the female from within masculine discourse. She does not call for women to find themselves a place in patriarchy, equal or the same as that of a man:

> Recovering fantasy, repressed or inhibited by a masculine tradition, is not sufficient in order to protect and elaborate a world of our own. This still signifies at best laughing together in the kitchen of a patriarchal family home, city, country, culture. We have to create another kind of home. (*Dialogues*, p. 140)

Irigaray is not proposing the kind of retrospective rewriting or reclaiming as practised by early feminist film theorists. Rather, she calls for a movement away from subjection to masculine discourse and for the creation of a female specificity:

> What this implies is that the female body is not to remain the object of men's discourse or their various arts but that it become the object of a female subjectivity experiencing and identifying itself. Such research attempts to suggest to women a morpho-logic that is appropriate to their bodies. It's aimed at the male subject, too, inviting him to redefine himself as a body with a view to exchanges between sexed subjects. (*je, tu, nous*, p. 59)

As the quotation suggests, this new language also has implications for the representation of male characters and of relationships between men and women. Central to this new approach is Irigaray's idea of the use of a curved mirror, a speculum – different from that of the flat reflective mirror as used, for example, by Lacan (cf. *Speculum*, p. 144) – as a way of getting inside women and accessing a different realm of representation. Importantly, this representation is not confined to the imaginary: for Irigaray, confinement to the imaginary can be a way of protecting oneself, 'becoming a refuge from the outside world'.[3] Irigaray's undertaking is to effect change at the symbolic level which enables people – both men and women – to share together, bringing about a new symbolic economy which allows a wider participation in society through relating with others.

There is a very collaborative aspect to Irigaray's work: it offers an invitation to engagement and dialogue, with the aim of effecting change in the reader and in the world. As Margaret Whitford describes, Irigaray is a 'philosopher of change', and 'is attempting to begin to state the conditions under which the status of the "female" in the symbolic realm might be altered' (*Luce Irigaray: Philosophy in the Feminine*, p. 15). The active, responsive reading required by Irigaray's texts facilitates the application of her thought to other fields, and the visual and morphological nature of part of her imagery and symbolism, such as her writing on flesh colours or feminine gestures, makes it an extremely valuable approach for film analysis (cf. 'Flesh Colors' and 'Gesture in Psychoanalysis', in *Sexes and Genealogies*). *In the Cut* particularly invites engagement with the female characters on a physical and gestural level, in spheres of experience such as the sensory and the auditory, as well as the visual, which demand active consideration from the spectator. With a culture of two subjects, which is Irigaray's aim (cf. 'You Who Will Never Be Mine', in *Key Writings*, pp. 8–12), she anticipates a different kind of looking:

> How many eyes do we have then, being two? Certainly we each keep our two eyes. But we probably have more eyes, one or two: to contemplate invisibility in the visible, in the light of day, but also to perceive in the night of interiority. The way of looking will be more contemplative, passive as well as active, capable of discovering an other or a world always unknown. What it is to see

is not already defined, and our eyes can thus remain open upon an infinity of views, of sights. (*Dialogues*, p. 150)

A fuller examination of the engagement of the spectator is beyond the scope of this article, but I simply highlight the possible similarities between reading Irigaray and watching a certain type of film – both active processes, demanding engagement in the text and relation to it on various levels of perception.

Luce Irigaray On-Screen

Irigaray invites a reconsideration, or re-reading, where the reader is attentive to aspects which may not be immediately apparent or as expected. When discussing the interpretation of a dream, for example, Irigaray appeals for the recall of spaces that are 'fixed in oblivion and waiting to come to life. Turning everything upside down and back to front' (*Speculum*, p. 138). This is one of the features of the cinematography and visual style of *In the Cut*: the film is 'jamming the theoretical machinery' with a 'disruptive excess' (*This Sex Which Is Not One*, p. 78), notably of detail, focus, sound and colour. The cinematography is disconcerting and challenging. In one shot there will be sections of the frame coming in and out of focus, unsettling spectators and making them aware that they should not be searching for a straightforward interpretation – this is not a vision of a city or of a woman which can be taken for granted.

As Frannie travels on the underground, she reads the 'Poetry in Transit' displayed in the carriage: a translated excerpt from 'Remansos', by Federico García Lorca. The camera follows the lines word by word as Frannie's voice-off reads the line: 'The still waters of the water under a frond of stars, the still waters of your mouth under a thicket of kisses.'[4] When Frannie leaves the train, she pauses on the platform to write down the phrase in her notebook. The camera focuses in extreme close-up on the tip of Frannie's ballpoint pen as she forms the words on the page, again accompanied by Frannie's voice-off repeating the line. The effect of this sequence is to align the spectator with Frannie's subjective point of view and to afford access to her thoughts. This also introduces a place which is not contained in the image on-screen or in the sound-track, but which is elsewhere: in Frannie's psyche.

When Frannie arrives home at her apartment, she is met by a police detective who wishes to question her about the discovery of a woman's body part in the garden outside her window. When Frannie allows the detective, Malloy, to enter her apartment, we are again aligned with Frannie's point of view as she observes Malloy's visual exploration of the pervasive phrases and poetry. Frannie's home contains an overwhelming array of phrases and words hanging on threads suspended around her flat, and her ornaments and décor are represented in particular detail. This has the effect of emphasizing once more the pre-eminence within the film of Frannie's psyche: we are shown so much detail about what interests her, and we are invited to appreciate the tools which she uses to represent herself. We are given access to her home, but this is not the domesticated realm of the wife or the mother. It is the imaginative, expressive den of a cultivated teacher and writer.

Frannie moves behind the camouflage of a mobile phone as if to observe Malloy unnoticed, and when she registers amused disbelief at his banal conversation, her wry expression engages the spectator in her reaction. It is not spoken, but her reaction involves us by letting us know that she thinks he is inane, and we laugh with her at Malloy. Again, we are sharing a space with Frannie which is outside of mere image and sound – it is the space of her subjective sensibility.

Applying Mimesis and the Camera as Speculum

The way in which *In the Cut* constructs and conveys Frannie's consciousness and subjective point of view is subtle yet radical. It is achieved through a complex and creative approach to film-making, an understanding of which can be enhanced and clarified by the writings of Irigaray and the strategies she proposes for the creation and preservation of feminine subjectivity. In *This Sex Which Is Not One*, Irigaray suggests mimesis as a means by which women can go outside of a masculine tradition, 'to try to recover the place of her exploitation by discourse, without allowing herself to be simply reduced to it' (p. 76). In order to disrupt the patriarchal hierarchy and symbolic systems, it would be possible to use mimesis 'to convert a form of subordination into an affirmation, and thus to begin to thwart it' (ibid.). This strategy offers an explanation of the way in which *In the Cut* is subversive: it takes on an established genre – the erotic thriller – and does something very different and surprising with the female role. The difference, among other things, lies in the film being close to, but different from, the generic expectations it arouses: the conventions of narrative logic suggest one interpretation, but when re-read they show something different with regards to the representation of the woman. While the conventions of *In the Cut* are those of the erotic thriller, they are also those of the male-cop-buddy film, the porn film and the 'slasher' film, which are traditionally considered male or even misogynist genres. There is, however, a gap between what we expect to see in the context of the familiar generic conventions and what is, in fact, portrayed. It is in this gap, arising out of an Irigarayan re-reading, that representations of female subjectivity can be located.

When saying that Lacan's flat reflective mirror is not appropriate to women, Irigaray suggests the use of the speculum as a concave mirror:

> to put into place a mode of specularization that allows for the relation of woman to 'herself' and to her like. Which presupposes *a curved mirror*, but also one that is *folded back on itself*, with its impossible reappropriation 'on the inside' of the mind, of thought, of subjectivity. Whence the *intervention of the speculum and of the concave mirror*, which disturb the staging of representation according to too-exclusively masculine parameters. (op. cit., pp. 154–5; italics in original)

The camera lens in *In the Cut* is used in this mode of specularization, in a subversive imitation of traditional feminine images. This camera is not simply a mirror: it tries to show how a woman constructs a world of her own, thereby partly revealing her 'journey into interiority – toward an internalized becoming'.[5] It is my contention that, in likening the film camera to a speculum – rather than a flat, reflective device – the camera can become a means of 'getting inside' feminine consciousness, revealing and examining interiority and subjectivity.

Interiority and Individuality

If there is ever to be a consciousness of self in the female camp, each woman will have to situate herself freely in relation to herself, not just in relation to the community, the couple, the family. (*Sexes and Genealogies*, p. 69)

This quotation calls for a concentration on women as individuals, and not as offshoots of men's representations or as necessarily part of a romance or relationship. This may be a prerequisite for an appropriate model of feminine subjectivity on-screen, and Irigaray provides ideas for how specifically feminine individuality might be imagined and represented. Irigaray calls for women to reinterpret the notion of virginity with positive meaning. For example, the sense in which she uses the term is about the capability of a woman to have and to keep a self of her own, and to preserve her difference, her own subjective sexuate identity. In this way, 'keeping one's virginity' signifies being capable of autonomy, singularity and preserving the space between two subjects, and thus being able to respect the other as other. This suggests possibilities for new representations of femininity on-screen. At the most basic level, there is a need for a woman to be shown on-screen living as an individual, not solely dependent on an other, or simply as part of a couple, that is, woman attending to her own sense of self. This might seem simplistic, but this *subjectified* portrayal of the activity of a single and solitary woman on-screen is rare, and therefore offers possibilities for non-standard depictions.

The use of the word 'virginity' is clearly a deliberately challenging stance by Irigaray. With the intention of redefining the term, and stripping it of its exclusively sexual and patriarchal connotations, Irigaray recalls that there was:

Hestia, the female divinity who guarded the flame of the domestic hearth. The divine is therefore watched over by the woman at home. It is transmitted from mother to daughter. When a daughter marries, the mother lights a torch at the altar of her own hearth, and, preceding the young couple, she carries it to their new residence. She thus lights the first fire of her daughter's domestic altar. The fire stands for the fact that the woman is the guardian of purity. Purity here does not signify defensive or prudish virginity, as some of our profane contemporaries might take it to mean, nor does it signify an allegiance to patriarchal culture and its definition of virginity as an exchange value between men; it signifies the woman's fidelity to her identity and female genealogy. (*je, tu, nous*, pp. 18–19)

This passage provides an example of the specifically feminine imagery and culture through which Irigaray indicates a way of interpreting her thought. The use of the term virginity here is really both practical and symbolic, but the term also has less tangible aspects in Irigaray's writing:

> Woman cannot therefore remain pure nature, even in motherhood. It is as a 'virgin' that she can give birth to a divine child. The word 'virgin' here doesn't signify the presence or the absence of a physiological hymen, of course, but the existence of a spiritual interiority of her own, capable of welcoming the word of the other without altering it. ('The Redemption of Women', in *Key Writings*, pp. 151–2)

This emphasizes the spiritual, fluid and subtle aspects of Irigaray's notion of virginity, as opposed to the 'material-natural sense' of the presence or absence of a physiological hymen (op. cit., p. 152). In the cultivation of such a spiritual virginity, Irigaray suggests that being able to keep silent may be a way of preserving a feminine autonomous belonging: 'It could be that girls keep their *lips closed* as a positive move. The positive meaning of closed lips does not rule out singing or talking. It expresses a difference' (*Sexes and Genealogies*, p. 100). This means of preserving self-faithfulness can also be seen as a way of protecting oneself from violation, keeping hold of a part of oneself.[6] According to Irigaray, focusing on one's interiority and subjectivity is needed for the capacity to stay in and return to oneself. It is not simply a matter of well-being, or devoting time to oneself.[7] Rather, it is the fundamental condition for a 'culture of two' that Irigaray envisages as founded in difference and allowing sexual difference to be cultivated. Usefully, it is also a way of talking about difference that moves from traditionally defined gender-based difference to the difference between two subjects. And it is this state of difference that Irigaray considers essential for the existence of feminine subjective specificity and love of self. The description of the effects of the objectification of women in this perspective adds to the understanding of the problems with the objectification of women in film:

> And when she is placed as an object by and for man, love of self is arrested in its development. She needs to accede to a love of herself, an affection of and in the invisible which can be expressed in that which touches itself without consummation. (*An Ethics of Sexual Difference*, p. 60)

It is this love of self which *In the Cut* attempts to represent by not placing Frannie as an object upon the screen, but rather by allowing her character to develop and reflect upon her own situation and experiences as subject, through gestures and language, but also through silence.

For Irigaray, silence as a positive gesture would enable woman to keep what is not yet manifest, as this is revealed by some Eastern traditions which talk about the sacred syllable *aum* (*Sexes and Genealogies*, p. 100). Silence is a necessary start for both interiority and dialogue. Silence is an opportunity for women to experience the world, themselves and the other without dissipation. With

regard to silence imposed on women in our tradition, Irigaray also suggests as a
strategy that women should

> Insist also and deliberately upon those *blanks* in discourse which recall
> the places of her exclusion and which, by their *silent plasticity*, ensure the
> cohesion, the articulation, the coherent expansion of established forms.
> Reinscribe them hither and thither *as divergencies*, otherwise and elsewhere
> than they are expected, in *ellipses* and *eclipses* that deconstruct the logical grid
> of the reader-writer. (*Speculum*, p. 142; italics in original)

Frannie finds and also creates blanks in the filmic discourse and reinscribes
these spaces other than as expected, thereby deconstructing the somehow conventional linear narrative. Frannie is silent, contemplative and non-responsive
verbally, but is exceptionally proficient in using written language to communicate – she is an English literature teacher who is writing a book on explicit
slang. She takes ownership of words which are misogynist, sexually violent and
derogatory towards women, including the detailed description of the death of
a female murder victim. Frannie asks how the woman was killed and Malloy
replies that she was 'disarticulated'; as soon as Malloy leaves her apartment,
Frannie notes down the word. Again, there is an extreme close-up of her pen
as she writes the word in her notebook, and the spectator is given access to the
place in Frannie's consciousness which is intrigued by language. In this way, the
images on-screen are concerned with Frannie's interiority rather than with the
conventional masculine discourse of violence and domination.

Body Movements and Sexual Pleasure

In exemplifying a place where a feminine syntax might be located, that is, 'a
syntax that would make woman's "self-affection" possible' (*This Sex Which Is Not
One*, p. 132), Irigaray suggests that it might be:

> deciphered [...] in the gestural code of women's bodies. But, since their
> gestures are often paralysed, or part of the masquerade, in effect, they are
> often difficult to 'read'. Except for what resists or subsists 'beyond'. In suffer-
> ing, but also in women's laughter. And again: in what they 'dare' – do or say
> – when they are among themselves. (op. cit., p. 134)

Frannie and her sister, Pauline, display laughter and ridicule at men and the
world around them, while their relationship is intimate and sensual. This sisterly
bond is portrayed in scenes where they are playful, emotional and supportive
by turn. Dressed in flesh-coloured underwear, appearing nude, in candlelight
or subdued lighting, they dance and sing, caress and confide, moving towards
'colour and [...] tonality as qualities of flesh, gender and genealogy' that defy
the 'mastery and abstraction of the living being', which Irigaray describes as
the activity of 'civilisations that give priority to nonfigurative writing, arbitrary

forms, and formal codes' (*Sexes and Genealogies*, p. 160). Frannie and Pauline display some of the actions and gestures which Irigaray encourages women to discover, 'gestures that have been forgotten, misunderstood, gestures that are also words, that are different from the gestures of maternity and shed a different light upon generation in the body in the strictest sense of the term' (op. cit., p. 181). The sisters dance and whirl, sing and laugh, and sit in silence together, all gestures considered by Irigaray as ways in which women can find self-expression. Irigaray's writing on the gestural code of women's bodies is integral to my reading of this film; in particular, the idea that girls might 'keep their lips closed as a positive move' (op. cit., p. 100). This is clearly a fertile proposal for film-making. The idea that there could be a manner of representing, involving actions, gestures and bodily experiences, which could enable women on-screen to be shown relating to one another and to the world around them in an original way: women engaging in specific action and movement, as opposed to the static or manipulated phallocratic spectacle of classical cinema.

Irigaray writes that 'a woman can usually find self-expression only when her lips are touching together and when her whole body is in movement. A woman is more at a loss when she is still than when she is moving, because when fixed in one position she is a prisoner, open to attack in her own territory' (op. cit., p. 102). Women in *In the Cut* are shown to be constantly moving and travelling – walking in pairs, running, roller-blading – in a city in which a serial killer is preying on young women. One of the major themes of the film is how women claim space and how men try to invade it. The invasion of space by men is threatening and deadly, whereas women are shown to move freely throughout the city, claiming space for themselves and displacing men. For example, Frannie's sister, Pauline, lives above a strip-club, and both she and Pauline are happy to go into the club, populated by female dancers and male customers, in order to order drinks from the bar or to find emotional support from the women who work there. Even this traditionally exclusive domain is in no way off-limits to Frannie.

Another strategy that is suggested by Irigaray – that is useful in terms of identifying where feminine subjectivity may be represented – involves women's sexual pleasure. Irigaray writes of the 'need to discover what makes our experience of sexual pleasure special' (op. cit., p. 20). She considers some pornographic scenes and analyses one of their components as 'a reduction of the body to a mere surface to be broken through or punctured' (*This Sex Which Is Not One*, p. 200), while 'the body's pleasure always results from a forced entry – preferably bloody – into an *enclosure*' (op. cit., p. 201; italics in original). Although widely described in the reviews upon release as being pornographic,[8] the sex scenes of *In the Cut* are erotic and visually pleasurable, and their focus is on Frannie's pleasure as she experiences her first two orgasms through masturbation and cunnilingus. Frannie's relationship with Malloy proceeds through emotional negotiation and encounters with sexual candour. Jane Campion has said of Frannie and Malloy that 'they are both truth seekers' – a poet and a detective (Lizzie Francke, 'Jane Campion', *Sight and Sound*, 13:11, p. 15). Campion also comments how the film's open-ended conclusion challenges the idea that a relationship can complete you, stating 'that's work you have to do yourself' (ibid.). In this sense, the representation of the burgeoning relationship between Frannie and Molloy can be considered as being, to some extent, consistent with what Irigaray says about the need to return to oneself in order to respect the difference with the other; which favours establishing the meeting with the other in a space of honesty, freedom and sensory perception: 'The other is the one whom I shall never reach, and for that very reason, *he/she* forces me to remain in my self in order to be faithful to *him/her* and *us*, retaining our difference' ('You Who Will Never Be Mine', in *Key Writings*, p. 9; italics in original). *In the Cut* offers a representation of a relationship between a man and a woman who recognize and respect their singularity and try to discover a way of being in relation with each other whilst retaining their own individuality.

In the film, the original and the subversive are attempts to create the representation of a woman who is 'becoming'. Her journey is not about well-being, redemptive moral realization, or recuperation into patriarchal discourse. It is a journey into her own interiority, with the discovery that an intersubjective relationship might enable a fully realized female subjectivity to flourish. As I hope to have demonstrated, the writings of Luce Irigaray provide a range of images, strategies, devices and notions that suggest expressions of a woman's interiority on-screen, but these are not prescriptive. Rather, they constitute a palette of possibilities with which a new visual language of the feminine can be created.

Notes

1 This article is reproduced in Mulvey's book, *Visual and Other Pleasures*.

2 *Speculum*, p. 135.

3 In May 2005, I attended a seminar organized by Luce Irigaray at the University of Nottingham. The seminar consisted of a week of presentations and discussions with a group of twelve other students writing their PhD on Luce Irigaray's work. During this week, Luce Irigaray commented on our own research and answered our questions. This quotation is taken from Luce Irigaray's comments during that seminar. I will hereafter reference quotations from the seminar as 'Luce Irigaray, seminar, University of Nottingham, May 2005'.

4 I use the term 'voice-off', as opposed to 'voice-over', to connote the existence of another place, off screen, which the voice inhabits. In this way, the voice can be appreciated as occupying a place of its own, not simply supplementing or complementing the image. I draw on this term from Brigit Sjogren, in *Into the Vortex*.

5 Luce Irigaray, seminar, University of Nottingham, May 2005.

6 Luce Irigaray, seminar, University of Nottingham, May 2005; and conference, 'In All the World We Are Always Only Two', June 2006.

7 Luce Irigaray, seminar, University of Nottingham, May 2005; and conference, 'In All the World We Are Always Only Two', June 2006.

8 Two examples of such discussions are: 'Sex in the Movies' by David Hudson, GreenCine, <http://www.greencine.com/static/primers/adult1.jsp> [accessed 01/09/2006]; and 'Has porn entered mainstream cinema for good?', by Mark Kermode, *Guardian*, 4 June 2006.

Chapter 6

Architectural Issues in Building Community through Luce Irigaray's Perspective on Being-Two

Andrea Wheeler

The University of Nottingham, United Kingdom

For architects, one of the most interesting and contemporary issues to emerge from Luce Irigaray's philosophy is the question of sustainability and how this is linked to problems of community. In this paper, I explore how Luce Irigaray's approach in essays such as 'How Can We Live Together in a Lasting Way' (published in *Key Writings*), the interview 'About being-two in an architectural perspective', and *Democracy Begins Between Two* have significance to those reflecting on the present problems of urban regeneration. My paper focuses, in particular, on the way the philosophy of being-two could challenge current thinking and assist the role of architecture in regenerating communities.

Government literature commissioned and published by the Office of the Deputy Prime Minister (ODPM)[1] has described a sustainable community as one that meets the diverse needs of residents, one that is sensitive to the environment, one that is safe, one that is inclusive, well-planned, well-built, well-run, one that offers an equality of opportunity and a high quality of life to all. Sustainable communities are described as responding well to the balance between social, environmental and global needs, including a global respect for other communities and their desires to make their own communities sustainable. Keys to developing sustainable communities are identified and described as fostering a sense of community identity, belonging, tolerance and respect, and managing such communities requires good services, good systems of governance, good leadership and active and effective participation by individuals and community organizations. This could, and often does, include educative and skills-building initiatives.

The Office of the Deputy Prime Minister's 2003 report, *The Sustainable Communities: Building for the Future* (p. 4), sets out twelve requirements of sustainable communities. The Royal Institute of British Architects (RIBA), in *Sustainable Communities: Quality with Quantity* (p. 5), adds six other criteria and expresses the desire to further planning legislation and extend these principles. Sustainable communities are next defined by Sir John Egan as the ones planned with care for the long term, by those who, to quote: 'think and act in the long term and beyond their own immediate geographic interest boundaries, and who involve users and local residents in shaping their policy and practices' (*The Egan Review*, p. 21). Sustainable communities are thus the ones that also have the intention of promoting and protecting the rights and desires of citizens both in their own and in neighbouring communities. Ultimately, such guidance is aimed at initiating some concern for the needs of future generations, care which has a global significance.

Nevertheless, whilst government guidance makes no suggestion that it can serve as a template for sustainable development, best practice examples are celebrated by awards that champion the idea that good practice in building design can also provide a host of social benefits, including the reduction of crime, illness and truancy from schools (cf. DCMS, *Better Public Buildings: A Proud Legacy for the Future*, p. 4). In a recent publication, *Building and Spaces: Why Design Matters*, The Commission for the Built Environment (CABE) states: 'Planning policy makes it clear that good design ensures attractive, usable, durable and adaptable places and is a key in achieving sustainability' (p. 20). Moreover, they claim that good design is indispensable to good planning. The Department for Culture, Media and Sport (DCMS) reinforces this opinion, quoting the statement made by Tessa Jowell: 'Most people now accept that you cannot breathe new life into cities, towns and communities without culture [...] The unprecedented £15 billion of lottery money, together with new investment from Government, has completely transformed communities all over the UK, putting culture right at the heart of that change' (*Culture at the Heart of Regeneration*, p. 3). Newcastle and Gateshead are cited as two significant examples where architectural projects constitute the success of the regeneration schemes. The major funds now available for regeneration projects include the Government's 'New Deal for Communities' and the 'Neighbourhood Renewal Fund', with a number of smaller funding bodies and the lottery funds making vast amounts available for redevelopment. In the East Midlands, for example, bodies such as the East Midlands Development Agency and Regeneration East Midlands provide training, grant funding advice and promote good practice.

Nevertheless, questions have always been raised over the potential of expensive cultural and, in particular, architectural projects to initiate any real benefit to communities. There are many lobby groups, such as the Empty Homes Agency (EHA), which criticize planning legislation for allowing profoundly unsustainable growth, whilst not meeting the needs of individuals and families for affordable homes, whilst leaving existing buildings empty (cf. David Ireland's *How to Rescue a House*). Moreover, the agency declares one of its key actions is to 'urge the Government to ensure that a full option appraisal is conducted of all viable options to bring property back into use prior to any demolition together with full public consultation' (*A Manifesto on Empty Homes 2005*, p. 4).

The problems of regeneration are complex for all those who are involved with them. Good design is not just a matter of conforming to planning guidance, but neither is it a response solely to an economic or social need.

Architecture is not simply a visual cultural form – which pleases or displeases our tastes, regenerating through its charm – nor is it purely the means to provide functional social requirements, at least as commonly understood.[2] The problems of community regeneration and the role of architecture with respect to them necessitate wondering what it means to live, an attitude that belongs to the philosophical as much as to the architectural tradition. There are numerous architectural theorists and writers who have explored the philosophical tradition to discuss these questions in terms of space and place. Many refer directly (such as Edward Casey in *The Fate of Place*) and sometimes indirectly to key philosophers from the phenomenological tradition, such as Martin Heidegger and Maurice Merleau-Ponty.

Architecture thus concerns us at many levels. Many architectural practices already employ creative strategies of community consultation and participation to elicit and respond to the desires of citizens in their plans. Peter Blundell-Jones, Jeremy Till and Doina Petrescu review this sort of practice in their edited collection *Architecture and Participation*. Blundell-Jones discusses the position of the architect Peter Hübner who, working with children and young people in an area of deprivation and low educational achievement, helped them to design and build their own school, a school that went on to become the centre for community regeneration and learning (cf. Blundell-Jones, 'Özcül postscript: the Gelsenkirchen school as built'). Many companies and organizations involved in participation suggest that place-making exercises by communities can create a sense of ownership, guardianship and concern for the environment, and there is good reason to endorse such approaches. Nevertheless, there is also good reason to criticize both the motives and the limits of such an undertaking.

The interest in recent publications such as *Eco-Phenomenology: Back to the Earth Itself* and *Rethinking Nature: Essays in Environmental Philosophy* reinforce the opinion that stimulating community relations from the level of individual engagement is valuable for encouraging more global environmental ethics. Ingrid Leman Stefanovic suggests that it is the foundational faith in a safe and healthy world which is illustrated in children's drawings and that underlies our own motives towards sustainable development programmes ('Children and the Ethics of Place', in *Rethinking Nature*, p. 61). However, collections of essays such as *Feminist Interpretations of Martin Heidegger* both celebrate the potential for and raise criticisms regarding such thinking. Trish Glazebrook, in 'Heidegger and Ecofeminism', argues that Heidegger offers the variety of ecofeminisms the philosophical grounding for an alternative conception of Nature, and yet she also recognizes the possibility of a feminist criticism. In 'Home and Home: Feminist Variations on a Theme', Iris Marion Young develops the complex issues surrounding ideas of home and belonging from the perspective of feminist philosophy, citing some of Luce Irigaray's works, and including her essay 'From *The Forgetting of Air* to *To Be Two*' in the collection – an essay which both celebrates Heidegger's thought and challenges the very relation or alternative conception or feeling for Nature that influences his thinking.

Thus, whilst the ambitions of establishing equal opportunities for all, reinforcing community identity through an awareness of belonging, and initiating a sense of guardianship and care for the environment can only be appreciated in the ethics of government literature, the philosophy of Luce Irigaray provides a way to review, from a relational level, such proposals and to question their real and effective long-term sustainability regarding the problems of community. The philosophy of Luce Irigaray criticizes not only the principles of sustainable development as they have been set out, but also the hidden desires, expectations and actions of architects, planners and urban management teams that are involved in community participation projects, though they have been so popular with the ODPM.

Regeneration projects warrant educative engagement with the community, a sort of building together of community identity, as well as physical place. This could assist in maintaining relationships of care and guardianship of the environment and natural resources. Both these sorts of objectives, and even a self-critical approach, are not unfamiliar territories to those carrying out participation exercises, especially to those adopting an Action Research methodology. However, responding to the desires of, as well as building with, the other – from the perspective of Luce Irigaray's philosophy of being-two – would go beyond any common participation practice and would provide new ways of thinking about community.

New Relational Perspectives in Architecture

In the section of *The Way of Love* entitled 'Rebuilding the World', Luce Irigaray suggests that our culture has above all neglected, and even forgotten, the horizontal dimension of human becoming. In *Democracy Begins Between Two*, she explains that it is through a sort of building between two – two who are both equal and different – that we could begin to found a new approach to community. She writes: 'What has not yet been imagined in thought is: how to remain together while still being two, how to be and become subjectively two, how to discover a way of coexisting as two beings, private and public' (*Democracy Begins Between Two*, p. 112). Moreover, in the paper presented at the Architectural Association, London, 'How Can We Live Together in a Lasting Way?' (in *Key Writings*, pp. 123–33) she proposes architectural initiatives that could challenge the generally unthought arrangements for living together which culturally reinforce unequal relationships between cohabitees, beginning in this way to open up new thinking about community.

For Luce Irigaray, there are more basic and natural relations between two than that maintained by patriarchal traditions, including through architecture. These relations are described in terms of 'sexuate' difference, the most misunderstood, most complex, most unthought difference in our cultures, which has distorted our belief, our relations to Nature and our relationships with the other.

For Luce Irigaray, to be truly human involves being in a relation to and with a different other in a way that is not stipulated by Western philosophical traditions. To culturally reach a relation in sexuate difference requires a sort of attentiveness and response to the desire of the other really not similar to those practices in participation exercises. She writes: 'To cultivate no longer means simply to reduplicate, to name, to educate, to construct, or to create the already existent universe, but to leave it to its becoming while accepting that it affects my own, without robbing it of its singularity' ('From the *Forgetting of Air* to *To Be Two*', in *Feminist Interpretations of Martin Heidegger*, p. 314).

Luce Irigaray's philosophy both deconstructs a past horizon and builds a new one with a dual attentiveness. She says: 'There are thus two acts to be carried out almost simultaneously: an act of constitution and an act of interpretation and departure from a cultural identity, departure from a land of exile that falsely separates man and woman' (*I Love To You*, p. 46). In the development of this new relationship with the other, the natural world has a role, but nature here is freed from the preconceptions of the Western philosophical traditions. Nature, then, can be of help to build a new culture:

> The natural, aside from the diversity of its incarnations or ways of appearing, is at least *two*: male and female. This division is not secondary nor unique to human kind. It cuts across all realms of the living which, without it, would not exist. Without sexual difference, there would be no life on earth. It is the manifestation of and the condition for the production and reproduction of life. Air and sexual difference may be the two dimensions vital for/to life. Not taking them into account would be a deadly business. (op. cit., p. 37)

Being-two presupposes a complex co-dependence, coexistence and co-belonging in sexuate difference, and it distinguishes Luce Irigaray's thought from other contemporary thinkers. The task for her is not only to imagine but also to stage an encounter between two differently sexuate subjectivities, and so to make something exist which is yet without any word, philosophy or architecture that are capable to take it into account. In *To Be Two*, amongst other texts, she writes of this relation with the mysterious living other:

> If you remain alive, my gaze, my senses are always aroused by your present intentions, and I cannot fall asleep in my knowledge of you, in the repetition of what I have already felt from you, as long as a stronger sensation keeps me awake. Your gestures, if they are inspired by your desire, attract my attention, my gaze. Its horizon is not closed but remains open upon your mystery, upon the irreducibility of your freedom, upon your intention. Turned towards you, my eyes are centred upon you, but they do not yet have, within, an image or a spectacle. They are always and already virginal when looking at you, at the expression of your desire. (p. 41)

The project towards sustainable development has to wonder whether its policies represent a valid approach, whether their strategies ought not only to encourage but also to maintain a viable behaviour. If Luce Irigaray's philosophy can be understood as a criticism of some of the proposals towards sustainable communities, such as issues of diversity and of equal opportunity, it above all stresses the fact that the question of sexuate difference is more complex than those envisioned in reports previously cited. For example, Luce Irigaray says that to only uphold diversity can be a way of escaping the question of difference:

> To promote only diversity, as is often the case in our times, runs the risk of remaining in an unchanged horizon with regard to the relations with the other(s). We then entrust this problem to customs, moral rules or religious feeling without questioning our culture about its capability of meeting with the other as such. Furthermore we are unable to open ourselves all the time to others different from us. We need to return to ourselves, to keep and save our totality or integrity, and this is possible only in sexuate difference. Why? Because it is the most basic difference, this one which secures for each one bridges(s) both between nature and culture and between us. It is starting from this difference that the other sorts of otherness have been elaborated. (interview with Andrea Wheeler, 'About being-two in an architectural perspective', *Journal of Romance Studies*, 4:2 (2004), p. 93)

Hence, from the level of community identity and belonging, Luce Irigaray asks us to question what it means to live as sexuate beings. She invites us to question what it signifies to dwell in a world where the dimension of sexuate difference pervades both our own being and our relation(s) with other(s), and to work towards the foundation of a culture of this difference. From an environmental standpoint, Luce Irigaray argues that the nature of care, of guardianship, of attentiveness to the natural world and its resources cannot be truly thought without an attention to the sexuate aspect. Moreover, to take into account sexuate difference, requires an implication which cannot remain only mental, as she explains: 'To work on this difference represents a difficult task, a task that cannot remain only mental, as our culture has taught us, but which requires a participation of the whole of ourselves, a sort of conversion of ourselves' (op. cit., p. 96). The very notion of being-in-the-world explored by eco-phenomenology suggests an inhabiting, but it is one that can be criticized as illustrative of an exploitative relation if it does not take account of the different ways of dwelling of men and women and of their different worlds: this can be explored as a question of love (cf. Andrea Wheeler, 'Love in Architecture').

The patriarchal model of care postulates a subject who is neutral, but it is not gender neutral. For example, in her essay 'Approaching the Other as Other', Luce Irigaray writes that man has mistaken cultivation with being accustomed to making everything that pleases him his own, to appropriating the all into his own world, in particular and especially women: 'On the level of consciousness, on the level of feeling, we make our own what we approach, what approaches us. Our manner of reasoning, even our manner of loving, corresponds to an appropriation' (*Between East and West*, p. 121). Such a culture is really extraneous to that proposed by Luce Irigaray. For her the other is a forever inappropriable living being: tangible, present and mysterious.

Building would thus imply a building of oneself, a letting-be of oneself and of the other, and a cultivation of the relation in two. The relation of care is really different to that of the patriarchal tradition. Such a care, or love, is yet to be cultivated, is yet to be. Irigaray claims:

Generally to build is understood as building something with material(s) to which it is given form(s). These views on building are rather masculine. From the beginning of our Western culture, man has tried to differ from nature by mastering this, which provides raw material, with his technique and technology. Building, then, implies cutting oneself off from nature, including human nature, especially represented by the mother and even by woman. Building is seldom understood as building oneself with respect for the nature that we are. This way of building, nevertheless, is in some way asked of woman, notably in engendering and loving. ('About being-two in an architectural perspective', op. cit., p. 97)

In the paper 'How Can We Live Together in a Lasting Way' (in *Key Writings*, pp. 123–33), Luce Irigaray suggests how the house of a couple could be split into two separate apartments; and children, when they arrive, would simultaneously have their own apartments as far as it is possible. This would favour both the development of each subjectivity and their being in relation. Moreover, the four elements and living growing vegetation would also play an important role in this restructuring of the home. The need for separate place is further discussed in terms of feminine becoming:

To reach building herself, woman has to preserve and cultivate her nature also in an autonomous and decided manner. She has to discover how to pass from her material or bodily nature to a cultural or spiritual nature appropriate to her. ('About being-two in an architectural perspective', op. cit., p. 97).

The effects of patriarchy can be concealed but conflicts can be illustrative of the fact that we have not yet begun to understand and cultivate sexuate difference. Reconsidering what it means to be human, what it means to be sexed, to be in a relationship of sexuate difference, reconsidering who and what we are now and what this implies for the future might be a way to explore further problems of sustainable communities and the exploitation of natural resources. Fostering a sustainable community from the perspective of being-two would need some care towards the development of differently sexuate ways of being, and these require some cultural changes. Architectural design and urban regeneration plans may be one approach to promote such changes. The attentiveness that Luce Irigaray's work appeals for could favour the rediscovery and the re-establishment of a form of community where equality is not considered in an abstract way but in relation to a real and natural difference and the implication of government policy corresponds to an active contribution. This means that such contribution goes beyond mere questions of involvement and of equality between citizens. As Irigaray says: 'All of us, and particularly architects, have to take into account the difference between the worlds in which each dwells, and have both to allow their existence and becoming and to care about the coexistence with the other, in respect of difference(s)' (op. cit., p. 99).

Notes

1 The Office of the Deputy Prime Minister (ODPM) has now become Communities and Local Government. Information about how the government defines sustainable communities is thus now to be found on the Communities and Local Government website at http://www.communities.gov.uk and in particular in the document *Sustainable Communities: Building for the Future* (2003) published on this site.

2 The popular philosopher, Alain de Botton, falls into this oversimplification by emphasizing this visual aspect of architecture in his publication *The Architecture of Happiness* and, in particular, in the TV series *The Perfect Home.*

Chapter 7

Touching Hands, Cultivating Dwelling[1]

Helen A. Fielding

The University of Western Ontario, Canada

Touch which allows turning back to oneself, in the dwelling of an intimate light. But which also goes to encounter the other, illuminated-illuminating, overflowing one's own world in order to taste another brightness. In order to give and to receive what can enlighten mortals on their path.

(Luce Irigaray, *The Way of Love*, p. 174)

Dwelling is essential to human being. It is no mere inhabiting of spaces; rather, in order to dwell we must erect structures and cultivate relations since dwelling happens in places, in room created by and between the things we build. Following Martin Heidegger, the art work that sets to work reveals relations that exceed what appears according to systems of calculative measurement, whereby man is able to assert control over everything through careful planning and adequate technology (cf. 'The Question Concerning Technology'). Dwelling takes place thanks to a gathering of the fourfold, Heidegger's term for the relations between humans, earth, sky and divinities (cf. 'Building Dwelling Thinking'). Humans, who are finite beings – they die – live on earth and under the sky open to the divinities, that is, alongside that which is not of their making nor under their control. The art work is a privileged *technë*, a privileged mode of experiencing and bringing to appearance that reveals a relation to being which transcends calculative measurement. It reveals a relation to being which sets up a world in which we might dwell, in which we might encounter that which is somehow other to us. In 1951, a time when so many were affected by the housing crisis in Germany, it is understandable that Heidegger chose to focus his lecture about dwelling on the construction of things, barely mentioning the cultivation of things that grow (cf. 'Building Dwelling Thinking'). Even so, although his thinking shifts from the earlier understanding of the *unheimlich* (the unhomely or uncanny) of the human as a violent 'making appear' to the later *Gelassenheit* or 'letting be', he remains concerned with *technë* as revealing what is (cf. *Introduction to Metaphysics*).[2]

But making is only part of the dwelling that belongs to being human. Luce Irigaray calls our attention to that which perhaps belongs more fully to the feminine and has been obscured in this age: the interior cultivation of the self necessary for a relation between two, and a cultivation of life, that is, of a becoming that is not merely dependent on man's making. This cultivation of the self and the other might belong more to the feminine in this age since a man encounters himself everywhere as 'ils' ('they' masculine), as one of the generic beings who have fabricated the world and themselves, rather than as a particular and sexuate individual (Irigaray, 'Importance du genre dans la constitution de la subjectivité et de l'intersubjectivité', in *Le partage de la parole*, p. 40). In *The Way of Love*, Irigaray asks why has man throughout History, privileged making? And how to interpret the relations between making and being, particularly with the meaning of 'letting be'. After all, 'Does not their traditional opposition mask an inappropriate articulation between nature and culture that prevents man from knowing himself in his truth?' (*The Way of Love*, p. 123).[3] Man's celebration of his *unheimlich* technological ability to make obscure the fact that humans are at least two, that man alone cannot be responsible for everything that is produced, and that the 'blossoming of man requires, in fact, a making and a letting be' (op. cit., p. 125).

The phenomenological move to demonstrate and to reveal what exists, is there, is insufficient for cultivating life. As one aspect of what it means to be human, taken on its own, it delineates above all the horizon of death. Thus an art work that allows us to meditate on *technē* both as revealing as well as cultivating relations, brings into relief Luce Irigaray's insights into the place of dwelling. Louise Bourgeois's outdoor sculptures entitled *The Welcoming Hands* (1996), as art works that set to work, provide for room that not only admits and installs the fourfold, but also allows for the cultivation of relations and of life.

Welcoming Hands

For Heidegger, building requires thought, since thinking accomplishes the 'relation of being to the essence of the human being' ('Letter on Humanism', in *Pathmarks*, p. 239). Indeed, thinking itself is a craft, a 'handicraft', for only a being who speaks – in other words, thinks – can have hands. Hands thus seem to provide a bridge between making and letting be, between erecting and cultivating, since the hand cannot be explained merely by its ability to grasp. It also 'reaches and extends, receives and welcomes' things and others (Heidegger, *What is Called Thinking?*, p. 16). It is with their hands that humans act – in German, *handeln*. Yet, notes Derrida, although Heidegger writes often about the hand, it is always a singular hand (cf. '*Geschlecht* II'). Louise Bourgeois's sculptures allow us to contemplate with Irigaray a 'being two'. They allow us to think about hands that touch and are touched.

The art work in question, *The Welcoming Hands*, consists of six distinct blocks of granite with varying configurations of intertwining bronze hands and is located in central Paris. It currently rests under and alongside two parallel lines of trees that run from the *Galerie Jeu de Paume* (which was once a handball court) in the direction of the *Orangerie*. If one walks away from the *Musée du Louvre* and across the *Jardin des Tuileries* towards the *Place de la Concorde*, the line of trees ultimately connects the *Champs Élysées* to the *Arc de Triomphe*, ending at the arch at *La Défense*. Were there a privileged approach to the work(s), it would be to follow this axis since, as one approaches the sculptures from this direction, they draw the eye downward into the earth.

The Welcome Hands 1 (no. 38) – Louise Bourgeois

The Welcome Hands 2 (no. 49)
– Louise Bourgeois

The Welcome Hands 3
(no. 61) – Louise Bourgeois

The granite stones set up the hands, holding them steady under the sky and on the ground. Like buildings, they are mostly lined up but not quite. They are of varying heights and shapes, colours and textures. They might also mirror or resound with nearby monuments, such as the phallic-like obelisk at the adjacent *Place de la Concorde*, where the guillotine stood during the revolution, or the statues that populate the *Jardin des Tuileries*, as well as the *Tour Eiffel* which can be seen in the distance. Yet these stones, unlike the other monuments, do not thrust into the sky, nor delineate massive straight lines. Set within this huge institutional layout – that includes gardens that are highly planned, as well as other art works – these sculptures are modest, quiet and easily missed. Still, if they are not missed, and if one attends to them, they bring into appearance new ways of relating. The shared root 'tec' can be found in both 'architecture' and '*technë*'. If *technë* is a making 'something appear, within what is present' (Heidegger, 'Building Dwelling Thinking', in *Poetry, Language, Thought*, p. 159), then Bourgeois's sculptures bring something forth into appearance from within the site that is established there.

The bronze hands that rest upon the granite stones are at once beautiful in their close to life-like *mimësis* of hands that are holding, leading, intertwining, as well as uncanny in the way that they first appear as amputated limbs spread out across granite tombstones. I thought, on first approach, that this work was perhaps a holocaust memorial. I was wrong. In fact, the sculptures were first created for Battery Park in New York City.[4] Originally positioned across the water from the Statue of Liberty, the hands were meant to welcome 'newcomers', new immigrants, as Bourgeois herself once was. Yet, the hands apparently caused concern since the adjacent Holocaust Museum was opening at about the same time, and officials worried that the hands 'suggested severed body parts from the death camps' (Amei Wallach, 'To an artist'). So there is something uncanny about these hands on first encounter. They are both familiar as human hands and yet they are not human. Moreover, it is strange to reveal hands as things, since when we are acting and doing they generally recede from view into the actions themselves, from which they usually remain undifferentiated. In Bourgeois's sculptures, the hands are clearly visible: her art works call us to think about hands, to reflect upon their materiality, their thing-like nature, as well as on that which they accomplish. They bring this uncanny strangeness of human making and cultivating to the fore.

At least three paths meet and cross at this place that the work(s) create. Two of the paths are in turn divided by rows of trees, creating the sense of multiple paths. A museum, as Jean-Luc Nancy points out in a talk given at the *Jeu de Paume*, a museum for temporary exhibits, a few years before Bourgeois's work was installed nearby, is a 'strange place where art only passes' (*The Muses*, p. 81). Art museums encourage us to encounter art works at a distance as aesthetic objects. Already there is something different about a permanent work erected outdoors in a public space that not only establishes an open place where events occur, but also where the sculptures can be intimately encountered. In a museum, sculptures cannot be touched – outdoors, they can. They invite us to be proximal to them, to stroke, explore and even caress them. Although the hands were originally created for another site, Bourgeois chose the new site within the garden and oversaw the location of the sculptures.[5] Reminiscent in one sense of a Richard Serra site piece, Bourgeois's sculptures are encountered by those who do not already know her work, who have perhaps not sought out an art work, but are merely passing through. They alter the rhythms and the movements of those who pass by, gathering them together in varying shifting configurations.

A Site for Dwelling

For Heidegger, truth happens in 'the open', the temporal and spatial region established by the work of art ('The Origin of the Work of Art', in *Poetry, Language, Thought*, pp. 61–2). In his account, art understood in terms of aesthetics is set apart to be viewed according to feelings and affect, whereas the art work provides a place where truth is revealed. Since there is a difference between being and beings, dwelling presupposes the open, a clearing within which we are thrown beyond the familiar. And yet, in this age of calculative systematicity, an encounter with the alien, with that which is other, is in fact that which we flee. Indeed, otherness cannot appear where production into appearance is collapsed into a kind of making appear according to instrumental planning guided by preconceived forms. Taking this further, Irigaray reflects, we can less and less be surprised by that which is other than man, since everywhere we encounter only forms which have been constructed or manufactured, materially or mentally, by him ('Being two, how many eyes have we', in *Dialogues*, p. 142)

Bourgeois's works do not merely establish an open where truth can unfold; they also establish a place where humans can interact and relate to one another. The stones are not elevated in order to impress or to allow maximum visibility. Rather, they are of varying but generally low heights that allow passersby to bend over them, to touch the hands, photograph them, draw them. One can walk around them. Children climb onto them, rock the smallest and lightest, and engage with them in very unmonumental ways. One jogger stops to stretch out her legs, supporting her calf against the granite. Another family creates a gathering with the nearby metal chairs and eats a picnic lunch laid out on one stone.

As noted previously, the works admit and install a place which shelters the fourfold. They are out in the open, on the earth and under the sky; the sun and light, the clouds and rain, play with and dance around the sculptures as well as the passersby. The bronze reflects, it responds to the sun, and as one walks around the hands, they seem to move as the light touches and refracts differently upon the multiple surfaces. In the sunlight, the hands seem livelier; the polished ends of the limbs are more vibrant. They look less like amputated stumps. Similarly, the colours of the stones change with the light and respond differently to the bronze accordingly. And light patches on the bronze expose zones where it has been repeatedly touched. Reverberating amongst themselves, these works create a place. One sculpture is set back, sheltered beneath the trees from the rain and sun. The trees, planted in parallel lines with their tops creating a second flat line, also seem to have a kind of architectural presence – they appear almost closer to the sky than to the earth, and the stones which hover beneath the trees in the clearing created below their branches appear more uneven by comparison. Even the hands and arms seem to parallel or echo the paths that intersect at various points at this place of crossroads.

The Cultivation of Relations

These works call us to reflect on what hands sense (Terrie Sultan, 'Redefining the Terms of Engagement', in *Louise Bourgeois*, p. 38),[6] as well as on what they do, both in terms of erecting structures and cultivating relations. Bourgeois reminds us that the work of hands is not only rooted in thinking but also in emotions. Hands touch and are touched; they caress and care for others as well as communicate thoughts and desires through their gestures. The hands are almost mimetic representations, perhaps somewhat akin to Rodin's hands, and a little larger than the hands that stop to stroke and touch them. But they reveal precisely that the real cannot be represented as such, that to really see means to see the invisible, the relational that modulates between things and people. Indeed, for Irigaray, representations are mere shadows of the real, its mere effects (*The Way of Love*, pp. 131–2). For what is real cannot be pinned down by images or forms. In these works, then, the hands reveal the invisible, that which cannot be shown as representation or as thing: the relation between two who are different. Hands make and demonstrate – these works themselves were made; yet they also create a site where people touch and are touched. Touching is reflexive. When we touch an other we also touch ourselves. Passersby touch the sculptures, measuring their hands against them, talking about them, reflecting upon these gestures. The sculptures, as art works, are not only about monstration, about the revealing of truth, the erecting of constructions, but are also about constructing identity. For it is not only a thing that can be a work of art; identity also needs to be created. How can our identities be understood, not as representations, but rather as emerging through the cultivation of relations with ourselves and with others, creating a space where the real takes place?

If, for Heidegger, the divinities refer to that which is other than human, to that which is beyond human making and control, it is not surprising that they have become assimilated to a celestial god. But the divine and the celestial, Irigaray reminds us, can also be cultivated between two living beings who are different, between two human beings who do not become appropriated to one another's image (op. cit., p. 147). For it is the 'dialogue between two living subjects [that] opens and closes again at each moment the question of what Being is' (op. cit., p. 83). Language might be the house of being, but if what is heard is only that which is said within its walls, then it does not provide sufficient space for the cultivation of relations between humans and for the appearance of the divine; instead, it pins things down in a movement towards death.

Alternatively, letting be opens up a space-time for the creation of co-belonging. It maintains a free space, a between-two, where the event of co-belonging can happen. Such a space is not itself a thing, nor can it be represented. Rather, it becomes a room – with vertical but also horizontal dimensions – in which the relation between two can take place, in which the being of each can be allowed to blossom (op. cit., p. 144). Bourgeois's sculptures allow for the vertical and horizontal dimensions of the blossoming of human life. The hands provide for a gathering of earth and sky, of mortals and the divine, but the gathering of mortals is in terms of the relations between two who are different, and the divine is revealed not only as the 'celestial [that] lies above our head, but also as that which can occur between us' (op. cit., p. 147).

For Irigaray, what is needed for dwelling is not only the attunement of building to thinking, but also the listening and attunement between two living beings who are different. This listening belongs in particular to the relation between two differently sexuate beings. The limit provided by being and remaining two then allows for the possibility of a relation between two different space-times where the embodied other cannot be appropriated to the temporal interiority of an intuiting subject. The hands that only demonstrate somehow are subjected to the privilege of vision, and belong to the body of a 'subject [who] is already ecstatic to the place that gives rise to him. He already lives [...] beyond the body that gives him sight' (Irigaray, *The Forgetting of Air: In Martin Heidegger*, p. 99). But the hands that belong to the self that cultivates relations alternate 'between moving and resting, going toward the other and turning back within oneself'. The 'duration [that] is woven' through this movement allows that 'time itself becomes space' (*The Way of Love*, p. 148). It is an embodied memory of the flesh, thanks to a sexuate identity, that permits us to stay with the other as well as with things. In Irigaray's words, 'Time and space remain open while continuously constituting a dwelling place in which to stay. Its measure is found in a perceiving of oneself and of the other, in a listening to oneself and to the other' (op. cit., p. 149).

In this way, Irigaray expands the fourfold. This includes not simply the vertical dimension of under the sky and on the earth, nor even simply a belonging of humans' being with one another, it also includes dwelling as a horizontal relation between two worlds: 'to go towards the other, to welcome the other into oneself, open non-vertical dimensions in the relation to the human and to the divine' (ibid.). What humans 'must measure is thus neither linear, nor uniform, nor homogeneous' (op. cit., pp. 149–50). Mortals are not only called to safeguard the earth as earth, letting earth be, they are also called to shelter the blossoming presencing of the other, which generates 'spaces of which the curves, the loops, can provide places in which to take shelter [...] for repose, for thought, for inward gathering. Also for distanciation, an estrangement which will permit coming together' (op. cit., p. 150). Touching oneself as well as touching the other requires proximity, but such a proximity necessitates distance, a non-fusion or confusion, if it is not to become 'seizure, capture, comprehension, all gestures of incorporation, introjection, apprehension in which the other as such vanishes' (ibid.).

Places that allow for dwelling, for the 'weaving of proximity with oneself', prepare us for an encounter with the other, that does not amount 'to including the other in my universe', which would make the meeting impossible (op. cit., p. 151). Rather, the mystery of the other appears as that mystery which it is – irreducible to the one. In Irigaray's account, the relation between two subjects who are different and who cannot be fully unconcealed or appropriated one by the other creates a space for the poëtic to take place. Heidegger's things might conceal as well as reveal, but they are unable to support a place where intimacy can grow. Whereas the naming that belongs to language can bring beings to appearance, the building of identity, for Irigaray, requires more than the construction of structures, or the demonstration of language. It also calls for the cultivation of relations, a perpetual movement, always with a difference, as a going out towards the other and a return to the self (op. cit., pp. 162–3).

Language does not only name to appropriate into one's own world, it also allows for communication, for being touched. Where there is a free space between two who are different, perception can become co-perception. Perception, then, does not capture what is there, reducing it to one world, a move which perhaps encourages cultural complicity but obscures the real (Irigaray, 'Being two, how many eyes have we', in *Dialogues*, p. 146). The very multiplicity of Bourgeois's sculptures – that require one to walk around them, and resist complete consumption at a glance, for there is always that which remains hidden from view – means that these works prevent the imposition of one form or image, and encourage a sharing of what is seen as onlookers gather around a sculpture, seeing it from different perspectives.

Different Relational Worlds

To dwell in the house of language does not suit human beings if this dwelling provides them only with one space-time. Sexual difference delineates different relational worlds, different space-time relations. In Freud's account, little Ernst comes to terms with his mother's absences through the verbal syllables *fort-da* that accompany throwing away and bringing closer to him a spool thanks to a piece of string. Ernst, Irigaray points out, 'was a boy', and not a girl, and his verbal articulation goes with a gesture of his hand and arm (cf. 'Gesture in Psychoanalysis', in *Sexes and Genealogies*, pp. 96–7). In her essay 'Gesture in Psychoanalysis', she hypothesizes that a girl would not symbolize her mother with a spool, as Ernst does, because the mother shares with her 'the same subjective identity', 'the same sex, and so cannot have the object status of a reel' (op. cit., p. 97). When a girl misses her mother, she becomes lost and in distress, or she 'organize[s] a kind of symbolic space' through her play, for example, with dolls, for dolls are not simply objects or tools for girls. Or she dances, creating a 'territory of her own in relation to the mother', a 'vital subjective space open to the cosmic maternal world, to the gods, to the present other' (op. cit., pp. 97–8). If she speaks it is 'in a playful mode [...] a language [which] corresponds to a rhythm but also to a melody' (op. cit., p. 98). The little girl would not control her distress through a game such as the *fort-da* because she does not have such distance from her mother. Rather than throwing and retrieving objects, displacing these maternal substitutes from place to place, her dance 'reproduces around [...] her an energetic circular movement that protects her from abandonment, attack, depression, loss of self' (ibid.). She spins round towards the inside or the outside of herself defining in this way a space of her own. It is a movement quite unlike that of the *fort-da*. It is not, then, the phallus that women need, Irigaray writes, but their autonomy. They seek 'to be free to *walk*, walk away and walk back, however it pleases them' (op. cit., p. 100; italics in original). They do not absolutely need to be wives and mothers through or for others, but rather to find their own space, 'an axis of their own, which on the microcosmic level moves from between the feet in the standing position up through the head, and macrocosmically from the center of the earth to the center of the sky' (ibid.).

Bourgeois's sculptures seem to provide for these axes. They are drawn into the earth – one can feel/see the gravitational downwards pull – and they bask under the sky, only slightly sheltered by trees. Not aligned precisely with the straight lines of the garden or of the city, this loosely formed circle of granite blocks permits passersby to stop, walk around, walk back, engage with the sculptures and with others with whom they are walking, or to contemplate the hands on their own. Because they are not installed in a museum, which imposes the self-conscious distancing of the *fort-da* game, passersby can come close to these sculptures, which allows for a relation of intimacy. They delineate a territory, a place, and I would suggest that the sculpture of the small and singular child's hand is provided a shelter by this so public yet private place that protects it from abandonment. People weaving by stop to touch it, to take photos, and to measure their own children's hands against it.

There is something unsettling and uncanny about these hands and arms, not only since they are severed from bodies, but perhaps also because they make what is familiar appear as other. Although many of Bourgeois's sculptures take up sexual difference overtly in phallic or breast-like shapes, these hands are not so obviously sexed, the more obvious difference being that of age, which also suggests different time-space relations. Her own hands apparently served as a model; but the hands are also, in Bourgeois's words, 'those of people of different ages, from babies to the very old and of many different colors' (Nadine Brozan, 'Chronicle').

For Heidegger, truth happens in the strife between world as revealed and earth, which remains concealed, and upon which world rests ('The Origin of the Work of Art', in *Poetry, Language, Thought*, pp. 48–9). On one level, this strife takes place rather literally in Bourgeois's works between the unyielding and impenetrable stone and the mimetic bronze hands. Yet what is also strikingly revealed is a strife between the uncanniness one experiences on first encountering these hands, and the tender holding and quiet calm they provide when one stays with them. As intertwined, chiasmically relating hands, each sculpture suggests a particularity of relation. In most pairs, one set seems vulnerable, hesitant, the other guiding and supportive. As already mentioned, there is something restful about these sculptures, which remain steady under the sky and above the ground, even as there is a constant swirl of movement around them: the noise of traffic from the six roads that converge at the nearby *Place de la Concorde* as well as the passing by of people as they walk through the Garden. Even if the shifting of the sunlight pulsing through the swaying leaves against the bronze, or the grey of the rain creating pools of water in cupped hands, create a constant movement, yet the hands hold firm amidst all these rhythms.

Perhaps what is strange is the way in which these sculpted hands show how the hands of the other can call to us to engage with them, in their otherness. Some of the pleasure offered by these works lies in the ways through which they call on us to move around them, bending, touching, engaging, moving from one to the other in no particular order – the varying stone heights lending themselves differently to bodies. Indeed, sculpture itself is a body. As Marie-Laure Bernadac suggests, the artist cannot separate her own body from her sculpture. For Bourgeois, 'what happens to my body is repeated in the stone' (Bernadac, *Louise Bourgeois*, p. 88). These works are not mimetic objects that favour self-affection in the sense of allowing the self to see the self seeing. Instead they let the familiar appear as other so that it can be encountered as other.

To Dwell with an Other

From Irigaray's perspective, Heidegger's position at least in part emerges from a masculine subjectivity that is unaware of itself. Perhaps even the 'mystery of the reign of techne' can be explained by this lack of awareness of masculine subjectivity and of sexual difference at the subjective level (Irigaray, *To Be Two*, p. 76). The privilege of *technë*, the privilege as such of a 'manufacturing outside of himself, a placing in front of himself, an external unveiling, a manifesting of truth in an other with force and skill', could be related, according to Irigaray, to 'man's relationship with the one who generates him' (ibid.). Following this reasoning, in order to separate from his mother, unlike her, man 'must fabricate things outside of himself' (ibid.). The *fort-da* mechanism allows the boy to set up divisions 'of time, of space, of the other, of the self' ('Gesture in Psychoanalysis', in *Sexes and Genealogies*, p. 102). In his attempt to become a subject, to differentiate himself, he confuses the familiar and the proximal with that which must be repudiated. In the *Introduction to Metaphysics*, Heidegger – as does Irigaray in *To Be Two* – comments on a passage of the tragedy *Antigone* by Sophocles where the chorus says that to be at home for humans has become to forget that they are not the sole creators of their dwelling place. It is to forget the abyss of the unknown, of the sway of being. In his later work on dwelling, Heidegger retreats from this language of violence and domination, arguing instead that the plight of homelessness is that humans 'must ever learn to dwell' ('Building Dwelling Thinking', in *Poetry, Language, Thought*, p. 159). If we are called to think about our homelessness, then we are already thinking beyond our own making and about our belonging to being, and homelessness might no longer be a plight. For Irigaray, however, poëtic thinking is not suffi-cient for providing a dwelling. It is also necessary that we remain open to 'a new kind of relationship with those who reside with us' ('How Can we Live Together in a Lasting Way?', in *Key Writings*, p. 133). Rather than encountering only the unknown of a universal being, she suggests that we also encounter the mystery of the being of the other, and that we cultivate our relations with one another and with ourselves, through a blossoming forth that has no end.

To dwell, then, is not only to persist with things, constantly questioning that which is familiar – it is also to be with an other as other. To dwell with an other requires letting the other be, safeguarding and sheltering the becoming of the other in a space that makes it possible for this other not to be appropriated into the self through knowledge, grasping or comprehension. Bourgeois's modest sculptures reveal a possibility of being two amongst others: it is another way of being and of living spatial relations than those of the *fort-da* and of technical systematicity.

Notes

1 Thanks to Chloë Fraser and Francine Wynn for their insightful suggestions, and to the Social Science Research Council of Canada for financial support.

2 In his essay 'The Uncanny', Freud shows how the *unheimlich* is closely related to the *heimlich* in that the familiar is revealed as strange. (See Freud, 'The Uncanny', in *Sigmund Freud: Art and Literature*, pp. 339–76.)

3 Here, 'History' refers specifically to Heidegger's understanding of a particular epoch, in this case Western culture, as being 'historical'.

4 Specifically, Bourgeois was 'commissioned by the Battery Park City Authority of New York City to create an outdoors sculpture for the new Robert F. Wagner Jr. Park in lower Manhattan. The Park faces the Statue of Liberty and Ellis Island.' (Louise Bourgeois, *Memory and Architecture*, p. 363.)

5 There are a number of sculptures, modern and contemporary, in the *Jardin des Tuileries*.

6 Terrie Sultan, 'Redefining the Terms of Engagement: The Art of Louise Bourgeois', (in Charlotta Kotik, *et al.*, *The Locus of Memory*). Sultan writes that 'Bourgeois' body frag-ments are surrogates for senses'; they also often 'act as gateways between exterior and interior surfaces, which themselves evoke similar distinctions between emotion and intellect' (p. 38).

Part III

Maternal Order Within and Beyond Patriarchy

Chapter 8

Swallowing Ice: A Study of Mothers and Daughters in Dacia Maraini's *L'età del malessere* and *Colomba*

Christina Siggers Manson

University of Kent, United Kingdom

Dacia Maraini's first novel was published in 1962 and she has continued to write novels, plays, poetry and screenplays ever since. One of Italy's leading contemporary writers, Maraini has been equally criticized and praised for her untiring criticism of women's treatment under patriarchy. Through her literature she aims to raise awareness of key issues regarding the struggle for female liberation, in particular the patriarchal control of women and their bodies. Maraini was an active member in the feminist movement in Italy, campaigning for the legislation of abortion and divorce, and promoting women's cultural activities.

In this essay I will consider the mother–daughter relationships that Maraini examines in depth in her novels *L'età del malessere [The Age of Discontent]* (1963) and *Colomba* (2004), which, in my opinion, best exemplify some critical aspects of Luce Irigaray's thinking regarding mother and daughter relationships in our patriarchal culture. These novels, although written four decades apart, share similarities in their negative examples of motherhood and in the interaction between mother and daughter. Irigaray's theories, in their critical but also constructive approach, could act as a guide for interpreting Maraini's fictional mothers and daughters, showing further how they could achieve a loving relationship.

L'età del malessere: Nourishing with Lifelessness

Teresa, the mother of the protagonist, Enrica, in *L'età del malessere*, is one of the few mothers in Maraini's work who attempts to alter her daughter's destiny, so that it does not resemble her own miserable existence. Throughout the novel Teresa is described as exhausted and lifeless, merely alternating between her office job and her housework. She has nothing to distract her from this tedium and appears to be empty inside. Maraini describes how, when Teresa puts on her dressing gown after work, her body seems to fold in on itself, losing its form like an empty sack (*L'età del malessere*, p. 37). Teresa finds no satisfaction at work or at home, and she is ground down by her work and family until she dies. Yet, in spite of her exhaustion, she attempts to advise her daughter on how best to proceed in life.

The advice that Teresa gives her daughter, however, is conflicting and therefore adds to Enrica's confusion, rather than providing her with clear guidance. Teresa's primary concern is that Enrica find a powerful, rich husband to support her; meanwhile, Enrica should advance with her studies in case this is not possible. Education, although seen by her mother as important, is merely a back-up plan – a suitable marriage is the ultimate goal. Trapped in a loveless marriage to a poor man, Teresa wants her daughter to have different opportunities and avoid the mistakes that she has made, either by marrying for money or through education. Having abandoned her own university studies halfway through the course, Teresa is aware of the significance of qualifications in allowing greater freedom of choice and the chance of fulfilment. She actively encourages Enrica to complete her studies:

> 'Have you studied?' she asked at last after a long silence.
> 'No.'
> 'I would like to know how you will get your diploma if you never study.'
> I did not reply. She went to get my books and opened them up for me on the table. 'Study', she insisted, pushing me towards the seat. (op. cit., p. 14)[1]

Such is the importance attributed to studying that Teresa physically pushes Enrica towards her books, making clear her feelings that only through education will Enrica have the hope of a different life. However, Teresa makes the mistake of commanding her daughter, instead of engaging in a dialogue with her. She believes that she knows what is best for Enrica's future and pushes her towards this destiny, rather than heeding her daughter's words and guiding her accordingly. The mother thus tries to take the daughter's choice away from her, depriving her of her own voice. Such behaviour makes me think of the interpretation of analyses of the respective languages of mother and daughter by Irigaray. In *I Love to You*, she concludes that, whereas the daughter strives for an intersubjective relationship with the mother,

> the mother does not show the same intersubjective respect for her daughter. While they remain two, they no longer have the same right to speak. The mother commands, the daughter is to listen and obey. The elder seems to repeat to her daughter what has been forced upon her as a woman. A dominant male culture has intervened between mother and daughter and broken off a loving and symbolic exchange. (pp. 130–1)

By forcing upon Enrica the teaching regarding marriage and femininity that she herself had received as a girl, Teresa complies in part with patriarchal expectations. On the other hand, she mixes this with the hope that, through education, her daughter can break the circle of secular feminine oppression and find self-fulfilment.

Yet what Teresa fails to recognize is that the best example she could give her daughter is to follow her own advice. By changing her own life first, before attempting to guide her daughter, Teresa's words would have more impact on the young Enrica. In the seminal essay 'And the one doesn't stir without the other', Irigaray points to the possible influence of a mother, who is not aware of her own problems, on the daughter:

By pouring your ice into me, didn't you quench my thirst with your paralysis? And never having known your own face, didn't you nourish me with life-lessness? In your blood, in your milk there flowed sandy mirages. Mixed in with these was the still-liquid substance which would soon freeze in all our exchanges, creating the impossible between us. Of necessity I became the uninhabitable region of your reflections. You wanted me to grow up, to walk, to run in order to vanquish your own infirmity. (*Signs*, 7:1, p. 64)

The mother-daughter relation, on which Irigaray comments in this text, also takes place in Italian culture in the film *Maternale [Motherhood]* (1978) by Giovanna Gagliardo. In the script, published in Italy alongside the text 'And the one doesn't stir without the other', the daughter embodies the mental paralysis of her mother, a paralysis of which the latter is unaware and which is revealed to her through her daughter. In a similar way in *L'età del malessere*, rather than fight against her own oppression, and thereby set a positive example for her daughter to aspire to, Teresa concentrates her efforts on ensuring that Enrica does not follow in her footsteps. Teresa seems to have accepted that her life has been of little purpose. Her only worry now is that her daughter break the vicious circle of female oppression and live a life vastly different from her own, an achievement that Teresa would see as a personal triumph, as a way to 'vanquish [her] own infirmity', as a woman and as a mother.

In *Between East and West*, Irigaray also asserts the importance of teaching from one's own experience – something that Teresa fails to do – stating that when 'what is taught is guaranteed by the life of the one who teaches [...] a concrete and spiritual knowledge is elaborated, a knowledge useful for a cultivation of life' (p. 58). In fact, according to Irigaray, the mother ought to be the first teacher of the child, in particular of the daughter, who is firstly a teacher about life. But how could a mother do that outside an experience of her own, asking her daughter to do what she herself is unable to do?

It is interesting that Maraini repeatedly describes Teresa as struggling to breathe as she nears the end of her life. Teresa's death from lung cancer is rather significant; stifled by everyone and everything around her, she is suffocated as her entire being is starved of air. Now, the mother is supposed to be the one who passes on oxygen to the foetus. How could she do that without breathing herself? Furthermore, as Irigaray insists, the cultivation of air is crucial to reach self-affection, a state that the mother must experience in order that her daughter could also reach it. Just as a spiritual virginity must be maintained by the mother in order to allow the duality between the daughter and herself to exist. In fact, mother and daughter have to be autonomous, one with respect to the other, and this requires that each one preserve her autonomy and virginity by cultivating her breath, which is the matter of her interiority, of her soul. Being able to keep her breath in herself, woman can reach her liberty and preserve her integrity, which cannot amount to conserving a physiological hymen but to protecting her own interiority. (Part IV, Spirituality and Religion, 'Introduction', in *Key Writings*, p. 147)

Teresa is unable to maintain her breath within herself, either physically or spiritually, and she expends all her energy simply trying to survive. The image of Teresa's body as an empty sack emphasizes her failure to protect her own interiority: as all her breath leaves her body, nothing remains. Teresa has given her whole being to others, to her husband and daughter, and to her employers. Only emptiness is left inside her.

At first, it seems that Enrica will be unsuccessful in breaking the bond that links her to her mother's fate. Mother and daughter fuse into one in Maraini's novel. When trying to imagine her mother as a girl, Enrica suddenly realizes that the girl in her mind is in fact herself (*L'età del malessere*, p. 61). She struggles to separate her own image from that of her mother. Later, following her clandestine abortion, Enrica sees her mother's face reflected in her own in the mirror:

> I went to the bathroom to dampen my burning face and in the mirror I saw my mum with two black rings under her eyes and a tired, bloated body that was sweating in her dressing gown with the greasy collar. I was like her. I made the same gestures. When I went back into the kitchen, even my dad started as though he had seen his wife. (op. cit., pp. 118–19)[2]

Looking in the mirror, Enrica sees both the mother's past and her own future, which seem inextricably linked: the daughter's fate appears set to follow the same pattern as her mother's. This merging of mother and daughter in the mirror echoes Irigaray's writing on the confusion between the images of mother and daughter in the mirror, reflecting back to each other their merging into the same woman's destiny:

> You look at yourself in the mirror. And already you see your own mother there. And soon your daughter, a mother. Between the two, what are you? What space is yours alone? In what frame must you contain yourself? And how to let your face show through, beyond all the masks? It's evening. As you're alone, as you've no more image to maintain or impose, you strip off your disguises. You take off your face of a mother's daughter, of a daughter's mother. You lose your mirror reflection. You thaw. You melt. You flow out of your self. ('And the one doesn't stir without the other', *Signs*, 7:1, p. 63)

In *L'età del malessere*, Teresa's mask and disguise are her work clothes, in particular her corset, which she longs to be rid of on coming home. Significantly, Teresa's corset restricts her breathing, as she fights to survive in a male-dominated workplace. The corset symbolizes the restrictions and objectification imposed on women in patriarchal society: it offers no benefit to women, but is intended to alter a woman's body shape to please the male gaze. It also acts here as a barrier between Teresa and the outside world, allowing her to construct an identity that is not true to her real nature. To meet with the requirements of patriarchal culture, woman must renounce an appearance of her own: 'Her clothes, her makeup, and her jewels are the things with which she tries to create her container(s) or envelope(s). She cannot make use of the envelope that she is, and must create artificial ones' (Irigaray, *An Ethics of Sexual Difference*, p. 12). As Teresa nears death, she ceases wearing her corset, permitting her natural body shape to show through once more, thereby inhabiting for a short time her natural envelope, which she was forced to renounce in order to compete in patriarchal society.

In the novel, Enrica eventually realizes that unless she actively refuses her mother's lifestyle, she is destined to repeat Teresa's mistakes and misery. Unable to understand her mother initially, Enrica's pregnancy forces her to reassess their relationship: 'I thought again of my mum and of myself who, as an old woman, would become like her, so tired and dirty and indifferent to everything' (*L'età del malessere*, p. 90).[3] Originally driven apart by the patriarchal expectations placed on women, her pregnancy allows Enrica to share a unique bond with her mother, one that a mother and daughter alone can experience. But it is only after Teresa's death that Enrica can truly appreciate her mother's advice and begin to reconsider her future. Although Teresa was unable to liberate herself, she manages to have enough influence on her daughter to effect a change in her. In a way, Teresa has to sacrifice herself, that is, to die, in order to help her daughter. The novel ends with Enrica ending her destructive sexual relationships and waking at dawn to search for employment.

However, it is seemingly only by renouncing the past bond with her mother that Enrica can hope to find any sense of future fulfilment. Her success, therefore, in making a truly fresh start can be questioned in the light of Irigaray's belief that female identity cannot be constructed 'in repudiation of one's physiology' (*I Love to You*, p. 107). By rejecting her mother, does Enrica not partly reject herself and her own female body? Driven apart by an inability to coexist in patriarchal society, Enrica and Teresa can never develop their relationship fully. Yet, without this cultivation of the mother–daughter relationship, a 'loving ethical order cannot take place among women' (Irigaray, *An Ethics of Sexual Difference*, p. 92). And it could be argued that in order to make the woman that she is blossom, Enrica ought to discover a way of coexisting with her mother outside any fusion or confusion between the two.

Colomba: The Search for (Self-)Affection

In *Colomba*, Maraini tells the story of several generations of the same family, focusing in turn on each member, as the protagonist, Zà, attempts to discover the truth behind her granddaughter Colomba's sudden disappearance.

Colomba, addicted to drugs and desperate for love, allows her boyfriend to keep her imprisoned in a caravan in the woods and sell her body to his friends. Whilst the narrative revolves around Zà's search for Colomba, a particularly interesting figure in the narrative is Angelica, who is presented both in the role of Zà's daughter and Colomba's mother. It is on the character of Angelica that I will focus my comments.

It becomes increasingly clear that neither as mother nor as daughter can Angelica find happiness or satisfaction, and she gradually descends into hysteria, because she is unable to cope with her disillusion at life. Angelica has difficulty sustaining relationships with both her mother and her daughter, a difficulty largely due to the sexual abuse that she suffered as a girl at the hands of her step-grandfather. Maraini implies that this abuse has changed the young Angelica from a 'sociable, affectionate and intelligent' girl into a 'moody and sullen' woman (*Colomba*, p. 158).[4] Seen in the light of Irigaray's comment – which contrasts to Simone de Beauvoir's belief that 'one is not born, but rather becomes, a woman (through culture)' – 'I am born a woman, but I must still become this woman that I am by nature' ('You Who Will Never be Mine', in *Key Writings*, p. 11), it is evident that Angelica's natural development has been halted by the sexual abuse that she has suffered. Angelica is therefore prevented from becoming the woman that she is by nature because of the intervention of a man. She withdraws from her mother, barely communicating with her and repelling any attempt at closeness to her.

In *An Ethics of Sexual Difference*, Irigaray highlights the difficulties faced by mothers and daughters in maintaining a close relationship when patriarchal society necessitates that they be in competition with each other for man's affection:

> If we are to be desired and loved by men, we must abandon our mothers, substitute for them, eliminate them in order to be *same*. All of which destroys the possibility of a love between mother and daughter. The two become at once accomplices and rivals in order to move into the single possible position in the desire of man. (p. 87; emphasis in original)

This idea is in keeping with both Enrica and Angelica's rejection of their mothers in *L'età del malessere* and *Colomba*, respectively. In the latter, mother and daughter have been wrenched apart by patriarchal violence as the intervention of one man – the step-grandfather – has driven a wedge between them. The emotional separation of Angelica and her mother, Zà, by sexual abuse is reminiscent of the enforced severance of Demeter and her daughter Kore in Greek mythology (see Luce Irigaray's comments in *Marine Lover* and 'The Return'). In the same way as Demeter and Kore, Zà and Angelica need to find a space that is theirs alone, a space that patriarchal interference cannot breach. However, as Irigaray explains, 'if women have no access to society and culture [...] they are abandoned to a state of neither knowing each other nor loving each other, or themselves' (*An Ethics of Sexual Difference*, p. 58). Certainly, in the case of Maraini's fictional mothers and daughters, patriarchal culture prevents these women from loving each other, and even themselves. It is therefore important that women construct a culture in which they can flourish: 'women have to constitute a social entity if love and cultural fecundity are to take place' (ibid.).

It is only after Angelica's death that Zà is truly reunited with the daughter whom she lost because of this violence. Viewing her body in the hospital, Zà is struck by the fact that Angelica's hair and body are soaking wet: 'water ran in streams down her copper-coloured hair, water covered her, water came out of her snow-white ears, water beaded on her throat' (*Colomba*, p. 298).[5] Angelica's dripping wet body recalls the amniotic fluid of her mother's womb, whilst also suggesting that Angelica has finally been cleansed of the supposed stain of abuse. Mother and daughter were unable to find each other again whilst both were alive, and they can only hope to return to each other outside of patriarchal society, that is, when one of them has left.[6] In a way, this is similar to the situation in *L'età del malessere*, since Enrica can only feel a true connection to her mother after she has died. In both cases, death is the only way in which mother and daughter can find a relationship.

In *Colomba*, as well as contaminating the relationship with her mother, the sexual abuse affects Angelica's bond with her daughter. Angelica is unable to fully mature and cannot find self-affection. Unable to love herself, it is difficult for the young woman to show positive love for her daughter. Angelica is desperate to be loved and depends on her husband's attentions for assurance of her self-worth. Driven by her jealousy of his interest in other women, Angelica spies on him and becomes increasingly neurotic, in spite of her mother's warning that 'if you degrade yourself in this way in front of him, you will lose your self-esteem and, if you lose esteem of yourself, he will also lose it' (op. cit., p. 261).[7] Unless Angelica can learn to love herself, she risks both losing her husband's love and corrupting the love that she feels for him. Zà's warning to Angelica ties in with Irigaray's belief that women hold the key to man's becoming, as well as their own. The fact that women can learn to cultivate and internalize their breath better than men means that they can assist man with his becoming: 'They are the ones who can share with the other, in particular with man, natural life and spiritual or divine life, if they are capable of transforming their vital breath into spiritual breath' (Irigaray, *Between East and West*, p. 91).

Another point: Angelica is doomed to remain discontented, because she constructs her life and her search for happiness starting from someone else's. She lives vicariously through her husband and, for example, waits desperately for his return home. Angelica does not have the financial freedom to leave behind the oppressiveness of the family home, unlike her husband, who enjoys the liberty to travel freely under the pretext of earning money to support the family. In *An Ethics of Sexual Difference*, Irigaray comments that:

> Tradition places her within the home, sheltered in the home. But that home, which is usually paid for by man's labor [...] encloses her, places her in *internal exile* [...] unless she is able, in some other way, to take on the envelope of her 'own' desire, the garb of her 'own' jouissance, of her 'own' love. [...] It is essential that she no longer depend on man's return for her self love.

Or at least not absolutely. But a whole history separates her from the love of herself. (p. 56; emphasis in original)

Angelica is unable to overcome this historical legacy. She cannot achieve self-affection because she does not meet the basic criteria outlined by Irigaray in *An Ethics of Sexual Difference* that are required for a woman's love of self: Angelica cannot separate herself from a woman's traditional role and needs to find 'love for the child that she once was, that she still is, and a shared enveloping of the child by the mother and of the mother by the child' (op. cit., p. 59). Instead, Angelica despises both the child that she was and the woman that she is now.

The only time that Maraini portrays Angelica as being happy is during her close friendship with Laura, the woman with whom her husband is having an affair. The complex relationship between the two women highlights several aspects of Angelica's personality, and echoes Irigaray's writing in 'The Love of Same, The Love of Other', in *An Ethics of Sexual Difference*. Angelica's attitude towards Laura is contradictory, both adhering to traditional patriarchal conceptions of female relationships and enabling Angelica to break from them. Irigaray talks of women's 'blind competition to occupy a place or space that is ill-defined but which arouses attraction, envy, passion. It is still not another woman who is loved but merely the *place* she occupies, that she creates' (op. cit., p. 89; emphasis in original). Accordingly, Angelica 'believed that she possessed her husband through Laura, who put their intimacy before that shared with her lover' (*Colomba*, p. 265).[8] Angelica feels that she can reach her husband through this other woman, using her as a means to obtain indirectly the love that she craves from him. However, for the first time in her life, Angelica also enjoys a close, even if ambiguous, relationship with another woman 'made up of understanding glances, affectionate smiles, and night-time confidences' (op. cit., p. 265).[9] Irigaray stresses the importance of cultivating love between women, as there can be '*no love of other without love of same*' (*An Ethics of Sexual Difference*, p. 89; emphasis in original). Through this blossoming friendship, Angelica seems to begin a tentative journey towards self-affection, which in turn manifests itself in increased affection towards her daughter (*Colomba*, p. 267). However, this journey is cut short when Laura falls pregnant and is unsure of the father's identity. The two women are ultimately forced apart by this unforeseen event. Laura's unwanted pregnancy results in the separation of the friends and Angelica subsequently embarks without restraint on her path towards self-destruction. In fact, the pregnancy of Laura reveals two problems not resolved in their relation: the place of the mother and that of a masculine partner.

Angelica's relationship with the world around her grows increasingly difficult and, after one failed suicide attempt, she finally ends her pain by crashing her car whilst drunk, killing herself and freeing her daughter from their destructive relationship. Again in Maraini's literature, the separation from the mother is necessary to enable the daughter to have some chance of survival. But this separation can happen only through the death of one of the two.

And, to return to the protagonist, Colomba, whilst growing up she witnesses her mother's complete emotional dependence on a man and consequently follows her example as an adult: the young woman allows herself to be imprisoned and prostituted in the name of love. It is Colomba's own desperate search for the affection that was lacking from her parents that leads her to submit to her boyfriend's abuse of her own body and trust. It is only because of her grand-mother's strength that Colomba survives.

Conclusion

Maraini's two novels clearly show that unless women can first find self-affection and initiate their own becoming, they fail to experience and show affection for their daughters. Both Angelica and Teresa, to different extents, are unable to love themselves and cannot subsequently develop the cultivation of a mother–daughter relationship. As Irigaray explains, 'women must love one another both as mothers, with a maternal love, and as daughters, with a filial love. *Both of them*' (*An Ethics of Sexual Difference*, p. 89; emphasis in original). Maraini's female characters cannot reach this and they are doomed to remain caught up in an unending search for love and self-knowledge.

Although there is more hope at the end of each novel with regard to the daughters' futures after both mothers have died, it is uncertain how successful they will be in escaping their mothers' legacies of paralysis. Both mothers, whether intentionally or not, have failed to pass on to their daughters a sense of self-worth, perpetuating the vicious circle of female oppression. In 'And the one doesn't stir without the other', Irigaray alludes to such a freezing effect in the mother–daughter exchange:

> With your milk, Mother, I swallowed ice. And here I am now, my insides frozen. And I walk with even more difficulty than you do, and I move even less. You flowed into me, and that hot liquid became poison, paralyzing me. My blood no longer circulates to my feet or my hands, or as far as my head. It is immobilized, thickened by the cold. Obstructed by icy chunks which resist its flow. My blood coagulates, remains in and near my heart. (*Signs*, 7:1, p. 60)

Irigaray's closing words in this essay perhaps best summarize the situation in which the mothers and daughters in Maraini's two novels find themselves: 'When the one of us comes into the world, the other goes underground. When the one carries life, the other dies. And what I wanted from you, Mother, was this: that in giving me life, you still remain alive' (op. cit., p. 67). This is a wish that goes unfulfilled in both of Maraini's novels. Both novels provide examples of problems that Irigaray highlights in a mother–daughter relationship which takes place in a patriarchal context, problems that are passed down through female generations if awareness and change do not intervene from women. What Maraini fails to do is to propose a concrete way of breaking this chain of patriarchal legacies. In contrast, Irigaray's thinking offers positive ways of cultivating the mother–daughter relationship in order to free it from these bonds. Irigaray suggests some measures that can be taken to succeed in this, beyond our evolution as women:

We have to care about the natural and spiritual autonomy of the child – the role of mediation of the placenta teaches us to do so. Holding real dialogues with the child, keeping the *I* and the *you* distinct, is also necessary. And further: teaching the child the existence and the fecundity of sexuate difference [...] in genealogy and in alliance, fraternity and friendship. Avoiding the authoritarian attitudes that destroy awakening and autonomy. Cultivating a dialogical relationship with the daughter, preventing reducing her to a same as oneself, the one who will do later what I do now. ('The Redemption of Women', in *Key Writings*, p. 158; emphasis in original)

Irigaray's suggestions here are intended to 'provoke reflection, favour meditation and help each woman to be conscious of her responsibilities' (ibid.). Only when women can do this will they become able to rethink the mother–daughter relationship and free it from its patriarchal setting.

Notes

1 ' "Hai studiato?" domandò alla fine dopo un lungo silenzio. "No." "Vorrei sapere come farai a prendere il diploma se non studi mai." Io non risposi. Lei andò a prendere i miei libri e me li aprì sul tavolo. "Studia", insistette spingendomi verso la sedia.' All translations of quotations taken from the original Italian edition are my own. This is also the case for the quotations taken from *Colomba*, which has not been translated into English at the time of writing. Page numbers given after references to the novels refer to the Italian edition.

2 'Andai nel bagno per inumidirmi il viso che scottava e nello specchio vidi la mamma con due ditate nere sotto gli occhi e il corpo stanco e gonfio che traspariva sotto la vestaglia dal collo unto. Ero come lei. Facevo gli stessi gesti. Quando rientrai in cucina, anche il papà trasalì come se avesse visto la moglie.'

3 'Ripensai alla mamma e a me stessa che, da vecchia, sarei diventata come lei, così stanca e sporca e indifferente a tutto'.

4 'socievole, affettuosa e intelligente', 'scontrosa e cupa'.

5 'L'acqua scorreva a ruscelli dai capelli ramati, l'acqua la ricopriva, l'acqua usciva dalle orecchie candide, l'acqua le imperlava la gola'.

6 I also consider Angelica's death in my article 'In love with Cecchino: opening the door to violence in Dacia Maraini's *Colomba* and *Voci*'.

7 'se ti degradi così davanti a lui, perdi la stima di te stessa, e se perdi la stima di te, la perde pure lui'.

8 'credeva di possedere il marito attraverso Laura che anteponeva la loro intimità a quella con l'amante'.

9 'fatto di sguardi di intesa, di sorrisi affettuosi, di confidenze notturne'.

Chapter 9

The Maternal Order Read through Luce Irigaray in the Work of Diamela Eltit

Mary Green

Swansea University, United Kingdom

And I can no longer race toward what I love. And the more I love, the more I become captive, held back by a weightiness that immobilizes me. And I grow angry, I struggle, I scream – I want out of this prison.

But what prison? Where am I cloistered? I see nothing confining me. The prison is within myself, and it is I who am its captive.

How to get out? And why am I thus detained?

(Luce Irigaray, 'And the one doesn't stir without the other', *Signs*, 7:1, p. 60)

The work of Luce Irigaray offers a fruitful approach to many aspects of recent Latin American literature and culture, especially in relation to sexual difference, gender and sexuality as represented in a variety of literary and cultural texts from the region.[1] In twentieth-century Chilean literature, for example, the lack of women's self-fulfilment explored in the oneiric novella and short stories of María Luisa Bombal (1910–1980) can be incisively examined through Luce Irigaray's own writing on this point (cf., for example, 'Così Fan Tutti', in *This Sex Which Is Not One*, pp. 86–105). Equally, her work on spirituality and a divine in the feminine (cf., for example, Part IV, Spirituality and Religion, in *Key Writings*) can offer fresh and constructive perspectives on many of the poems of Gabriela Mistral (1889–1957), which have, until recently, been read by critics merely in terms of Mistral's disillusionment with Catholicism.

The aim of this essay is to draw on key tenets of Luce Irigaray's work on the mother–daughter relationship to briefly examine the significance of the emphasis given to this relationship in the narrative fiction of the contemporary Chilean author, Diamela Eltit, specifically in her third novel, *El cuarto mundo [The Fourth World]* (1988), and her short story, 'Consagradas' ['Consecrated'] (1996).[2] Throughout her *œuvre*, Eltit brings to the fore the complex and ambiguous relationship between mother and child, and in particular between mother and daughters, and the lack of representation of the mother as such at a symbolic level, two aspects that are fundamental to Luce Irigaray's work on motherhood and sexuate difference. I take a particular interest in how Eltit aims to effect a wider critique of the social and symbolic structures of Chile through a focus on the maternal figure and mother–child relations. I have already found the writings of Luce Irigaray to be extremely useful for elucidating diverse facets of the representation of motherhood in Eltit's novels, and thus for opening up new interpretations of Eltit's work which, because of its experimental quality, has been too easily dismissed by critics as 'hermetic'.[3]

Eltit's *œuvre* spans two periods of recent Chilean history: the dictatorship of General Augusto Pinochet (1973–1990) and the Transition to Democracy (1990–). In contrast to many Chilean writers and intellectuals, she remained in Chile during the Pinochet dictatorship, publishing her first novel, *Lumpérica*, in 1983, and co-founding an artistic collective which carried out unorthodox acts of protest against the military. To date she has published seven novels, but she has also moved beyond the realm of narrative fiction to publish, among other texts, a collection of critical writings; the transcript of the delirious monologue of a male tramp; and a collaborative photoessay of love in a psychiatric institution.[4] As noted above, her *œuvre* is marked by its defiance of linguistic and narrative norms: it draws upon a rich and highly poetic language, there is no plot in the traditional sense, and it is punctuated by ellipses.[5]

Three of Eltit's novels were published during the period of dictatorship, including *The Fourth World*. The military usurped power in 1973, following a brutal coup which led to the death of the democratically elected Marxist president, Salvador Allende, and many of his supporters, and resulted in disappearance, torture and exile for thousands of Chileans. The military's aim, in their own terms, was to 'cure' the nation of the 'Marxist cancer' that had spread throughout society and so establish social order. To this end, the nationalistic and Catholic-inflected public speeches of the military emphasized the role of the patriarchal nuclear family in their campaign to re-establish the *patria* ['fatherland'], and their discourse glorified women only as wives and mothers. Women were thus reduced to an essentialist notion of 'woman' as a mere function of reproduction, and enrolled onto the continuing reconstruction of Chile through their maternal role. As Giselle Munizaga explains, women were expected to 'accept the sacrifices imposed on them by fulfilling their objective of keeping the fatherland alive through their children' (*El discurso público de Pinochet*, p. 32).[6] The structures of patriarchy and political authoritarianism were thus intertwined, a point that is constantly probed through Eltit's novels written during the dictatorship.

The governments elected during the Transition to Democracy have also emphasized the nuclear family in their public discourse as a means to bring stability and order to an extremely polarized society, many sectors of which were left traumatized by the legacy of the dictatorship. The values championed by the governments of the Transition have again been strongly influenced by the moral position of the Catholic Church, which reveres the maternal figure as the pillar of the family. The Chilean cultural critic, Nelly Richard, explains that the governments of the Transition have emphasized that the family unit should be 'a moral and legally constituted family which must allow – essentially – the natural-biological destiny of each body to coincide with the maternal and paternal vocation towards roles programmed by a transcendent ideal of universal values' (*Residuos y metáforas*, p. 205).[7] In short, she argues that in spite of the threat to traditional

social values brought about by the effects of globalization, the official line continues to be that ' "the essence of a woman is to be a mother" ' (op. cit., p. 207).[8]

In these periods of recent Chilean history, the following affirmation by
Luce Irigaray is certainly applicable: 'Globalisation, the depopulation of certain countries, social and political distress all need palliatives: the family unit is
one of them' (*Everyday Prayers*, p. 46). The substratum of Chilean society during
both periods is 'the woman who reproduces the social order, who is made this
order's infrastructure' (Luce Irigaray, 'Women-Mothers, the Silent Substratum
of the Social Order', in *The Irigaray Reader*, p. 47). Luce Irigaray's assertion that
our culture 'is based upon the murder of the mother' (ibid.) is pertinent to the
Chilean context, and Eltit's focus on the maternal figure can thus be more fully
understood in terms of Luce Irigaray's claim that 'if we make the foundations
of the social order shift, then everything will shift' (ibid.).

Also of relevance to the readings presented here is Luce Irigaray's contention that there is a lack of symbolic representation of the mother–daughter
relationship and of a maternal genealogy in patriarchy, and she stresses the
potential for women in seeking to define or rediscover such representations.
As she says: 'In our societies, the mother/daughter, daughter/mother relationship constitutes a highly explosive nucleus. Thinking it, and changing it, is
equivalent to shaking the foundations of the patriarchal order' (op. cit., p. 50).
However, as things stand, she explains, the existing definition of women is too
often limited, even if only implicitly, to man's (m)other, and so women are prevented from effectively separating their own identity from that of their mother.
For Luce Irigaray, this results in women's inability not only to view the mother
as a woman, and not merely as a mother, but also to represent the relation to
their mother and to origins in their own terms (cf. 'The Bodily Encounter with
the Mother', in *The Irigaray Reader*, pp. 35–7).[9] However, she says that re-establishing the existence of a genealogy of women would be one of the means to
rearticulate and symbolize the relation between mother and daughter:

> It is also necessary, if we are not to be accomplices in the murder of the
> mother, for us to assert that there is a genealogy of women. [...] Let us try to
> situate ourselves within this female genealogy so as to conquer and keep our
> identity. (op. cit., p. 44)

It is thus beginning with granting representations to the mother–daughter
relationship through the articulation of a female genealogy, Luce Irigaray suggests, that women will no longer be 'accomplices in the murder of the mother'
(ibid.), and will not have to compete for the place of the mother.

The Fourth World: Beginning to Change the Mother–Daughter Relationship

Eltit's third novel, *The Fourth World*, was published in Chile two years before rede-
mocratization and during the year in which a plebiscite was held that heralded

the end of the Pinochet dictatorship. The novel is written in the context of a return to democracy and in a society swept into the global economy, some devastating effects of which are played out in the dysfunctional family home depicted in Eltit's novel.

The novel is recounted by fraternal twins, one male and one female, and each narrates one section of the novel in contrasting styles. While the male twin employs a verbose and conceited style, that of the female twin is fragmented and often opaque.[10] The novel begins just prior to the conception of the twins and ends with the birth of their own child: a baby girl that collapses into the novel that the reader has just completed, both of which are shown to enter the marketplace as commodities. There are multiple levels to this novel, but what is important to note is that Eltit uses the idea of fraternal twins as a metaphor to address what she terms 'the problem of the couple, considered so nuclear in society [...] what better metaphor [...] than these foetuses who rub against each other, annoy one other and invade each other's space' (Sandra Garabano and Guillermo García Corales, 'Diamela Eltit', *Hispamérica*, 62, p. 70).

The second section of the novel, narrated by the female twin, is the focus of my reading here. Acting as a counterpoint to her brother's account, this section is marked by a delirious language, through which the female twin attempts to give voice to her multiple identities as mother, daughter and sister/lover. It is only at the very end of the novel that she is able to represent herself as a woman. She picks up the narrative where her brother had left off, beginning with the description of her conception of a child, the result of the very first instance of fraternal incest: 'A strange fertilization took place in the room when the seminal residue trickled out and I felt the remainder sting like a whiplash' (*The Fourth World*, p. 69). The conception of the twins'/lovers' baby thus transgresses the incest taboo, the founding rule of kin relations, and subverts the military's insistence on the nuclear family as the basis of moral values and social order. While the pregnant female narrator's explicit detail of her sexual relationship with her twin brother/lover also defies the maternal ideal of purity and moral superiority propagated by the military, it soon becomes evident that their relations are founded on male possession and female submission, and thus structured according to phallic authority and power. Their 'fraternal' relationship, then, falls along vertical lines, perpetuating women's subjection to what Luce Irigaray terms 'a culture in the masculine' (Part IV, Introduction, 'Spirituality and Religion', *Key Writings*, p. 146).

The depiction of the sexual relationship between the twins/lovers is the most critical feature of this section of the novel, and it almost occludes the insight into the mother–daughter relationship that is also included here. The female twin/ daughter is shown to be bound to her nameless mother through feelings of sin and shame, a mother imbued with the biblical transgression of Eve, and passed on to her daughter, who continually confesses on her own behalf for her frantic sexual drives and on her mother's behalf for her adulterous thoughts. Constant references are made by the narrator to the guilt that she, as a daughter, carries on behalf of her family: 'I remained attentive in order to bear their guilt, and mine, carrying the ancient, degrading sudaca humanity on my back. Falling.

Falling. Explosive' (*The Fourth World*, p. 81).[11] The sense of guilt and ignominy experienced by both mother and daughter reflects, among other things, a religious culture that 'lacks models of woman's love relations' and which illustrates 'a lack of respect for feminine genealogy' (Luce Irigaray, 'The Redemption of Women', in *Key Writings*, pp. 154–5). In Luce Irigaray's terms, the daughter has merely moved into the place of the mother. As she says: 'to become a mother would supposedly be to occupy that place, without having any relationship to the mother in that place' (*An Ethics of Sexual Difference*, p. 102).

The lack of a model of love between women and the absence of respect for a feminine genealogy also afflict the relationship between the female twin, as a mother, and her as yet unborn child, whose sex is clearly identified at the end of the novel as female. No expression of love or even gentleness is expressed by the mother towards the child that she carries within her. In spite of the possible damage caused to the foetus, she never fails to respond to the sexual demands of her brother/lover, above the maternal care that she neglects to offer her own child *in utero*. Only rarely does she make reference to her unborn daughter and always as an increasing obstacle to the twins'/lovers' sexual pleasure.

It is only with the disintegration of recognizable social and familial systems, so that the family unit, in Luce Irigaray's words, can be 'regrounded on the couple rather than on patriarchal authority' (*Everyday Prayers*, p. 46), that we are given a glimpse of how the mother–daughter relationship may be rearticulated. Mother and daughter are now more independent, including with respect to motherhood, and the feelings of sin and shame that had previously bound them together dissolve. This also allows the female twin to begin to imagine her mother, albeit hazily, in more positive and meaningful terms as a woman. The attempt to symbolize this relationship permits the female twin, as a daughter, to separate her identity from that of her mother and assume her own identity as a woman.

This results, in turn, in the reconfiguration of relations between the sexes, since it is at this moment that the female twin enters into a dialogue with her brother/lover for the first time. In contrast to the frenzied sexual urges and corporeal fusion that had marked their previous encounters, their dialogue is now founded on expressions of mutual care and love. Rather than attempting to seize or possess the other, each voice is clearly differentiated, not only by opposition, and respectful of the other voice. Through the dialogue of the twins/lovers, we receive a glimpse of what Luce Irigaray terms 'an encounter with the other', based on a respect for 'difference(s) between subjectivities and their own participation in exchanges, linguistic or other' (Part IV, Introduction, 'Spirituality and Religion', in *Key Writings*, p. 147, p. 146), and thus a means to reimagine relations between men and women.

The novel ends with the birth of the baby/novel: 'Far away, in a house abandoned to fraternity, between April 7 and 8, diamela eltit, assisted by her twin brother, gives birth to a baby girl. The sudaca baby will go up for sale' (*The Fourth World*, p. 114).[12] Eltit clearly does not underestimate the oppression facing women in her society, who are branded as 'a use-value for man, an exchange value among men; in other words, a commodity' (Luce Irigaray, *This Sex Which*

Is Not One, p. 31). However, by merging the birth of the baby into the creation of the novel that has just unfolded, Eltit transposes procreation from the level of the biological to the realm of culture, and so offers hope for the future. As Luce Irigaray explains:

> Engendering in difference is not limited to procreation: culture, community, the word are also engendered by two. This presupposes an elevating of sexual difference to the level of a sexuate subjectivity and not to let it remain as a simple biological corporeal reality. ('The Redemption of Women', in *Key Writings*, p. 157)

The baby/novel, 'engendered by two', represents a body/text that has emerged from the alliance of two voices and two sexuate subjectivities, and is thus engendered with respect for difference. The baby/novel thus has an opportunity to turn back to her place of origin, to her mother, and to her mother's mother, allowing her to insert herself within a female genealogy. Although further symbolization of the mother–daughter relationship is undeniably necessary, the baby/novel contains within her a representation of her mother as a woman and as a speaking subject, and thus a means to rearticulate the relation to her mother in terms that may permit a new feminine subjectivity to emerge.

'Consagradas': Consumption and Repression of the Mother–Daughter Relationship

Eltit's short story, 'Consagradas', is included in a collection by various Chilean women writers which takes as its focus the theme of the mother–daughter relationship. In contrast to many of the other stories, Eltit's contribution stands out, not only because of its ambiguity and fragmented narrative style, but also because of the disturbing cruelty and viciousness depicted in the relationship between mother and daughter. The emotions between them are expressed primarily in terms of fury and ferocity, with only occasional instances of tenderness appearing throughout. The daughter, we learn, is 60 years old and still bound to her mother and to the family home, within the claustrophobic confines of which the story is set, and from which the father is largely absent. Both mother and daughter remain nameless, confounding their possibility of being ' "identified with respect to the other" ' (Luce Irigaray, *This Sex Which Is Not One*, p. 143). The mother–daughter connection as portrayed by Eltit is truly damaging and asphyxiating, in a similar manner to the description of the mother–daughter relationship in terms of suffocation, engulfment and imprisonment as put forward by Luce Irigaray in her essay 'And the one doesn't stir without the other'.

'Consagradas' opens with reference to the cough and asthma attacks that afflict the daughter throughout the story and which cut off her access to breath, a fluid which, in Luce Irigaray's terms, is 'given us gratis and free of interest in the mother's blood, given us again when we are born' (*An Ethics of Sexual Difference*, p. 127). The asphyxiation that the daughter experiences could thus symbolize her estrangement from the maternal body, but it is precisely these attacks that lead her to desperately seek out her mother to help prevent her suffocation. However, rather than offering succour or comfort, her mother inflicts further harm on her daughter. Eltit's story revolves around the mutilation enacted on the daughter by her mother, who bites off and devours the fingers of her daughter's right hand, one by one, until they are all gone. The mother thwarts her daughter's aim of protecting what she refers to as the most valuable part of herself, leading the daughter to realize that, in her words, 'I will never be exactly myself again' ('Consagradas', p. 102).[13] In this way, the mother's actions result in the progressive haemorrhaging of the daughter's life and identity, which corresponds to the haemorrhaging of her blood after each act of mutilation by her mother.

In 'And the One Doesn't Stir Without the Other' – which is a comment on the film, *Maternale [Motherhood]* (1978) by the Italian director, Giovanna Gagliardo, as indicated in the French version of the text – Luce Irigaray writes of how the consuming of the one by the other can sometimes illustrate the mother–daughter relationship in our tradition:

> Will there never be love between us other than this filling up of holes? To close up and seal off everything that could happen between us, indefinitely, is that your only desire? To reduce us to consuming and being consumed, is that your only need? (*Signs*, 7:1, p. 62)

Her depiction of the reduction of the love between mother and daughter to the 'filling up of holes' can also be seen in Eltit's story, in which the mother fills up her gaping mouth with her daughter's fingers, sealing off any relationship between them other than one founded on consumption. The mother's progressive devouring of her daughter's fingers leads the daughter to become repulsed by her hand and to question the value of her existence: 'if I survive it will remain sliced, without fingers, my hand, and then what?' ('Consagradas', p. 99).[14] The mother's actions thus induce self-loathing in her daughter, but she is unable to move beyond the corporeal destruction wrought by her mother, and, in spite of her mother's monstrous and depraved acts, she continues to obey and revere her.

The daughter makes clear that her mother fails to recognize the connection between them, 'because my blood makes you vomit, spasmodic, without understanding – imbecile – that my finger, that I, that all of me, am blood of your blood' (p. 97).[15] Her mother is thus unable to acknowledge their consanguinity, reflecting Luce Irigaray's comments that 'Blood rights are so completely neglected that "consanguineous" is now defined as "sired by the same father" and, what is more, set in opposition to the word "uterine"' (*Speculum*, p. 125). The mother's inability to recognize the value of the maternal blood line that connects her to her daughter highlights the extent to which a father–son genealogy structures kin relations. In the absence of the father, it is the mother who forecloses her daughter's return to origins, to what Luce Irigaray describes as 'this first body, this first home, this first love' ('The Bodily Encounter with the

Mother', in *The Irigaray Reader*, p. 39). The daughter is prevented from placing herself within a female genealogy, and is unable to symbolize any relationship to her mother.

The mother–daughter relationship thus remains ensnared in consumption, this time through the mother's consumption of her daughter's blood. Their relationship seems to be a symptom of the rapid consumption of commodities that is one of the most prevalent characteristics of present-day Chilean society, following the military's imposition of a neo-liberal market economy and its continuation by the governments of the Transition. In Eltit's story, the rupture of the mother–daughter bond appears to underlie economic consumption, whereby the mother–daughter relationship is subordinated to a patriarchal political and economic order.

The story also embodies Luce Irigaray's comments on the continual disappearance of mother and daughter into each other (cf. 'And the one doesn't stir without the other', *Signs*, 7:1, p. 62, p. 65). By the end of the story, the mother has become reduced to an animalistic state, barking and howling like a mad dog, but she uses her daughter as a means to shore up her identity, imitating her daughter's every gesture, as the daughter indicates: 'My mother copies me unashamedly in the same way [...] as a sunset imitates another sunset' (p. 101).[16] The daughter exists only as her mother's 'predestined guarantor. The profile of yourself that another would have stolen from you' (Luce Irigaray, 'And the one doesn't stir without the other', *Signs*, 7:1, p. 66), a point that is also evident from the way in which the mother hoards and reveres her daughter's rotting finger, stroking it at night in self-congratulation. However, the mother's imitation of her daughter is equally harmful to herself, since she also induces the asthma attacks that repeatedly afflict her daughter, actively seeking the suffocation that engulfs her, and cutting herself off from the air that symbolizes her own connection to the maternal body and her capacity to really come by herself into the world.

By the end of the story, the daughter describes herself merely as an 'orifice' that is about to disappear ('Consagradas', p. 103), portraying herself as a gaping hole in a way that reflects her mother's gaping mouth. References are made to the daughter's orifice throughout the story in terms of auto-eroticism, that is, as the part of her body by which through touch she gains sexual arousal, and as a hole which she often attempts to cover over. Now, however, she is unable to either touch or conceal herself, since all the fingers of her hand have been devoured by her mother. Deprived of the possibility of what Luce Irigaray terms 'self-affection' (*This Sex Which Is Not One*, p. 133), the daughter comes to represent only a lack or an absence, 'a negative image that provides male sexuality with an unfailingly phallic self-representation' (op. cit., p. 70).

To Conclude

While *The Fourth World* clearly highlights the repression of the mother–daughter relationship in a patriarchal regime, a reading of this novel through the work of

Luce Irigaray allows us to envision, in the final pages, how the rearticulation of the mother–daughter relationship can lead to a reconceptualization of male–female relations, which, in turn, forms the basis of the transformation of social and symbolic structures. Luce Irigaray's emphasis on the powerful potential for women in attempting to provide representations of the mother–daughter relationship is thus expressed in Eltit's novel. However, the publication of 'Consagradas' eight years later offers a more disillusioned perspective on Eltit's part. The story sets out a damning critique of a supposedly democratic society, in which the respect for difference put forward in *The Fourth World* has vanished. In a context of globalization and consumerism, 'Consagradas' urgently draws attention to the violence and consumption inherent in the mother–daughter relationship that is buried beneath the symbolic constructs of a patriarchal society. Disturbingly, the maternal figure is shown to be complicit in upholding the patriarchal structure of consumption on which contemporary Chilean society appears to be based.

To conclude, then, I hope to have given an insight – even if rather negative, given the context – into how the work of Luce Irigaray can serve to explore the significance of the textual emphasis on the mother and the mother–daughter relation in Eltit's work. Luce Irigaray's writings not only allow for a fuller understanding of the impact of the lack of symbolization of the mother–daughter relationship, but they also offer a means to recover this relationship. Her work has far-reaching implications for realizing how the reformulation of the mother–daughter relationship can potentially destabilize and disrupt patriarchal structures, and allow women to construct an identity that is founded on mutual recognition of and love for the mother, as both a woman and a mother.

Notes

1 I am very grateful to Luce Irigaray for reading and commenting on this text, and for inviting me to work with her on this volume, during which time I have gained many new insights into her work.

2 Quotations from *El cuarto mundo* are taken from the English edition, *The Fourth World*, translated by Dick Gerdes. All translations of quotations taken from the original Spanish edition of 'Consagradas' are my own, since this story has not been translated into English at the time of writing.

3 See Mary Green, *Diamela Eltit: Reading the Mother*, in which I draw on Luce Irigaray's work to examine aspects of the representation of motherhood in Eltit's first six novels which are not covered here. This monograph is based on my PhD thesis, which I was completing when I attended Luce Irigaray's seminar at the University of Nottingham in May 2004.

4 To date, four of Eltit's novels have been translated into English and two into French.

5 Given Eltit's emphasis on 'unearthing' buried representations of feminine and maternal subjectivity, the highly poetic quality of her writing and its non-conformity to grammatical, syntactical and lexical norms suggest a correspondence with Luce Irigaray's stress on the need to find another 'logic' of writing in granting the feminine its own specificity (cf. *This Sex Which Is Not One*, p. 153).

6 'aceptar los sacrificios que éste le impone cumpliendo con su objetivo de mantener

viva la patria a través de sus hijos – los jóvenes'. The English translation of this quotation is my own.

7 'una familia moral y legalmente constituida que debe hacer coincidir – esencialista-mente – el destino natural-biológico de cada cuerpo con la vocación materna y paterna de roles programados por un ideal trascendente de valores universales'. The English translation of quotations from Richard's text are my own.

8 " 'el esencial de la mujer es ser madre" '. Richard is here quoting the Christian Democrat senator, Adolfo Zaldívar.

9 A revised version of this essay has also been published as 'Body Against Body: In Relation to the Mother', in Luce Irigaray, *Sexes and Genealogies*, pp. 9–21.

10 The female twin remains nameless until the very end of the novel, when she is identi-fied as 'diamela eltit', dissolving the boundary between author and narrator. The male twin is referred to by the female name of María Chipia, bringing to the fore the gender confusion prevalent in the novel.

11 'Sudaca' is a Spanish word used to refer to Latin Americans in a pejorative way, and is the term used to define the racial lineage of the family portrayed in *The Fourth World*.

12 The published English translation of the novel uses the word 'brotherhood' here instead of 'fraternity', but I have modified the translation to more accurately translate the Spanish 'la fraternidad', used in the original version of the novel.

13 'que ya no seré nunca más exactamente yo'.

14 'si sobrevivo quedará mocha, sin dedos, mi mano y entonces ¿qué?'

15 'porque mi sangre te hace vomitar, espasmódica, sin comprender – imbécil – que mi dedo, que yo, que toda mí, soy sangre de tu sangre'.

16 'Mi madre me copia descaradamente de la misma [...] manera en que una puesta de sol imita a una puesta de sol'.

Chapter 10

Feminist Generations: The Maternal Order and Mythic Time

Gillian Howie

The University of Liverpool, United Kingdom

The familiar historical story of the philosophy of sexual difference may have been narrated by many feminists in various voices and tones, but always seems to retain a commitment to the overriding principle that somehow difference is a value in and for itself.[1] Rita Felski writes that this story has become a grand narrative which manages to confuse the logic of intellectual debates with the condition of the world as a whole (*Doing Time*, p. 117). Prising out some of the points of tension within latter-day feminist theory, Felski calls for a difference-based feminism which manages to refuse identities defined within male norms, and which, at the same time, does not reject equality. The recognition that 'equality' is not synonymous with 'sameness' could lead to 'an expanded notion of equality that can also respect difference' (op. cit., p. 130). It is essential, claims Luce Irigaray more than twenty years earlier, that women among themselves invent new forms of organization and new forms of struggle which bring difference(s) to light, which are respected and confirmed through civil law (*This Sex Which Is Not One*, p. 166). Calling for transformations in the law, in symbolic processes, and in the logic and style of discourse, Irigaray dovetails ethics, political struggle and civil rights. Underlying this, 'the principle of morality and ethics [...] consists concretely in the respect for real differences' (*I Love to You*, p. 52), and the belief that we need a way to conceive such differences.

The staged story of recent struggles and generations was articulated most clearly by Julia Kristeva in 'Women's Time' (in *Feminist Theory*, p. 36). The first, nineteenth-century generation is seen as responding to a shared exclusion from political, social and economic life. Suffragists and existential feminists aspired both to gain a place in linear time as the time of project and history, and to extend the social contract so that it could include political citizenship for women. Whether all women active in this movement could be described as feminist is a moot point. But by the second stage in feminist history, a clearly defined feminist movement emerged in the 1960s and the 1970s. Reflecting on the gains of the suffragists and disappointed by the fact that substantive change had not followed the modification of formal legal and political structures, feminists concerned themselves with broader social relations. This second generation of feminists is thought to have concentrated on issues which specifically affected women: reproduction, mothering, sexual violence, expressions of sexuality and domestic labour. Demanding recognition 'for an irreducible identity', second generation feminism, according to Kristeva, was situated at the intersection of archaic memory, mythical time, and the time of marginal movements (op. cit., p. 38). From this demand to be inserted into history, complemented by a radical refusal of subjective historical limitations, rose a signifying space which became occupied by a new generation.[2] Since Kristeva's essay, a new generation of women has grown up and a new terminology, with which to reflect on feminism, has emerged. This new generation shed feminist attachment to 'universalism, naturalism and essentialism' (cf. Elizabeth Grosz, 'A Note on Essentialism and Difference'), and embraced what Felski describes as 'a doxa of difference' (*Doing Time*, p. 116).[3]

From its early formation (1991–5), this third stage – now described as a wave – was marked by the question of whether or not third wave and post-feminism were synonymous, or whether third wave feminism was an extension of second wave feminism, especially with its critical interrogation of the logic of identification. An extension it may have been, but it also defined itself against the second wave. In 'Making waves and drawing lines', Cathryn Bailey suggests that whereas second wavers saw themselves as carrying many of the basic values and aims of the first wave, third wavers seem to define themselves more negatively, primarily against the values associated with the second stage.

The idea that second wave feminists somehow policed morality and sexuality, thereby enforcing binary identity, runs through much third wave literature. For some, the idea of generational difference can be reduced to a matter of birth dates, specifically post-1960. For others, birth dates are relevant because the experiences that inspired individuals to become feminists in the era of Reagan, for example, are radically different from those of the previous generation (Rita Alfonso and Jo Trigilio, 'Surfing the third wave', *Hypatia*, 12:3, p. 3). Alfonso defines the third wave as a distinct political generation, a group of people who share formative social conditions at approximately the same point in their lives and hold a common interpretive framework shaped by those historical circumstances. Indeed, second wave feminism is often located within the Academy as part of the establishment to be overcome.

Third wave feminists are undoubtedly right to note the coincidence of a decline of activism and a rise of municipal feminism: the incorporation and mainstreaming of feminism into academia. Certainly tensions between generations have been exacerbated by the disciplining structures of a university system that encourages the pressure for academics both to individuate themselves and to submit to fairly explicit institutional norms if they are to survive professionally. Conservative modernization, sweeping academia, rewards those who are integrated into managerial structures, but also engenders a tendency to aggressive individualism that tends to promote originality, which must appear as newness and the disavowal of the old.

However, the presentation of second wave feminism as monolithic, combined with a history of forgetting the complexity of political activism and simplifying the richly diverse cultural terrain, has led Louise Bernikow to describe the relationship between second and third waves as political matricide (quoted in Madeline Detloff, 'Mean spirits'). Such tension in the movement is not without precedent. We have to acknowledge the strife within the second wave movement itself: conflicts that, on one hand, forced women into recognizing the relevance of specific location and to admit to the universalizing tendencies within feminism but, on the other, led inadvertently to the collapse of activists' groups and editorial boards.

Yet despite our own recent history, it is still the case, surely, that in order to escape spaces, roles and gestures assigned by men, in order to overcome a de facto rivalry, and to discover a new form of social existence, it is important for women to join together, 'among themselves' (Irigaray, *This Sex Which Is Not One*, p. 164). The violence of rape as an instrument of war, young girls abandoned in orphanages because they are girls, sex trafficking, girls judged by religious law to be sexually promiscuous when they report rape, domestic violence, the gender pay gap: all this and more is still true despite 'girl power'. Our ability to narrate historically at all depends on a woman-to-woman sociality which requires a new covenant, one that links the past, present and future. Another style of collective relations, free from the sororal anxiety permeating the generational account of the women's movement, and perhaps the movement itself, requires another style of collectivity, another relationship to space and time: 'an active transition from what is most vegative to what is most divine' (Irigaray, 'Creating a Woman-to-Woman Sociality', in *The Irigaray Reader*, p. 193).

Notwithstanding Kristeva's protestations that 'generation' implies less a chronology than an attitude, the generational account actually maps social, intellectual and political history onto a linear line of historical progression. Rather than coexisting generations, it is linear generation which is woven through the wave metaphor. The wave metaphor suggests that one wave is followed by another, supercedes and incorporates the previous wave, and, despite some currents, that the movement is forwards. This sense of a wave sublating the previous one, including it and moving onwards, echoes in the memory of feminists who would like to claim this time for their own and of feminists who are disposed to disavow their younger selves.

In a recent interview, Irigaray perceptively notes that if stages in the feminist movement correspond to waves, it can be as an image which suggests an affinity with water, the fluid and the sea: a ceaseless and restless movement (Gillian Howie, 'Interview with Luce Irigaray', in *Third Wave Feminism*, p. 319). Unstable and affected by things external to itself, this movement could not assume a definitive meaning or form. Cleaving this image from historical teleology, she draws attention to the fact that such an image refers us more to a mythical, rather than to a historical, time. To consider woman-to-woman sociality, we ought to reconsider both temporalities, that is, how historical time intersects with mythical time. Two questions then follow: What is this mythical time? How can we articulate mythical time together with historical time?

If we try to reconsider the status of woman in the symbolic realm, we run up against the problem of thinking the new within the constraints of historical time. Yet, at the same time, rumination guided solely by historical sense is harmful to a living thing, whether that be a woman or a culture. A living thing will, according to Nietzsche, only be fruitful and strong if it protects itself from falling back into the past, and it can only do so if it is bounded by a horizon: 'if it is incapable of drawing a horizon around itself, and at the same time too self-centred to enclose its own view within that of another, it will pine away or hasten to its untimely death' ('On the Uses and Disadvantages of History for Life', in *Untimely Meditations*, p. 63). In a similar vein, Felski reminds us not to collapse feminine subjectivity into its historical determinants because women in history have never been merely passive vehicles for phallocentrism (*Doing Time*, p. 122). Confidence in the future perhaps depends on being able to sense when one ought to feel historically and unhistorically, even though, and because, it is impossible to think that which must be thought (Theodor Adorno, *Metaphysics: Concepts and Problems*, p. 145). Here, then, a utopic moment: the impossible 'unhistoric' thought that is the condition for woman-to-woman sociality is itself a condition for historical narrative.

For Irigaray, a metaphor rather belongs to the logic of a phallogocentric system of representation. Yet without such metaphors, women are 'a blank space', a lack of representation. So Irigaray considers a third way between the two alternatives of phallogocentric representation and the absence of feminine representation 'by resolutely focusing on the blank spaces of masculine representation, and revealing their disruptive power' (Elizabeth Berg, quoted in Margaret Whitford, *Luce Irigaray: Philosophy in the Feminine*, p. 71). A metaphor establishes a relationship at once and yet leaves something to imagination. If we conceive mental activity in its relation to bodily activity, then we could say that conceptual metaphors, such as that of the wave, could be motivated by underlying pre-linguistic schemas concerning space, time, movement and control. This embodiment hypothesis would direct us to corporeal levels of experience: to the two main boundaries of skin and physical object.

The symbolic, as the order of discourse and meaning, intervenes in the imaginary and the imaginary exerts influence and flows through the hinterland of the symbolic. To invoke an imaginary domain is to accept that 'literal space cannot be conflated with psychic space and reveals that our sense of freedom is intimately tied to the renewal of who we are and who we wish to be as sexuate beings' (Drucilla Cornell, *The Imaginary Domain*, p. 8). The freedom is in part revealed through projection forwards, an identification with oneself, a space where individuals may become, in a future that has yet to be realized. The metaphorical association of waves with ebbs, flows, cross-currents, as a way to understand altercations within feminist theory and the women's movement, directs us back to the sea and then ultimately back to the corporeal level of experience.

Picking up the Cartesian metaphor that equates *res cogitans* with a pilot of a ship, Irigaray asks what is this sea that the pilot must navigate as it threatens to overwhelm him? The Cartesian 'I' will attempt to subject the sea to a whole range of techniques that will transform her, the sea, into an object of use. 'The "I" thinks, therefore this thing, this body that is also nature, that is still the mother, becomes an extension at the "I"'s disposal for analytical investigations, scientific projections, the regulated use of the imaginary, the utilitarian practice of technique' (Irigaray, *Speculum*, p. 186). The 'I' that navigates through waters chartered by himself, is the same 'I' who attempts to manage the sea and all that is extension, and who reasons to the existence of an infinite being, reproducing (for) himself a (mother)-father in his own image (op. cit., p. 187). In these thoroughly Cartesian images we can detect the omission and exclusion of actual sex from the masculine imaginary.

If knowledge is subtended by the unacknowledged mother then a place for maternal genealogy should be made in the symbolic. If the 'I' that thinks 'woman' only does so because she, the mother, has already been incorporated into the masculine imaginary, then let us take the sexing of the 'I' subject and the 'she' seriously. Not the single, neutral or neutered subject from which generates the world – copula without copulation – nor a subject who derives power from appropriating the non-place of the mirror. Instead, let us conceive a subject already two, maybe a particular subject recognizing the particularity of the other as sexed, even when that sex is not yet known. This would be a subject already in tune with the otherness of a specific other through a qualitative difference.

As a critical intervention into Lacanian psychoanalytic theory, we could say that symbolic castration is naturalized by projecting lack, or chaos, onto the female body, and that this enables men to avoid facing their own castration or separation anxiety. This deflection is then disguised through numerous naturalized representations of women (Whitford, *Luce Irigaray: Philosophy in the Feminine*, p. 84). Unless women find a way to represent their relation to the mother and to maternity, and so to an origin outside masculine paradigms, we will 'always find ourselves devalued' (op. cit., p. 86). More significantly, without a way to imagine, conceive or represent their relationship to the maternal origin, women will tend towards rivalry, a rivalry at the very least encouraged by the competitive aggression of the market. Let us consider the maternal order as a way to reimagine this relationship.

In discussion with Helen Rouch, Irigaray draws attention to the mediating role of placenta. Placental mechanisms, designed to block maternal immune reactions, are only put into operation if there has been recognition by the maternal organism of foreign antigens. Placenta is not an automatic protection system. Clarifying this, Rouch explains the distinction between placenta and organ transplant; she points out that the embryo is half-foreign to the maternal organism, and as such the mother's body 'should' activate its defence mechanisms to reject this other self. But the placenta, which is also an other, prevents this mechanism from being activated, but only locally and in a way that allows the mother to maintain her defensive capabilities against potential infection (cf. 'The Maternal Order', in *je tu nous*, pp. 37–44).

This negotiation brings into question the patriarchal presentation of the child–mother relationship as a fusion that needs the interjection of paternal law for separation. What appears within the Cartesian phantasy to be boundless, needing to be charted, traversed and controlled, thus already contains a different sensibility and a sensibility of difference. What if she were there in the beginning? Already two, or more? The singularity of the relations between mother and child/children *in utero* suggests a distinctive imaginary: a qualitative difference. This original mythical time then is posed through the 'I' of the mother rather than through symbols of anxious and masculine infancy, where love is recycled as a loss of plenitude which demands, in reparation, loving self-renunciation on the part of the wife or mother.

All such myths are perilous. Any association of the feminine with maternity or generation may strike some as free play within the masculine symbolic. We risk assimilating all forms of difference to an idealized version of the feminine, avoiding 'the many tensions and conflicts within particular axes of difference' (Felski, *Doing Time*, p. 123). It is true that any mother gambles with her identity, just as she can have a sense of possession that claims ownership: 'this being is mine an adjunct to, or incorporated within, my project'. It is also the case that any attachment to strict historical generation invokes dependency upon, or reaction to, God-Father-King or to its matrilinear equivalent, that is, upon genealogies of power and knowledge. Although, at the same time, as we try to avoid unidirectional lines of power-knowledge, let us not forget the wise woman who in today's culture of youthful insistence has neither use nor exchange value. To avoid the reduction of self to function, to displace genealogy and hear the intentionality and becoming of the other, we should stress that the maternal order and temporal order need not coincide. These are not absolutes, merely an attempt to convert a form of subordination into affirmation, a moment of silence into an image of redemption that, we can accept, always risks falling back into the same.

Let us return to the suggestion that the wave metaphor articulates a mythical time. The term 'myth' identifies a sacred narrative often linked to the spiritual or religious life of a community, while 'mythic time' would be linked to the universal and local beginnings of the community. The mythic, but not phantastical, maternal order introduces a new sensibility into the generational account. The generational account of the women's movement, as we have seen, is often characterized in terms of conflict, resistance and denial. It is the unconscious ground where perhaps 'professional' feminists bury both our mothers and the shadow of our own gender. I suggest that the thought of the maternal order, so well expressed in *je, tu, nous*, offers a new hermeneutic of difference and a more developed sensibility: an image of the recognition by the mother of the other and her sensed responsibility towards this other where the self and the other are continually renegotiated.

The maternal order suggests a way to think the antecedence of the ethical relationship before any determination of the other. In *I Love To You*, Irigaray notes that to recognize a sexuate identity in oneself is already to overcome instinctual and egological immediacy by recognizing the negative in the self: 'I am sexed' implies 'I am not everything' (*I Love To You*, p. 51). It is not only a way to reflect myself back to me. The negative can thus maintain the duality of sub jectivities. Similarly, 'I recognize you means that I cannot know you in thought or in flesh. The power of the negative remains between us' (op. cit., p. 103;

translation amended). This irreducibility can be thought prior to and required for an ethics of listening to the other, a being called to the other if you will, as it 'prepares the way for the not-yet coded, for silence, for a space for existence, initiative, free intentionality, and support for your becoming' (op. cit., p. 117). If speaking from the already known introduces a stasis, a hiatus of the becoming of the one and the other, then you, who are not visually present, cannot be known or claimed so easily (Irigaray, *The Way of Love*, p. 17). Could that not also invoke the *in utero* relationship?

Here the 'I' can think but without reification, called by the other yet unable to determine who this other is. It is, may be, the site of the non-reduction of the other to a mere object. This relationship cannot concern an Other, through whom each other is substitutable. No one can be substituted without a loss of identity. For lack of this particularity, Levinas' phenomenology of the caress falls back within the boundaries staked out by philosophical constitution of the masculine subjectivity (cf. Irigaray, 'Fecundity of the Caress', in *Face to Face with Levinas*, pp. 231–2, p. 255). The irreducibility of the self to the other bars the alienation of the other's freedom in my subjectivity, yet, and at the same time, there is an irrefutable and touching *mit-sein*. There is an emptying of a certain consciousness, a *kenosis*, commanded by the ethics with respect to the world of the other which inflicts a sort of wound that never heals. It is the respect for the other as other that commands me. From this we can build a 'we': a being-with.

According to Nietzsche there are three species of history: monumental, antiquarian and critical. These three species correspond to ways that people live. The first corresponds to a living individual who acts and strives towards something, the second to the way an individual preserves and reveres, and the last refers us to an individual who suffers and seeks deliverance. Now since we are all the outcome of previous generations, with their passions, errors, conceptions, we cannot free ourselves from this historical chain. The best we can do, says Nietzsche, is to confront our inheritance and implant in ourselves a new instinct, a new habit, a second nature. 'It is an attempt to give oneself, as it were *a posteriori*, a past in which one would like to originate' ('On the Uses and Disadvantages of History', in *Untimely Meditations*, p. 76). Although this second nature is more fragile than the first, for those who employ critical history for the sake of life, there is knowledge that this new second nature may become a first. Thus we read our history as a negotiation between the aspiration for new habits and instincts, the demands of a future life, but with knowledge of the past, within constraints imposed by that past, and knowledge of the present that can only be yielded by knowledge of the past. How can we, feminists or women who are part of a liberation movement, hear the past in light of the new without an anxious displacement: footfalls that echo in the memory down paths which we did, or did not, take?

The idea that, although I am called to you, I am unable to determine you helps to reorientate cognition. Such cognitive reorientation would begin by accepting the irreducibility of the particular other to the self, and then insist that no one other can be exchanged for another one. In this way it is also a thought against the economic substitutability of the commodity market. The understanding that 'I am not everything', the negative relative to the self, creates a space for potential meeting and listening. Unless there is this meeting and listening, feminist discourse will continue with points of silence, omission, and consequent conflicts. The account of a not-yet determined other brings to the surface the particularity of the self–other relation – allowing us then to consider whether the relations are economic, political, social, psychological, desiring or whatever. Without this, it is not easy to make visible inequalities of power, money and access to material resources. The call to hear the other cannot ignore, and is not embarrassed by, the newly sensitive skin, peeled away, the wound that never heals: love. 'We still know nothing of the salvation love brings, individual and collective salvation' (Irigaray, *I Love To You*, p. 29). This mythic moment of the maternal order not only helps to reorientate cognition, but also unlocks ways to approach embodied – relational and unique – difference: the otherness of the other. From within the theory of sexuate difference and the maternal order emerge pathways through feminism and between feminists.

The metaphor of waves as a way to conceptualize stages in the women's movement brings us back to the sea, to the maternal order that then can introduce an ethical sensibility with which to understand the generational and historical direction of feminist theory and the women's movement. From within the mythic time of the maternal order, which is – it has to be stressed – not bound by linear temporality, is generated a discursive and ethical orientation that helps us to articulate the historic ebbs and flows of the women's movement. The recognition of otherness, of alterity, whilst not the supreme goal of feminism, may well be the condition of historical narrative and woman-to-woman sociality, which is itself the condition for political intervention: 'I can agree to recognize a reality that is foreign to me, that will never be mine, but which determines me and with which I am in relation. [...] Such a change in the nature of the constitution of subjectivity and the recognition of the other as an other, irreducible to me and unthinkable in terms of my spirit, could be the opening-up of a period of History yet to come' (op. cit., pp. 56–7).

Notes

1 There have been notable exceptions from as early as 1986 with Sandra Harding's 'The instability of the analytical categories of feminist theory', *Signs: Journal of Women in Culture and Society*, 11:4, 664.

2 Although all of Luce Irigaray's work is generally concerned with sexuate difference, it too follows three stages: the first as a critical reading of Western tradition which uncovers the masculine nature of a subject who claims to be neuter, neutral and universal; the second is interested in qualitative distinction and is a creative exploration of alternative subjectivity for women, and the third stage focuses on the possibility of an ethical relationship between men and women.

3 The wave metaphor has come under some pressure recently. See, for example, Stacy Gillis and Rebecca Munford, 'Genealogies and generations: the politics and praxis of

third wave feminism', *Women's History Review*, 13:2, 165–78; *Third Wave Feminism: A Critical Exploration*, ed. by Stacy Gillis, Gillian Howie and Rebecca Munford; and *Catching a Wave: Reclaiming Feminism for the 21st Century*, ed. by Rory Dicker and Alison Piepmeier. The most comprehensive account of the Third Wave can be found in *The Women's Movement Today: The Encyclopaedia of Third Wave Feminism*, ed. by Leslie L. Heywood.

Part IV

Interpreting and Embodying the Divine

Chapter 11

Disinterring the Divine Law: Rediscovering Female Genealogy in the Rites of Death

Sabrina L. Hom

McGill University, Canada

Hegel: Death and Divine Law

In *Phenomenology of Spirit,* Hegel sets forth two ethical principles: the human law and the divine law. The human law is explicit, fully conscious, and governs men in the public realm, while the divine law is unconscious, 'subterranean', and its obligations are fulfilled exclusively by women. The human law defines the ethos of public life and, through the public logic which shapes and justifies the activities of the family, much of private life as well. The divine law concerns the obligations of a woman towards a dead kinsman. The conflict between these laws destroys harmony, seemingly forever, and dooms the feminine ethical principle to its repressed and ironic status in the state.

In the earliest Greek life, prior to the historical moment represented by the struggle between Creon and Antigone, the two ethical principles are in harmonious coexistence, and are both acknowledged by the community. In Sophocles' *Antigone*, Creon, the king of Thebes, forbids the burial of the traitor Polynices, but his orders are disobeyed by Polynices' sister Antigone, who recognizes that the imperative of the divine law is that she buries her brother. As a result of Antigone's crime, Creon orders her to be walled alive into a crypt. Once she is entombed, Antigone hangs herself. Antigone's condemnation brings resistance from the citizens – who perceive the imperative to bury the dead – and tragedy to both the city of Thebes and Creon's family. In fact, Antigone and Creon are governed by intractable and incompatible laws: the 'divine law', which impels Antigone to care for her dead brother, and the 'human law', which impels Creon to protect the city. These laws are reconciled through the appropriation of the divine law to the ends of the state. This process is accomplished, firstly, through war, which Hegel considers necessary to maintaining the unity of the state, and which turns women's care for the individual dead to the service of a cult of war heroes; and, secondly, by the repression of elements of the divine law, represented by Antigone, that resist appropriation.

The divine law is concerned with the care of the dead, a series of practices which serve to spiritualize death and memorialize the dead; this work is crucial in Hegel's schema. In death, the citizen 'has raised himself out of the unrest of the accidents of life into the calm of simple universality' (*Phenomenology of Spirit*, §451). While this activity is necessary to the development of Spirit,[1] the death of the citizen in fact represents a crisis for Spirit. The individual, who had mastered nature, spiritualized his body, and discovered his community with other subjects, now falls catastrophically back into impotent passivity, natural determination, and inert isolation. The vital and turgid male body, which prefigured consciousness's voracious swelling towards self-completion, has gone limp and bloodless, a mere object. Death feminizes the male body, or rather represents a return of the male body to a less spiritualized form: the dead man is passive, weak, the object of men's gazes and animal depredations; he is recognized only in the sphere of the family.

Furthermore, the cohesion of the community of mutual recognition that underlies Spirit is threatened by the loss of a subject: a man's death creates a fissure in that specular edifice of public life in which, wherever a man looks and imagines, he finds a reassuring reflection of his subjectivity. Since death is a constant and defining risk for male subjectivity,[2] the return to object-like, natural passivity in death is a radical and necessarily ever-present threat to the community. The death of an individual leaves a dangerous trace – a corpse that not only threatens contagion, as in the case of Polynices, but also evinces the contingent, inert, animal destiny of each in the community over-against the progressive, self-conscious destiny of Spirit. The dead man's unseeing eyes, pecked docilely by birds, would seem to mock the community of mutual recognition, founded, as it is, on the power of the gaze.

Against the fleshy and accidental destiny of the corpse, the rite of burial establishes a universal and necessary destiny, one that can be reconciled with the community and no longer threatens its logic. Women's work in caring for the dead respiritualizes the dead man and ensures the integrity of the community. By deliberately burying the dead man and intervening in his natural decomposition, the family asserts rational control and mastery over death. Where death was, in its particulars, accidental – a man need not die at any given time or from any given cause – and, in its universality, a natural determination, the act of burial sees that the dead man 'shall not belong solely to nature but shall be something *done*, and the right of consciousness be asserted in it' (op. cit., § 452; italics in original). The women of the family deliberately bury the body of their dead relative so that his destruction will not be a simple act of nature – as would be the case if, as Antigone fears, wild animals were to eat her brother's corpse. The care of death guarantees that, even at his most passive and renaturalized moment, man does not fall back into indifferent nature. The dead man is maintained as a rationally determined agent by his family's efforts to protect his body from natural depredations, and preserved as a particular individual in the memorial his family constructs for him. These guarantees arise both from the immediate rites that follow a death and from the structure of family genealogy, which produces a family line which memorializes the dead man's name.

As we see in Hegel's account of the family, subjectivity requires not only an initial foundation but continued sustenance. In burying the dead man, the women of the family '[wed] the blood-relation to the bosom of the earth, to the elemental imperishable individuality' (ibid.), ensuring that he will always have the rejuvenating care that sustains subjectivity. Nature here has two aspects: the wild animals and forces of decay that would degrade and destroy the corpse, and the imperishably nurturing maternal Earth. By burying the dead, the family appropriates the Earth's resources for his eternal care, ensuring both his immortality – as the Earth is immortal – and his mastery over nature. The dead man's family 'thereby makes him a member of a community which prevails over and holds under control the forces of particular material elements and the lower forms of life, which sought to unloose themselves against him and to destroy him' (ibid.). Burial rites represent human dominion over the forces of decay and depredation that threaten the dead man, and over the nourishing maternal Earth herself.

The 'universal individuality' of the dead man is perpetuated not only in the anonymous womb of the Earth but in the memory of his family. A duty of the dead man's family, less noted than burial itself, is the ongoing task of enshrining the dead man as part of the 'ancestral pantheon', as an 'imperishable presiding part of the family' (op. cit., §. 452). As a 'household god' or a venerated ancestor, a man's individual name and life is remembered across the generations. It is as a member of this ancestral pantheon – that is, as the forefather and sire of a lineage, sustaining the community despite his own death – that man performs his 'supreme service to the community' (ibid.); in this enshrinement the accident of the dead man's death takes on a universal meaning. Women's work in memorializing the dead involves both the isolated actions of veneration that preserve 'imperishably' the dead man's individuality and the more general work of perpetuating his line and, therein, his name.

Hegel casts this divine law as thoroughly enmeshed in the phallic logic of the state, albeit unconsciously: in raising the dead man to universality and reintegrating him into the community, a woman is accomplishing masculine mastery of death and overcoming nature. This work seems, firstly, to offer no benefit to woman, rather benefiting only the surviving men (in sustaining their community) and the dead (in sustaining their subjectivity); and, secondly, to act specifically against women's interests in sustaining a familial and state apparatus that appropriates her labour, refuses her pleasure, and imposes a logic of war and death on the community. Luce Irigaray has excavated these aspects of the divine law in 'The Eternal Irony of the Community' in *Speculum: On the Other as Woman*,[3] even as she points out that the divine law also represents a vestige of, and a gesture towards, an alternative to the phallic economy.

Women and the Care of Death

After the victory of human over divine law, women's work in the service of divine law is alienated labour: its product is enjoyed by a woman's kinsmen and their fellow citizens, but not by women themselves. The work of caring for the dead does not directly benefit women, since they do not have public agency to preserve, and do not participate in the community beyond the family.

The care of death is performed by women at great cost; this cost is clear in a figure such as Antigone, who sacrifices her life to her funereal duties, but is no less present in any number of women who sacrifice their blood relations to their natal families and their rights to their children in order to build a memorial to their husbands' names. While women bear the costs of the care of death, they are systematically denied the crucial goods that accompany the receipt of such care. In a public realm that is obsessed with death, murder and war, those who lack care of death suffer and fall behind. Where the entry points to subjectivity and citizenship are points at which death must be risked, the passage through these points is, at best, a difficult and agonizing possibility for those who do not have familial guarantees of memorialization. Without sustaining care, women's subject positions in the public realm are a precarious achievement. According to Hegel, it is only the funeral rites performed by women such as Antigone that ensure that men's necessarily rational subjectivity does not collapse into meaningless accidents at the moment of death. Antigone must suspect that, with no one to bury her properly or enshrine her memory as a household deity, her hard-won subject position as a public agent will evaporate. In fact, after Antigone has accomplished her ethical duty and before her heartening return to the earth, her resolve falters, and she laments her imminent death – not only because she will lose her life but because she will lack mourners (*Antigone*, lines 876–80).

Even if Antigone had living family members to ensure her proper burial and mourning, these initial burial rites would be only the beginning of the process of memorialization. As a woman, whose genealogy is nameless and hidden, she will not be instituted as a household god or the progenitor of a lineage. The suppression of female genealogy is of a piece with the denial of female individuation. As Luce Irigaray points out in *Speculum*, the paradigm of patriarchal genealogy produces a lineage of individuated males, while there is no place for women's individuation, only a generational cycle in which women successively hold the place of maiden, mother and grandmother. Women are only placeholders in this paradigm, providing a site in which to reproduce a name and a subjectivity that is never their own.

Unless the non-individuated maternal site is unfolded, allowing for individual subject positions to arise among generations and lineages of women, there cannot be a history of female ancestry and therefore no institutionalized means of intergenerational memorialization for women. Hidden and nameless maternal genealogies are denied the material support of male genealogies, for they do not represent the inheritance of property or social status through the generations. By perpetuating the memories of men in the form of their namesake sons, women work to build a necropolis of patriarchal 'houses' over the ruins of matriarchal descent. This is not only an appropriation of women's labour and a denial of a basic good to women but a strategy to repress a potential site of resistance to human law. The appropriation of the divine law concerning caring for the dead by the male economy of war is completed, Luce Irigaray observes, when the women of Hegel's community come to mourn the loved sons they have sacrificed to the city's good at war, in memorials that are as much a part of the fabric of the state as of the family.

Lacking a name of their own in the memorial logic of the polis, women are impoverished in their very ability to speak and to represent themselves. The undying family name marks the individual who possesses it as one worthy of entering into the community of mutual recognition, as one who can bear and return the gaze of the other, and as an enduring subject who will not threaten the integrity of the community by reverting wholly to nature. Women, who are merely bearers, not possessors, of the name, lack the signifier of subjectivity. Where women lack the ability to recognize and be recognized, they are unable to represent themselves – either as human or as divine, alone or as part of a couple.

In *I Love to You*, Luce Irigaray explains that the lack of a proper name and corresponding subject position disadvantages women linguistically, denying them the ability to take up the position as subject of their own utterances. Luce Irigaray's research demonstrates that women rarely appear as the subject of their own speech or that of men. The patriarchal logic of name, memory and memorial work ensures that the subject 'I' is always already gendered as masculine, with the feminine as an auxiliary to this subjectivity. In this symbolic field, it is impossible to speak as a woman, which hinders women's ability to represent themselves as subjects while reinforcing a logic of the same in the whole of discourse. This linguistic impoverishment impedes communication between men and women, who, Luce Irigaray argues, essentially speak different languages; even more so, it impoverishes the language that might bond women together at the human and spiritual levels. Luce Irigaray observes in her research that mothers are particularly lacking in the language to discourse with their daughters (*I Love to You*, p. 74). The impossibility of speaking as a woman means, in part, that the bond between mother and daughter remains unspeakable and unconscious, and is deprived of cultural and spiritual significance.

Without the ability to represent herself and her mother as two, intimately intertwined and yet of two different generations, the little girl cannot imagine the relationship between herself and her mother, and lacks the capacity for 'rehearsal, repetition, re-presentation of her relationship to beginnings and to reproduction' (*Speculum*, p. 77). When the little girl can imagine herself and her mother as women, Luce Irigaray thinks of a healthy, 'ludic' relationship between mother and daughter – one in which the daughter plays out, with her baby doll, the role of her mother, depicting the mother as desiring the girl child. In this ludic relationship, the child's 'play with representations of the self' allows both an identification with the mother and a means to dream up a life for herself that is different from that of her mother. Deprived of maternal ancestry, then, a woman is cut off from the matrilineal relationships that most threaten patriarchy and is refused a potentially revolutionary perspective from which to reimagine her own relationship to maternity.

In her seminar at the University of Nottingham in June 2006, Luce Irigaray challenged me to step outside of the Hegelian logic of death, in which women are denied goods specific to the phallic economy, such as specular subject-recognition and the mastery of death. Within such a framework, it seems that women's great concern is exclusion from the life of the state and of Spirit. While Luce Irigaray mentioned that the integration of women into the public life of the state, and particularly into civil society, is imperative, she also points to the disruptive principle of blood immanent in the care of the dead. Blood could inaugurate a revolution that reconfigures the logic of the family and polis, and reintegrates these into the divine – a realm which, Luce Irigaray stressed, I had not reflected on sufficiently. This insight led me to adjust my larger project – an investigation of the effects of the Hegelian funeral economy on women – in a more positive direction, in order to better acknowledge the potential of blood, not to allow women to better integrate into the paradigm of Hegelian subjectivity, but to disrupt the funeral logic of the state. The final sections of my paper explore the principle of blood and offer examples of practices that can help in the personal rediscovery of blood.

Luce Irigaray and the Significance of Blood

Luce Irigaray explained that I had focused too much on the suffering and appropriation of Antigone, and particularly on her relation to the death drives and masochism. It is true that for Antigone, the principle of blood is already affected by the oedipal logic of patriarchy, and that Antigone suffers and dies as a result of the phallic appropriation of death. Luce Irigaray, however, taught me that to read Antigone with such a focus is to neglect the powerful feeling that motivated Antigone, even unto her suicide. While the maternal blood that motivates Antigone is necessarily marked by the patriarchal logic of the ancient Greek family, it nonetheless provides a powerful current of resistance against human law and indicates a disruptive reality that cannot be represented within the Hegelian world. Antigone's self-asphyxiation at once epitomizes Creon's stifling oppression of the feminine and represents a striking act of self-determination; it is worth noting that she takes her own life in a way that does not shed her blood and respects the divine law that Creon transgresses: that the living should be above ground and the dead buried. Far from being forgotten, Antigone is still remembered – perhaps by those tapping into a subterranean current of blood – particularly by women concerned with resistance. Antigone is a riveting figure because she reveals both the cruel and thorough nature of the Hegelian human law and the possibility for peoples and individual women to rediscover the power of blood.

Antigone's action in the service of the divine law indicates an enduring bond between daughter and mother, a powerful axis that threatens the patriarchal order. As Luce Irigaray points out, in caring for her brother, Antigone is reconnected with her mother and in fact carries out her mother's desire. Of course, insofar as the mother's desire is not simply for a child but for a son, the divine law is already appropriated to the oedipal logic of the patriarchal family (though perhaps only in part, because Polynices is the younger twin). To the extent that Antigone assumes and carries out her mother's desire, her tribute to the feminine principle of blood begins to slip into the patriarchal logic that refuses to individuate the relation between mother and daughter, treating them rather as moments in the execution of a maternal function in fact reduced to the desire for and reproduction of the phallus. Hence, in 'The Eternal Irony of the Community', Luce Irigaray does not share Hegel's nostalgia for the alleged harmonious coexistence of the brother and sister, human and divine laws prior to their tragic, final conflict. She points out that the moment for which Hegel longs is already preceded by a kind of 'rape': the distortion and appropriation of the divine law, a distortion that would begin, as she said to me, with its separation from and opposition to human law. However, Luce Irigaray argues that the divine law carries the vestige of a moment prior to this distortion and appropriation by patriarchal logic, which she describes as 'red blood'.

Luce Irigaray correlates the divine law to 'blood', the fluid, vital and natural (yet also intrinsically human) principle that is repressed in the development of Spirit. Blood represents the matrilineal principle that connects the mother to the child. In the maternal womb, the blood is a medium of exchange between the mother and the foetus; it represents the enduring link between mother and child, and between co-uterine siblings. In the adult woman, menstrual blood marks a fecundity that indicates her sexed relation to nature and to the creation and sustenance of life. Like death itself, blood is repressed and obscene, a sign of gore and violence, within the logic of the phallic economy; however, it retains an original aspect of vitality and nourishment.

Blood provides the fundamental and evident links of familiality – particularly, those between mother and child, and between co-uterine siblings – which cannot be fully assimilated to patriarchy. Antigone's claim that she would not sacrifice herself, as she has for her brother, to bury a husband or a child, indicates a co-uterine bond that exceeds any allegiance she might have to a husband and to a child generated with him.[4] Even after these links have been repressed or appropriated to the logic of the patriarchal family and city, they retain their own ethical significance, one which is independent of human law, and they maintain special and largely invisible bonds to the city which no longer exist within phallic logic: specific and loving relations between mother and daughter, living and dead.

The principle of blood is instantiated in the divine relation between Demeter and Kore. When Luce Irigaray speaks of the loss of divine female ancestry, she often refers also to the fall of the mystery rites that worshipped these goddesses, since obscuring divine female ancestry correlates to obscuring divine female spirituality (*Thinking the Difference*, p. 100). Demeter represents the fecundity of the Earth, while her daughter represents virginity – a notion that Luce Irigaray has re-read and widened as a principle of women's self-determination and integrity, both physical and spiritual. Together, Demeter and Kore also evince a historical representation of the spiritual significance and sanctity of matriarchal lines of descent, of the desire of the mother for a daughter and of a daughter for the mother *qûa* woman, and such representations are rarely present, Luce Irigaray points out, in our time. The loss of figures such as Demeter and Kore is not only a loss of female divinity but of female ancestry, language and self-representation:

> we women, sexed according to our gender, lack a God to share, a word to share and to become. Defined as the often dark, even occult mother-substance of the word of men, we are in need of our *subject*, our *substantive*, our *word*, our *predicates*: our elementary sentence, our basic rhythm, our morphological identity, our generic incarnation, our genealogy. (*Sexes and Genealogies*, p. 71; italics in original).

The rebellious principle of blood is perhaps best shown in the particular love that bonds Demeter and Kore: it is a love that resists those economic norms that traffic in women; it transgresses the boundaries between the worlds of the living and of the dead; and it values virginity and fecundity against the gods' practice of rape and war. The mother and the daughter have no interest in the power struggles between the male gods, Zeus and Hades, and concern themselves instead with growth and, particularly, with the human cultivation of nature. Hence, Demeter and Kore represent also a bridge between the natural, the human and the divine. When Zeus and Hades conspire in the rape of the daughter and the destruction of the mother–daughter pair, Demeter resists this trade between father and husband, and acts to preserve the virginity of her daughter. While the sharp and adversarial distinction between the realms of Zeus and Hades – the realms of the living and of the dead – is fundamental to the logic of kingdoms, the blood tie between Demeter and Kore is indifferent to such a distinction. Blood is, in the case of Demeter and Kore, the sign of the power of female genealogy; the site of women's representations of themselves as divine; and a means for the spiritualization of virginity, fecundity and even death.

As the mark of fecundity and vitalism, blood is a point of resistance to the logic of death and war imposed by the victory of human law. It may seem strange to correlate the divine law, now exclusively concerned with the care of the dead, with the respect and preservation of life. Unlike the warfare and struggle that characterizes public life, however, which is concerned with ending the life of an other and mastering one's own death, the work of caring for the dead is fundamentally concerned with sustenance and continuation. The burial of the dead – which, as Hegel puts it, comprises the return of the dead man to the nourishing bosom of the Earth – is a gesture of quasi-maternal care. As we see in the example of Demeter's love for Kore, a love undiminished when the daughter goes to the underworld, in the logic of blood, death is neither radical nor terminal, and it does not disrupt the weaving of care and connection supported by blood. The sister's care of the dead brother represents not only his reintegration into the fabric of a community, a community which, in the case of Polynices, has effected his death through a logic of fraternal competition, but also his reintegration into the loving couple of sister and brother, mother and son. Therefore, burial here reconfirms not only the logic of the polis but the bonds of love. These acts of sustenance and love, deeply intertwined with the work of giving and sustaining life, are hardly a concession to the phallic logic of death; rather, they effect the return of death to life.

After the triumph of the human law, blood has been dispersed, and women's preference for younger, less authoritarian men is ruthlessly crushed through mobilizing these young men for war (*Speculum*, p. 226). The work of memorializing the dead, so dangerous for the state in the moment of Antigone's confrontation with Creon, is appropriated to memorialize young men's sacrifice of their lives to the state. What remains, to allude to Luce Irigaray's famous turn of phrase, is woman as 'the eternal irony of the community', that is, as a disruptive and unexpected surprise. Luce Irigaray's early work, devoted to analysing the history of philosophy, is in part founded on the ironic scene of a woman observing contradictory currents in men's writing, inconsistencies of which the writing subjects are unaware. These inconsistencies, hidden to the subject of philosophy, include omissions and contradictions that often reveal weaknesses in the philosopher's logic or open up an alternative with respect to his certainties.

At least, a disruptive irony would persist in spite of the phallic economy of death, one that indicates the possibility of reappropriating the divine law from the Hegelian schema of death and mastery. While it is in the interest of Spirit that the natural accident of a man's death should be recast as chosen and mastered, women's work in caring for the dead is not actually concerned with mastery but rather with the shadowy work of reconciling the masculine community's need for mastery with the exigencies of nature. As such, the care of the dead represents an intriguing middle point between natural determination and rational self-determination, one that resists the binary logic of animal/human, life/death, and reason/nature. In reconciling the needs of the human community with nature, the divine law indicates the possibility that the tensions between nature and culture in the work of Hegel might not necessarily end in conquest and repression but rather in mutual accommodation. Drawing out from the shadows the ethical law of caring for the dead, then, presents a challenge and an alternative to Hegel's logic of mastery.

Hegel's own dismissal of blood – which, Luce Irigaray demonstrates, is necessarily excluded from Absolute Spirit – at the same time acknowledges the necessity of blood in the process that achieves Spirit. Like the divine law itself, blood remains a crucial element in the sustenance of the community, albeit one that is apparently excluded from the community as such. In Hegel, then, blood may be dispersed and degraded, but it must also remain in some subterranean or appropriated form – one which, Luce Irigaray suggests, can be rediscovered and reappropriated.

The Return to Blood

In *Democracy Begins Between Two,* Luce Irigaray decries the fact that 'woman is still subjected to the state of nature' (p. 42), as she lacks a civil and a spiritual identity. 'The cause of this', she writes, 'is the lack of a passage, within the family itself, from natural to civil identity' (op. cit., p. 52), a passage that can only be reconstructed through institutions, like sexed civil rights, that counter the traditional repression of sexual difference. At the same time, it is necessary to rediscover a passage from natural to spiritual identity within the family, and I propose that the divine law presents such a passage. A going back to and reappropriating the divine law promises not only to right certain civil wrongs against women but also a return to the spiritual principle of blood – a principle fundamentally opposed to the warlike and possessive logic of the state, and which maintains a spiritual connection to nature, life and female ancestry.

Given the power and promise of the divine law and its trace of blood to disrupt the patriarchal state, it is in the best interest of women to return to this principle. To disinter the divine law, the one buried in the time of Antigone, is to rediscover a point of resistance to the economy of war and death, to rediscover matrilineal ancestry, and a relation to the divine which suits women. Luce Irigaray has successfully disinterred a divine in the feminine in traditions such as yogic breathing and the Christian figures of the Virgin Mary and her mother, Anne. In what follows, I will offer an account of the rediscovery of the values of female genealogy through the spiritual practices of Chinese traditional religion. This account, while purely anecdotal, demonstrates the possibility of rediscovering female ancestry – and, with it, a divine in the feminine – through existing cultural traditions, and also provides us with a set of techniques which can aid in the task of re-establishing and revaluing female genealogies.

Chinese traditional religion is an ancient form of ancestor veneration thought to predate the Buddhist and Taoist practices also common in China. It entails the belief that the dead live in a spiritual world in many ways parallel to that of the living. Deceased ancestors, like living family elders, should be cared for by descendants, and require attention and worship, generally in the form of real or symbolic sacrifices of food, clothing or money. Burial sites must be looked after, and the names of male ancestors remembered. Ancestors are revered as quasi-deities, who demand sacrifices and offer protection and aid. The care of ancestors represents veneration for the fecundity of the previous generations, and also a special tie to the Earth where they lived and died, as the burial site is maintained by a family member. Since the duty of taking care of the ancestors falls to the family, a rite of burial becomes an occasion for the highly ritualized, public display of a family's constitution and limits. Traditionally, the duties of caring for the dead are granted to a dead man's sons and daughters-in-law; unmarried daughters have a lesser role, and married daughters are excluded from the familial rituals. The women who guard and execute these rituals are in fact the elder women of the family, the daughters-in-law rather than natal members of the family.

In recent years, I have observed in several Chinese-American families, including my own, a shift in the representation of kinship in the funeral rituals. These rituals have integrated natal daughters and granddaughters, both married and unmarried, into the fabric of the family for the purposes of burying their male and female ancestors. This change is surely influenced by the increased value placed on female children in China and the West over the past century; smaller families also make it likely for families to lack sons and grandsons, and

American culture tends to accord married daughters a role in the natal family. In the simplest terms, such a change reflects a desire on the part of elder women, the guardians of the tradition, to represent the kinship to their daughters and granddaughters at the level of divine ritual. In reimagining burial rituals to incorporate female as well as male genealogies, female elders offer their descendants the means to live out the divine law in a way that respects, rather than obscures, the principle of blood. These reimagined rituals are a rare opportunity to represent blood relations between women, both at the familial and, to some extent, the public level – as funeral rituals produce public events such as announcements and processions. Finally, insofar as the care of the dead and the remembrance of ancestry correspond to a spiritual task within Chinese traditional religion, the matrilineal bonds, too, become spiritualized.

Rediscovering and reimagining funeral traditions can provide women with a means to return to female ancestry and female divinities. Reinvented with a concern for women's genealogy, memorial practices, such as memorizing ancestors' names and visiting their graves, can help to establish alternative or multiple genealogies, genealogies that are not confined to the same exclusive lineage by which each person is assigned one, perhaps two, family names. The rituals of caring for the dead – a vestige of a divine law that has been appropriated to the ends of the patriarchal family and state – can thus be rediscovered, for example in the funeral rituals described above, as a place to affirm the bonds of blood. By readopting and adapting cultural traditions of care and memorialization for the dead, women can both preserve existing cultural diversity and unearth one of the possibilities of culture between women.

As ancestor veneration is a tradition in which the correlation between the rediscovery of female genealogy and female divinities is unusually clear, I do not accord this tradition any special primacy in the pursuit of female spirituality. I present this example because I believe that a dedication to a culture of difference requires us to recognize that all cultures hold their particular lessons and possibilities for the rediscovery of the female divine, and because for me, as I suspect is the case for many women, this rediscovery of female divinity was facilitated by my relationships to the women of my family. Finally, I find that the way in which the changing roles of women between generations and cultures are integrated, by older women, into ancient traditions is a promising sign that feminist activism does not need to produce a war between generations of women nor a struggle to destroy existing culture but can rather promote a collaborative process between mothers and daughters to rediscover hidden hope in their cultures.

Notes

1 As is demonstrated in Karen Burke's paper in this volume. Burke's incisive analysis of death in Hegel enriches and exceeds my own on many points.
2 The community of men originates in the potentially fatal struggle between the two parties who will become master and slave, and it is perpetuated through the risky habit of war; it is through the fear of always-looming death that the slave realizes his freedom.

3 Usually translated into English as *Speculum of the Other Woman*. However, 'Of the Other Woman' is a subtitle and ought to be translated as 'On the Other as Woman'.

4 While it is difficult, under the rubric of blood, to understand Antigone's declaration (*Antigone*, line 1020) that she would not act thus to bury her husband or, particularly, her child – indeed, this passage is considered problematic in most readings – this statement can perhaps be understood as a defence of the hidden principle of maternal blood over-against the colonizing principle of patriarchal descent. Antigone's matrilineage is distinguished by its irreproducibility, as maternal lines of descent and relation are actively suppressed and cut off. Antigone's matrilineal relations will be erased by marriage, to be replaced by a family – husband, children and in-laws – defined by norms of marriage and paternity rather than blood. Within this logic, Antigone's relation to her own children will reproduce the paternal grandparents' line, but cannot reinscribe or re-present her relation to her mother as does her relation to Polynices, her mother's son. I suggest that this claim of Antigone's is best understood as a defiance of the logic of patriarchal definitions of family, which instantiates kinship by means of law rather than blood, which is nonetheless founded in this logic. Antigone values her brother above all other because he is the only apparent link to her mother.

Chapter 12

Writing the Body of Christ: Each Flesh Becoming Word

Emily A. Holmes

Emory University, USA

In 1987, Luce Irigaray published a review of *In Memory of Her*, Elisabeth Schüssler Fiorenza's classic work in feminist biblical hermeneutics and theology.[1] While Irigaray praises the book for its insights into early Christian history and for its views that 'let in a breath of fresh air and a bit of spirit as well' ('Equal to Whom?', in *The Essential Difference*, p. 64), she was ultimately disappointed: 'sociology quickly bores me when I'm expecting the divine' (op. cit., p. 80). In her review, Irigaray implies that Schüssler Fiorenza is more interested in discovering women's historical equality with Jesus' male disciples – what Schüssler Fiorenza in fact refers to as the 'discipleship of equals' (*In Memory of Her*, pp. 130–54) – than in claiming for women 'an equal share in the divine' ('Equal to Whom?', in *The Essential Difference*, p. 74). In contrast to Schüssler Fiorenza's historical-critical approach to the early Christian tradition, Irigaray offers her own theological reflections on Jesus' significance. For Irigaray, the most interesting thing about Jesus is not his radical social teachings and practices, but the divine character of his incarnation and the possibilities it indicates for 'a spiritualization and divinization of the flesh'. Nevertheless, as Jesus was male, he 'is the manifestation of only a part of this: he is God made man. But at least he's flesh and blood, living in the confines of a body and therefore sexuate' (op. cit., p. 72; translation modified). Following Schüssler Fiorenza's discussion of the historical elimination of women from central roles as Christian witnesses to the Jesus movement, Irigaray speculates that the denial of Christ's sexuate incarnation in part 'results from the exclusion of women from preaching the Gospels and from the priesthood' (op. cit., p. 74). Because 'women, who were his witnesses as much as men, were eliminated from all evidence relating to him' (op. cit., p. 70), Christ's divine body, his revolutionary attitudes towards marriage and women, his use of touch to heal and console, and his respect for the fruits of the earth over sacrifice in his memorial meal are more easily forgotten. Irigaray further hypothesizes that the Christian witness of Jesus might have been very different had his women followers written of their experience of his incarnation and been the ones to transmit the central ritual of the Eucharist in memory of him – and of her.

Twelve hundred years into Christian history, women did provide a witness to the effect of the incarnation of God in their spiritual lives, writings and practices. The later Middle Ages saw an outpouring of women's religious devotion, including women's theological writing, unlike anything before or, for that matter, since. The increasing number of convents founded by the new monastic and apostolic orders, women's participation in various heretical movements, and the invention of quasi-religious opportunities for women remaining in the world all speak to the rise of a women's religious movement.[2] The explanations offered for this movement are numerous, including the popular 'surplus women' theory, and demographic and economic factors were certainly at work. But, theologically, the women's religious movement can be linked to a renewed emphasis on the incarnation of God, the suffering humanity of Christ, and the role of the sacraments in medieval Christian religion, these shifts in medieval piety being partly a response to the radically dualistic Cathar heresy. Carolyn Walker Bynum, in particular, has traced the dominant imagery found in texts describing medieval women's piety to their bodily identification with Christ who, by becoming wounded flesh that is broken and eaten, was understood to have identified with them (cf. *Holy Feast* and *Fragmentation and Redemption*). Women's bodies thereby became the privileged site for miracles attesting to God's presence in the world through their extreme feats of suffering, inedia, food miracles such as lactation, as well as for their erotic longing for union with God (cf. Martha J. Reineke, ' "This is my body" '). Others, however, have noted important differences between the hagiographical texts, largely written by men, that are the basis for most of Bynum's claims, and medieval women's own theological writings (cf. Amy Hollywood, *The Soul as Virgin Wife*).

Two Beguine writers in particular, Hadewijch of Brabant and Marguerite Porete, along with Franciscan tertiary Angela of Foligno, granted their own texts the status and authority of scripture by claiming God as their co-author, prompting historian Bernard McGinn to place them among the 'female evangelists of the thirteenth-century' ('The Four Female Evangelists'). Their texts manifest important variations arising not only from differences of language, geography and influence, but also from artistic choices of genre, style and imagery. Each of these women writers, however, despite their important differences from one another, shares a mystical emphasis on union with God without distinction between God and the soul (cf. McGinn, *The Flowering*).[3] For each writer, moreover, Christ's humanity is the means to union with his divinity. The incarnation is central to the thought of these women mystics, often introduced in surprising and counterintuitive ways through images of pregnancy and birth that extend their interpretation of the incarnation to other bodies and even to the entire cosmos.

What makes these women distinct from contemporary accounts of the largely affective mysticism of the *mulieres religiosae* is the fact of their writing. By writing of their spiritual understanding and by interpreting the meaning of the incarnation – the Word of God become flesh in the person of Jesus Christ – for themselves, they implicitly reject the hagiographical tradition that encouraged women merely to experience union with Christ physically through suffering acts of extreme asceticism and paramystical phenomena.[4] These women writers claim the authority not only to interpret their own experience, but to assume a pedagogical and theological ability to instruct others. Their frequent self-reflections on their own writing display the anxiety, and the courage, such interpretive boldness required in order to become a speaking or writing subject.

The possibilities for women's speech, writing and subjectivity are the theoretical focus of Luce Irigaray as well.[5] Her work interrogates how female bodies and desire signify within language, disrupt the paternal symbolic, and might constitute a feminine subjectivity in a culture of sexuate difference. In this essay, I discuss Luce Irigaray's theoretical writings on *parler-femme*, or speaking (as) woman, with reference to the writings of three medieval women mystics on the Christian doctrine of the incarnation. As early as *Speculum*, in the review discussed above, and also in her more recent writings on spirituality (for example in the section on 'Spirituality and Religion', in *Key Writings*, pp. 145–94), Irigaray links her own philosophical and linguistic interest in women's subjectivity to the theological question of the incarnation. Her overriding interest in sexuate difference extends all the way to the divine, but rather than rejecting the Christian belief in the incarnation as upholding a male standard of both humanity and divinity (as some feminist theologians do, such as Mary Daly in *Beyond God the Father*, and Daphne Hampson in *Theology and Feminism*), she embraces the notion of a bodily, sexuate divinity. For her, however, the incarnation necessarily remains incomplete and unfinished. Because orthodox Christianity limits the incarnation to the unique body of Jesus of Nazareth, the Word of God has not been made female flesh.[6] Without an incarnation in the feminine, women lack a divine model of their own subjectivity, an issue Irigaray takes up again in later essays, especially 'Divine Women' (*Sexes and Genealogies*, pp. 55–72). But Irigaray's preoccupation with the incarnation as a way to establish women's subjectivity turns up in other ways as well. In fact, her early interest in markers of sexuate difference in linguistics and the language of women, what she calls *parler-femme*, can be seen to have theological significance. For Irigaray, the problem of the incarnation for women is not merely the maleness of Christ, nor a representation of God as woman, whether in the form of a divine Mother, Christa, or an incarnate Spirit. It is not only the problem of an eternal divine Word made flesh, but, more crucially, the issue of female flesh made word and also silence.[7] This approach to women's subjectivity and their relation to the divine makes the incarnation first and foremost a problem of bodies and a problem of language.

After discussing Irigaray's early writings on speaking (as) woman and the relation of *parler-femme* to the mystical discourse of *La mystérique* (cf. *Speculum*, pp. 191–202), I turn to a brief description of the writings of Hadewijch of Brabant, Angela of Foligno, and Marguerite Porete. I contend that the theoretical writings of Luce Irigaray, along with a critical reading of medieval women's mystical texts, position the contemporary feminist theologian to reinterpret the incarnation in the feminine: not as eternal and disembodied masculine Word made flesh, but as female flesh becoming divine word, in and through the cultivation of spiritual practices, such as the writings of these medieval women.

Luce Irigaray on *parler-femme*

For Luce Irigaray, *parler-femme* has multiple meanings, not limited to but including speaking the feminine, speaking of and to women, speaking as woman-subject, and action or speech by or on behalf of women (*par les femmes ou au nom
des femmes*).[8] What Irigaray proposes by *parler-femme* is an economy of significa-
tion that is not based on the phallic exchange of metaphors, that is, a substitution of signs which aims to pass from a material and concrete meaning to
a more abstract meaning, but rather on *metonymy*, for example, at the bodily
level, that of the two lips in contiguous relation. Thus the language of *parler-
femme* arises from desire, but what makes it distinctively feminine is that it is iso-
morphic with a different morphology: a female body that is fluid, multiple, not
one, unlike the unity and identity of the phallus. The speaking subject remains
in contiguity with her body; her language would not be a substitutionary chain
of signifiers but a speaking of desire in which language remains touch, also to
and with the body.[9] Although, according to Irigaray, often women are not yet
subjects of enunciation as women, she already finds evidence of *parler-femme* in
the way women's bodies signify, the way they speak what otherwise cannot be
said except through laughter, gestures and hysterical symptoms.[10] Establishing
the link between those bodily gestures and a symbolic language is the problem
of enunciation,[11] that is, to create the conditions for women to speak as women
subjects, without denying or disavowing their bodies, their self-affection, their
mothers, and their relationships with other women (see Margaret Whitford's
interpretation of *parler-femme* as *langage* – rather than *langue* – in *Luce Irigaray:
Philosophy in the Feminine*, pp. 38–49).[12]

Part of the problem of women becoming speaking subjects, according to
Irigaray, is that language rests on a hidden and unacknowledged debt to its own
material – and maternal – conditions. For women to assume speaking subjectivity entails a twofold transformation of language: (1) the debt to the maternal
must be acknowledged, that is, the body of the mother that subtends language
must be brought into consideration, and (2) the woman-subject must be separated from her confusion with the mother. In order for women to become subjects of enunciation, they need language as a sort of 'shelter' for what Irigaray
calls their 'becoming' (op. cit., pp. 45–8). In her later work, Irigaray also links
this transformation of language with God, both as divine verb or Word and as
a divine figuration which could be appropriate to women (cf. 'Divine Women'
and 'Women, the Sacred, Money', in *Sexes and Genealogies*). Without a 'God in
the feminine', Irigaray worries that women remain fixed in the role of, at best,
the mother through whom God becomes man (op. cit., p. 62). The unacknowledged debt to the maternal in phallocentric language thus parallels the unacknowledged debt to Mary in the incarnation of Christ: in both cases the woman
is 'sacrificed' or paralysed as mother. As that which subtends language and the
becoming-divine of men, the maternal-feminine is excluded from access to
her own language, her own divine representation, and her own incarnation.
A divine in the image of women would, according to Irigaray, serve towards
the perfection of women's subjectivity, as the infinite horizon towards which

women might 'become' in an ongoing process of 'transfiguration' of flesh and speech.[13]

In light of Irigaray's embodied linguistic theory of *parler-femme*, as well as her more recent writings on spirituality and the breath, her work helps position the contemporary feminist theologian to reconceive the Christian doctrine of the incarnation in terms of women's bodies' advent to language, that is, as female flesh-made-word in a way that reconfigures the opposition between Word and flesh. It therefore becomes possible to reread thirteenth-century women's texts as a kind of mystical *écriture féminine* in which that which is repressed as feminine – body, desire, affect, birth and death – erupts into speech and writing, even in the midst of a patriarchal social and religious historical context.

Irigaray's *parler-femme* can thus be seen to have startling affinities with the mystical writings of Hadewijch, Angela, and Marguerite Porete.[14] Just as many contemporary feminists have struggled with finding a voice and inventing the words to say what has never been said before (for example, Audre Lorde, 'Poetry is Not a Luxury'; and Marie Cardinal, *Les Mots Pour Le Dire*), for medieval women the act of writing was equally fraught with anxiety: not only were they writing theology in the context of a church that denied them teaching authority, but they were daring to write their ineffable experience of God.[15] These medieval texts are also marked by the features of 'feminine' writing and speech: paradox and wordplay at the level of syntax; a refusal of the either/or of binary logic; the use of multiple genres and dialogical positions; a delight in bodily images of Christ, Mary and the mystic herself; and a libidinal economy that 'gives' without return to a master signifier.[16] Irigaray's theoretical work thus provides a productive framework in which to understand the eruption of women's theological speech in the thirteenth century as their female flesh made word through their participation in writing the body of Christ.

Indeed, at the heart of *Speculum*, Irigaray finds an example of *parler-femme* in the writings of the medieval mystics. 'La mystérique' forms the central chapter of the work and continues the mirror imagery of the book as a whole. While the chapter opens with quotations from Ruusbroec, Eckhart, and Angela of Foligno, allusions to other women mystics can be identified as well (cf. Philippa Berry, 'The Burning Glass', in *Engaging with Luce Irigaray*, p. 235). Irigaray claims that mysticism 'is the only place in the history of the West in which woman speaks and acts so publicly' and with a cultural and political impact (*Speculum*, p. 191). The centrality of women in late medieval mysticism is due in part to the traditional and grammatical femininity of the soul, but more especially to the outpouring of women's texts, vitae, bodily phenomena, miracles and so on, that have been so well documented in recent years.[17] More important for Irigaray's concerns, she finds in mysticism an alternative discourse to the 'dry desolation of reason', a place where 'subject' and 'Other' mingle and embrace, where *jouissance* flourishes, and where language and subjectivity are interrogated, annihilated and reconfigured (op. cit., pp. 191–2) This 'la mystérique' – in which one can also hear 'l'âme hystérique' – is culturally coded as feminine, not simply because of the centrality of women or the grammatical femininity of the soul, but as an alternative discourse that threatens to disrupt phallogocentric reason. Here, 'within a still theological onto-logical perspective' (op. cit., p. 191), Irigaray glimpses an expression of something other, through a speech pre-eminently associated with women in the Middle Ages, the *parler-femme* of the mystics.[18]

Irigaray rightly observes that this speech was made possible by the mystic's identification with the feminized body of Christ. The incarnation and crucifixion lie at the heart of women's production of mystical speech.[19] The wounded body of Christ provides a divine mirror to female morphology, which, as Irigaray argues in *This Sex Which Is Not One* (p. 23), has never been represented as anything other than a wounded or amputated version of the phallic standard. When the mystic gazes upon the body of Christ, she sees and loves herself: 'In this way, you see me and I see you, finally I see myself seeing you in this fathomless wound which is the source of our wondering comprehension and exhilaration. And to know myself I scarcely need a "soul", I have only to gaze upon the gaping space in your loving body' (*Speculum*, p. 200). In the passages in which Irigaray discusses the divine mirroring between Christ and the feminine soul or mystic, she shifts to the first person and the subject 'I' appears.[20] While her writing in this chapter is poetic and allusive, her argument ultimately seems to point to a particular moment in late medieval European history in which identification with the wounded, bleeding body of Christ rendered it possible for women's subjectivity to accede to language, in particular through the production of a mystical discourse. That is, identification with Christ, who out of love has made this accessible through his incarnation, allows women's own frequently demonized flesh to become Word through mystical writing and speech.

Three Medieval Women Mystics on the Incarnation

In the longer version of this essay – my dissertation, 'Writing the Body of Christ' – I offer close readings of the writings of Hadewijch of Brabant, Angela of Foligno, and Marguerite Porete towards the construction of a feminist theology of the incarnation. Beginning with the relation between bodies and language, flesh and word, as theorized by Irigaray, I note that the theological writings of these medieval women are made possible by an interpretation of the incarnation that extends its significance from Christ's body to other bodies – Mary's body, the mystic's own body, the bodies of her audience – and practices, including the practice of writing. Focusing on features of mystical writing that resemble *écriture féminine*, and in particular on the use of images of pregnancy, birth and maternity, I interpret the ways in which female flesh becomes word. Not only do these tropes of natality figure the incarnation and extend it beyond the unique body of Jesus Christ to other bodies, these images also serve as figures for the mystics' own texts, to which they 'give birth' in response to or as an effect of the incarnation. By writing the body of Christ along with her own body into the text, each writer offers a novel interpretation of the incarnation in terms of bodies, language – writing and speech – and practices that has significance for the status of other bodies, even today. I therefore sustain that the

Christian message of the incarnation is one that must be practised. Men and women have to live into their incarnation through ethical and spiritual practices, including the practices of reading, interpreting and writing undertaken by the medieval women I discuss.

Hadewijch of Brabant, a Dutch Beguine of the thirteenth century, wrote in a wide variety of genres: visions, letters, poems in stanzas, and poems in rhyming couplets.[21] She is unique among medieval women writers not only for the diversity of forms in which she wrote, but also for her maternal model of the spiritual life, according to which she instructed her fellow Beguines to take Mary as an example, and to conceive and give birth to divine love in their spiritual practices. Hadewijch understands the incarnation of God from the perspective of Mary's experience of conception, pregnancy and birth. By taking Mary as the model of spiritual life and interpreting her biological experience in spiritual and allegorical terms, Hadewijch effectively extends the incarnation to all others, and especially women, but also men, whose spiritual practices similarly give birth to love.[22] The legacy of Hadewijch's spiritual practice is found in her poetic writings, which convey her Marian model of spirituality and her own flesh made word through her *parler-femme*. Hadewijch's interpretation of the incarnation in terms of the birth of divine love within the soul makes possible her own creative production of texts out of love for God and for her fellow Beguines.

Angela of Foligno, an Italian Franciscan tertiary who died in 1309, offers a more concrete and visceral example of writing the body of Christ through her practice of *imitatio Christi* (cf. *Il Libro della Beata Angela da Foligno*, translated as *Complete Works*). Her literary itinerary, as outlined in her *Memorial*, commences with her somatic display of paramystical phenomena – screaming on the floor of the church of St Francis in Assisi – through which she is 'writing the body' in the classic sense of the hysteric, whose physical symptoms manifest what cannot be spoken (cf. Hélène Cixous and Catherine Clément, *La Jeune Née*). Through her sessions with her Franciscan relative and confessor Brother Arnaldo, her physical symptoms gradually recede as she begins to interpret her experiences and speak her desire. Her theological reflections deepen and she gains spiritual authority, eventually becoming the 'mother' of a group of Franciscan sons and daughters. The resulting *Book of Blessed Angela* is a collaborative text: the *Memorial*, written together with Brother Arnaldo,[23] and the *Instructions*, a collection of letters, teachings and anecdotes, written for her spiritual disciples. In both parts of Angela's book, the incarnation plays a central role leading to a sacramental worldview – 'this world is pregnant with God!', she writes in *Complete Works* (p. 170) – and the experience of the Word within her own flesh: 'Then God showed me the Word, so that now I would understand what is meant by the Word and what it is to speak the Word. And he said to me: "This is the Word who wished to incarnate himself for you." At that very moment the Word came to me and went all through me, touched all of me, and embraced me' (op. cit., p. 315).

Marguerite Porete was executed as a relapsed heretic in Paris in 1310 for disseminating her book, *The Mirror of Simple Souls*. Her book is written as an allegorical dialogue among Love, Soul and Reason, all of whom are personified as ladies, who together discuss the soul's ascent to God through various stages that lead to what she calls 'annihilation', because the soul is brought to nothing in union with God. Porete's book presupposes and resists the popular somatic women's piety of her contemporaries as she transfers the suffering of the body to the suffering and eventual annihilation of the will, partly in order to free the body from the burden of extreme asceticism, which she relegates to a lower stage of the spiritual life.[24] Ultimately, the movement of the soul's annihilation in God is Christ-like in form (cf. Ellen Babinsky, 'Christological transformation'). Like Christ, the soul sacrifices her own will in a kenotic gesture that annihilates her particular subjectivity. But that annihilation is not complete: oddly material metaphors of wax, parchment and singing testify to the persistence of the soul in the form of a new, resurrected and deified, subjectivity that is fully identified with divine love. It is this new subjectivity that sings – and writes – in Porete's text, despite the annihilation of the soul and the challenges it seemingly presents for writing. In Marguerite Porete's text, the body of Christ is found written in her subtle incarnational theology of the soul. As her characters describe the soul's Christological movement from annihilation to deification, a new subjectivity emerges that speaks 'I' only because she is fully identified with the 'I am' of divine Lady Love, herself posited as the origin of Porete's text.

Hadewijch, Angela and Marguerite each presuppose a popular female sanctity, based on physical identification with Christ's suffering humanity. Each emphasizes the centrality of the incarnation to salvation history and the spiritual life, and recognizes that women's primary access to Christ's divinity is through his humanity. But each writer takes her understanding of the incarnation further: these women experience and interpret the body of Christ in ways that make possible the divinization of their own bodies and their own writing, as flesh becoming word. By writing the body of Christ into their texts, each offers an interpretation of the incarnation as having significance for other bodies and, through spiritual practices, for the mystic's own creative writing.

Motivating my reading of these women's texts are explicitly theological concerns. Rather than undertaking an interpretation of the incarnation with a claim about the transcendent pre-existence of God who chooses – whether violently or out of love – to enter the temporal realm of human flesh, these medieval texts make it possible to think the incarnation from the opposite direction, beginning with women's bodies marked first by sexuate and also other differences. Because women's bodies have historically, and philosophically, been associated with matter, flesh, sex, sin and death, the incarnation – the creedal profession of the embodiment of God – is a fertile site for feminist intervention. As Irigaray quips, at least this god is flesh and blood ('Equal to Whom?', in *The Essential Difference*, p. 72). But despite medieval women's impressive ability to claim access to the sacred based on their identification with Christ's suffering, feeding, feminized body, the problem – for some contemporary feminist theologians, at least – remains that 'what is not assumed is not redeemed', or as Rosemary Radford Ruether asks in *Sexism and God-Talk*, 'can a male savior save women?' (p. 116).[25] No matter how 'wounded' – itself an extremely problematic conception of the 'female' body based on castration – the body of Christ remains male. In other words, from the perspective of sexuate difference, the incarnation appears to remain partial and limited.[26]

Some theologians refer to this limitation as a scandal of particularity, emphasizing the uniqueness of the incarnation event in the body of Jesus of Nazareth (see, for example, the writings of Søren Kierkegaard and Karl Barth). Others tend to universalize the incarnation by extending its significance to human divinization (cf. Friedrich Schleiermacher, *On Religion* and *Christmas Eve*). The Greek fathers made similar arguments, but divinization historically often turns out to be based on the exclusion and repression of women and bodies. More recently, Gianni Vattimo has reinterpreted the incarnation as secularization: to claim in faith that God has a body empties God's transcendence of all absurd and capricious elements that would do violence to reason, and instead opens up the significance of that body to the ongoing history of interpretation (cf. *Belief* and *After Christianity*). Recent feminist writings on the incarnation have focused on its significance for other bodies, and even for non-human bodies, through ethical and spiritual practices of respect and care (for example, Sallie McFague, *The Body of God*; and Stephanie Paulsell, *Honoring the Body*). This ethical effect of the incarnation that leads to divinization is the main point of Luce Irigaray's response to Elisabeth Schüssler Fiorenza.[27] A feminist interpretation of the incarnation that begins with women's bodies can best assess the effect of the Christian belief in the incarnation by asking not how, or why, Word became flesh, but how female flesh can become divine.

In this constructive aspect of my project, I retain the impulse and spirit of universalizing interpretations of the incarnation in a way that preserves and acknowledges difference and particularity, including Jesus' own particular male body. By focusing on specific texts written by women and their interpretations of the incarnation, I attempt to avoid the totalizing gestures and homogenization that make all human beings into images of a male Christ. While we can understand the effect on women's bodies of the incarnation of God in the male body of Jesus as allowing for the creative writing on women's paramystical bodily symptoms and miracles, more importantly we can observe the effect of the incarnation of God in what it makes possible in the thirteenth-century texts that I discuss: women's own writing, in which not only Christ's, but their particular female flesh becomes divine word in a writing and speech marked by the desires and drives of the body. These texts, read through the lens of issues raised by Luce Irigaray, open up the interpretation of the incarnation from a unique, special revelation in a particular male body to a more general theological feature of the relationship between word and flesh, matter and spirit, in a multiplicity of bodies and texts marked by difference and desire, pleasure and pain, possibility and loss.

In their texts, the women mystics recognized this effect of the incarnation on other bodies. By identifying with the birthing, bleeding and broken body of Christ – who identified with them by becoming human – and yet by further transforming that identification into speech, readings and written texts, they inscribe their own bodies into the unfolding Christian tradition. Their interpretations of the incarnation proceed through spiritual practices, both active and contemplative, and particularly through their practice of writing, with its contemplative aims and active effects on the community of their readers.

A Dialogue with Luce Irigaray

When I presented this thesis to Luce Irigaray, she was receptive, and, in an engaging dialogue, she raised several questions for me to consider in the development of my work. The primary concern for Irigaray is that these medieval women mystics do not retain their self-affection and do not find the divine within, but instead go outside themselves, like the woman lover of the Song of Songs, in search of the divine Other. To be sure, many women mystics speak of self-annihilation or losing themselves in God instead of transfiguration or cultivation of the self, and their violent language of abjection raises serious questions for feminists interested in the conditions of women's subjectivity. Marguerite Porete, for example, expresses the precise situation of women under patriarchy when she writes, 'He is, and I am not' (*The Mirror of Simple Souls*, Chapter 122). Angela of Foligno has fantasies of dismemberment and death through which she might grow closer to her beloved, Christ.[28] Hadewijch wrestles with the seemingly fickle nature of divine love and experiences its absence as painful to the one who seeks divine favour (see especially her *Strophische Gedichten* (Poems in Stanzas)).[29] It is true that, within a patriarchal Christian context, these women were seeking God outside themselves, and that their self-affection seems to be replaced with painful self-degradation, whether in physical acts of mortification or, more frequently, in spiritually suffering the absence of the Beloved.

And yet, at the same time, these women discovered an interior beauty that corresponds to the love of the self and the love of God within. Like their early modern spiritual sister Teresa of Avila, who describes the soul as an interior castle 'made of a single diamond or of very clear crystal' (*Interior Castle*, p. 28), medieval women mystics found God within themselves, and they found themselves beautiful. For Marguerite Porete, once the soul has been stripped by grace of all its accretions, she becomes nothing other than a purely reflective mirror of God – so reflective that there is no difference between God and her (*The Mirror of Simple Souls*, Chapter 118). Hadewijch describes how Mary becomes the mother of God through her spiritual conception of love, prior to any biological conception, and she contends that all Christians might equally incarnate God as they, too, give birth to God from within (see especially Poem in Stanzas 29 and Poem in Couplets 14). Angela of Foligno discovers God within herself when she hears a voice saying 'You are full of God', and experiences the delight of the divine within (*Complete Works*, p. 148). Even within a patriarchal context, these women found within themselves what theologian Wendy Farley calls a 'pure luminosity' as the deepest reality of their being (*The Wounding and Healing of Desire*, p. 162). Christian language, images and spiritual practices provided the context and the means for the discovery of the divine within and, consequently, for a type of self-affection.

My research emphasizes the remarkable ability of these medieval women to write some of the richest, most provocative and most beautiful texts in the Christian tradition. When Luce Irigaray asked me whether writing can ultimately provide enough self-affection as a means of redemption for women – in comparison, for example, to the cultivation of the breath and an active receptiveness, of silence and the self-affection that it entails (see especially 'The Redemption of Women', in *Key Writings*, pp. 150–64) – I reflected that Christianity has always understood reading, especially Scripture, and writing as spiritual practices: salvation comes through the Word (for instance in Origen, *On First Principles*, Book IV). Writing, moreover, allowed these medieval women to speak to the other – not simply to the divine Other, but also to their contemporaries, to other women and to the other of history: that is, those of us who have received their work with gratitude. Working out of this Christian tradition, my concern is to recover spiritual practices that allow women, and also men, to understand the significance of the incarnation of God as the possibility for their sexuate flesh to become divine. The *parler-femme* of the women mystics, as seen in the way they write their own bodies along with the body of Christ, is one of these practices that can be recovered today. While writing may not ultimately be enough for the 'transfiguration of the flesh' of which Luce Irigaray speaks, women's mystical writing provides an opening for a feminist reinterpretation of the Christian tradition, beginning with an incarnation in the feminine. I think Luce Irigaray is right to suggest that other spiritual practices must accompany and follow writing: various forms of prayer, contemplation, the cultivation of silence and of the breath, notably through singing, and so on (cf. 'Fulfilling Our Humanity', in *Key Writings*, pp. 186–94).

This fruitful exchange brought a new perspective to my research by tracing the *parler-femme* of the mystics back to its origins in the body and especially the breath. Breathing is at the heart of both speech and silence, of both word and flesh, and thus may be the key for understanding the passage between them: the mystery of the incarnation as word made flesh and flesh made word, becoming divine through the cultivation of the breath. Christians might call this divine breath the Holy Spirit, breathed upon the disciples by Jesus. This same Spirit inspired the sacred texts of the Christian tradition. These texts, such as the writings of the medieval women mystics I have discussed, are thus not dead letter but, according to their authors, were the gift of God's breath. Writing the body of Christ, these women mystics equally breathed their own flesh into writing and thereby wrote their own incarnation as divine. We breathe a spiritual life into their writings by reading and interpreting them today.

Notes

1 Luce Irigaray, 'Egales à qui?', *Critique*, 43:480, 420–37. Published in English as Luce Irigaray, 'Equal to whom?', in *The Essential Difference*, pp. 63–81. Subsequent quotations are from the English translation. This text is a review by Irigaray of the French translation of Elisabeth Schüssler Fiorenza, *In Memory of Her: A Feminist Theological Reconstruction of Christian Origins*.

2 Such as Premonstratensian, Cistercian, Dominican and Franciscan convents; Cathar, Waldensian, Lollard and 'Free Spirit' heresies; and quasi-religious Beguines and tertiaries. See Carolyn Walker Bynum, *Holy Feast and Holy Fast: The Religious Significance of Food to Medieval Women*, especially Chapter 1, 'Religious Women in the Later Middle Ages'; and Bernard McGinn, *The Flowering of Mysticism: Men and Women in the New Mysticism (1200–1350)*. Both refer to Herbert Grundmann, *Religious Movements in the Middle Ages: The Historical Links between Heresy, the Mendicant Orders, and the Women's Religious Movement in the Twelfth and Thirteenth Century, with the Historical Foundations of German Mysticism*. See also Paul Vandenbroek, *Le jardin clos de l'âme: l'Imaginaire des religieuses dans les Pays-Bas du Sud, depuis le 13e siècle: Société des Expositions Palais des Beaux-Art de Bruxelles, 25 février-22 mai, 1994*, which contains an essay by Luce Irigaray, 'La voie du féminine'.

3 Some of these writings may have influenced Meister Eckhart's own speculative mysticism of indistinction (cf. *Meister Eckhart and the Beguine Mystics: Hadewijch of Brabant, Mechthild of Magdeburg, and Marguerite Porete*, ed. by Bernard McGinn).

4 Which can easily be interpreted, and dismissed, as pathological or hysterical (cf. Cristina Mazzoni, *Saint Hysteria: Neurosis, Mysticism, and Gender in European Culture*). As Amy Hollywood has argued, by shifting their focus from the body to the will, Mechthild of Magdeburg and Marguerite Porete, in particular, transform and spiritualize physical suffering (cf. *The Soul as Virgin Wife: Mechthild of Magdeburg, Marguerite Porete, and Meister Eckhart*, especially Chapter 7).

5 Among other 'French feminists', such as Hélène Cixous and Julia Kristeva, who share certain similar concerns, despite their important differences in methodology and conclusions. The term 'French feminist' should be kept in quotation marks, given the non-French origins of the most prominent 'French feminists' (Irigaray is French but was born in Belgium; Wittig was from Germany; Kristeva is from Bulgaria; and Cixous grew up in French Algeria) as well as their uneasy identification with feminism and the politics of identity (cf. Christine Delphy's scathing critique of the Anglo-American appropriation of 'French feminism' in 'The invention of French Feminism: an essential move', *Yale French Studies*, 87, 190–221). Nevertheless, they all mostly write in French and about the French language. As for feminism, in different ways they are all contesting masculine and patriarchal norms for the construction of what counts as knowledge, meaning and truth in order to open the possibility for other ways of thinking, speaking and writing that might take account of sexual/sexuate difference (cf. Elizabeth Grosz, *Sexual Subversions: Three French Feminists*). In other words, their feminist intervention is not only at the level of liberal economic or political access, though in general they support these efforts, and beyond (see in particular Luce Irigaray, *Democracy Begins Between Two*), but also at the level of the symbolic organization of language, representation, knowledge and meaning that makes political and economic systems possible.

6 Heretical movements have occasionally addressed this seeming lack, such as the thirteenth-century Guglielmiti of Milan, who revered the woman Guglielma as the incarnation of the Holy Spirit. It was believed that Guglielma would appoint a woman pope and soon initiate the third age of history: the feminine age of the Spirit (cf. Stephen Wessley, 'The Thirteenth-Century Guglielmites: Salvation Through Women', in *Medieval Women*; and Barbara Newman, 'The heretic saint: Guglielma of Bohemia, Milan, and Brunate', *Church History*, 74:1, 1–38).

7 See Irigaray's discussion of the importance of silence in relation to women's closed lips and self-affection, in 'Gesture in Psychoanalysis', in *Sexes and Genealogies*, especially pp. 99–102.

8 In Luce Irigaray's words: 'Speaking (as) woman is not speaking of woman. It is not a matter of producing a discourse of which woman would be the object, or the subject.

That said, by *speaking (as) woman*, one may attempt to provide a place for the "other" as feminine' (*This Sex Which Is Not One*, p. 135; emphasis hers; and also 'When Our Lips Speak Together', pp. 205–18).

9 See, for example, Irigaray's description in *This Sex Which Is Not One*, which I have left in the original French: '"Elle" est indéfiniment autre en elle-même. De là vient sans doute qu'on la dit fantasque, incompréhensible, agitée, capricieuse [...] Sans aller jusqu'à évoquer son langage, où "elle" part dans tous les sens sans qu' "il" y repère la cohérence d'aucun sens. Paroles contradictoires, un peu folles pour la logique de la raison, inaudibles pour qui les écoute avec des grilles toute faites, un code déjà tout préparé. C'est que dans ses dires aussi – du moins quand elle l'ose – la femme se re-touche tout le temps. Elle s'écarte à peine d'elle-même d'un babillage, d'une exclamation, d'une demi-confidence, d'une phrase laissée en suspens [...] Quand elle y revient, c'est pour repartir d'ailleurs. D'un autre point de plaisir, ou de douleur. Il faudrait l'écouter d'une autre oreille comme *un "autre sens" toujours en train de se tisser, de s'embrasser avec les mots, mais aussi de s'en défaire pour ne pas s'y fixer, d'y figer*. Car si "elle" dit ça, ce n'est pas, déjà plus, identique à ce qu'elle veut dire. Ce n'est jamais identique à rien d'ailleurs, c'est plutôt contigu. *Ça touche* (à). Et quand ça s'éloigne trop de cette proximité, elle coupe et elle recommence à "zéro": son corps-sexe' (*Ce sexe qui n'en est pas un*, p. 28; emphasis hers).

10 'Je pense que là où elle serait le plus à déchiffrer, c'est dans la gestualité du corps des femmes. Mais, comme cette gestualité est souvent paralysée, ou entrée dans la mascarade, effectivement, c'est parfois difficile à "lire". Sinon dans ce qui resiste ou subsiste "au-delà". Dans la souffrance, mais aussi le rire des femmes. Et encore: dans ce qu'elles "osent" – faire ou dire – , quand elles sont entre elles' (Irigaray, *Ce sexe qui n'en est pas un*, p. 132). Irigaray also finds evidence of *parler-femme* in a certain practice of poetic writing that aims to shift the conditions of speech, to provide a place for the advent of the other, through a different syntax, without subject or object, entailing proximity, but not appropriation.

11 'Le problème du "parler-femme" serait justement de trouver une continuité possible entre cette gestualité ou cette parole du désir – qui, actuellement, ne sont repérables que sous forme de symptômes et de pathologie – et un langage, y compris un langage verbal' (Irigaray, *Ce sexe qui n'en est pas un*, pp. 134–5).

12 *Parler-femme* thus refers to the position of enunciation and consequently to the conditions of women's subjectivity.

13 'If she is to become woman, if she is to accomplish her female subjectivity, woman needs a god who is a figure for the perfection of her subjectivity [...] the deformity associated with women [...] all this is symptomatic of the fact that women lack a female god who can open up the perspective in which their flesh can be transfigured' (Irigaray, 'Divine Women', in *Sexes and Genealogies*, p. 64).

14 In addition to other contemporary feminist theories of language that interrogate the relation between word and flesh, such as Hélène Cixous' *écriture féminine* and Julia Kristeva's theory of the maternal semiotic, which also bear an affinity to mystical discourse.

15 Their anxieties can be seen not only in their rhetorical use of humility tropes – God chose me because I am so unworthy and uneducated – but also in their frequent struggles with language to make it express what they mean, a language which fails, or even more strongly, blasphemes and lies. This struggle with 'the symbolic' may be a feature of some women's writing more generally; one thinks of Virginia Woolf's or Harriet Jacobs' efforts to put pen to paper. For a theological account of the sheer courage it took a thirteenth-century woman to begin to write, see Stephanie Paulsell, 'Writing as a Spiritual Discipline', in *The Scope of Our Art: The Vocation of the Theological Teacher*, pp. 17–31.

16 Such as the phallus, according to Lacan, or God the Father, according to Thomas Aquinas.

17 See note 2, above.

18 According to Luce Irigaray, mysticism is the only part of the Western tradition in which one can hear the voice of woman. Consequently, the mystics are key for going outside the Western patriarchal tradition. For her, they are just as important as the philosophical tradition, and thus she reads Angela of Foligno next to Kant. (Personal communication, seminar of Luce Irigaray, University of Nottingham, 22 June 2006).

19 She writes: 'one man, at least, has understood her so well that he died in the most awful suffering. That most female of men, the Son. And she never ceases to look upon his nakedness, open for all to see, upon the gashes in his virgin flesh, at the wounds from the nails that pierce his body as he hangs there, in his passion and abandonment. And she is overwhelmed with love of him/herself' (Irigaray, *Speculum*, pp. 199–200).

20 For example: 'What if everything were already so intimately specularized that even in the depths of the abyss of the "soul" a mirror awaited her reflection and her light. Thus I have become your image in this nothingness that I am, and you gaze upon mine in your absence of being [...]. A living mirror, thus, am I (to) your resemblance as you are mine' (Irigaray, *Speculum*, p. 197). Irigaray also seems to allude to Jacques Lacan's discussion of the mirror stage and retrieving an alternative possibility of subjectivity, or the formation of the 'I', through a mirror that could reflect feminine specificity. Irigaray suggests that a concave mirror, or a speculum, might provide a better representation of the ego-ideal for women in sexuate difference.

21 The critical editions of Hadewijch's works are edited by Jozef van Mierlo, S.J.: *Hadewijch: Visionen*, 2 vols; *Hadewijch: Strophische Gedichten*, 2 vols; *Hadewijch: Brieven*, 2 vols; and *Hadewijch: Mengeldichten*. There is an English translation by Mother Columba Hart, O.S.B., *Hadewijch: The Complete Works*.

22 See Irigaray's reflections on Mary's virginity in 'The Redemption of Women' and 'The Age of the Breath', both in *Key Writings*, along with Chung Hyun Kung's reinterpretation of Mary's virginity as her autonomy and self-definition, in *Struggle to Be the Sun Again: Introducing Asian Women's Theology*.

23 In Irigaray's terms, Angela and Arnaldo wrote 'in two'. The text of the *Memorial* is a product of two voices, written in sexuate difference.

24 For example: 'This Soul neither longs for nor despises poverty or tribulation, Mass or sermon, fasting or prayer; and gives to Nature all that it requires, with no qualm of conscience; but this Nature is so well ordered through having been transformed in the union with Love, to whom this Soul's will is joined, that it never asks anything which is forbidden' (Porete, *The Mirror of Simple Souls*, Chapter 9). This was one of the articles on the basis of which Porete's book was condemned as heretical.

25 Gregory of Nazianzus; of course, the church fathers would maintain that Christ's humanity was inclusive of women, even though women could not represent Christ.

26 As Irigaray points out, Jesus himself did not claim to be the final and complete revelation: 'if I do not go away, the Advocate will not come to you' (John 16:7). Gianni Vattimo also emphasizes this verse in his quasi-Joachite interpretation of the incarnation, the Holy Spirit and history (cf. *After Christianity* and *Belief*).

27 'But is Christianity a religion based on a love of the poor and the hope of salvation for the ignorant? While far and away preferable to exploitation and disdain, these qualities of Christianity strike me as but one of its aspects or effects. It is the social outcome of the respect for the incarnation of all bodies as potentially divine; nothing more nor less than each man and each woman being virtually god. If Christ's redemption of the world lacks

this meaning, then I see no other worthy of such historical loyalty' (Irigaray, 'Equal to Whom?', in *The Essential Difference*, pp. 68–9).

28 Angela writes: 'I was even disposed, because of his love, to wish that all the parts of my body suffer a death not like his, that is, one much more vile [...]. I could not imagine a death vile enough to match my desire' (*Complete Works*, p. 128). Her desire for humiliation and abjection, that paradoxically becomes divinization and exaltation in Christ, extends to her trip to care for lepers: 'And after we had distributed all that we had, we washed the feet of the women and the hands of the men, and especially those of one of the lepers which were festering and in an advanced stage of decomposition. Then we drank the very water with which we had washed him. And the drink was so sweet that, all the way home, we tasted its sweetness and it was as if we had received Holy Communion. As a small scale of the leper's sores was stuck in my throat, I tried to swallow it. My conscience would not let me spit it out, just as if I had received Holy Communion. I really did not want to spit it out but simply to detach it from my throat' (op. cit., p. 163).

29 For a feminist critique of the violent language in Hadewijch's mystical writings, see Julie B. Miller, 'Eroticized violence in medieval women's mystical literature: a call for a feminist critique', *Journal of Feminist Studies in Religion*, 15:2, 25–49.

Chapter 13

Sharing Air: Becoming Two in the Spirit[1]

Roland J. De Vries

McGill University, Canada

The narrative of the Annunciation has always had pride of place in the classical Christian tradition, expressing as it does the heart of the gospel message concerning God's presence with and for men and women. Indeed, no aspect of the church's life and teaching, whether its theology, iconography, or spirituality, has remained untouched by the narrative of Gabriel's visitation to Mary. In the writings of Luce Irigaray, also, the story of the Annunciation has been given pride of place, which is evidenced by the frequency with which she turns, or returns, to this biblical narrative. In the few pages that follow, it is my intention to demonstrate how Luce Irigaray's interpretation of the Annunciation gives expression to two important aspects of her later writings. In the first section of the paper it will be observed that Luce Irigaray's interpretation of the Annunciation expresses her distance from the classical Christian tradition and, more specifically, her refusal of the traditional Christian conception of the divine. In the second section it will be observed that Luce Irigaray's exposition of the angel's visitation to Mary also gives expression to her vision of an ethical and fecund intersubjectivity between man and woman. Each of these aspects of her thought – her distance from traditional Christianity, and her vision for the relationship between man and woman – is closely related to the other, and their interrelatedness will become evident as we consider her interpretation of the Annunciation.

Having considered how Luce Irigaray's interpretation of the Annunciation gives expression to her distance from the classical Christian tradition and to her vision of a transformed relationship between man and woman, in the final section of this paper I will consider a question that is mine in a more personal way. The question is whether someone who identifies with the classical Christian tradition – as I do – and who is unable and unwilling to abandon the basic theological presuppositions of that tradition – as I am – is able to enter into a meaningful and fruitful conversation with Luce Irigaray. That is, am I able to move beyond the task of merely describing and repeating her thought in order to embrace aspects of her ethical vision? I will offer a tentative 'yes' in answer to this question. Although Luce Irigaray's account of sexuate difference is in many ways bound up with her refusal of the classical Christian tradition or its interpretation, I will sketch out an account of intersubjectivity between man and woman, within a theocentric perspective, which is indebted to her ethics of sexuate difference. More specifically, I will speak of the relationship between man and woman in terms of a sharing of air, that is, in the Spirit.

Luce Irigaray, Christianity and the Divine

In considering her relationship to Christianity, we do well to begin with Luce Irigaray's own account of her relationship to that tradition. In *Key Writings* she reflects on her personal experience:

> As many people in Europe, I was born and educated in a Christian context. Also, as many people, upon becoming an adult, I left my own tradition, at least the conscious part of it. Later, I came to understand that a religious dimension is an important aspect of our culture and that it is crucial to consider both how we have been determined by this dimension and how we can, in the present, situate ourselves with respect to it. (Part IV, Spirituality and Religion, 'Introduction', p. 145)

In the light of these reflections it is apparent that while Luce Irigaray is attentive to Christianity as an important part of Western culture, and while she wishes to situate herself in relation to this aspect of Western culture, the orthodox or classical interpretation of Christian tradition is not hers in a determinative sense. Indeed, her reference to 'becoming an adult' should be read as a criticism of those who remain 'naively' situated within the Christian tradition, as a criticism of those who fail to mature by achieving at least a critical distance or perspective with respect to its traditional reception. Thus, she goes on to argue: 'I also have understood that we have to become adult and responsible towards our tradition and that which it has produced in ourselves: that is, neither to remain children nor to become iconoclasts' (ibid.). Luce Irigaray's posture towards Christianity, then, is neither one of mere acquiescence nor of complete repudiation, but is one which seeks a third way between these two possible responses. Continuing to speak of a mature and adult engagement with Christianity, she describes the intention of her work as follows:

> Thus, I tried to make apparent the main spiritual aspects of my tradition, and to render them fruitful for a becoming divine of my feminine subjectivity. I think that such work was necessary for my own liberation, but also for a human liberation in which the Christian tradition represents a crucial historical step and has still a decisive function to secure when it is faithful to its spiritual message. (ibid.)

The language employed by Luce Irigaray suggests that while she accepts the Christian tradition as her own and remains 'decisive' for her, she has also taken a significant step 'beyond' traditional Christianity. Indeed, in her essay 'The Redemption of Women', she assumes a decidedly more critical tone with

respect to the usual teachings of Christianity as she questions the incarnation of
Jesus Christ, in the body of a woman, at the behest of God the Father:

> For years I have tried to navigate on the raft of such truths, such dogmas. I
> trusted them, was wounded by them, and then distanced myself from them.
> I have come back to them, but to question and no longer to submit to them
> blindly. To me, this task seemed a necessary one, but also for all women and
> all men in search of their liberation. (*Key Writings*, p. 150)

She continues:

> I have therefore returned to my tradition in a more enlightened manner,
> more autonomous as a woman, and with a little Far Eastern culture which
> has given me some perspective on my own beliefs and taught me much about
> the figure of Jesus. (op. cit., pp. 150–1)[2]

It is clear, then, that the Christian tradition is significant for Luce Irigaray
on account of its mutual implication with Western culture. Since each person
is shaped by the religious, historical and philosophical context into which he
or she is born, and cannot simply step outside that tradition, each person must
both recognize one's tradition and endeavour to move forward in the process
of human becoming. From Luce Irigaray's perspective, to the extent that our
tradition contributes to our becoming man or woman, it should be embraced;
on the other hand, to the extent that our tradition prevents such becoming, it
must be repudiated or overcome. Of course, this raises a number of important
philosophical and hermeneutical questions, but the central issue, we might say,
is her attribution of 'epistemic primacy' to human becoming. To say that this
account of human becoming has epistemic primacy is to say that the Christian
tradition must be rejected, modified or overcome depending on whether it
coheres with her philosophy of sexuate difference, rather than vice versa. That
is, unlike someone situated within the traditional Christian tradition, whose
account of human becoming would be established on the basis of the theological presuppositions of that tradition, Luce Irigaray's view of human becoming is
apparently established on other grounds.[3] Her account of human becoming, as
is evident to those who are familiar with her work, is developed in her own allusive and richly textured philosophy of sexuate difference. While Luce Irigaray
does not repudiate Christianity, and if her thought embraces important aspects
of Christianity, it is nevertheless fair to say that she is at odds with classical interpretations of Christianity in important ways.

Turning to the Annunciation, we might identify the ways in which Luce
Irigaray's interpretation of this narrative is indicative of her distance from traditional Christianity. In *I Love to You*, she introduces her engagement with the
scriptural narrative by suggesting that hers will differ from the 'usual' reading:

> The Annunciation is given the following rather univocal interpretation nowa-
> days: Mary, you who are young and still a virgin, thus beautiful and desirable,

the Lord, who has power over you, is informing you through his messenger that he wishes to be the father of a son to whom you will give birth, Mary can only say 'yes' to this announcement because she is the Lord's possession or his property. The mystery of the angel remains. (p. 140)

Leaving aside the important question of whether this is an accurate account of the 'usual' interpretation of the Annunciation, we observe that the Annunciation is, for Luce Irigaray, one of those dormant seeds, frequently present in Western religious texts, which invariably matures in the direction of God the Father (*An Ethics of Sexual Difference*, p. 68). Whether in terms of the text's own trajectory or in terms of the interpretive assumptions of its readers, the narrative of the Annunciation fails to appreciate sexuate difference as Luce Irigaray understands it. Nevertheless, the Annunciation is a text with a sufficient link to the philosophy of sexuate difference that she is willing to offer an alternative reading. Given the way that she has characterized, at least in some texts, the usual reading of the narrative, we can assume that her interpretation will avoid construing the God–Mary relationship as one in which either partner has power over the other, or in which one partner takes the other as a possession or as property. Also, her reading is one in which the mystery of the angel, as a mediating figure, will not recede into the background as unimportant, but will regain an appropriate prominence.

It is somewhat unusual, we might say, to find Luce Irigaray addressing herself to the Annunciation in the context of a discussion of intersubjectivity between man and woman, as she does in *I Love to You*. It is unusual because the Gospel of Luke represents the Annunciation as an encounter between God and a human person, and not between a man and a woman. What we should realize, however, is that Luce Irigaray's interpretation of the Annunciation gives expression to her conviction that man and woman are, or ought to become, themselves divine beings. This is to say that her vision of intersubjectivity between sexuate beings presupposes a refusal of the traditional Christian view that God is a being or entity wholly other than the human, and, furthermore, asexual or neutral. Indeed, some of her texts interpret our traditional conception of the divine as a male creation/fabrication rooted in the need, but inability, of the Western boy-child to come to grips with the transcendence of the maternal *you*. Hence the fact that the (male) subject has remained both autological and solipsistic and has projected transcendence onto God in order to establish a solid foundation for his own subjective Truth (with a capital letter), while building his subjectivity on a forgetting of the mother and on a concomitant denial of sexuate difference. As she writes:

The first other in the life of a man, the first human *you* with whom he communicates, is predominantly a feminine-maternal *you*. But the reality of this *you* becomes fused with an undifferentiated nature from which he must emerge and distinguish himself, and that he must deny as a possible partner in any communicative exchange. Every constitution of the subject which begins in and with the mother-nature will thus be solipsistic, autological. The *you* may finally be given back to the father, to God-the-Father, and later to the other masculine subjects situated inside a world constructed in spite of or against the first *you*. ('Beyond All Judgement, You Are', in *Key Writings*, p. 68; italics in original)

Luce Irigaray's interpretation of the Annunciation as an encounter between two human beings, then, gives voice to her refusal of a mere projection of transcendence onto God.[4]

As many interpreters of her writings have noted, and as is already implied in our discussion to this point, Luce Irigaray does not repudiate the notion of the divine. Rather, she seeks to rethink and redeploy the notion of the divine as integral to the human and will go as far as to suggest that the divine is necessary for our becoming man or woman. In 'Divine Women', Luce Irigaray has argued that 'A divine dimension is what we need to become free, autonomous, sovereign. No human subjectivity, no human society has ever been constituted without the help of the divine' (*Sexes and Genealogies*, p. 62). As it stands, of course, woman lacks a divine in her own image. As long as this lack persists, however, woman

> cannot accomplish her subjectivity in accordance with a goal of her own. She lacks an ideal that would be a possible aim and way to achieve her becoming. Woman dissipates herself, women scatter and become agents of destruction and annihilation for lack of an other of themselves that they can become. (op. cit., pp. 63–4; translation amended)

While woman is born a woman, she must also become the woman that she is by birth, and for this process of becoming she requires a horizon, some shadowy perception of achievement, towards which she moves – a divine in the feminine can be, among other things, this horizon, this shadowy perception of achievement (op. cit., p. 67).[5] Although Luce Irigaray is arguing that woma(e)n require(s) a God just as ma(e)n have a God, we should be careful to clarify that a feminine God will not look like the God of patriarchy. While the masculine God has functioned as an ego-ideal for ma(e)n, for woma(e)n the divine will not be 'a fixed objective, not a One postulated to be immutable but rather a cohesion and a horizon that assure, for us, the passage between past and future' (ibid.; translation amended). This god in the feminine will not reflect the idealized human subject of Western philosophy and history – a God as a foundation for Certainty and Truth. Furthermore, this god will correspond to a subjectivity particular to woman, a subjectivity which is not yet a reality. Thus, Luce Irigaray argues that a god in the feminine is still to come.

By situating her interpretation of the Annunciation within a discussion of intersubjectivity between human beings – and firstly between man and woman – Luce Irigaray seems to express her refusal of the divine as an ontologically other being, and gives voice to her conviction that man and woman are divine in their own right. Her reading of the Annunciation, then, represents more than simply a refusal of the classical Christian conception of the divine. Indeed, one might go further and suggest that her intention is to consider the best of the Christian tradition, to reclaim that which has been overlaid with centuries of patriarchal theological accretions. Although we cannot fully explore this aspect of her thought, to which we will return briefly in each of the following two sections of the paper, this positive orientation towards the Christian tradition becomes evident when Luce Irigaray argues that the becoming divine of the human is already expressed in the divine life of Mary and Jesus – 'who are both inhabited by the breath of the Spirit' – and that this becoming divine of a woman and a man grounds the possibility of an ethical and fecund alliance between sexuate beings ('The Age of Breath', in *Key Writings*, p. 168). With this in mind, we proceed to analyse something of Luce Irigaray's account of intersubjectivity between man and woman, and do so by considering breath and silence as they are expressed in her interpretation of the Annunciation.

The Annunciation: Sharing Between Two

According to Luce Irigaray, an ethical and fecund relationship between man and woman, rooted in the recognition of sexuate difference, requires that silence exist as a mode of interaction between two. In her reading of the Annunciation, we can say that silence makes its appearance in the space created by God's question:

> Mary [...] do you want to be my lover and for us to have a child together, since I find you worthy of this, even though you are young, inexperienced and without any possessions? It is only thanks to your *yes* that my love and my son may be redemptive. (*I Love to You*, p. 140)

God does not announce that an end has been definitively set for Mary. God does not announce an accomplished thing to Mary. Rather, God poses a question and then . . . silence . . . waiting for her reply. Having posed the question, all that God can do is to wait patiently as the angel carries the message to the young woman. The silence of God, as God waits for Mary's reply, evokes for me the words of Luce Irigaray about the need for silence in an intersubjective relation: 'This silence is a space-time offered to you with no a priori, no pre-established truth or ritual. To you it constitutes an overture, to the other who is not and never will be mine' (op. cit., p. 117). We might say, furthermore, that God's silence is made possible by the angel's departure from the presence of God. That is, the departure of the angel from the presence of God makes it apparent that God is not immediately present to the woman, that God is not present to Mary, that he can speak to her with a commanding or appropriating voice. The mediating angel, even as it traverses the abyss of sexuate difference, transforming the abyss into a threshold of encounter, demands and guarantees the silent listening of God.

Luce Irigaray returns to the theme of silence in *To Be Two* (pp. 62–3), where she suggests that silence is threefold; there is a silence particular to the becoming of man, a silence particular to the becoming of woman, and a silence particular to the becoming of their relationship. If the silence on the part of man and the silence on the part of woman take part in their respective becoming, the

third silence can act as a mediation between them and make possible an ethical and fecund intersubjectivity. According to Luce Irigaray, this third silence
is a space between the two subjectivities which 'must not be overcome either
in words or in representations, but must be protected, cultivated, generated,
also historically, so that it becomes more refined and shared' (op. cit., p. 62).
Extending this argument, she writes:

> An availability prepares a free space for a common mediation, or rather for
> the search for possible mediations for the two. This space is not emptiness
> but *a silence deliberately safeguarded for the task that the relation with the other repre-*
> *sents.* Not starting from nothing but from what each already is, provided that
> neither be considered as the totality of the real. And that each be disposed
> to dialogue with a real which is not one's own but with which one has to
> enter into relation as human. (*The Way of Love*, p. 88; emphasis mine)

If man and woman are to achieve an ethical intersubjectivity, each must acknowledge the negative which lies at the heart of each human being – each must
acknowledge that he or she is only a part of humanity. Indeed, in *I Love to You*,
Luce Irigaray writes that a silence between the two is 'made possible by the fact
that neither *I* nor *you* are everything, that each of us is limited, marked by the
negative, non-hierarchically different' (p. 117; italics in original). On the basis
of this negative, non-hierarchical difference, then, and on the basis of my awareness that the other is forever a mystery to me, silence is, among other things, a
refusal to name or to circumscribe the one who differs from me sexually. Silence
is a refusal to deploy language and communication as they have been deployed
according to the logic of the One – precisely as a means of denomination and
circumscription.[6] The respect and cultivation of this free space of silence, of
course, will require a high degree of self-control on the part of both man and
woman – particularly on the part of man, whose tendency to objectify and name
the other through language is decidedly more pronounced than that of woman,
at least in our Western tradition, according to Luce Irigaray. If man and woman
are to fulfil the human together, then each must respect the becoming of the
other, a respect which can and must be expressed notably through the space of
silence they cultivate between them – a free space for possible encounter(s).

This free space of encounter between man and woman, Luce Irigaray has
said, is not an empty space – it is a space of silence. In order to understand
more clearly what this free space of silence consists of, we should note that Luce
Irigaray's notion of silence is tied closely to her account of breathing and air. In
I Love to You, she writes: 'Listening to the other, sparing them some silent time, is
respecting his or her breath, too' (p. 121) According to her, the element of air
is by definition shared – air is that in which all men and women share and which
ought neither to be possessed nor appropriated. In view of this, an ethical intersubjectivity is a relationship in which both man and woman gain an access to
air of their own and in which man and woman each live and breathe as autonomous beings. 'Once born', Luce Irigaray says, 'we all must, should, breathe for
ourselves' (ibid.). In terms of the Annunciation, the virginity of Mary is recast by

her as an expression of the autonomous breath of Mary: 'Mary is a virgin because she was able to keep and to cultivate a spiritual relation to breathing, to the soul [...] The conception of a divine child depends on the quality of breathing and on the exchange of words that precedes it' (*Between East and West*, p. 78). To clarify the relationship between silence and air, we can say that silence is the preservation of a free space in which man and woman each acknowledge the right and need of the other to breathe. The silence of God before Mary is nothing less than God's willingness to allow Mary her own space to breathe, her individual access to air as an autonomous and spiritual woman.[7] Rather than insisting that she follow his will, God enters into conversation with Mary and poses a question to her. And, having posed the question, God's silence is a space-time offered to Mary so that she might breathe, so that she might either take up the invitation of God or refuse it, according to her own intention.

We can become clearer on the relation between silence and air by briefly noting that we are probably, here, in the realm of Luce Irigaray's sensible transcendental. Luce Irigaray's philosophy of sexuate difference, from the outset of its formulation, has challenged the dualistic assumptions and logic of much of the Western philosophical tradition. As a result, she considers culture and spirit as a movement in continuity, and bound up, with the natural and the physical – this over-against Western (masculine) culture in which the cultural and the spiritual are built on precisely a denial of natural belonging. Hence, her later work has emphasized that the physical act of breathing is tied to the spiritual becoming of man and woman. To become a man or a woman is to engage in an autonomous process in which I accept responsibility for my own breath, for my own relationship to the air that sustains my life and that of the other: 'Breathing in a conscious and free manner is equivalent to taking charge of one's life, to accepting solitude through cutting the umbilical cord, to respecting and cultivating life, for oneself and for others' (*Between East and West*, p. 74).[8] As one begins to 'take charge' of one's life, and to cultivate one's breath, one's life, as a man or a woman, becomes spiritualized in such a way that the natural is caught up with and embraced within the spiritual/cultural – no division, then, between physical and spiritual breathing. The becoming of the human amounts to the physical and spiritual becoming of both man and woman, through the cultivation of breath.

In terms of the Annunciation, then, neither God nor Mary can uniquely determine the path into the future. Having posed his question – 'Mary [...] do you want to be my lover and for us to have a child together?' – God must wait in silence, being aware that his overture alone cannot renew humanity. God cannot command Mary's assent, but must, in an engagement with her as a feminine subject, invite her to participate, according to her own intention, in the unknown, unfolding future. God must allow Mary a free space of physical and spiritual becoming, in relation to air – he must leave her room to breathe. As Tina Beattie puts it: 'Mary is not a passive object to be appropriated by the divine will, but a woman whose desire must be aroused and whose response must be solicited in tenderness and in loving concern for her well-being' (*God's Mother*, p. 175). As Luce Irigaray herself expresses it: 'Words and listening shared voluntarily between the lovers enable a divine child to be conceived' (*I Love to You*, p. 141). The future is only ever something which the two, who together constitute the human, can initiate and accomplish: 'In order to carry out the destiny of humanity, the man-human and the woman-human each have to fulfil what they are and at the same time realize the unity that they constitute' (*The Way of Love*, p. 105).

Sharing in Air – A Theocentric Perspective

We turn, finally, to that question which I have described as my own in a more personal way, the question of whether one who finds himself situated within the classical Christian tradition can embrace aspects of Luce Irigaray's ethical vision. Upon first reading her works, and first encountering her vision of a renewed intersubjectivity between man and woman, I found this vision compelling. Even more, I was left with a sense that important aspects of her ethical vision could be embraced within the framework of my own theological convictions. Of course, in the space of this short paper I cannot fully explore this possibility. Thus, in this concluding section my intention is to offer a formal statement of what a theocentric ethics of sexuate difference consists of and, subsequently, to offer a brief reflection on the sharing of air between man and woman in this theocentric framework. My intention here is not to appropriate Luce Irigaray's words or thought, but to give a sense both of that which I have tried to learn from her and of that which I cannot receive.

In *Works of Love*, Søren Kierkegaard proposes an account of human intersubjectivity in a theocentric perspective. He argues that while 'worldly wisdom is of the opinion that love is a relationship between two persons; Christianity teaches that love is a relationship between: a person – God – a person, that is, that God is the middle term' (*Works of Love*, pp. 106–7). He goes on to suggest that

> however beautiful a relationship of love has been between two people or among many, however complete all their desire and all their bliss have been for themselves in mutual sacrifice and devotion, even though everyone has praised this relationship – if God and the relationship with God have been omitted, then this, in the Christian sense, has not been love but a mutually enchanting defraudation of love. (op. cit., p. 107)

According to Kierkegaard, then, the relationship between two people is mediated by God, which might be diagrammed as follows:

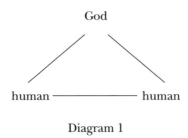

Diagram 1

As is clear from the diagram opposite, to suggest that God is the middle term in a relationship is not to say that God stands between the two, so that they are prevented from relating directly to each other. Rather, it is to suggest that each person lives in relation to the God who created him or her, and that this relationship to God informs the relationship to the other.[9] While Kierkegaard's own writings frequently reflect patriarchal assumptions, this does not prevent us from reformulating his account of intersubjectivity in a way that more closely approximates Luce Irigaray's conception of sexuate difference. On the basis of the scriptural assertion (cf. Genesis 1:27) that God created the human as both man and woman – neither the one nor the other constitutes the human – we might reframe Kierkegaard's theocentric account of intersubjectivity so that it considers, at least in part, Luce Irigaray's vision for an ethical and fecund intersubjectivity between the sexes. This might be diagrammed as follows:

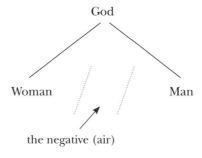

Diagram 2

This alternative diagram of Kierkegaard's account of intersubjectivity (Diagram 2) makes apparent that I aspire to a theocentric ethics in which man and woman each remain responsible before the God who created and redeemed them, yet in which neither the one nor the other is permitted to take a god-stance towards the other.[10] Neither one may presume to define or appropriate the other; rather, each is invited to respect the other as possessing a distinctiveness given by God.[11] In Luce Irigaray's ethics of sexuate difference, the negative persists between man and woman in such a way that each is invited to respect the Being and becoming of the other as autonomous. In continuity with the classical Christian tradition, however, the theocentric account of sexuate difference assumes that it is the Holy Spirit of God who equips and strengthens man and woman for the life and the task to which each is called in Jesus Christ.[12] In view of this, we can conceive of the gap between man and woman in terms of their sharing in the air of God's living Spirit. Within the classical Christian tradition, we should note, there is a close association between air or wind and the Spirit, which authorizes our attempt to think of intersubjectivity between man and woman precisely in terms of a sharing in air. In the space that remains to me, then, I will offer a brief reflection on precisely the possibility of a sharing of air between man and woman.

In the context of the Hebrew Bible, the prophet Ezekiel is a figure in whom we find an affirmation of the unity between the physical and the spiritual, a unity between the movement of air and the movement of God's Spirit. In Ezekiel's ecstatic vision of the Valley of Dry Bones, God speaks to Ezekiel and invites the prophet to participate in the renewal of God's people, who are symbolized by a valley full of bleached human bones. God says to Ezekiel: 'Prophesy to the breath, mortal, and say to the breath: Thus says the Lord God: Come from the four winds, O breath, and breathe upon these slain, that they may live.'[13] The prophet Ezekiel offers the following account of what transpired next: 'I prophesied as God had commanded me, and the breath came into them, and they lived, and stood on their feet, a vast multitude.' In this prophetic vision, Ezekiel gives voice to the mutual implication of wind and Spirit in classical Christianity – a mutual implication revealed also in the narratives of creation. God's life-giving Spirit comes in with the wind, which blows from the four corners of the earth. This is not to say that the Spirit of God is bound to the element of air, since the Spirit's movement is always mysterious and free. Nevertheless, within the scriptural tradition the movement of God's Spirit is frequently symbolized by and coterminous with the movement of air – that is, air and the Spirit can be said to arrive and proceed in one movement, according to the freedom of the Spirit. This, as suggested above, authorizes us to speak of human fulfilment precisely in terms of man and woman's sharing in the Spirit of God and, thereby, in air. In this framework, our sharing in the Spirit of God cannot be cut off from the physical act of respiration – as is, in my opinion, the case for Luce Irigaray's sensible transcendental; rather, it is God's Spirit that sets us free to become both physically and spiritually alive in one moment. We should clarify, however, that merely to breathe, as physical act, is not to share in the life-giving movement of the Spirit, since in the absence of God's Spirit, the becoming of man or woman remains stunted.[14]

Within the New Testament, the free movement of the Spirit continues to be expressed through the movement of air and also fire, we should note, as in the narrative of Pentecost. When the disciples had gathered together in the upper room, after the ascension of Jesus, 'suddenly from heaven there came a sound like the rush of a violent wind, and it filled the entire house where they were sitting' (The Acts of the Apostles 2:2). However, beyond this insistence that God's Spirit is present and active through air in both the physical and spiritual becoming of man and woman, we note the New Testament's insistence that the enlivening Spirit of God comes to each person with a vocation or task, for the common good (First Corinthians 12:7). Thus, the Spirit not only makes ma(e)n and woma(e)n physically and spiritually alive, but also gives each one a task or vocation for the good of the human. As a result, spiritual existence can no more be divorced from the act of physical respiration than from the task to which each one is uniquely called in the Spirit. In applying all of this to the relationship between man and woman, it can be said that a gap or interval persists between man and woman in such a way that I, as a man, may never define nor circumscribe woman. Furthermore, a gap or interval persists between man and woman in such a way that I, as a man, am required to acknowledge that she lives and breathes in the Spirit independently of any intention of my own. Here, the unity of man and woman in the Spirit does not consist in anything accomplished or intended by man or woman, but consists in that which the

Spirit accomplishes by its free movement. In conjunction with the thought of Luce Irigaray, we are here able to affirm that 'Listening to the other, sparing them some silent time, is respecting his or her breath, too' (*I Love to You*, p. 121).[15] To preserve silence between two, within a theocentric ethics of sexuate difference, is to acknowledge that the other is not mine, and cannot be appropriated, possessed, defined or circumscribed by myself. She receives her vocation in the Spirit, and is set free to breathe in the Spirit. Between us a space of physical and spiritual silence is, then, preserved and cultivated, so that we are each enabled and encouraged to fulfil our life and vocation in the Spirit. The future belongs to man and woman as they live and breathe, independently and together, in the Spirit.

In conclusion, we might helpfully return to Luce Irigaray's thought and attend to her exploration of what she refers to as the third age, the age of the Spirit. She writes:

> In my opinion, the third age, the age of the Spirit [...], corresponds to the age of cultivation, by man and woman, of the divine breath they received as human beings – if I trust the narrative of Genesis as a basic myth of our tradition. The God-Father creates humanity by sending his breath into matter, into earth, the text tells us. Then sin occurs, the loss of divinity for man and for woman, and the necessity of the second age, the age of the redemption through the generation of a woman – Mary – and of a man – Jesus – who are both inhabited by the breath of the Spirit. In the third age [...] the task of humanity will be to become itself divine breath. ('The Age of Breath', in *Key Writings*, p. 168)

Here, Luce Irigaray's continuity with the important aspects of the Christian tradition is in evidence, as she points to the mutual implication of air and spirit as this is expressed in the creation narrative of Genesis. Indeed, it is precisely this continuity between her and classical Christianity on the question of the mutual implication of air and Spirit which has made possible my engagement with her on this subject. For Luce Irigaray, the third age, that of the Spirit, is the age of an alliance between man and woman – in the previous time represented in a genealogical way by Mary and Jesus – in which each takes charge of the negative that belonging to a sexuate identity entails and recognizes the mystery that the other represents. It is an age in which man and woman breathe as autonomous beings, in which each respects the inner breath of the other, and in which they also share air, thus paving the way for a new future. I have appealed to this account of intersubjectivity in my own description of man and woman's sharing in air and in the Spirit, which is to say that Luce Irigaray's thought has provided a rich resource in my own theological exploration of intersubjectivity between sexuate beings. Let it also be clear, however, that the discontinuity between her and classical Christianity is present in her conception of the third age of the Spirit, inasmuch as her emphasis on the divinization of man and woman correlates with her questioning of the divine as an ontologically other being, and with her refusal of the Triune God of classical Christianity as the only possible trinity. With reference to the third age of the Spirit, for example, we find Luce Irigaray arguing that this age ought to be 'centred on the divinization of humanity incarnated (flesh becoming divine through our own breath), and not on representations of divinity – images, various figurations, abstract ideals, dead words: all kinds of idols' ('The Age of Breath', in *Key Writings*, p. 169). Which would require 'the cultivation of *one's own breath as divine presence*, in ourselves and between us' (ibid.; emphasis mine). Thus, while my path must diverge from that of Luce Irigaray on the question of the divine nature, this is not to say that the conversation between us has not been, and may not remain, a fruitful one. Perhaps a final, more poetic word will provide yet another sense of the fecundity of the encounter.

> From the four corners of the earth the wind blows toward us and upon us and through us. And as it blows, those who were dried up flesh and bone receive the gift of life. The breath of God revives and the breath of God invigorates. By the breath of God they stand on their feet, man and woman – they breathe (The Prophecy of Ezekiel 37:9-10).

> This wind is no man's possession, no woman's possession – it belongs neither to me nor to her. This wind is God's own breath, which blows where it will and when it will (The Gospel of John 3:8). It belongs to me neither to dictate the moment of the breath's appearing nor to prevent its sharing among those upon whom it has blown.

> Before God, she breathes and is filled with the Spirit. Before God, I too may breathe and be filled with the Spirit. Each has a share in God's breath, and each receives life and a task in the Spirit (First Corinthians 12:7).

> To love her is, in the Spirit of self-control, to allow her a free space of becoming. To love her is to remember that God gives her life and a task in the Spirit. To love her is to cultivate a free space of silence between us so that we might live and work together according to the Spirit's intention. To love her is to acknowledge the freedom of one who lives and breathes in the Spirit.

Notes

1 My thanks to Luce Irigaray for comments provided on earlier drafts of this paper.
2 Here it becomes clear that Luce Irigaray's posture towards the Christian tradition is a decidedly positive one, since the narratives of the Christian tradition remain those to which Irigaray will appeal in the development of her thought.
3 This language of epistemic primacy is taken from Bruce D. Marshall, *Trinity and Truth*, pp. 17–49.

4 We should add, of course, that Irigaray also sees the usual reading of the Annunciation as perpetuating patriarchal assumptions, whereby the man, with the aid of God, commands woman, rather than entering into respectful communication with her (cf. *I Love to You*, p. 124).

5 In fact, Penelope Deutscher argues that one's participation in the divine, for Luce Irigaray, can be thought of as coterminous with one's participation in one's sexuate genre (cf. *A Politics of Impossible Difference*, p. 92, p. 97).

6 Luce Irigaray writes: 'Instead of leading the other to their suite in a house of language already built in its foundations, the subject then comes to a standstill in front of the irreducibility of the other. The subject is silent – a silence which is not the one already captured in the unfolding of an existing speech, a silence which suspends this unfolding in order to open the space of another unfolding' (*The Way of Love*, p. 36).

7 Luce Irigaray also speaks of this free space of silence in terms of a 'letting be': 'A letting be that is open – in oneself and to the other – to a still unknown speech and silence' (*The Way of Love*, p. 50).

8 Here we cannot fail to mention Luce Irigaray's argument that woman has a closer relation to breath and to the cosmos than does man, and that woman might therefore become a natural and spiritual guide for man in his natural/spiritual becoming. We should also note her insistence that the problem of man's projection of transcendence onto God will only be resolved when sexuate difference is recognized: 'Between man and woman, thanks to love, including carnal love, an awakening to transcendence can take place that corresponds to the reign of spirit as spiritual breath, as soul' (*Between East and West*, p. 90). Thus, the recognition of sexuate difference would overcome the dualism of masculine culture and, through the guidance of woman, might lead man to respect his breath and nature (see, especially, *Between East and West*, pp. 84–91; and also 'The Age of Breath', in *Key Writings*, pp. 165–7).

9 Here, Luce Irigaray would almost certainly object that to identify God as creator is to participate in reinstating an original matricide. She would likely also argue that the setting up of this third term will lead, again, to a privileging of the masculine.

10 Although the Christian tradition has invariably read the creation narratives as defining woman in terms of man – as complement, as similar, as inadequate approximation – I believe that there is nothing in the narratives that prevents us from reading them as giving voice to the conviction that the human is two. The human is only fulfilled through the sharing of two who are different, who are irreducible to one another.

11 Kierkegaard develops the idea of each person's distinctiveness in a way that might make his thought more amenable to the reality of sexuate difference (cf. *Works of Love*, pp. 264–79).

12 Thus, it is a decidedly Trinitarian ethics of sexuate difference towards which we are moving here, though we focus on the pneumatological dimension.

13 Some translations of the Hebrew Bible employ the word 'Spirit' in place of the word 'air', thus giving a sense of the mutual implication between Spirit and air throughout the biblical tradition.

14 This is not to deny Luce Irigaray's argument that Christianity has, at times, been implicated in a dualism which ignores the body and denies the importance of respiration for spiritual life.

15 For an idea of the objections that Luce Irigaray might offer in response to this account of the relation between Spirit and air, see Chapter 12 of *I Love to You*, from which this quotation is taken.

Chapter 14

A Future Shaped by Love: Towards a Feminist Geography of Development and Spirituality

Eleanor Sanderson

Victoria University of Wellington, New Zealand

Desiring to Speak of the Soul

Man loses the intuition of what he is, and lets himself be governed by that which distances him more and more from himself. Even what are called the human sciences approach this real from the outside, with the aid of calculations and techniques that make the 'soul' dissolve before even reaching the question of what constitutes the Being of man in his ground, his existence, his particularity with respect to other kingdoms. Deprived of soul, a coherence from then on will be provided for him thanks to a totality foreign to what animates his life and his becoming: an essence, or a unique divine being of which the properties are immutable. Unities defined through abstraction at a moment of the human journey and which prevent this journey from unfolding between its first and last terms. (Luce Irigaray, *The Way of Love*, p. 122)

The 'soul' seems indeed much hidden, forgotten – repressed – in the human science disciplining of geography and development that my soul moves within.[1] There are moments when the soul breaks out and people speak of the strangeness of its absence, and wonder how they are to integrate such life within their academic or theoretical practice. In human geography such questions are addressed by Terry Slater ('Encountering God') in relation to spiritual experience, and Seamus Grimes and Jamie Nubiola ('Reconsidering the exclusion of metaphysics in human geography') in relation to metaphysics, all asserting the need for human geography to relinquish its ignorance of these dimensions of our space and time. Within development studies, attention to spirituality – which has been markedly absent – is now emerging.[2] Kurt Ver Beek ('Spirituality') asserts the integral understanding of spirituality for many of the people involved in 'development' and challenges its taboo status within development studies. Such absences and taboos can be seen as symptomatic and indicative of the foundational framing of Western society and philosophy as critiqued by the work of Luce Irigaray. This critique has particular pertinence for my research, which explores a feminist geography of development and spirituality, while working with a Mother's Union in Tanzania (referred to as Umaki) and a Melanesian settlement in Fiji (referred to as Holy Family Settlement) to articulate an embodied cartography of development space. Through exploring the inherent spatial nature of Irigaray's *œuvre*, and specifically her challenge to create a genuine dialectic between space and time, this article indicates the transformative potential of such a challenge within contemporary feminist geography and the intersection between the disciplines of geography and development studies.

Approaching the Space of the Culture of Two

A culture of two is immediately spatial. The preservation of both needs a movement from the self to the other and a return to the self. The development of communication between two requires the emergence of a new space. Irigaray suggests that this sort of communication would intend to move the other in the place of the 'communication *with*', that is, the place of the 'heart and the still sensible word' (*I Love to You*, p. 125; emphasis in original). Communication then is a '*touching upon*' in which there is 'nature and spirit, breath, sensibility, body and speech' (ibid.). It involves a space 'between', but also a space within our own interiority: in recognition that we are not the other, we can 'open a space of interiority' within ourselves (Irigaray, *To Be Two*, p. 36). Drawing near to the other needs us to draw near to one another, which requires a change within the self: 'the space becomes settled between the outside and the inside' (Irigaray, *The Way of Love*, p. 65). A space of interiority is necessary for the other to enter into our world: a virgin space.

A space between and a space of each enable and necessitate a dialectic between the two, which demands the cultivation of our perceptions. Perceiving through the senses fosters 'a relationship between the you which exists in space' outside of myself 'and the you which exists in my thoughts and my heart'; which can provide a 'spiritual measure to my sensibility' (Irigaray, *To Be Two*, p. 47). A development of sensory perceptions here results from an interaction between subjectivity and objectivity founded on a culture of the relation between two, where one can never fully assume or integrate the other. Irigaray considers this development a higher work of the subject than the task of imprinting the world with 'his' subjectivity. The challenge for the subject is now 'to constitute himself as human, to construct the objectivity of his subjectivity as human [,...] a subjectivity [...] essentially relational', and, as Irigaray asserts, to be human is to be 'capable of providing in oneself a place not only for the other but for the relation with the other' (*The Way of Love*, p. 80). 'This relational dimension' of our humanity 'is forgotten' in Western culture, 'As is forgotten the fact that the human is not one, but two' (op. cit., p. 89).

The foundation of sexual difference, the foundation of humanity as two, as an intrinsically spatial foundation, brings us to a new sense of space. Irigaray warns that 'the relation between each one, between each one and the whole' cannot be 'transpropriated in a unique reflection-place – a different, more spatial, version of the spirit of people' (op. cit., pp. 135–6). Instead, this space is opened outside and within ourselves through faithfulness to each other, needing a culture that does not entrap us with codes that overpower the memory and the becoming of that to which we are faithful. This is a space that is 'not solely internal to each one', nor simply 'external', but corresponds to a 'more complex' and 'subtle' 'undertaking of humanity' (op. cit., p. 139). Achieving such a space is questioned by Irigaray as being possibly the ultimate undertaking of humanity. This is perhaps because such a space is the space of love: 'love takes place in the opening to self that is the place of welcoming the transcendence of the other' (Irigaray, *Between East and West*, p. 115). Irigaray also points here to this love as the way to transubstantiate our flesh – a new stage to be realized by humanity.

The spatial dimension of Irigaray's philosophy is therefore also connected to time, but presupposes a cultivation of space and time still unknown (*The Way of Love*, pp. 125–7). This still unknown element is the cultivation of self in its own singularity, which then enables a culture of two. Such a culture and language founded upon our sexuate reality 'at first glance [...] seems simple, but is extremely difficult, because everything, or almost everything, must be reinvented' (Irigaray, *To Be Two*, p. 105). This includes our conceiving of a dialectic of time and space.

Space and time in a culture of sexual difference allow us to be faithful to becoming of the self and the other. This necessitates a change in 'our manner of reasoning, even of loving [which] corresponds to an appropriation' seeking to dominate and contain reality (Irigaray, *Between East and West*, pp. 121–2). This means of understanding and fashioning knowledge deadens the life of the world and of each other by our wanting to have them within the space of our own heart or mind (ibid.). Space and time in this gesture do not enter into a dialectic process. As such, our relationality as humans is threatened. Irigaray also points to this threat in the growth of information in time and space that is part of Western culture today. The danger, she highlights, then comes from the growth of our knowledge without a sufficient growth of our awareness of ourselves and of the otherness of the other, and of 'the ability to communicate between us and with the world' (op. cit., pp. 93–4).

Irigaray's later work is directed towards engendering this consciousness and communication. For example, the 'to' in 'I love to you' provides a different way of relating to space and time from that of 'I love you':

> *To you:* spacing in order to pass from affectivity to the spiritual, from interiority to exteriority [...] I return towards you, I try to speak, to tell to you: a feeling, a will, an intention, for now, for tomorrow, for a long time. I ask of you a place and time for today, for soon, for life, mine, yours, for the life of many. (*I Love to You*, p. 149; emphasis in original)

The 'sensible transcendental' is also indicative of the space–time dialectic Irigaray calls us to. In *Everyday Prayers*, she articulates and fosters the sensible transcendental as a possible experience in the relation to the self and the other in fidelity with the rhythms of the universe. These prayers are words that 'can help memory along the way of becoming [...] arranging for oneself and for the other [...] dwellings to inhabit, as a body and as a soul, [...] in which to wait and share' (*Everyday Prayers*, pp. 50–1).

Passage from the Culture of Two to the Culture of Many

From these perspectives, I come back to present realities in constructing and engendering understanding and knowledge within geography and development studies. Geographies of development equally require an implicit connection between time and space. As highlighted in the opening quotation of this chapter, Irigaray stresses the violence of the methodology used by social sciences, explicated particularly in her essay 'Between Us, a Fabricated World', in *To Be Two*. This methodology – pointed to in sociology, psychology and ethnology, among others – begins with being imposed upon us from the outside, delineating us from 'different kinds of knowledge, transforming our to be in different types of apparent beings' and 'in so doing they distance us from our to be' (op. cit., p. 75). The science that seeks to uncover our 'to be', instead destroys it. Hence the duty to 'refuse to allow parts of ourselves to shrivel and die that have the potential for growth and fulfilment' (Irigaray, *Sexes and Genealogies*, p. 69); in this instance, it is a question of the soul, and the consequential lack of differentiation between space and time. Without an appreciation of the culture of two there can be no passage to a culture of many – a culture implicitly required in geographies of development.

Irigaray brings together a critique of the shortage of cultivation of our sensory perceptions and the truncation of our humanity in the concerns that she raises in regard to globalization. These concerns relate to our lack of the 'subjective and objective means' to work out this historical reality (*Between East and West*, p. 139). A historical reality, it must be noted, that also distances ourselves from ourselves through a 'fabricated' and 'manufactured' world (Irigaray, *To Be Two*, p. 38), and through the dominance of money in which 'humanity has alienated its freedom and its culture' (Irigaray, *To Be Two*, p. 50). In the face of this threat of an uncontrollable globalization and universalization, notably of culture, Irigaray calls us back to the wisdom of love, which is the outworking of her foundation of sexual difference (op. cit., p. 129). The development articulated in Irigaray's essay 'Spiritual Tasks for Our Age' also has to do with the generic conceptualization of 'development' as

> *a spiritual dynamic* in each one. This requires that the development of each leaves an opening for the encounter with the other as other. Development is thus accomplished through the search for a personal absolute that accepts being questioned, modified, and fecundated by the development of the other towards their absolute. (*Key Writings*, p. 173; emphasis in original).

These words resonate with the many voices speaking within the broad terms of post-development and post-colonialism, and which challenge the erasure of the self through the lack of such a dynamic in past and present inter-relationships, calling for development to take place in a culture of many. Shrestha Nanda ('On Becoming a Development Category') makes an explicit connection between a sense of self and humanity, and the lack of dignity associated with the terminology of 'under-development'. One of the strongest proponents of post-development, Joke Schrijvers, asserts that development is founded on the basis of Western superiority in regard to knowledge, technology and 'civilization' (*The Violence of Development*, p. 9). Development is a geopolitical construction (cf. Gilbert Rist, *The History of Development*), that therefore demands deconstruction and reconstruction through non-Western but indigenous knowledge (cf. Gustav Esteva, 'Development'; Arturo Escobar, 'The Making and Unmaking of the Third World through Development'; Ronaldo Munck, 'Deconstructing development discourse'; and Vincent Tucker, 'The Myth of Development'). Maja Rahnema, for her part, equates post-development with 'hearing the voices of the great losers and their friends' (*The Post-Development Reader*, p. xi). The 'under-developed' are defined and determined by lack – just as woman is in foundational psychoanalysis.

The work of Irigaray, in pointing to the association of woman with 'lack', and in challenging the 'fullness' of Western/masculine discourse, inspires a different foundation from which to speak of 'development': a foundation on sexuate difference articulated so far in this essay. The spatial emphasis inherent to Irigaray's thought also parallels the critique offered by post-development in fracturing the temporal superiority and trajectory of 'development' through its recourse to particular spatialities. To take away the predominant conceptualization of 'lack' – at first concerning woman's identity – we must start with humanity as two and intersubjective relations between these two in order to elaborate a new subjectivity of and between many: 'Financial imperialism, for its part, creates a proliferation of hierarchies of haves and have-nots where the value of being and of becoming human are not taken into account; reinforcing real relations among human beings is required to counteract this' (Irigaray, 'Spiritual Tasks for Our Age', in *Key Writings*, p. 184).

There has been a proliferation of 'people-centred' approaches to development, specifically through the theory and practice of 'participatory development'. These approaches attempt to call into question the traditional power dynamics of development and seek to assert 'bottom-up development' approaches (e.g. Robert Chambers, *Whose Reality Counts?*). In response to these, there is a rich body of research that both affirms and questions them. The concerns highlight the complexity of participation and emphasize the need to ensure that the familiar bias towards elites is not maintained (e.g. Joe Mannion and Eammon Brehony, 'Projects for the people or of the people'), and, more significantly, that the knowledge constructed does not primarily reflect the legitimacy of the 'Developers' – as the Western masculine subjects (cf. David Mosse, 'Authority, gender and knowledge'; Alison Goebel, 'Process, perception and power'; June Lennie, 'Deconstructing gendered power relations in participatory planning'; Bill Cooke and Uma Kothari, 'The Case for Participation as Tyranny'; and Eleanor Sanderson and Sara Kindon, 'Progress in participatory development'). In effect, these challenges concern the absence of real relations among human beings, as understood by Irigaray. Developing a culture of many, whilst potentially moved towards, has not necessarily been achieved. One indication of such a culture not being fully achieved is the absence of the soul, as illustrated in the opening of this essay.

Expressions of the Soul

I have tried to approach the 'real' through the human sciences from the 'inside' (Irigaray, *The Way of Love*, p. 122), both by drawing from a growing feminist emphasis on embodied geographies (e.g. Catherine Nash, 'Remapping the Body/Land') and through the participatory research emerging within geography (cf. Rachel Pain, 'Social geography').[3] The exploration in such research is founded upon the concept of 'cartographies of development space'. This concept employs critical geography's exploration of space and place with the subversive appropriation of cartography to articulate 'unmapped' geographies of development and to explore possibilities in feminist cartography,[4] resorting to 'mimicry [...] so as to make "visible" [...] what was supposed to remain invisible' (Irigaray, *This Sex Which Is Not One*, p. 76). This mapping is focused from the personal embodiment of development geography, that is, from the embodied view out, rather than from the macro-view down to the body or the person. Using participatory practice, I have sought to perform a cartography of development space with a re-visioning of cartography as a more critical and dynamic community-centred approach, mediated through the collaborative engagement of the two case study communities – Umaki and Holy Family Settlement – while acknowledging the complexity of the practice and of the term 'communities' (cf. Irene Guijt and Meera Shah, *The Myth of Community*).

My research approach is a response to Gillian Rose's assertion that feminist geography needs more intricate cartographic tools in order to enter the 'Paradoxical Space' which she advocates for feminist geography: a space that is 'multiple and intersecting, provisional and shifting' (*Feminism and Geography*, p. 155). Such a space resonates with Irigaray's expression about the economy of fluids as that which guarantees the system whilst being excluded from it (cf. 'The "Mechanics" of Fluids', in *This Sex Which Is Not One*, pp. 106–18). Rose defies the geographic discourse by using the work of Irigaray, destabilizing the implicit masculine subjectivity of the former perspective through a performative text entitled 'As if the Mirror Had Bled' (in *Body Space*). She defies the language of geographic discourse both by writing through different characters of the academic geography world – for example, the young, enthusiastic female lecturer – and by specifically questioning the distinction between real and imagined space which is perceived to exist within geographic discourse.

Correspondingly, my own research is not purely descriptive of development space: it *is* development space. Implicit within development is the idea of change, and the changes within the development space of my research are indicative of a degree of the intersubjectivity to which Irigaray calls us. The paradoxical spaces articulated in our cartographies challenge the reductionism found in development geography and in development theory and practice, and begin with privileging interpersonal relations. For example, the following words were the final evaluation of our research given by one of the Umaki leaders:

You have drawn us to you. Other people might stay away from this place, but you have gone out into the villages and you have met with us, and that has really encouraged us and built up our hearts. We have shared together and shared with you. (Mama Jesse, Umaki, Tanzania)

To build up the heart is the founding gesture of development space for Umaki. In their self-expression they say that 'the heart is the home and the home is the heart'. On the mud wall of an Umaki member's house are written the words 'My heart', decoratively surrounded by images of nature. Above the doorway, similarly decorated, are the words 'Jesus is coming'. The heart is synonymous with the home and open to the orphaned, the refugee and to every other. To fully appreciate the weight of this gesture requires an appreciation of the responses of these women to the refugees from the Rwandan genocide – which occurred principally during 1994 and involved the mass killing of hundreds of thousands of ethnic Tutsis – and the growing number of orphans from HIV or AIDS in their area. Here, Mama Martha and Mama Usof describe their hospitality work:

If there's someone in the group who's sick we have times when we go visiting. If someone's sick in their group, each of us will take peas or bananas or beans, or something like that, and we will all take them on our heads and go to visit. We will try to go together. And we do the same for people who've lost a loved one, a husband or a child, or mother. And even for someone who's had a child, we'll go and when we go, we study the Word of God to fellowship together. Now that we are all together, we are very close. We do the work to share together, to fellowship together. (Mama Martha, Umaki, Tanzania)

In everything of life we know what's happening in the lives of each other, whether you've had a child or whether you're sick. And it's the love. We're all in love. (Mama Usof, Umaki, Tanzania)

'Working together' and 'being together' were some of the strongest marks of identity and future desire, likewise expressed within Holy Family Settlement. The embodied perspective of development that emerged from Holy Family Settlement emphasized community, culture and the meeting of physical needs, all encompassed within a spiritual spatiality:

Here in Holy Family Settlement, like we love each other. Some other places, like, they just care about their own family, like that, but here we care about each family in the village. (Amila, Holy Family Settlement, Fiji)

Oh, I think in the future is just to build up our, you know, spirit life . . . Mm, life. That's the meaning, yeah . . . because only that thing going to build up the life that we know, to be . . . what to say? To be good and everything's hard will come, you know? (Lay, Holy Family Settlement, Fiji)

Whilst I am mindful of the underlying complexity in what is being said, and the potential challenge to valorization, these expressions do point to the prominence of inter-relationality, socially and spiritually, as the framing within which negotiations of 'development' occur.[5] They emphasize the attention to interiority as well as to exteriority, and their expressed connection. The development space and the interactions that constitute the research with Umaki and Holy Family Settlement, as presented above, show a desire for and cultivation of a 'culture of two'. Whilst not specifically discussing sexual difference as a basic dimension within these 'communities' – although it was sometimes included in my conversations with Umaki members –, a culture of sexual difference, as developed by Irigaray, is a starting point for a culture of all differences.[6] Such a culture concerns the cultivation of interiority *and* exteriority in a socio-spiritual intersubjectivity, and it is the expression of humanity that can be seen in the articulation of development space within my research communities. Furthermore, the family and relationships within the family are a locus of concern, and as such may have the potential to progress through a passage from a natural to a civil identity for the family, a passage which, Irigaray stresses, is urgently needed (cf. 'How to Ensure the Connection between Natural and Civil Coexistence', in *Key Writings*, pp. 225–6).[7] The absence of such a passage is considered by Irigaray as the source of difficulties in natural and civil coexistence in bigger communities, such as the European Union: between different races, even within the community; and between the different sexes and different generations within families (ibid.). Both the 'communities' in my research are confronted with the consequences and existence of such difficulties.[8] These are difficulties that cannot be disconnected from the imposition of a Western cultural imaginary through colonization, within which Christianity has a complicated relationship.

Towards a Future Shaped by Love

In the intersubjective relations of the communities in my research, in this development space, and in the place that this research took me to – the seminar of which this book is in part our expression – we embrace and privilege the embrace. From that embrace I return to myself, helped to cultivate my own interiority – an interiority that refuses to relinquish the embrace out of faithfulness to the priority given to the embrace above theoretical constructs, as emphasized by Irigaray: 'Under all these artificial constraints of time and space, I embrace you endlessly' ('When Our Lips Speak Together', in *This Sex Which Is Not One*, p. 217). Such a cultivation of interiority, and also of perceptions, has implications for a feminist geography that inherently concerns spatiality and the inter-relationality of applied research. The task of not objectifying the other, the subject of our research and also the 'research subject', into the economy of the same, particularly the same of the Western imaginary that renders visibility and invisibility – such as the invisibility of spirituality – is not an easy one. The complexity and apparent impossibility of this task is highlighted by Jennifer Robinson ('Feminism and the spaces of transformation') in her analysis of the potentially transformative space available from Irigaray's work. Yet, when understood within the cultivation of interiority, and corresponding exteriority, familiar within spiritual practice, this transformative space is the most accessible, the most near to us. Near, that is, if we give our attention to the near and not to the constructs of our cultural practice that distance us further and further from ourselves unto the dissolution of the soul. This is the heart and the home of a development space articulated within the communities of my research – a geography of development with a spatial conceptualization, stretching towards the culture of two and its passage to a culture of many, as envisioned within Irigaray's work. The reconceptualization of the dialectic between space and time provided by Irigaray offers possibilities for geographies of development that may assist our collective becoming in moving away from the currently perceived 'impasse' of development (cf. Frans Schuurman, *Beyond the Impasse*).

The future then would be shaped by love, a love as is articulated by Irigaray, through privileging the nearness of intersubjectivity within 'communities'. Irigaray's work, like our work, gives prominence to becoming, to a connected coherency between interiority and exteriority. This future horizon moves our aim from a development activity with an other to a becoming with an other, in a reciprocal and founded on real relation, with the desire to cultivate our humanity. The awareness of ourselves would be neither characterized by fullness nor lack, but by an interiority cultivated in openness to being with the other.[9] Such a horizon brings us to a place of silence as well as of speech, to a place of virginity; a place where we are able to close our lips and let other's lips also remain closed.

> As we finish
> These exchanges
> Of words and breath
> Refreshed by the
> Liberty to love
> We will leave with
> Our own silence
> That is not nothing[10]

Notes

1 I use 'soul' here in the Hebrew understanding of 'nephesh', relating to our entirety, our living being, and not in the Greek disassociation between soul and body. It is also in this comprehensive understanding that Irigaray talks about the soul, notably in reference to the Eastern tradition of yoga.

2 Development studies is a discipline concerned with the theory and practice of international and community 'development', and the past, present and future trajectories of our world in this regard. 'Development' occurs in single quotation marks throughout this article to indicate that it is a contested term. It is also important to note that a distinction is sometimes made between 'development' and 'Development', whereby 'development' refers to people-centred participatory approaches and 'Development' refers to the more international level predominated by neo-liberal economics.

3 'Embodied geographies' are an aspect of human geography concerned with geographies of the body and the role of bodies in negotiating geographic processes. 'Participatory research' seeks to enable research participants to strongly inform and direct the research process. It must be noted that there is considerable overlap between 'participatory development' and 'participatory approaches' within research, particularly action-orientated research.

4 'Critical geographies' are concerned with the power dynamics implicit within the discipline of geography and seek to use geographic research to challenge and subvert perceived power imbalances. 'Cartography' refers to the conception as well as the practice of mapping and has historically been a central component of the discipline of geography.

5 Irigaray has given a substantial critique of the dominant masculine imaginary of Christianity, which is not directly countered within these communities. See, for example, 'Divine Women', in *Sexes and Genealogies*, pp. 57–72.

6 For an explicit commentary on this transition from sexual difference to cultures of difference, see Alison Martin, 'Introduction: Luce Irigaray and the culture of difference'.

7 Again, I am mindful of the call by Irigaray for a necessary civil identity for each person within the family, with the understanding that such a motivation may not necessarily be shared within these communities.

8 This is in regard to the history of political unrest in Fiji and in Umaki's proximity due to the genocide of Rwanda.

9 This place of 'being with' is obviously distinct from any sort of rape, as both subjectivities need to move to the place of 'being with'.

10 This poem was written as a gesture of our appreciation towards Luce Irigaray, following our participation in the seminar which she organized at the University of Nottingham in May 2005.

Part V

New Philosophical Horizons

Chapter 15

Expression and Speaking-*with* in the Work of Luce Irigaray[1]

Donald A. Landes

State University of New York at Stony Brook, USA

> For there to be an exchange, it is essential that the other touch us, particularly through words. (Luce Irigaray, *The Way of Love*, p. 18)

If Luce Irigaray and Maurice Merleau-Ponty are both correct, and philosophy must reflect upon experiences that have not yet been exhausted, on concepts that have not yet been 'worked-over', and on moments that would give all at once the subject and the object, pell-mell, then perhaps I am justified in structuring this work around the 'with'. This short word immediately evokes ideas of sharing, of co-production, of a between, and recent thinkers have explored the richness of the related French word *partager*, which bears with it the meanings of sharing *and* separating, of simultaneously interrupting and connecting, separating and bringing together.[2] In adding the short preposition 'with' to the end of some of our most solipsistic and philosophical activities – speaking-*with*, thinking-*with*, etc. –, we might be able to join with Luce Irigaray in her project of rethinking the tradition from a focus on difference, and specifically on the sharing between two people across difference.

It is not irrelevant that Irigaray chooses to begin her reading of *The Visible and the Invisible* with the first sentence by which Merleau-Ponty begins the fourth and enigmatic chapter of that text, 'The Chiasm – The Intertwining'. That phrase, mimicked in my first sentence above, calls for us to rethink the tradition in light of the experiences that remain irrecusable and enigmatic thickets of meanings – always present but always escaping firm and timeless grasps. As is evident in many of Irigaray's readings of other philosophers, she is often exploring *with* them, taking them at their word and yet placing those words in the context of an exchange, a dialogue between herself and a presumed closed text or horizon. In *The Visible and the Invisible*, Merleau-Ponty chooses to explore the experiences of 'seeing, speaking, even thinking' (p. 130), while Irigaray notably brings to the text the argument of the experience of intrauterine life to question his position (*An Ethics of Sexual Difference*, p. 152). And perhaps we might see other moments in Irigaray's work as answering Merleau-Ponty's call for philosophy to begin again, to discover a new beginning, by including the 'with'. Seeing-*with*, speaking-*with*, and thinking-*with* are themes in Irigaray's work as she places the history of philosophy into dialogue with sexuate identity, and thus difference.

For my part, I would like to explore the possibilities of rethinking philosophical treatments of 'expression' towards thinking the implications of expression-*with*, but this would be too large a project to pursue on this occasion. What I hope to offer here is a more narrow exploration about Irigaray and Merleau-Ponty, and to make some productive suggestions towards how the thought of expression-*with* might complete itself. In her dialogue with Merleau-Ponty, Irigaray is able to recognize the power of Merleau-Ponty's formulation of flesh and chiasm, and at the same time to systematically demonstrate the fundamental blindness from which he suffers, a blindness to the *in principle* invisible of the relation in difference. And perhaps most importantly, she suggests that the possibility of an exchange requires the interruption of the reversible structures so foundational for the phenomenological ontology of that work. In order to explore this suggestion, and rethink expression – a very important concept for Merleau-Ponty throughout his corpus – I will suggest that we need to think towards what we might characterize as a loving-horizontality.

It should perhaps be noted that, from the beginning, Irigaray does not make the term 'expression' thematic in her work. When this term does appear, it is rather in a critical context where it is associated with 'subjective affect' or 'sentiment', and yet I will suggest in this paper that expression, as I conceive of it, is certainly helpful in understanding her work on a productive exchange across difference.[3] Love plays a central role in Irigaray's work, and allows her to think past tropes of authenticity, whether they be Heideggerian or colloquial, and this emphasis allows us to rethink expression outside of the context of either authenticity or mere subjective affect. This will lead into a final section, devoted to the productive and important work offered by Irigaray on *speaking-with*. A subtle account of expression, emerging from Merleau-Ponty, harmonizes with the structures of exchange suggested by Irigaray, and by thinking with her in terms of *expression-with*, we can begin to understand the need for such strategies.

Developing Expression . . .

It may be worth while offering the reader a context as to why I approach expression through Irigaray and Merleau-Ponty. In a very real sense, reading Irigaray's essay 'The Invisible of the Flesh' (*An Ethics of Sexual Difference*, pp. 151–84) raised some important questions for me: is an understanding of expression always already masculine, and, moreover, were my attempts to find a universal account of the structure of expression also marked male despite my efforts to rethink or rehabilitate expression to identify a rich and authentic embodied speaking? A true question is not a mere syntactical formulation – it haunts, it demands to be recognized, it refuses to be set aside – and this particular question physically manifested itself as uneasiness. I was no longer comfortable speaking for a universal subject. I became uneasy with the presuppositions such a universal account required regarding the flattened out, or homogeneous, nature of the speaker(s). What were the hidden norms of such a descriptive or speculative phenomenology?

Now it is important to be clear, if brief. In terms of expression, I was not convinced by approaches to expression that involved the externalizing or encoding of thoughts, previously existing in the mind of the speaker. Nor was I thinking of some emotional or romantic account of artistic expression, for example the kind of activities Irigaray associates with the word 'expression', as noted above. Rather, in a search for a more satisfying proposal, I had initially turned to writers such as Ludwig Wittgenstein, R. G. Collingwood, Martin Heidegger and especially Merleau-Ponty. I was convinced that a rich and authentic speaking, as presented by Merleau-Ponty in the chapter entitled 'The Body as Expression, and Speech', in *The Phenomenology of Perception,* was the answer. In this reflection, Merleau-Ponty offers an embodied presentation of speech in which speaking is the accomplishing of thought, and I felt that if only I could figure out the relationship between this early work on expression and his difficult concepts of flesh, chiasm, institution and reversibility as they emerge in *The Visible and the Invisible,* then I would have a complete answer. Yet little did I know at that point that this last term, reversibility – a term Merleau-Ponty convincingly takes from the image of the touching-touched into the very field of speech – would be the thread that Irigaray would pull to undo and begin to rethink the entire closed ontology of the homogeneous flesh of the world.[4] It would, however, be impossible to adequately pursue this aspect here, so let me just make a few comments about expression as I was developing it with these thinkers.

Expression, I would suggest, is not the formulation of a pre-existing idea, encoded through alphabetic and grammatical rules into sound or ink, and then interpreted by the other. Expression is the existential act of a lived-body, a real, physical presence in the expressive field. And as an act, it is as much an insertion into the 'weighty'[5] as the realization of a potential. The intelligible comes down into the sensible as a word, a paint stroke, a gesture, but that which is spoken was not a definite 'thing', such as a completed idea, before it was spoken. And moreover, the materiality of the expression – the sound, the ink, the paint – falls away from the last limit of the expressing body, leaving a trace, an artefact. In fact, it is Irigaray who helps us to think this union, as she suggests: 'there ceases to be a division between sensibility and intelligence, and they are most certainly not hierarchically ordered [...] Speech is intelligible because it remains sensible' (*The Way of Love*, p. 126). Thus, we must have an approach to expression that maintains its creativity and respects its materiality.

And yet, having turned to Irigaray, it is now clear that there is something missing from this account, from those accounts from which I was drawing inspiration: namely, the 'other of difference'. The horizontal spreading out of sensible expression was from a subject in command of the vertical arrival, even if this subject is an embodied tacit *cogito*. And although Merleau-Ponty characterizes listening to a speech as the speech of another actually accomplishing my thought,[6] a model that on first glance seems to make possible a rethinking of

communication and dialogue, the model remains one of *speaking to* – or at least
for, since my words accomplish your thoughts – and certainly not *speaking-with*.
Indeed, this account seems to reveal one of the possible sources of violence in
any speaking, for if my speech can accomplish your thoughts, then we ought
to pause over the violation of agency suggested in communication and reflect
on the strategies for engendering the loving-dialogue offered by Irigaray, and
to which I will point below. And even if this speech leaves that which is reached
for open, vague, waiting to be determined by its actual concrete expression,
through its negotiation with its physical medium, there is still no other who
presents themselves to me in difference, there is still our tending towards a
presumed common world rather than a shared creation.[7] And perhaps most
importantly, the work of speaking remains the work of a solitary speaker. The
absence of an other who is different, and the violence of these forms of communication, was the source of uneasiness revealed through reading Irigaray, and
to which she generously offered her insights in her seminar at the University
of Nottingham. There is also, of course, the uneasiness that accompanies the
move from the safety of speaking with a reversible other about a common world
– which we might characterize as the safety of the Western tradition – to speaking with a real and irreversible other in an attempt to create a shared world – a
speech, in Irigaray's words, that 'is always at risk'. To this later uneasiness I will
turn below. For now, let this suffice to give the context of my research and the
landscape of the question of expression.

Moving Forward with Irigaray and Merleau-Ponty

Although this is not the moment to work through the detailed exegesis of the
'dialogue' Irigaray has with Merleau-Ponty – literally inserting a different voice,
her voice, into the monologue of large sections of the last chapter of his last
work –[8] it is a nice opportunity to reflect on a number of points that I was able
to discuss with Luce Irigaray during the seminar for people doing their PhD
on her work which took place in the University of Nottingham in June 2006.
I focused my presentation on how Irigaray argues that in his collapse of the
'look' and vision, in his faith in the complete and ultimate reversibility of the
flesh, and in his attempt to find in his world, including in its presumed natural
aspect, the universally knowable or sayable, Merleau-Ponty fails to account for
the irreversibility of sexual difference.

The flesh of the world, as Irigaray suggests Merleau-Ponty conceives it, is a
homogenous substance. The faith, however, that Merleau-Ponty puts in having
the invisible remain invisible, though not *in principle* so, is shaken with the realization of an irreversible sexual difference. It perhaps could be concluded that
the flesh of the world, at least as Merleau-Ponty's 'elemental', merely effaces
difference again. However, the folds of flesh could also be re-read as guarding
a secret: the impossibility of reduction to the same, the possibility of multiple
worlds. What is more, an irreversibility would leave some 'failing in the very tex-
ture of the flesh'.[9] After Irigaray, we can no longer think of the material char-

acter of the flesh as irrelevant to the relationships established between bodies and persons.

In order to question this faith, Irigaray suggests an experience that has yet to have been worked over, one that indeed is suggested by many of Merleau-Ponty's metaphors, but one that also throws into question his very first steps that privilege the visible model over the tangible. This experience is that of intrauterine life. In this case of relationship between woman and foetus, mother and unborn,[10] 'one [...] is still in [...] night does not see and remains without a visible (as far as we know); but the other seer cannot see' it (*An Ethics of Sexual Difference*, p. 152). If the world of the mother is organized and unified around this invisible, then the invisible itself would be the presentation of a style that corresponds to a nothing, and so the mother in a sense would see nothing –

> except from this zero of the infant's nocturnal abode? The invisible of its prenatal life. This intimate secret of its-their birth and shared knowledge [...]. What-has-not-yet-been-seen of and by its-their look. Seeing the universe in function of or beginning with that – which will never appear as something seen within the field of the visible. (op. cit., pp. 152–3)

This relationship between a non-visible and a non-seer immediately shows us that Merleau-Ponty's foundation is not innocent, nor is it generalizable to all experience. How are we to think now the chiasmatic crossing of the un-crossable, without reverting to a crossing-out?

It is perhaps worth noting that a large portion of this chapter from *The Visible and the Invisible* is not considered by Irigaray in her reading. For example, the paragraphs most directly related to expression do not find their way into her text, undoubtedly because her focus in that text is elsewhere. In these passages, however, Merleau-Ponty offers some resources for thinking about the presentation of the unpresentable. In considering what he calls the 'most difficult point' (*The Visible and the Invisible*, p. 149) and 'the paradox of expression' (op. cit., p. 144), Merleau-Ponty points towards certain 'individuals' that are only present in the flesh as 'what is absent from all flesh' (op. cit., p. 151). We are not able to hear or see the ideas, but rather we sense these domains like the 'presence of someone in the dark' (op. cit., p. 150). Perhaps it is in these moments of considering the infinitely agile reversibility of expression that we can come closest with Merleau-Ponty to an understanding of the irreversibility at issue for Irigaray.

Rather than taking up these considerations about expression, Irigaray examines the imagery and metaphors invoked by Merleau-Ponty, and establishes that an appropriation of pregnancy metaphors is, consciously or not, at work in memorable moments of his work. The question is, as Irigaray seems to suggest: why is the evocation of intrauterine life forced into the apparatus of the visible? Could this be man's nostalgia to domesticate 'her' invisible, in a way her irreversibility? The seer (or perhaps Merleau-Ponty?), tries to establish the flattening of the world, one in which, despite any fold, does not inhibit *in principle* their visibility as such. Of course, this flattening does not deprive the phenomenologist from all recourse to the vertical, and furthermore, it results in a blurring of the horizontal, and a dissolving of those differences that are crucial for relations between irreversible interlocutors. Thus, it seems that Merleau-Ponty still privileges the polarity of seer/visible while, in undoing this privileging, Irigaray returns us to a sort of 'carnal look', an act that takes place before, and even after, the visible and has been appropriated by vision (*An Ethics of Sexual Difference*, p. 153). It is perhaps this move that allows us to think vision on the model of touch, rather than vice versa.

Connecting Carnal Touch and Expression

In the process of questioning Merleau-Ponty's reversible structures, Irigaray alludes to the possibility that the other of sexual difference may be reached through touch, even if the distance cannot be bridged by vision, when she suggests: 'That in which their differences consist is experienced in touch but is never "seen"' (op. cit., p. 167). This is not, however, merely an inversion of the traditional emphasis on vision; rather, touch plays a founding role for Irigaray, one that cuts across the division into our five senses. It seems that for Irigaray, touch is, among other things, the modality of intimacy and the 'mediation of life itself',[11] thus neither an apparatus of traditional totalization nor a reduction to sameness. Touch is not merely the coming into contact of flesh, for according to Irigaray, we can be touched by words and we can touch the other with our words. Speaking and touching can be thought together.

As Luce Irigaray reminded me in our exchange in the seminar, contact or communication is always at risk, notably of repeating those power dynamics of oppression and violence, but we cannot for all that reject speaking with each other, because the attempt at sharing communication has the distinct chance for authenticity. This authenticity, however, can neither accept the colloquial nor the Heideggerian senses of the word, but rather must be rethought on the model of dialogue, specially loving dialogue. If speaking, then, is also touching the other with the tongue, my tongue, perhaps it is doing so across a spacing large enough for the love of the union to appear to cool into linguistic exchange. But we can and do touch each other with our words, and when there is touching there is always a question of a loving-touch versus a violent or oppressive-touch.[12]

Irigaray quotes Merleau-Ponty, who suggests that in the gesture of speaking, the speaker 'offers himself and offers every word to a universal Word' (op. cit., p. 177). This closed circuit, speaker and Logos, which Irigaray reads as the 'most solipsistic construction', precludes that there will be air, openness, creativity, but just the interminable operation of the turning in the horizon of the same, effacing the memory or experience of difference (op. cit., p. 178). Since this 'one' can no longer imagine the other, Irigaray has touched upon the moment of 'incarceration' which the masculine speaker has submitted himself to, the self-ascribed law of the universal Word: *Thou shalt not speak with the other . . .*

And yet Irigaray begins to suggest the possibility of a non-closed language, a language without the guarantor of a universal Word. If those with whom we speak are not thought of as substitutable for each other, then the circuit must always remain open. For the other of sexual difference, whose very visibility guards a secret which the phenomenological gaze may neither trump nor master, is also an other with whom it is possible to speak, it would not be possible, as Irigaray frames it, to 'overhang or encircle such a production of speech' (ibid.). She continues, suggesting that a true dialogue between the *in principle* irreversibles must be 'ceaselessly engaged in seeking its rhythm, its measure, its poetry, its house, its country, its passages, its shortcuts, toward itself, toward the other, others – the same or foreign – its ethics. A speech that is always at risk' (op. cit., pp. 178–9). For Irigaray, a language across difference is only possible if we can provide a passage through this silence and solitude which characterize the speaking of the subject who offers herself or himself to the universal Word. Above all, we need to be able to offer ourselves to each other, speaking and listening, and remaining safe from any kind of appropriation. We need to be able to speak-*with* as we touch each other with our words.

Expression-*with*

We began by touching upon the development of both my interest in, and positive account of, 'expression'. Reading Irigaray's work on Merleau-Ponty brought an uneasiness to the surface, an uneasiness that led me to the seminar with Luce Irigaray at the University of Nottingham. With the help of the seminar participants, and considered responses from Luce Irigaray, I have begun to think through the notion of 'expression-with', towards which I will conclude by giving some indications here. The task of following out the suggestion that a speaking-*with* is possible, though always at risk, remains an open task that calls for our attention, and Irigaray herself moves beyond a statement of a rich speaking, or expression, that remains a speaking *to* or *for* and stays in the ultra-solitude of the self-ascribed law of the universal Logos, towards an account of expression that is at risk because always in dialogue with an irreducible other – an 'expression-with'.

The two main texts that I have in mind in developing this theme are *I Love To You* and *The Way of Love*. Indeed, 'love' is a word that I have been using throughout in order to signal some type of relationship that Irigaray is pointing us towards. At different times above, and in my exchange with Luce Irigaray during the seminar, I found myself invoking quasi-technical terms such as: loving-exchange, loving-dialogue, loving-relationship, and a loving-speaking, all of which might be best thought of, as Irigaray has suggested to us, through reconsidering our relational being in terms of horizontality. The question of loving is undoubtedly of paramount importance to Irigaray's thought, and she has established that love is a fluid and living exchange, not reducible to static possession, for the loving relationship presupposes at least two active participants in a shared creation.[13] Love, it seems, is Irigaray's answer to the long solitude of the Western philosopher.[14] Thus, loving, and in particular horizontally loving, indicates a new way of thinking of authenticity, as between at least two there is

no longer a solitary speaker who owns his own facticity and destiny, but a couple who engender together and each other. These indications seem to firmly
indicate 'love' as playing a role in Irigaray's thinking as important as the role
played by 'authenticity' in Heidegger's thought. This should not, however, be
considered a collapse of the two terms, because love in the sense that Irigaray
gives it cannot be imagined anything solitary, nor anything about ownership,
but rather a reciprocal horizontal relation between at least two.

Let me turn, finally, to expression, and consider what we might learn from
a loving dialogue both discussed and demonstrated in the texts of Irigaray. As
mentioned above, Irigaray avoids the word expression for strategic reasons, for
she seems to associate it with a subjective outpouring of affect or sentiment.
And yet in her optimistic moments of describing the attitudes needed for a loving dialogue across difference, I find a real affinity with the type of expression
I have been trying to develop. If expression can be envisioned as an existential
act in which neither that which is expressed nor the being of the body that does
the expressing are situated in a completed ontology, then perhaps we can best
think of expression-*with* as joining the spirit of Irigaray's thought. An existential
statement of expression would have to find itself in pursuit of an exploration of
human becoming, rather than human being, and this stress on becoming is a
leitmotif of Irigaray's recent work. Indeed, consider her 'Preface' to the English
publication of *The Way of Love*, where she suggests that:

> For such work, descriptive and narrative languages, those to which we most
> often resort today, are no longer appropriate. They correspond to something
> or someone who already exists, and is even already in the past, or put into
> the past by what is said. The task here is different. (*The Way of Love*, p. viii)

And she continues, characterizing the task, I would suggest, as one of expression:

> It is a question of making something exist, in the present and even more in
> the future. It is a matter of staging an encounter between the one and the
> other – which has not yet occurred, or for which we lacked the words, ges-
> tures, thus the means of welcoming, celebrating, cultivating it in the present
> and the future. (ibid.)

What immediately jumps out of this passage is the emphasis on the encounter,
on the need to enter into relation through a means which does not exist prior
to the exchange, indeed a communication-with rather than a mere communication of information. We must recognize that in a loving exchange, the partners do not remain hermetically sealed poles sending out information-packed
messages, and conversely deciphering those packets received from the other. In
a loving exchange, the partners must develop with the encounter, together, yet
not fuse together; otherwise we have no right to speak of it as loving. But this is
unmistakably expression, in the rich and subtle sense of existential expression,
with the brilliant Irigarayan twist of adding, resolutely, the 'with'.

I believe that this shows us exactly how important expression – as finding the words and creating, always tied to a real living body that has real material features – is or could be for Irigaray. This type of speaking 'implies another relation with language, a relation which favours the act of speech in the present, and not a language already existing and codified' (op. cit., p. ix). And by placing the emphasis on expression rather than on merely speaking, I believe we can properly find the importance of the creation of a relationship, now having to be radically rethought on the notion of the creating-*with*. Speaking-*with* runs the risk, in my opinion, of appearing to be a mere communication, while expression-*with* inevitably points us towards exchange and communion. This last point is important, as Irigaray answers Heidegger's invitation:

> to try to find where we could make an experience of speaking. My way of answering is that, if such an experience can take place in poetic language [...], it first of all exists in a present dialogue with an other different from myself. There we can and we must experience what speaking means. (op. cit., p. xi)

In order to have this experience, the important direction is not moving upwards towards truth in speaking the universal Word, nor speaking out to the other in conveying an inner experience complete and ready to be shipped out, but simultaneously moving inwards and outwards towards the perfection of the relation between speakers – a movement away from verticality towards loving-horizontality, a movement that must be fluid and shifting as the partners bring their lives together in a shared moment.

And perhaps most importantly, given the stress I have placed on the gestural aspect of expression, Irigaray emphasizes how the loving speaking relation needs a silent gesture of approach and touch, and 'it happens that speaking is necessary to create the silence in which to approach' (op. cit., p. 15). With this, Irigaray draws our attention to the necessity of a shareable space for the exchange, which is as important for us to cultivate as any individual contribution to the dialogue. These many rich themes are related to touch as well, as Irigaray suggests: 'for there to be an exchange, it is essential that the other touch us, particularly through words' (op. cit., p. 18). This touching through words fits well with the materiality of expression, and leads to the question of how this experience is one of expression-*with*. As we touch each other, we must also wonder about the caress or the strike, about the loving and the violent touch, because Irigaray even characterizes the activity of finding a dialogue across difference as language 'finding its ethics'.[15] Irigaray's reflections call us to think of the ethics of speaking and touching beyond the realm of any simplistic moral system, any reductive consideration of human rights or universal laws, and to envision closely the concrete relationships between lovers as an ideal towards which to fashion a generalized ethos of loving-horizontality.

Finally, let me note the danger or the risk of the emphasis on speaking. If I am right and fair when characterizing the project as one of expression-*with*, we must notice that Irigaray is putting her faith in us as speakers to resist the temptation that speaking creates, that is, the movement downwards into the old problems of solitude and speaking *to* or *for*. Keeping attention must be our 'constant task', a phrase and an obligation that Irigaray deploys in these very moments of danger.[16] Irigaray's fascinating response to this risk, at least as I read her work, is to offer us the attitude, the strategy, or the openness needed to render a true exchange possible. These are not methods, if by a method we hear a guarantee of an outcome, an algorithm with the certainty of a programme; rather, they are strategies, postures, which make a fertile exchange across difference possible.

It seems to me that the important guiding thread in such strategies is Irigaray's emphasis on human becoming. In *I Love to You,* she often plays with the productive interaction between nature and becoming, suggesting twice that although there may be a natural identity, one must cultivate and endeavour to become what or who one is (*I Love to You,* p. 39, p. 107). This, I believe, is indicated nicely when we think of expression as bringing about that which was not yet become, and also as having an essential effect on the expresser. If we now think of expression as a shared activity, as expression-*with*, we may begin to see the expressive field as the very space for becoming that seems so important for understanding Irigaray's fluid and dynamic reference to identity. Expression no longer is employed from the perspective of producing a product, but rather of opening the space in which an exchange and a development of a shared world is possible. The expressive field becomes the object and the subject of a phenomenology of expression, decentring the inquiry and allowing us to take up Irigaray's project in this domain.

In order to cultivate such a space of becoming which, Irigaray suggests, reveals that as participants we must begin from a stance of recognition. It is paramount that we recognize the other as always outrunning any attempt through which we might erroneously try to grasp him or her in their totality, and also that each other is a concrete other, and not merely one instantiation among many others of a single universal. The stance of recognition results from 'the power of the negative', which, Irigaray suggests, reveals that 'you are irreducible to me, just as I am to you. We may not be substituted for one another' (op. cit., p. 103). Along with this recognition comes the realization that the other is a real that cannot be possessed by the phenomenological gaze: 'I cannot see right through you. You will never be entirely visible to me, but, thanks to that, I respect you as different from me' (op. cit., p. 104).

Through such a recognition, we have to establish a connection, a communication, which Irigaray describes as the 'transcendence between us' (ibid.). Our coming into relation is beyond the grasp or control of either participant. This relation, however, is brought through speaking with each other, and touching each other, which, for Irigaray, do not amount to relations different in kind. And the need to listen, to allow the other to think and to breathe, indicates that there must not be a difference in kind between speaking and silence either, so long as that silence is one which respects the other – and also oneself – in their mystery. Thus, it is the case that we must cultivate a silence that makes possible an exchange, a silence fostered through words too, 'a silence that is the primary gesture of *I love to you* (op. cit., p. 117; italics in original). And there is the need to touch each other: 'With this sharing, the carnal act becomes an act of speech, speech that respects woman and man, and is mindful of silence and breath' (op. cit., p. 124).

This short offering can only begin to point towards the important ways of rethinking expression as expression-*with* and thus help us to reconsider this traditionally solitary activity. But we should be careful and wary of drawing conclusions with the pretence of finality too soon, if at all. Rather, let this reflection suffice to open up a space for expression and for the work of Irigaray, in the spirit of the exchange and the *with*, I will end here with the words of Luce Irigaray, who reminds us that the intentions of the loving exchange:

> would be to draw the other to the *site* of communication *with*, the *site* of the heart and the still sensible word. Its aspiration would be to awaken the other to an exchange in which the word is born and remains between two bodies, maintaining them in themselves by respecting their differences and spiritualizing them without removing them from their flesh. (op. cit., p. 125; emphasis in part added)

Notes

1 I would like to thank Luce Irigaray for her generous feedback on an earlier version of this piece, offered both during the seminar organized by her at the University of Nottingham in June 2006 and in personal correspondence. I am also grateful for the comments and responses from all of the other seminar participants, as well as for helpful readings contributed by Mary Rawlinson, Lisa Diedrich and Kathleen Hulley at Stony Brook University, and for the support of the Social Sciences and Humanities Research Council of Canada. Of course, I remain solely responsible for any errors or shortcomings in the finished product.

2 The theme of sharing can be found throughout the work of Luce Irigaray, especially in her recent text *The Way of Love*. It can also be seen as a recurrent theme in the work of Jacques Derrida, for instance in *On Touching-Jean-Luc Nancy*, and in the work of Jean-Luc Nancy, particularly *Le partage des voix*.

3 For one critical mention of 'expression' in relation to mere affect or sentiment, see Luce Irigaray, *I Love To You*, pp. 115–16.

4 It is worth noting here that this paper presumes an intuitive relation between the concepts of 'irreversibility' and 'irreducibility', a relation that clearly appears in the work of Luce Irigaray. Indeed, it seems that Merleau-Ponty's faith in the reversible structures of the flesh of the world leads him to assume the reducible nature of the other, but a more careful study of the relation between these two notions certainly seems called for. Thanks to Luce Irigaray for identifying this connection for me in personal correspondence.

5 For an important discussion of weight and thought, see Jean-Luc Nancy, *The Gravity of Thought*, and Gregory Recco, *Philosophy and Literary Theory*.

6 'The orator does not think before speaking, nor even while speaking; his speech is his thought. In the same way the listener does not form concepts on the basis of signs

[...] The end of the speech or text will be the lifting of a spell' (Merleau-Ponty, The *Phenomenology of Perception*, p. 209).

7 The notion of an *a priori* common world is closely linked for Luce Irigaray to the belief of the possible substitution of one individual for another since they are, at root, identical transcendental rationalities. The notion of shared world, between irreversible subjects and hence the existence of more than one single world recurs especially in her more recent thought.

8 The 'dialogue' referred to can be found in *An Ethics of Sexual Difference*, pp. 151–84.

9 Thanks to Luce Irigaray for this phrase, given in personal correspondence, May 2007.

10 It is difficult to even label the participants in this relation, as any such act seems hopelessly political. But we can see here already emerging a different type of participation to the traditional Platonic model of Universals and particulars. It may be worth saying that in this relation, we are wrong to think that we can discuss the participants as separate individuals, but the political weight behind this question would require much more space and reflection. For now, I wish only to point with Irigaray towards this relation and the experience it denotes.

11 Thanks to Luce Irigaray for the second part of this phrase, given in personal correspondence, May 2007.

12 For an exploration of 'touch', we must refer to Jacques Derrida's recent text on the work of Jean-Luc Nancy. Of particular interest for the current considerations, it would be important to think through Derrida's account of Husserl and Merleau-Ponty, but most importantly his explicit references to the work of Luce Irigaray in considering sexual difference and the touching of two lips. For this discussion, see Derrida, *On Touching-Jean-Luc Nancy*, p. 164, and p. 347, n. 5. Indeed, Derrida and Nancy reject any universal 'the' sense of touch. If touch is always this touch, touching someone or something, then the generic category covers over the always present determination of the exchange, somewhere between love and violence.

13 And certainly not the lover and beloved as it emerges in the traditional interpretation of Diotima's speech in Plato's *Symposium*. For Irigaray's reading of *Symposium* and her reinterpretation of Diotima's speech, see *An Ethics of Sexual Difference*, pp. 20–33.

14 Even more so if we remember her insistence that philo-sophia could equally be rendered the 'wisdom of love', rather than the traditional translation, the 'love of wisdom' (cf. *The Way of Love*, p. 1 and *passim*).

15 For a concise statement of Irigaray's reading of Merleau-Ponty and Levinas on the caress, see 'The Wedding Between the Body and Language', in *Key Writings*, pp. 13–22.

16 This phrase, and many themes important to the thoughts presented here, appear in 'Sorcerer Love', in *An Ethics of Sexual Difference*, a text that also begins to characterize the loving relationship engendering the beyond in the here.

Chapter 16

On Rivers, Words and Becoming an Other: The Importance of Style in Luce Irigaray's Work

Laine M. Harrington

University of California at Berkeley, USA

Prelude

The work of Luce Irigaray has come to us via different avenues. This is not surprising, for her work traverses numerous boundaries, engaging disciplines as diverse as linguistics, literature, art, religion and spirituality, nature and the environment, ethics, philosophy, politics, science and psychoanalysis. We could say, then, that her work comes to us on a grand scale and is, in a sense, inclusive of the world. But, I must go further here, for her work is not only inclusive of our world, it also goes beyond its wholeness, towards its otherness. Whether amongst human and not human, or between human and human, that is, male and female, difference abounds, for we are not the same. This sense of otherness appears throughout Luce Irigaray's writings, certainly, as previously mentioned, in terms of their varied content. However, as commented on by many, style – or, I would say, her river of words – plays a critical role in her work. Indeed, her work cannot be addressed without also addressing her style.

Starting from a critique of the masculinized *logos* with its implications of reflection, polarity and oneness, Luce Irigaray has created another way of expressing the world. She goes not only to the depths of the river of *logos*, to its mouth, its beginning, its source, she also goes further and creates her own discourse, and another way of thinking. Certainly, her critique of *logos* in *Speculum* – where she 'begins with Freud and ends', as she says, 'at the beginning, with Plato' – is well known. This paper, in part, will pick up from Plato and move retrogressively to the work of Heraclitus, with, among other thoughts, his famous 'not stepping into the same river twice'. Both Plato's and Heraclitus's *logos* will help set the stage for understanding the necessity of an Irigarayan evolution to otherness with respect to our Western world, for an understanding of how Luce Irigaray's style of writing speaks as other, as different than the *logos*.

Plato's *Logos*: Reflection, Duality, Oneness

> White. Immense spaces. White, a rush of breath. Be swift,
> marry this breath. Remain in it. Make haste. Let it not
> abandon me. Let me not turn from it. Be swept up: my song.
>   You give me a white mouth. My white mouth, open,
> like the angels in the cathedrals. You have stopped my tongue. What remains
> to me is only song. I can say nothing but sing.
> (Luce Irigaray, *Elemental Passions*, p. 7)[1]

Initially, Luce Irigaray's work with *logos* comes from her groundbreaking text, *Speculum*, where she traverses backwards the whole of Western history. Using the notion of mirror – with semantic links to speculation and speculum, but also to world – she stresses the mirroring, or reflection, that Western patriarchal culture has required of women. In 'Plato's Hystera', for example, Luce Irigaray comments on *logos* as a masculinized system of *mimesis* that guards Truth by cleverly reproducing (i.e., reflecting) itself, and only itself (*Speculum*, p. 258). Linking the notions of sameness and discourse, she addresses the implicit 'systems of duplication, the rules of duplicity' that occur within such a system, thereby contributing to the absence, the negation of the feminine – as she writes 'One Speaks, the Others are Silent' (op. cit., p. 256).

Plato's notion of *logos* reveals itself through his theory of forms, or *eidos* ('idea'), where his regard for reflection is expressed as a hierarchical preference for the ideal world over the real. As Luce Irigaray alludes, embedded in Plato's *eidos* is the theme of duplicity, which requires that there is a 'higher', which reproduces itself as a 'lesser', and that this 'lesser', the 'base', reflects or, in a sense, exists only in opposition to that which is its 'higher'.

We see these notions within Plato's assembly of numerous dichotomies – for example, body vs. soul, injustice vs. justice, pseudo vs. genuine, bad vs. good, false vs. true – where, in all cases, he appears to side with the latter. Doing so, he reveals his bias towards the unity offered by equations based on verticality. After all, equation seeks to make two or more things equal where, for example, the soul sides with the perfect and 'unchanging Form', and body sides with 'imperfect mutable participant' (A. W. Price, 'Plato: Ethics and Politics', in *Routledge History of Philosophy, Volume I: From the Beginning to Plato*, p. 406). From such a viewpoint, a sense of wholeness is made to exist by linking the two: soul with the ideal and body with the real. However, in a Platonic world of Ideas, we must make clear that whether it is a part of the ideal or of the real, whether 'perfect' or 'less', there is room for only oneness. Or, as Luce Irigaray explains, 'The Idea of Ideas, alone, is itself in itself. Confusing signified, signifier, referent, *Idea holds nothing outside itself* (*Speculum*, p. 298).

Whereas these notions abound in most of Plato's dialogues, we have also to consider the context in which his conception of *eidos* appears. Plato's thought is steeped in the ancient Greek philosophy of the day, and is constructed according to a logical, harmonic, well tuned and ordered universe that adored traditional polarities, that is, dualities based upon reflection and oneness. Certainly, these notions had influence upon both Plato and the earlier Heraclitus. As David Jacobs explains, 'The Presocratic Greeks [of whom Heraclitus is one] receive distinction because the starting-point of the Logic [a term derived from *logos*] is the same as the starting-point of the history of philosophy' (Hegel, 41, as cited in *The Presocratics after Heidegger*, p. 5). To explicate these matters further, I will turn to a brief etymological introduction to *logos*.

Initially, the root of *logos* (λεγω) means 'to gather', or, more precisely, to gather things together, 'which from some standpoint are alike' (E. Hoffmann, 'Die Sprache u.d. archaische Logik', Heidelberger Abh. Z. Philosophie u. ihrer Geschichte, p. 77, as cited in *Theological Dictionary of the New Testament*, p. 72). Further implied in this notion of gathering together is order, for when things of like value are gathered together in a whole, in the name of not only their intrinsic order, an order external to them also prevails.

In actuality, the term *logos* is translated as word, speech, thought, or discourse. And, whereas word and thought supposedly hold different meanings, the symbiotic nature of their relationship suggests reflection, such that right speech – word – reflects proper thinking – thought – and vice versa.

As with the Platonic *logos*, such attempts at unity and order also imply dualisms that, from an Irigarayan perspective, continue to take part in a logic of the same. With its focus on the proper reflection between word and thought, *logos* suggests putting words and thought in order, such that each replicates the other, which, in a larger picture, also mirrors the harmony of the cosmos, of the world. Let us consider the process of narrative. Certainly, the outward parameters that define a narrative imply order, but so does each word within it: this one comes first, that one next, and so on until complete. In addition to meanings that evolve from this sense of order, *logos* also finds its way to the realms of numerics and law. There, we find another meaning for *logos* that also provides some aspect of order. We could note, for example, the various activities of 'computation, reckoning, account, measure, ratio, and proportion' (cf. Gordon H. Clark, *The Johannine Logos*, p. 15; and *An Intermediate Greek-English Lexicon*, ed. by H.G. Liddell and Scott, pp. 476–7). As we shall see, such notions of *logos* based on measure and proportion will become critical as we turn from Plato to the earlier Heraclitus.

Heraclitus' *Logos*: Fluctuation, Proportional Equivalence, Oneness

To sing for you. But that 'for you' is not a dative. Nor that song, a gift. Not received from you, not produced by me, nor for you, that song: my love with you. Intermingled. Escapes from me. A cloud. (Luce Irigaray, *Elemental Passions*, p. 7)

Many know of Heraclitus from Fragment 91, in which we find these words about the 'impossibility of stepping twice into the same river', or the notion that everything is always in flux (from Heraclitus's fragments numbered and printed according to Diels-Kranz, as cited in *Fragments*, trans. by T. M. Robinson). Many think this fragment about the 'impossibility of stepping twice into the same river' relates to the flowing nature of things, and thus turns away from early Greek affections towards oneness and reflection. However, it would be fitting to consider the context of Heraclitus's work. For example, he also states that we are unable 'twice to touch a mortal being in the same condition' (Robin Osborne, 'The Polis and its Culture', in *Routledge History of Philosophy, Volume I: From the Beginning to Plato*, p. 99). Certainly, in these cases, Heraclitus's words are bound to a discourse about nature, where all things appear linked through their constant change. But, this notion of change operates in a coherent and unified manner, is fixed, and in some way is based on duality and oneness. In other words, Heraclitus's river is included in a theory of fluctuation that relies on an exchange between equals, and thus remains entrenched in a logic of opposites and of oneness.

Many agree that Heraclitus was one of the earliest persons to write to such an extent regarding pairings, as things set in opposition to one another. We know this from his fragments, which treat not only non-human but also human pairings as reflected in the opposites of night and day, sea and earth, warm and cool, wet and dry, winter and summer, disease and health, hunger and satiety, weariness and rest, good and bad, just and unjust, war and peace, mortal and immortal, young and old, up and down, straight and crooked, divine and human, etc. (cf. Osborne, op. cit., p. 96, p. 102; and Edward Schiappa, *Protagoras and Logos*, p. 94).

Within these pairings, Heraclitus includes the oppositions of male and female. The context of the day also suggests the relationship between these opposites. As Ann Bergren explains, a number of the Presocratic philosophers – both pre- and post-Heraclitus – implicated male and female as one of the oppositional pairings. Bergren writes, 'Parmenides claimed the sex of the child depended upon the position of the womb (right for males, left for females); Empedocles, upon the temperature of the womb at conception (hotter for men, colder for women); and Anaximander the side from which the father's seed came (right for males, left for females)' ('Helen's Good "Drug"', in *Contemporary Literary Hermeneutics and Interpretation of Classical Texts*, p. 201). And, as we know from Luce Irigaray's work on the Platonic *logos* and also from Edward Schiappa's work on the Presocratics, oppositional pairings also included a meaning where, generally, 'one of the two things in opposition was considered in some way preferable to the other' (Schiappa, *Protagoras and Logos*, p. 92).

Hence, whatever the 'rationale' set aside to support these oppositional pairings, the qualities of these pairings are such that the polarities are not of equal value. At some point, one of them takes over the other, bringing to mind the earlier noted attribute of sameness. Thus, it would not be surprising that within Heraclitus's theory of fluctuation, which is founded upon the permanence of change, we find a logic based not only on measure and proportion, but also upon oneness. Or: when one thing ebbs, it also flows. We sense the harmonic implications in Heraclitus's notions of sea and earth: as one thing diminishes, the other increases in proportionate measure. One could say: the same for the same. And, while it is well known that fire for Heraclitus was the main – though not the only – element, it is also well known that these 'changes between fire, sea and earth balance[d] each other', and [were] driven according to the rationality of the universe (G. S. Kirk, J. E. Raven, and M. Schofield, *The Presocratic Philosophers*, p. 197). For example, in Fragment 30,[2] fire gets lit and is extinguished always in proportionate measure; in Fragment 31b,[3] the sea is 'poured off' and made equal to its level before even the existence of the earth; and in Fragment 31a,[4] sea and earth come to existence as, again, fire ebbs and flows.

Thus, although the fluidity of fire – or water, or the earth – allows for infinite becoming and creates balance, the *logos* of Heraclitus relies on the permanence of the elements – fire, water, earth – in keeping measure and proportion. Osborne supports this notion by adding that any 'discontinuity in change finds itself reflected in the equivalence of exchange' ('The Polis and its Culture', in *Routledge History of Philosophy, Volume I: From the Beginning to Plato*, p. 100), that 'what we have after the change is [...] the same value [...] measured to the same *logos* (op. cit., p. 101). And, if this is so – if Heraclitus's *logos* represents not change, but permanence, and if his *logos* calls for proper measure and proportion based on oppositional pairings that suggest false equality – then I would claim that his not 'stepping twice into the same river' does not relate to the movement, nor to the flow, of a river. Rather, it is the river that remains the same. And as Same, as 'One', it can only be stepped into once, because once in, there we also remain.

Certainly, *logos* is a term with an extendable definition that takes part in a complex history, fecund in its ideologies associated with Sameness. Similar to its early associations with Heraclitus, *logos* presupposes a unity based on a conception of oneness that requires a 'supreme intelligence controlling the universe', a 'He' who directs the course of nature (Clark, *The Johannine Logos*, p. 19). As a Western cultural institution, *logos* has played a dominant role, and has perhaps expected that a feminine discourse could complement it such that each word of the other – or thought, or speech, or discourse – would become an accomplice in sameness, thus disregarding a place for any type of asymmetrical 'otherness'. Certainly, in our Western culture, *logos* as a unifying structure for reflection, duality, proportional equivalence, and oneness guarantees the 'Truth'. However, as we shall see, this kind of Truth leaves little room for the feminine as other.

The Importance of Style in the Work of Luce Irigaray

But you do not hear it. So many words divide us. Divide from the song. How could this white outpouring reach you? The strength of innocence remains inaudible. Bereavement of the tongue, such a whiteness is not heard.
(Luce Irigaray, *Elemental Passions*, p. 7).

Early on, Luce Irigaray understood that to undertake to outline a philosophy in the feminine would entail another language, another discourse. Familiar with the work of Plato, Heraclitus – and others such as Jacques Lacan, Sigmund

Freud and Ferdinand de Saussure – as she is, she knew she could not honestly express feminine subjectivity by remaining within the same *logos*, the same logic, the same discourse as that which she tries to interpret in order to reveal its confinement in sameness. To do so would display a lack of integrity. Thus, asking, 'How to cry out that I was living inside you? That I spoke through your mouth?' (*Elemental Passions*, p. 26), Luce Irigaray searches for her own language through 'a woman's phenomenological elaboration of the auto-affection and auto-representation of her [own] body [...] What this implies is that the female body is not to remain the object of men's discourse or their various arts but that it becomes an issue of a feminine subjectivity experiencing and identifying itself' (*je, tu, nous*, p. 59, translation amended).

Foreshadowing the third stage of her work, in which she now advocates two different subjectivities – one could say: a new woman and a new man – rather than the one – so-called neuter or neutral subject – of the *logos*, Luce Irigaray argues that such a move for the feminine ought also to consider the existence of the masculine subject, 'inviting him to redefine himself as a body with a view to exchanges between sexed subjects' (ibid.). Thus, she turns to the necessity of becoming other on the part of woman, explaining that 'many women, and men for that matter, still do not believe that woman can be anything other than the complement to man, his inverse, his scraps, his need, his other. Which means that she cannot be truly other' (*I Love to You*, p. 63).

She thus tries to express women's sense via another discourse, another style. Doing so, she creates a feminine language that relies on 'a "style," or "writing," of women [which] tends to put the torch to fetish words, proper terms, well-constructed forms [...] a "style" [which] does not privilege sight; instead, it takes each figure back to its source, which is among other things *tactile* [...] comes back in touch with itself in that origin without ever constituting in it, constituting itself in it, as some sort of unity [and] [...] is always fluid' (*This Sex Which Is Not One*, p. 79). We find this approach to style in many of her works: *Speculum*; *This Sex Which Is Not One*; *Marine Lover*; *The Forgetting of Air*; *je, tu, nous*; *I Love to You*; *To Be Two*; *Everyday Prayers*, to name just a few, and certainly in *Elemental Passions*, here quoted, where she writes philosophy in a very different way, with another discourse, among other things, to make clear that 'women and men can only be wed beyond an already defined horizon' (p. 4). Even now, writing in English, she chooses every word carefully, attentive to expression, aware of the nuances that particular constructions have had historically. Thus, the fluidity of her words remains outside of the river of sameness that the *logos* provides, articulates the feminine, creates another discourse carried out through her style which more suits feminine subjectivity.

In an Irigarayan world, then, becoming an other suggests difference. More than this, it implies respect for all, and a breaking away from the discursive stream in which we have lost ourselves. To be able to say that, she needs to resort to difference in language and to step away from the prefabricated world constructed by masculine discourse towards her own words, her own style.

Opening one of her pages, the words pour forth, cascading over boulders, traversing the impossible places that catch us, pulling our footing from beneath.

White water, a rush of breath: are you asking me to remain in it? If I do, I am afraid it will carry me away, this river. Certainly, things are not as they seem: the same. Then write me a story, he says. Name the parts of a river: a mouth, the delta, the bed. Are there more? Only to be received, she says. With honesty and grace.

Afterword

Spilling out without a break. Without any obstacle save an
imperceptible limit or term, everything is suffused with
air impregnated by my life. Unseizable suspense, it
nourishes the body of your words.
Call yourself. Give, yourself, names.
Recall yourself once more: I insist, into the air.
Seeing, hearing, speaking, breathing, living, all these wait [...]
(Luce Irigaray, *Elemental Passions*, pp. 7–8)

Finally, I am here, at this river, the hillside, a series of adobe tablets
Overhead a thousand birds: my eye on the one who veers away.
I hear more than see its thunder, a rapture amongst all the elements –
I go from the rafts to the fishers to the salmon,
a line drawn outward, then two.
The wind is everywhere,
and infinitely would I carry your words across these depths,
If they were mine, I could.

How else could she tell him?
Faithfully, she tried
Takes a walk upstairs
Red door the same as red mountain,
a sheet of sand
drawn over her,
Stones smooth with times of beauty and abandon.

Upstream, my soul has been taken by your words, or a spirit,
Some would say a song that tumbles forth,
A ribbon of a river, like the Nile in early spring, Blue and White:
A delta for love,
a mouth for speech, a bed for rest,
a bank for our economy of difference.
These are the things that hold a river,
it took me days to know,
but only days.

Otherwise, we have come here at least 12,000 times.
The Mackenzie, The Magdalena,

The Tonegawa, Tigris and Euphrates
Or, Pearl and Yellow, Danube, and la Seine.
I sit here and realize
She has given me back to myself, this river.
Source and tributary,
a language not yet said,
or even if at the tip of a tongue
Fresh water.
and better than a question,

to receive her at her mouth,
just ahead of the channel,
both beyond and outside,
where she surpasses even her own boundaries.
And infinitely would I carry your words across
these depths.

If they were mine, I could.

Notes

1 The translations of *Elemental Passions* have been amended for this paper.
2 'This system, one and the same system of all things, no god, nor any human being made it, but it always was and is and will be an ever-living fire, catching light in measures and extinguished in measures' (Osborne, 'The Polis and its Culture', in *Routledge History of Philosophy, Volume I: From the Beginning to Plato*, p. 100).
3 'Sea is poured off and is measured out to the same proportion (*logos*) as it was formerly, before the birth of the earth' (ibid.).
4 'Fire's turnings: first sea, and of sea the half is earth, the half "burner" [i.e., lightning or fire] . . . [earth] is dispersed as sea, and is measured so as to form the same proportion as existed before it became earth' (G. S. Kirk, J. E. Raven and M. Schofield, *The Presocratic Philosophers*, p. 198).

Chapter 17

Masculine and Feminine Approaches to Nature

Karen I. Burke

State University of New York at Stony Brook, USA

What relationship does humanity have to nature? What relationship should there be? How do we relate to each other and to ourselves as natural? Luce Irigaray offers an intriguing answer: human culture involves the active cultivation of the natural, so that there is continuity between nature and culture. Rethinking the relationship of humanity to nature underlies Luce Irigaray's visionary proposals for a different future, proposals that span the realms of politics, spirituality, linguistics, philosophy and medicine. In this paper, I explore her idea of the cultivation of nature as both an original philosophical insight into the question of the relationship of humanity to nature and as a positive practical proposal.

Nature refers broadly to the natural environment, to our own bodies, and to other living beings; for each, Luce Irigaray proposes relating to nature through cultivation and culture. Thus her idea transcends the usual boundaries between the disciplines of environmental ethics and the study of sex and gender. As Luce Irigaray suggests, the cultivation of nature implies a rejection of the common assumption that nature and culture are separate. Usually, 'nature' refers to a wilderness untouched by human intervention or to some sheer materiality within us, to plants and animals – but not to humans – ecosystems, the elements, sea, land, and sky. 'Culture' denotes society, institutions, intellectual and scientific achievements, the economy and laws. I suspect that most Western dictionaries define nature and culture as antonyms. Despite these conceptual antagonisms, many of our environmental problems suggest that our cultural activities influence and affect nature. Our human activities – such as using electricity in our homes, driving, and purchasing goods made by industry – are all contributing to the change of the climate, and all air pollution affects both human health and the health of 'wild' ecosystems. A perspective sensitive to environmental concerns, like that of Luce Irigaray, challenges us to rethink the idea that culture is separate from nature. In exploring her idea of the cultivation of nature, an understanding of nature and culture themselves that is not founded on their antinomy will emerge. This paper begins with a brief section characterizing the traditional Western approach to nature. I will then discuss Luce Irigaray's really original view that culture involves the cultivation of nature, which is both highly specific and practical. I will conclude by discussing her ideas concerning the cultivation of the body, the cultivation of gender, and the cultivation of the environment.

The Domination of Nature

The powerful speech given by Luce Irigaray in 1986, 'A Chance to Live', concerning the nuclear accident at Chernobyl, articulates many of her criticisms of the masculine ways of relating to nature which dominate nature and our culture (*Thinking the Difference*, pp. 3–35). Meditating on the horrific way in which people feared even the rain as possibly being radioactive, she points out that Chernobyl was 'a foreseeable accident [...] another in a series of symptoms of the state of our culture, symptoms that can be found in both theory and practice' (op. cit., p. 4). I turn to this published speech as a central place in her writings where she diagnoses this disease in our relation to nature and as a poignant articulation of her sensitivity to the natural world and its reciprocal effects on us.

Luce Irigaray writes in this essay: 'No society can exist without its constituent bodies. This tautology is continually forgotten for reasons of male subjective economy, at least in our patriarchal cultures' (op. cit., pp. 16–17). Society requires bodies, but this tautology is forgotten. Only in forgetting the analytically true dependence of society on natural living bodies can we believe that culture is separate from nature. How and why could Western society collectively forget that society depends on natural life, on the bodily life of its citizens? Luce Irigaray suggests that this collective forgetting is due to the male subjective economy. In growing up, the little boy must separate himself from his mother and from the material conditions of his existence:

> Male society has characteristics which some people claim are universal, but which are in fact attributable to the sex of the people that compose it. Thus, without a sexual culture, a (partially dialectical) pattern of cultural relations between the genders, man – in his logic, discourse, behaviour; his entire subjective economy – constantly oscillates between the *yes* and the *no* that he says to all forms of mothers in establishing his identity. [...] Man needs these yesses and noes to maintain a distance between himself and the matter that produced him. More often than not, he seeks to remain in denial of this primary mother or matrix. His denial of reality is an attempt, by various means, including very subtle reasoning, to impose *a second nature* that eventually destroys the first or causes it to be forgotten. (op. cit., pp. 17–18; italics in original)

Forgetting his natural existence, his ties to nature and to his mother, would be, in our tradition, a necessary component of the masculine subject's achievement of his freedom, his membership in masculine community, and his spiritual identity.

The conceptual separation between culture and nature, that is then accomplished by the masculine subject to assert his own independence and deny his natural origin, is also the imposition of a second nature, a new reality replacing natural reality. Luce Irigaray connects the technological domination of nature with the creation of this second reality: the world we live in is a world more full of machines than nature, even if they are convenient domestic machines in our homes. The technological relation to nature also *neuters* nature. Referring to the 'mechanical conditioning' of our fabricated environment today, Luce Irigaray notes that 'Sexualization, which is one of the essential characteristics of living matter, has not been cultivated in our societies for centuries, and our age of technology is attempting to eliminate it' (op. cit., pp. 7–8). Another tautology we collectively forget is that a machine does not have a sex. Living in a world of machines which mediate even our very life processes, we forget that living matter is essentially sexed – animals and plants are sexed, and only single-celled organisms and fungi are alive but not sexed. All sexed life is neuter only in death, or is neutered by death. And since we live in a second nature in which we dominate nature through technology, and since technology incorporates natural materials only as dead resources, in most of our societies 'destroying life seems to be as compulsory as giving life' (op. cit., p. 7). Luce Irigaray calls this the most fundamental contradiction of our societies.

Hegel: The Death of Nature and its Resurrection as Spirit

As Luce Irigaray confirmed to the students in her seminar at the University of Nottingham, in June 2006, Hegel's philosophy is significant for her thought. Hegel is one of the only major Western philosophers to reject the false dichotomy of nature and culture, and who aimed to demonstrate their continuity. In 'A Chance to Live', Luce Irigaray praises Hegel for recognizing our relationship to nature as problematic:

> Hegel was particularly aware of this shortcoming of an ethics of our relationship to the natural world as it concerns the genders and their ancestries; Antigone is sacrificed because she pays her respects to the blood and gods of her mother by honouring her dead brother. Hegel wrote that this sacrifice hobbles the whole rest of the becoming of the spirit. (op. cit., p. 16)

Nevertheless, Luce Irigaray notes that Hegel's attempt to 'spiritualize nature' fails in the same ways as do other parts of Western culture: it requires death, the neutralization of sexed life, and sacrifice. While much more can be said on this matter, I will here briefly show how even Hegel's thinking is marred by the tradition of the domination of nature by culture. The closer one looks, the further one sees how deeply Luce Irigaray's criticism cuts.[1]

All of Hegel's philosophy concerns the continuity of nature and spirit, but here there is only room to discuss one key moment in his thought. It is a place to which Luce Irigaray has persistently returned in her own engagements with

Hegel:[2] the moment in *Phenomenology of Spirit* when Spirit first emerges as self-conscious, and where Hegel discusses the family and thus gender (cf. Chapter VI, Spirit, § 438–76). Hegel shows that the family is both a moment of natural unity, in that all of its members are related to one other, and also a moment of spiritual unity, in that it is a legally recognized and fundamental unit in modern society. There are, nevertheless, two important tensions between its natural and spiritual unity. The family faces two threats to its natural unity: since the members of the family are each separate living organisms, they are born and, especially, they die at different times, and they belong to different genders. Spirit must overcome these tensions in becoming self-conscious, when it must incorporate or 'spiritualize' the natural. In this section, Hegel articulates how Spirit overcomes the death and sexual difference of individual family members. The way in which Spirit resolves these tensions is particularly significant for feminism and the life of women, since Hegel presents arguments justifying the confinement of women to domestic life.

The death of the beloved family member happens contingently through natural and accidental processes, such as disease. Yet Spirit renders this death 'spiritual' when the family performs the ritual burials of the dead body. As Luce Irigaray notes, Hegel sees the duty of the blood relatives of the deceased as 'to ensure *burial for the dead*, thus changing a natural phenomenon into a spiritual act' (*Speculum*, p. 214; emphasis in original). The family members of the deceased take the dead body, which is subject to decay and decomposition by random natural factors, and symbolize it as eternal, as part of Spirit. The body is placed in the earth and marked by a permanent gravestone bearing the person's name. As Hegel puts it, the family

> weds the blood-relation to the bosom of the earth, to the elemental imperishable individuality. The Family thereby makes him a member of a community which prevails over and holds under control the forces of particular material elements and lower forces of life, which sought to unloose themselves against him and destroy him. (*Phenomenology of Spirit*, § 452)

The earth is the only individual immortal through its physical composition, so by placing the corpse in earth the body becomes part of the earth and participates in its immortality. Hegel explicitly connects the transition of body into Spirit and the relation of man to physical nature – but again, only in death. Burial thus twice recuperates and immortalizes the family member, as both soul and body: his soul is symbolized as a permanent part of the human community, and his body is rejoined to the earth in physical 'community'.

For Hegel, death brings the dead family member – a man, significantly – into universality, replacing the disconnecting assortment of particular experiences that characterized his life (op. cit., § 451). In fact, Hegel even says that 'death is the fulfilment and the supreme "work" which the individual as such undertakes on its [the ethical community's] behalf' (op. cit., § 452). The accomplishment of Spirit occurs at the level of the universal, and the individual's death facilitates the transition to the universal. Society cannot leave the sacrifice of individuals up to chance, so embedded in this section is one of Hegel's calls for the necessity of war. For him, war serves almost as a kind of opportunity for the particularity of individuals to be sacrificed to the greater universal of the nation, and the nation engages in war for this very end:

> In order not to let them [families] become rooted and set in this isolation, thereby breaking up the whole and letting the [communal] spirit evaporate, government has from time to time to shake them to their core by war. [...] Spirit [...] checks their tendency to fall away from the ethical order, and to be submerged in a natural existence; and it preserves and raises conscious self into freedom and its own power. (op. cit., § 455)

Without war, families could remain submerged in their natural unity and forget their greater calling to the universal, to the nation. So war agitates against this tendency of families, and the deaths of many sons – as it reads in the last line of the quotation – serve freedom. If the greatest work that an individual may do for the universal is to die, then war benefits not just Spirit but the dead individuals themselves.

Performing the ritual burials of the dead soldier-sons, the care of death falls to the women in the family.[3] Then Spirit overcomes the tension between the different genders in the family by assigning traditional gender roles to the family members. Man and woman each fulfil different tasks that together and in coordination fulfil the goals of the family unit: the man heads out into the world to earn a living and the woman remains at home to take care of the family members. For Hegel, the brother's movement into full self-consciousness and the sister's persistence in the natural unity of the family is a solution for Spirit. He announces the gendered division of labour as this solution:

> He passes from the divine law, within whose sphere he lived, over to human law. But the sister becomes, or the wife remains, the head of the household and the guardian of the divine law. In this way, the two sexes overcome their natural being and appear in their ethical significance, as diverse beings who share between them the two distinctions belonging to the ethical substance. (op. cit., § 459)

Only as individuals are they man and woman, but as the universal ethical beings operating in unity and coordination in the family, their bodies are, strictly speaking, only relevant to Spirit in that Spirit takes bodies to destine individuals for their traditional roles. Man is destined for Spirit and the human law, while woman remains the guardian of the divine law. The significance of the female body for Hegel is its confinement to the simple universality and unity of the family, while the man has a role in the family but also moves on to the self-consciousness and freedom characteristic of further developments of Spirit. Even the sexual desire of man and woman is governed by this logic. Hegel says that the husband, because he is also a citizen, 'thereby acquires the right of desire and, at the same time, preserves his freedom in regard to it' (op. cit., § 457).

The man has the right in the spiritual realm to his naturally occurring physical desire, but the woman's desire is illegitimate. Without a passage to the spiritual realm, the woman can have no sexual desire of her own: her desire remains purely contingent, particular and natural in the rawest sense, as well as illegitimate. In contrast to what Luce Irigaray will suggest with 'the cultivation of desire', which I explain below, for Hegel even man has a simple desire with a right superadded to it: his desire may be legitimate but it remains uncultivated.

The Cultivation of Nature: The Transition from Living Nature into Spirit

The transition that Hegel proposes from nature to Spirit requires death, sacrifice, war and the neutering of sexed life. Nevertheless, as Luce Irigaray acknowledges, his intentions were similar to her own: 'Hegel always bet on the continuity between living nature and Spirit in his debates with pure empiricists and idealists' (*Sexes and Genealogies*, p. 140). Yet his ideas did not live up to his wishes: 'Hegel is doomed to do what he wished not to do [...] This failure in Hegel's thought, though not entailing the a priorism of Kant or Fichte, maintains a break in the spiritualization of the living and of nature' (ibid.). This failure consists in his requirements that the corpse, the dead body, be spiritualized, and that the neutrality of death come to replace the sexed reality of embodied persons. The logic of the sacrifice of life – living nature and sexed human beings – pervades Hegel's view of the transition from nature to culture.

Luce Irigaray instead proposes a true spiritualization of nature, one that spiritualizes the natural during life, and thus spiritualizes living nature. Hers is a feminine approach to nature while that of Hegel she sees as a masculine view, that is, bound to the struggles of the masculine subject as discussed above. Juxtaposing Hegel's account to that of Luce Irigaray accentuates key features of her proposal. For her, it is not the dead body but the living body that has to be cultivated during life. For her, the cultivation of nature, or the spiritualization of nature, begins with the natural as its starting point, and then moves to transform, modify, cultivate and spiritualize it. Spirit does not have to leave the body to be spirit; spirit is a spiritualization of the body. Thus there will be no imperative for death and war embedded in the transition from nature to spirit. The universal does not require the neuter; there is a masculine universal and a feminine universal. The human relation to nature will not just be a masculine one, dominating our whole culture, but both masculine and feminine ways of relating to nature are called for by Luce Irigaray. Boldly she remarks that rethinking and re-enacting a new transition between nature and culture is not just her own personal endeavour:

> It is a task for everyone. No one is beyond it, and it makes no one naturally a master or slave, poor or rich. We are all of us, men and women alike, sexed. Our principal task is to make the transition from nature to culture as sexed beings, to become women and men while remaining faithful to our gender.

This task, which exists for all men and women, must not be confused with reproduction. (*I Love to You*, p. 30)

Here she specifies only our own nature, and not external nature. This raises the following question: why juxtapose two topics usually discussed in isolation from each other, the body and the environment? Luce Irigaray sees this usual division as a relic of patriarchy: 'In patriarchal traditions individual and collective life both wants to and believes it is able to organize itself outside of the surroundings of the natural world. The body – also called microcosm – is then cut off from the universe – also called macrocosm' (*Between East and West*, p. 55). The feminine approach to nature that Luce Irigaray articulates, taking seriously the idea that culture is not separate from nature, also implies a commitment to treating the body and the environment together, as interdependent. A body cannot survive, let alone be cultivated, if it lacks nutritious food, fresh air and water, and sufficient warmth – and for all of these it depends on its environment. Similarly, talking about environmental problems such as pollution, without acknowledging their effects on our health, perpetuates the false idea that nature is simply external to us and that we should care about it only through disinterested altruism.[4]

The cultivation of nature is not merely an abstract concept, even if the constraints and conventions of philosophical writing have thus far led me to use it that way. Luce Irigaray uses many versions of the phrase 'the cultivation of nature' in denoting the many objects of cultivation: desire, breath, living perception, gender, life and nature. Cultivation will be a set of specific practices, specific also to the object of cultivation, attentive to its own natural proclivities, inclinations, or potentials. One could not cultivate a tomato plant in the same way as a carrot, nor breath in the same way as perception, nor a river ecosystem in the same way as a desert ecosystem. Cultivation attends to the specific natural differences inherent in its objects. Luce Irigaray's phrase, '*la culture de la nature*', is a phrase in French that I translate as both 'the cultivation of nature' and 'the culture of nature', and I had been wondering whether or not this was true to her intention. During the seminar with Luce Irigaray, she indicated to me that both translations are appropriate. She uses 'cultivation' to refer to our active and practical engagement with and development of the natural, and 'culture' to indicate the result of collective processes of cultivation, and also a historical stage. She proposes both the cultivation of life and a culture of life. Nietzsche, reacting against the influence of Hegelian philosophy in his essay 'The Use and Abuse of History', concludes with a call to the reader to discover 'the idea of culture as newer and finer nature' (*The Use and Abuse of History*, p. 73). Luce Irigaray has made such a discovery.

The Cultivation of the Body

All our words for natural entities have connotations of their opposition to culture: 'body' often implies the low, the carnal and the debased, in contrast to the elevated spiritual. These connotations must be shed when reading Luce Irigaray. The cultivation of the body is a set of specific practices and habits through which we develop our bodies, and thus ourselves, and develop our capacity to perceive, and thus our capacity to relate to other living beings. She understands the body not as a passive tool used by our active soul, but as the locus of the development of self and soul. Breathing is an important example. For Luce Irigaray, we do not breathe merely to access oxygen, as if it were the fuel for a bodily machine. Instead, our breath is our soul. Earlier Western philosophers such as Empedocles share this view and the Eastern yogic tradition maintains it today. Luce Irigaray writes: 'the soul corresponds to the life of the body cultivated to the point of acquiring the autonomy and spiritual becoming of the breath' (*Between East and West*, p. 75). Here she links breathing with freedom. To clarify this, consider the way that we ordinarily think of breathing as either involuntary or voluntary. Cultivating one's breath develops our voluntary – wilful or free – breathing. This might sound unusual, but that is because Western culture, as Luce Irigaray explains:

> does not teach us how to cultivate breathing. Which means teaching us to assure our existence in an autonomous manner and to spiritualize our vital breath little by little while keeping it free, available, nourishing for the body itself, and for others. Becoming spiritual amounts to transforming our elemental vital breath little by little to a more subtle breath in the service of the heart, of thought, of speech and not only in the service of physiological survival. (op. cit., pp. 75–6)

Luce Irigaray has turned to the yogic traditions of the East to learn these practices, as she discusses in *Between East and West*. Conscious, free, voluntary breathing brings our will into our physical acts, renders them more spiritual and more our own. We then breathe for ourselves as bodies and not only for mere survival. And as Luce Irigaray reminded me in editing this piece, we also breathe to meet with the other.

The cultivation of the body involves many more dimensions. Throughout her work, Luce Irigaray mentions examples such as the cultivation of perception, the cultivation of love, of sexuality, of touch, of sensitive and sensuous language. She also discusses the cultivation of desire, the transformation of too immediate an amorous energy, the culture and cultivation of life. The cultivation of the body is a cultural practice of spirit emerging in and through embodied life: 'By reading certain texts on yoga, for example, we learn that spiritual substance does exist and is not experienced as a property exterior to the self. In other words, the interior or interiority of a body is cultivated and is not to be reduced to the obscurity of the natural' (*I Love to You*, p. 31). Luce Irigaray's understanding of our embodiment has tremendous implications for medicine, for instance. She advocates preventative medicine instead of the usual practice of medicine only once a condition exists and brings suffering. Yet, we cannot discuss health in isolation from society, and discussing women's health in particular, she writes that women 'are deprived of a subjective order by which they can unify their corporeal vitality. A body can only be sound if it has a personal or spiritual project or objective, keeping it together and bringing it to life, (*je, tu, nous*, p. 105). Thus, we need a feminine culture wherein women can have these objectives and achieve both spiritual and physical health.

The Cultivation of Gender

The theme of the spiritualization of living nature leads Luce Irigaray to argue for a cultivation of gender: 'Life can only be thought about, guaranteed, protected if we give consideration to *gender* as one constituent of the human race, not only in reproduction, but also in culture, spirit' (*Sexes and Genealogies*, p. 132; italics in original). As I have been emphasizing, she sees the supposedly neuter universal in society to be linked to the masculine subject: her vision is that the feminine subject will find a place in culture too, that there should be a culture of the feminine alongside the already existing culture of the masculine. She calls for sexed rights to replace the neuter rights we have now. Developing civil identities as both masculine and feminine instead of a neuter citizenship, developing masculine and feminine universals instead of relegating the feminine and the body to the private realm, would mean, claims Luce Irigaray, that women would begin to develop a public subjectivity honest to their natural inclinations without reducing them to naturality, to the naked capacity for bearing children.

This is an often misunderstood aspect of her work. To some feminists, especially in the United States, Luce Irigaray here seems too close to anti-feminist arguments that reduce women to nature, that claim that women have a minimal role in greater society because they are naturally incapable of it. But as Simone de Beauvoir pointed out in the Introduction to *The Second Sex*, such anti-feminist arguments make the mistake of taking a social consequence for a natural predetermination: 'it is, in point of fact, a difficult matter for man to realize the extreme importance of social discriminations which seem outwardly insignificant but which produce in woman moral and intellectual effects so profound that they appear to spring from her original nature' (p. xxxii). Luce Irigaray has been wrongly accused of making this same mistake; her proposals would, in fact, serve to remedy the isolation of woman in the family and in the natural.

Luce Irigaray is, as she says, a theorist of sexual difference. During the seminar, she clarified what she means by 'sexual difference'. She explained that sexual, or rather sexuate, difference corresponds to a *relational identity*: for example, the feminine subject identifies with her mother during childhood while the masculine subject distances himself from his mother. Sexual, or sexuate, difference is not a simple naturality, a deterministic materiality. Luce Irigaray rejects the idea that women are determined by nature, but maintains that feminine identity is linked with natural capacities that are specific to women.

A culture of the feminine, as Luce Irigaray proposes, would involve the instantiation of feminine universals, of feminine spirituality, and of laws that would give women a feminine civil identity. In *Democracy Begins Between Two*,

Luce Irigaray gives the example of a 'right to free choice of maternity' as a possible feminine right (p. 100). Contrasted with the usual concept of a 'right to abortion' which it would replace, this new right would better suit the reality of women's choice to become mothers. A 'right to abortion' can only be exercised in the case of an already existing pregnancy, so it operates retroactively, and it incorrectly implies that women only become mothers reluctantly. It continues to be a difficult right to guarantee in law.[5] Conversely, a 'right to the free choice of maternity' could be exercised by women throughout their lives, and would pay tribute to the deliberation, choice and autonomy characteristic of becoming a mother. It is both incorrect and degrading to think that women simply carry babies against their will, due to nature and the biological father's action. In advocating a civil feminine identity, Luce Irigaray means to rescue women from being reduced to the natural, not perpetuate their isolation in the natural, a tendency that also denigrates the environment: 'The exclusive emphasis on woman's role as mother has gone in step with a lack of respect for the natural order' (*Sexes and Genealogies*, p. 131).

The Cultivation of the Environment

Luce Irigaray also advocates a change in our relationship to external nature. I name this new relationship the 'cultivation of the environment', although this exact phrase never appears in her work. The cultivation of the environment would only arise through specific practices rooted in a consciousness of the way that a particular ecosystem intrinsically tends to work. For instance, water in mountain streams has its own way of purifying itself as it flows downstream; the cultivation of water would seek to understand and then encourage these natural purification mechanisms of water, instead of our usual practice of purifying water by chlorinating it, which succeeds in killing micro-organisms but also pollutes it with a known carcinogen. The cultivation of a forest ecosystem might mean the reintroduction of the main predator, as wolves were reintroduced into the US National Park of Yellowstone, setting the natural ecosystem back into its own logic, though one mediated by conscious human participation.

I believe that Luce Irigaray's idea of the cultivation or culture of nature could be the foundation of a full-fledged environmental ethic. To take seriously the idea that culture is a culture of nature, a development out of and upon nature but not separate from it, requires not only a re-evaluation of the way in which we relate to our own bodies, but also a re-evaluation of the way in which we relate to the rest of the natural world. For Luce Irigaray, we can introduce consciousness, freedom and careful human intervention into the living natural world, accomplishing a cultivation of the environment benefiting both us and it. Just as specific legal reforms developed from the idea of the spiritualization of the body, specific legal reforms would also be part of an environmental ethic of the culture of nature. Pollution, losses of biodiversity, and genetically modified organisms could all be criticized, from this viewpoint, as operating against the cultivation of nature by controlling, manipulating, exploiting and irreparably harming it. Even more important, however, will be the positive programme for managing natural places and communities of organisms. Legal and financial support will be given to the careful study of the natural mechanisms and balances; and action will be taken to aid ecosystems on their own terms.

How have the ideas of nature and culture themselves taken shape through the course of investigating Luce Irigaray's idea of the cultivation of nature? We will have to abandon the idea that culture is a creation of humans as disembodied minds or language users, an idea that although common should seem absurd at the end of this paper. Culture, then, is a refinement or perfection of living nature, an accomplishment rooted in natural capacities, an achievement of specific bodily existence: culture corresponds to cultivated nature. It is not enough to say that culture is 'part of nature' because that wrongly implies that culture can be reduced to nature, which it cannot. Culture is something more than nature would be without cultivation. And then what is nature? It is the way we refer to the materiality of our existence and that of the natural world, the elements of earth, air, fire and water upon which our physical survival depends, and even a part of which is studied by science. It is the set of possibilities and potentialities that we do not create but can develop. While uncultivated nature is that out of which culture blossoms, neither can be reduced to the other.

I am grateful to Luce Irigaray for all that I have learned from her, in her writings and in the seminar, and even in my communication with her as the editor of this volume. Even the title of this paper speaks to the greater understanding I reached through participating in the seminar. As we were concluding the seminar, Luce Irigaray suggested a new title, replacing 'The Cultivation of Nature' with 'Masculine and Feminine Approaches to Nature'. Until then I had wrongly thought that Luce Irigaray intends to replace *all* thinking about the relationship of culture to nature with the idea of the cultivation of nature. Yet, as she writes, 'there is, for each gender, a relation between nature and culture that is specific to it' (*Democracy Begins Between Two*, p. 6). She envisions a future in which both masculine and feminine ways of relating to nature might coexist. A small example can illustrate such symbiosis. While considering noise pollution and its harm to our hearing, she notes that hearing is 'a component of the most advanced and universal aspects of culture' (*Thinking the Difference*, p. 23). Of course, machines cause noise pollution and, as discussed above, she considers the technological approach to nature to be masculine, but her solution is not to abandon all technology and return to an agrarian past. She recommends 'restricting the number of roads for motor vehicles both inside and outside cities by creating many footpaths and quiet zones [...] [and] focusing research on the invention of quiet machinery' (op. cit., p. 23). She suggests that we use new technology and laws restricting certain uses of technology to help preserve our hearing, a solution which blends the masculine and the feminine. So, while the bulk of this paper articulates the feminine view of the cultivation of nature, the title indicates Luce Irigaray's ultimate vision: the peaceful and fruitful coexistence of masculine and feminine ways of relating to nature.

Notes

1 In a longer version of this paper (unpublished), I extend this analysis much further. Further exegesis of Hegel reveals how incisive Luce Irigaray's criticism is and how deeply entwined, for Hegel, are the notions of death, the neuter, sacrifice, mourning and war for the transition of nature into Spirit. In this longer version I inquire into an additional moment of transition from nature to Spirit in Hegel's thought: the conclusion of the *Philosophy of Nature*, as all of nature cedes to Spirit (§ 371–6). Here Hegel is explaining the transition between the strictly 'natural' world, that of plants and animals, to the human world, initially subjective Spirit. Here, too, the transition pivots around the death of the individual animal organism and of sexual difference: Spirit relieves itself of bodily mortality and sexual difference – and hence of living bodies in general.

2 Three major places in Luce Irigaray's work discuss this moment: first, the chapter 'The Eternal Irony of the Community', in *Speculum*; then the chapter 'The Universal as Mediation', in *Sexes and Genealogies*; and thirdly, the opening chapter of *I Love to You*, 'Introducing: Love Between Us'.

3 Sabrina Hom's contribution to this volume elaborates on this point in much greater detail.

4 This is not to suggest that Irigaray might advocate an anthropocentric environmental ethic (such as, that we should preserve the rainforest so that its biodiversity may someday provide a cure for cancer). Such an idea also stems from a false separation of humanity from nature.

5 In the United States, *Roe v. Wade* established a precedent for the legality of pregnancy termination based on the right to privacy, a right which is itself under attack.

Contributions of Luce Irigaray

*Director of Research in Philosophy at the Centre National
de la Recherche Scientifique (C.N.R.S), Paris*

Chapter 18

Teaching How to Meet in Difference

Luce Irigaray

The work that made possible this text did not aim to speak about children. Rather, it lets them speak. It allows the girls and boys to speak, and particularly to say things that they usually keep to themselves or whisper to each other. Of course, the matter is not to deprive them of their secrets but to invite them to speak freely, notably about things that teachers do not want to listen to, things that children would thus have to leave outside school, even to forget in order to go to school, to join in language, in culture and civic relationships.

Towards a Global Education

But to leave these things outside school, language and social relations amounts to leaving oneself outside school, to abandoning oneself in order to be subjected to models that are strange and abstract with respect to our real being. As a result, we are more and more lost, both nostalgic and indifferent, and also aggressive. We become confused in a world of somebodies from which we try to rise up through competitiveness and violence. But this does not bring ourselves back to ourselves; on the contrary, such behaviour increasingly removes ourselves from ourselves, and makes us more and more lost and aggressive.

In fact, the models imposed on boys and girls in school render them uncivil although they aim to teach them public-spiritedness. In reality, they split children – as all of us – into two parts: one so-called cultivated part and one so-called natural part which ought to remain at home, possibly in darkness, perhaps only in bed, in any case lacking words or education concerning desire and love. Now these dimensions of ourselves have to be included in a civic education in order to escape paralysing conformism, loss of oneself and a correlative aggressiveness. Of course, the question is not only of teaching about sexual organs for having sex or conceiving, as some progressive people have imagined. And neither is the matter about employing all our relational energy in playing sports so that we exhaust desire – our culture caring more about competitive sports than about relations between citizens. This, by the way, merely allows boys and girls to remain or return amongst the same as them without confronting each other in bodily difference. Incidentally, I could also add that during this research that

I carried out with children, it occurred that I suggested, in a physical education class, exercises in which boys and girls confronted each other in one way or another. The results were surprising, notably because more energy arose from such a mixed confrontation.

Thus the first aim of the work, that gave rise to the analysis and interpretation of words and drawings by children, was to provide them with a civic education. This undertaking took place after an attempt to obtain rights for women, children and foreigners from the European Parliament. On this occasion, I once more understood that our culture knows only sameness, and that, in order to awaken consideration and respect for difference(s), we have to start in the school. Politicians are too old – as almost all of us are – to perceive and agree with that which is at stake in difference. At the very best, they talk about difference in ideological and moralistic discourses relating to foreigners whom we ought to integrate into our countries. Integration, of course, does not amount to coexistence. Integration is a way of reducing difference to sameness.

After understanding that it was too late to convince politicians, I decided to return to school. I accepted a contract as consultant of the Centre National de la Recherche Scientifique (C.N.R.S) with the Emilia Romagna Region to define programmes for civic education in difference. Thus the main objective was not a sexual education but a civic education in difference, which requires a sexuate education. Such an education cannot exist without our becoming conscious of our sexuate identity and that of the other – whether it is the same as ours or different from ours. The most originally real and polyvalent relationship arises from our sexuate belonging. It creates the first bridge between us: as children, adolescents, lovers or parents, but more generally as persons or citizens. If we deny this initial attraction, we deprive ourselves of the most important source of relationships between us, and construct these starting from artificial codes which annihilate real relational energy. But if we do not cultivate this energy, we run the risk of not going further than instinct – all kinds of instincts: sexual possession and also procreative or parental instinct, gregarious instinct, etc. In my opinion, wanting to remain in sameness amounts to a sort of instinct that is not revealed as such and thus is left uncultivated – a need for an animal territory, for example, which can also be a cultural humus or grounding. But this does not allow us to enter into human relations, which requires liberty, respect for otherness, and the passage from instinct to desire.

If we do not progress in human liberation at the level of relations with the other – be they a lover, a child or a foreigner – it is because we lack a sexuate education. Sexual instinct is the most initial and universal instinct. It is necessary to take it into consideration and include it in education in order to be able to enter into respectful relations with all sorts of others. All the moralistic discourses about the other – and there are so many today! – forget that to succeed in being respectful towards the other requires a cultivation of energy, first of all of sexual energy. Such discourses remain at an ideological or moralistic level, which serves to cut us off precisely from the other as such. Moralism and ideology are shared between an individual and people of their own group:

they belong to the code of a certain group and take part in what binds them together. Thus moralism and ideology are not endowed with a relational energy and are proper to those who belong to the same people. Energy, above all, arises from sexual and sexuate attraction. This has to be cultivated in order to allow for respectful and reciprocal relations, and the construction of a world fitting for the two being in relation with one another at each time.

To put the emphasis on the number two does not signify that I allude only to a traditional couple, nor to an intimate or affective relation. Being two is the way of emerging from this undifferentiated group of someones or somebodies to which our culture leads us, and in which we lose our singularity, our difference(s) and our relational desire and energy. In fact, a society would be formed starting each time from two, whose relations result in a lively interweaving. If the two is always confused in the many, a multiple formed of someones, we are living in common artificially. We are only conforming to the same norms, models and rules that level us to an average. Of course, an average is a quantitative estimation that is founded in sameness. As such, we have not begun to envision the cultivation of energy which could result from relating to each other with respect for difference(s). In such an alternative perspective, the regulation of energy would come from us, from the development of our desire, and would not be imposed on us by norms external to us. There are relations between subjects which freely, but with respect for one another, assure coexistence in a community or a society, and, finally, become the basis of a human culture.

School Experimentation

If I now return to school to meet children, you will understand, I hope, that the aim of my project was not only a sexual education – even if this is critical – but a civic education in difference. I started from sexuate difference because it is the most crucial difference for realizing such an objective.

From the beginning of each encounter with the children, I helped them to discover that the difference between boys and girls is not only sexual in a limited sense, but sexuate, that is to say that this difference does not only concern their sex and a few bodily characteristics, but also their whole subjectivity.

Nevertheless, to reach this stage it is useful to begin with sexual difference strictly speaking. If you repress or ignore this dimension, you will never teach anything about sexuate difference. In fact, this is what happens in our culture, and particularly in our education. Paradoxically it is puritanism that has maintained our subjection to instinct rather than allowing a culture of desire to pave the way for entry into human relationships. It is also partly puritanism which has led us to a society of somebodies in which we have become merged without remembering our singularity, nor that of the other, and in which we have lost our longing for relations between us. It is important to go beyond puritanism, to overcome it, not only to reach a so-called sexual liberation but a total human liberation based on whom we really are.

Thus I began to speak with the children about sexual difference. And I encouraged them to feel at ease with the question. I left them to talk about their sexual organs, saying that all of us, males and females, have a sex, I as well as they, and that we have either the same sex or a different sex. I added that being sexually different not only means having different sexual organs, but that other things also differentiate us. I asked children, with boys and girls speaking alternately, to talk about some of these differences. They then evoked such differences as longer or shorter hair, more or less feminine or masculine clothing, as well as, for example, the fact that the boys are more violent and the girls more sentimental. After a few minutes, I suggested that they could perhaps see other differences by themselves by carrying out a written exercise, and later other activities as, for example, making drawings. I asked for their agreement, and insisted on the fact that the matter was not of a grammar test, but that the written sentences had to be personal and beautiful as in a literary text. To stimulate their engagement with this work, I added that their sentences or other answers would appear in a book and an exhibition. I completed the book and the exhibition a few months after the research with the children, and went to present the book in the various classes, writing a personal dedication in the book of each participant. I also invited the boys and the girls to visit the exhibition.

How to share words between different subjects?

The first exercise proposed to boys and girls consisted of writing sentences including, each time, one or two given words. I myself wrote these cue words one by one on the board, waiting for all the participants to finish their sentences before writing a new cue. All the words required a relation to be established. For example: *with, together, to share, to love, I tell him* or *I tell her,* but also *I . . . you, I . . . him, I . . . her,* etc. I had previously observed with other populations – of adults or adolescents – that these types of cues threw up interesting responses. After a few sentences had been composed, I sent three girls and three boys to the board – two by two, one girl and one boy – to write their responses to a given cue. The children were then invited to think about the differences, and also the resemblances, between the sentences of the girls and of the boys. As they were still free from a priori ideological associations and judgement, they found many things that older people could not discover.

After coming to a better awareness of their own identity and of the differences between them in this way, the participants were encouraged to communicate in respect for their difference(s). For example, I asked each boy and each girl to propose to a friend of the other sex something that they could do together which would please them both. If the proposal could be made orally – that is, if time permitted – some very dynamic and interesting exchanges took place. When it was not possible, the participants wrote a short letter with their proposal. You can read a few of them on page 213 and in the book *Chi sono io? Chi sei tu?* (Biblioteca di Casalmaggiore, 1999). [English translation: Who am I? Who are you?].

What types of utterances are produced by children approximately eight years old? I indicate the responses of the first boy and the first girl to various cues. Of course, 'first' here refers to a random numbering system used to identify the respondants – who never disclose their name to preserve their intimacy – and the number one implies no value judgement.

I (io)[1]

> Girl: I love Dilan. ('Io amo Dilan.')
>
> Boy: I love baseball. ('Io amo il Base-ball.')

You (tu)

> Girl: You love Gian Michele. ('Tu ami Gian Michele.')
>
> Boy: You hate women. ('Tu odi le femmine.')

I . . . you (io . . . tu/te)

> Girl: You and I, we have the same tastes.
>
> ('Io e te abbiamo gli stessi gusti.')
>
> Boy: I hate you ('Io odio te.')

I . . . he/him (io . . . lui)

> Girl: He and I love each other. ('Io e lui ci amiamo.')
>
> Boy: He and I play Game Fair.
>
> ('Io e lui giochiamo con il Game Fair.')

I . . . she/her (io . . . lei)

> Girl: She and I love the same boy.
>
> ('Io e lei amiamo lo stesso ragazzo.')
>
> Boy: She and I hate each other. ('Io e lei ci odiamo.')

with (con)

> Girl: I talk with Marco. ('Con Marco io parlo.')
>
> Boy: I hit the ball with the racket.
>
> ('Con la mazza batto la palla.')
>
> [Or, less frequently: I play basketball with him.
>
> ('Con lui gioco a Basket-ball.')]

together (insieme)

> Girl: Marco and I have a child together.
>
> ('Insieme a Marco facciamo un figlio.')
>
> Boy: I always play together with them.
>
> ('Insieme a loro gioco sempre', the context of answers
>
> indicating that 'loro' designates boys)

to love (amare)

> Girl: I am madly in love with Gian Paolo.
>
> ('Io amo Gian Paolo alla folia.')
>
> Boy: I love basketball. ('Io amo il Basket-ball.')

to share (condividere)

> Girl: I share with Dilan even though I never really knew him.
> ('Io condivido con Dilan anche se non l'ho mai
> conosciuto veramente.')
>
> Boy: I share the computer with my mom.
> ('Io condivido il computer con mia mamma.')

Without yet analysing all the differences between the sentences, one might note that:

the boys prefer
- subject–object relations,
- relations with the same as them, when relations exist between persons,
- the one–many configuration,
- hierarchical or family relationships;

the girls prefer
- relationships between subjects,
- relationships in difference,
- relationships between two persons,
- horizontal relationships.

Boys and girls thus belong to really different relational worlds, and communication between them will be impossible before they become aware and respectful of their difference(s).

It has been stated as an objection to me that the girls' responses show an alienation dating from birth, if not before. How could this be true when, on the whole, research carried out on significant populations of girls and boys proves the contrary? Girls demonstrate that they are more precocious literarily, artistically and linguistically than boys. They are more creative as well. I include some illustrations of this drawn from the book *Chi sono io? Chi sei tu?*, which is made up of material gathered in October 1998 during encounters with children and adolescents frequenting various schools in the small city of Casalmaggiore (Cremona province in Italy).

For example, to the cue: *Make up a sentence using the word 'you' (tu)*:

Girls:

> – You are the only person who makes me understand what it means
> to have feelings for another person that one loves.
> ('Tu sei l'unica persona che riesce a farmi capire che cosa vorrebbe
> dire provare sentimenti per un'altra persona a cui si vuole bene.')
>
> – I remember that, one time, I had the courage to face the boy I loved
> and to say in his face 'I like you a lot'. After that day, I never had the
> courage to look at him until I understood that love had no limits.
> ('Mi ricordo che una volta ho avuto il coraggio di dire in faccia al
> ragazzo che amavo "Tu mi piaci molto". Da quel giorno non ho

avuto il coraggio di guardarlo fino a quando ho capito che l'amore
non aveva limiti.')

- You are resplendent like the moon that lights up the night.
  ('Tu sei splendido come la luna che illumina la notte.')

- You are a universe I can take refuge in.
  ('Tu sei un universo nel quale mi posso rifugiare.')

- For me, you are like the air; but remember, without air we cannot
  live.
  ('Tu sei come l'aria per me, ma ricorda: senza l'aria non si vive.')

Boys:

- You are a very nice person, but girls hate you because you are a
  brute.
  ('Tu sei molto simpatico e gentile, ma le femmine ti odiano perché
  sei brutto.')

- I like you a lot.
  ('Tu mi piaci molto.')

- Who do you think you are?
  ('Tu ti credi di essere chissà chi . . .')

- You are a very nice person.
  ('Tu sei molto simpatico e gentile.')

Beyond the fact that the sentences of the girls – these girls and boys are now
around thirteen years old – are longer, more complex and more beautiful, it
can be observed, above all starting from the Italian sentences, that the girls
speak to a boy while the boys do not address themselves explicitly to a girl: they
speak to another boy or produce a discourse in the neuter. Not paying attention to this means that the interlocutor always remains of masculine or neuter
gender. For this reason, the dialogue between him and her is again impossible.

We can also observe the responses of another group to another cue. The sentences are this time composed by boys and girls around sixteen years old. The
cue was: *Make up a sentence using the word 'to desire' or 'to want'* (desiderare).

Girls:

- I desire your love, but I do not want it if you cannot love me.
  ('Io desidero il tuo amore ma non lo voglio se tu non mi puoi
  amare.')

- I desire sincere friendship and affection between girls and boys.
  I desire it a great deal.

('Desidero un'amicizia e un affetto sincero tra ragazzi e ragazze.
Lo desidero fortemente.')

- For the future, I want a peaceful life, but above all I want to have a
  family to spend beautiful and unforgettable moments with.
  ('Nel mio futuro desidero una vita serena, ma soprattutto desidero
  avere una famiglia con cui trascorrere i momenti più belli e
  indimenticabili.')

- I am dying to see your smile while you talk to me and to touch you
  while you laugh, just once more.
  ('Desidererei da morire poter rivedere il tuo sorriso mentre mi
  parli, poterti sfiorare mentre ridi solo un'altra volta.')

Boys:
- I want to know myself better and be happy.
  ('Io desidero conoscere meglio me stesso e stare felice.')

- I want, always and in whatever way, to have a good time.
  ('Io desidero sempre e comunque divertimi.')

- I want to remain on good terms with my friends.
  ('Desidero restare in buon rapporti con i miei amici.')

- It is natural to desire the other sex.
  ('E' naturale desiderare l'altro sesso.')

This sample shows the same characteristics as the others. Once again, the girls'
responses demonstrate a more developed linguistic and literary aptitude, along
with more alert and lively relational abilities and tastes. More laconic, perhaps
even stereotypical, the boys' sentences reveal an impoverished relational life,
particularly as regards the other sex.

Stereotyped interpretations

Is it possible to assert that the indisputable cultural richness of the girls'
responses is a symptom of alienation? Would that not mean a refusal to recognize their qualities and merits? Does that not still occur in the world of education? Education is still based on the characteristics of the male subject, and
seldom takes interest in the values of the female subject. Subject–object relations, competitive relations with a peer, or peers, within a one–many configuration, and hierarchical relations define the dominant model. What is lacking
is a culture of horizontal relations between different subjects. These values,
so fundamental to human subjectivities and communities, are not taught, but
assumed to belong to the more or less natural universe of the couple or the
family. This error paralyses human development at both the individual and collective level.

Because of a lack of awareness of, or education about, her own subjective specificities, the girl projects all her love, all of her ideals, the whole of herself, onto him – a him who inhabits another world, and who cannot respond to such feelings, desires, or needs. She imagines that he does not want to love her, that she cannot please him, when he is simply incapable of loving her. He does not have the luxury of a choice in the matter. Needing some maternal support from her, a support that he together claims and rejects, he goes on to develop an attachment to the girl, or to the woman, who helps him the most sexually and emotionally. It is true that emerging as a man requires a separation from the mother. The girl falls into the trap of the ambivalent feelings of the boy; her relational and cultural vitality is paralysed, and becomes stereotyped, and at times demanding. The mutual misunderstanding is in fact absolute: she imagines the boy as a prince, or a god, whereas he remains in a tragic relational void, reinforced by the excessive valorization of his sex, a sex he does not even really know what to do with, apart from acting out more or less violently. Education, by supporting the tendencies of the male subject, encourages his isolation until a quasi autism, where the fear of nightmares is accompanied by phantasms of illness or death. I here include two stories written by eleven year old boys in the first year of middle school in Casalmaggiore:

- Once upon a time, Quaccio Mele wanted to pick apples. But while he was gathering them, a poisonous spider bit him and he became sick. He went to the hospital and they operated on him.

   When he left the hospital, he sent his little brother Sbirulino to pick apples. But Sbirulino did not notice anything, and ate the poisoned worm inside the apple. His Mommy brought him to the hospital, but it was too late. The poor little boy died. That is the end of the story. ('Allora c'era una volta Quaccio Mele che voleva raccogliere mele, ma mentre le raccoglieva un ragno velenoso lo morse e lui si ammalò. Andò all'ospedale e l'operarono.

   Quando uscì dall'ospediale, manda il fratellino Sbirulino a raccogliere mele, ma lui non se accorse e si mangia anche il verme velenoso che c'era dentro. La mamma lo porta all'ospedidale, ma era troppo tardi. Poveretto morì. Così finisce la storia.')

- Right after school, Billy went home. He had to cross a field where he saw a big white house that had not been there yesterday. He walked up to it, went in, and saw a great hall with frescoes on the ceiling, and great marble staircases. He went up and saw four doors. He opened the third; it was an empty room. Then he decided to leave, but the walls began to wave back and forth. ('Billy appena tornato da scuola andò verso la casa. Doveva attraversare un campo; vide una casa grande e bianca, che ieri non c'era. Si avvicinò, entrò e vide un grande atrio con degli affreschi sul soffito, delle grandi scale di marmo. Le salì e vide quattro porte. Aprì la terza ed era una stanza vuota. Allora decise di uscire, ma i muri oscillarono.')

The other stories written by boys in the same class also show that boys live alone in a world of phantasms, where exile, abandon, anguish, conflict, illness, and death predominate. For those around thirteen years old – third-year middle-school students – we could add war and murder to the magic already encountered among the younger boys. In their stories, the main character is always male. If this character is not alone, those who are with him are family members, or adults, or friends who are there to help him with a challenge he must meet. But enemies are also present, along with dangerous animals.

In the boys' world, there is no place for a girl or a woman. Sometimes the very young boys refer to Mommy or to a witch, and the older ones to a female mythological character, the enemy of the hero, who seeks to kill him, aided by his wife. When the female world is not completely absent, it is thus represented extremely negatively. The boys' universe is shown to be homocultural or homosocial in the sense that the hero's partners, or the other characters, when there are any, as well as all phantasms, goals and modalities of action or discourse, belong to the male world. All that is accompanied by a creative and linguistic weakness. The stories' themes, as well as other aspects of the text, are generally not invented by the boys themselves but are inspired by the media or culture in general; this is not the case in the girls' responses.

When eleven year old boys are asked to imagine a dialogue between a man and a woman – the only people on earth, as specified by the instructions, whether they are at the beginning of this world or of a new world – their responses are as follows:

- Dialogue between the man and the woman is still a long way off, according to me, and I think that they will speak to each other through gestures.
  ('Secondo me il dialogo fra l'uomo e la donna è ancora lontano e io penso che si parleranno gesticolando.')

- In my opinion, dialogue cannot start right away, but later.
  ('Secondo il mio parere, il dialogo non può iniziare subito, ma in seguito.')

- In my opinion, dialogue between them two cannot begin until they both know how to talk.
  ('Secondo me, il dialogo fra loro due non potrà iniziare finché tutti e due sappiano parlare.')

- He will speak it (the first word) to Eve because she was the only person he can confide in.
  ('La dirà ad Eva [la prima parola] perché lei era la sola persona a cui si poteva confidare.')

    – Dialogue will become more and more frequent, and will be spoken by
      all.
      ('Il dialogo verrà parlato sempre più spesso e verrà parlato da tutti.')

Talking together is also imagined by the boys as if it were like eating together.
When adolescents write notes inviting a female friend to do something with
them, it is almost always an invitation to go out to eat together:

    – Dear X. I kindly ask you to go to the cinema with me. After that, we
      will go to eat a pizza. If you don't want to, it doesn't matter. It is only a
      way of getting to know you better.
      ('Cara X, Ti chiedo gentilmente di venire con me al cinema, dopo di
      che andremo a mangiare la pizza. Se non volessi è lo stesso, per me è
      solo un modo di conoscerti meglio.')

    – Dear Tizia. Do you want to go to the pizzeria with me and then go to
      the cinema until one o'clock? With affection. (name and first name).
      ('Cara Tizia, Vuoi venire in pizzeria con me e poi venire al cinema
      fino all'una? Con affetto. [nome e cognome].')

    – Dear . . ., I would like to invite you to go out with me tonight. We will
      meet in the Mongolfiera pizzeria at half-past eight. You will see: we will
      enjoy ourselves.
      ('Cara . . ., Voglio proporti di uscire con me stasera.
      Ci vediamo alla pizzeria 'Mongolfiera' alle ora 8:30. Vedrai ci
      divertiremo.')

    – Dear . . ., I wonder if you would like to come with me tonight to eat a
      pizza: after we have finished the pizza, I would like to go to the cinema
      to see Titanic.
        When the film is finished, we will go for a romantic walk on the
      beach in the moonlight. Finally, I will accompany you home.
      ('Cara . . ., Mi chiedevo se stasera volessi venire con me a mangiare la
      pizza, poi finita la pizza andrei al cinema a vedere Titanic.
        Finito il film, andremo a fare una romantica passeggiata sulla
      spiaggia al chiaro di luna. Infine ti raccompagnerò a casa.')

Girls' notes propose very different things in a loving context that often includes
an invitation to enter into dialogue. What follows is an example of a note written by a thirteen year old girl:

    – Dear Daniel,
      Ever since I saw you again, my eyes have been shining with joy, like the
      sun and the moon shine on earth.
        On earth, all the plants thirst for water, while I thirst for your love.
      And that is enough, I think, to make you understand how strong my

love is for you. I can tell you that it is enough to give life to a mad soul: mine.

In my universe, there is room for only two stars: we two.

Love me, Daniel; you will not regret it.

Until later [signature].

('Caro Daniele,

Da quando ti ho rivisto, i miei occhi si illuminarono di gioia come il sole e la luna illuminano la terra.

Sulla terra, le piante sono assetate di aqua mentre io sono assetata del tuo amore. E questo penso che basti a farti capire quanto è grande il mio amore per te, e ti dico che questo basta per fare nascere una anima folle: la mia.

Nel mio mondo, c'è posto solo per due stelle: noì due.

Amami Daniele, non te ne pentirai.

A presto [firma].')

How to share space and environment in difference?

Girls and boys, from a very young age, express themselves in a really different way, through language and through their behaviour in general. Examples can be provided from encounters with nursery-school children, as well as from non-experimental observations of daily life. To maintain that difference in their way of expressing themselves is only the result of social stereotypes amounts to denying that girls and boys come into the world in a different relational context. To be born a girl of a woman, that is, of someone belonging to the same gender and with the ability to engender as she does, or to be born a boy of a woman, that is, of someone of a different gender and with whom subjective relations will be complex, notably because it will be impossible to engender like her, leads to a different constitution of subjectivity, that needs to be recognized and cultivated. For a girl, the conditions for becoming of intersubjective relations are favourable, whereas a boy will have to interpose objects and the elaboration of a homocultural or homosocial world in order to emerge from the maternal world and to affirm himself as a masculine subject. One could add that female subjects make love within themselves and not outside themselves, engender in themselves and not outside themselves. This represents an important difference with respect to men, and what is more a woman can contain, in maternity and in love itself, the other gender within herself.

Of course, I could say many other things about my work with children and quote many other examples. I hope that some of you will take the time to visit the exhibition if it is mounted again and, at least and above all, for those who speak Italian, to look at the book *Chi sono io? Chi sei tu?* and at the *Report* that I wrote at the end of my contract as consultant with the Emilia Romagna Region.

Anyway, I would like to explain something about the drawings that children made on this occasion. In fact there are three sorts of drawings:

- drawings that the girls and the boys made while waiting for the group to finish their work: these drawings are often on the same page as the answers to the cue; they bear witness to creativity and also to differences between girls and boys;
- free drawings that were made in the first part of an encounter devoted to drawing itself. One can already observe a great difference between the masculine and the feminine drawings: in the way in which nature, houses, human bodies, encounters between persons, etc., are represented, but also in the use of colours and forms, to allude only to some differences;
- drawings made with the following cue: make a drawing to offer to a friend of a different sex, that is to say, for a girl if you are a boy, for a boy if you are a girl. This cue awakens enthusiasm and creativity from the part of the girls, but resistance and even refusal from the part of the boys. I do not think that the boys are really conscious of that, as is the case for the occurrences of the word 'hate' in the first responses (cf. p. 207); the question, rather, is of their difficulty with being two, in particular for talking or doing something with someone of another sex.

In the drawings, we find the same tendencies as in the verbal sentences:
- the girls:
  - are more creative,
  - prefer relating with another person than with objects,
  - choose a representation in two – directly or indirectly,
  - prefer nature to the technical and fabricated world,
  - prefer a reciprocal relation,
  - prefer colours to forms,
- the boys:
  - generally show less creativity,
  - prefer relations with objects,
  - put the emphasis on themselves rather than on a relation with an other,
  - prefer the technical world to nature,
  - prefer forms to colours.

The way in which a child speaks or lives in is not an unimportant matter. It bears witness to the child's manner of dwelling – of relating with himself/herself, with the other(s), with the world in general. It reveals the child's own world, a world in which he/she lives, a world which takes part in some way in the identity of the child. The traditional education system does not take this into consideration enough. When it begins to pay attention to the specific identity of the child, this attention generally results either in psychological assistance or in secondary strategies used solely in certain classes, for example in art classes. What is then at stake is solely the sensibility of each child, for which a certain space is allowed for expressing itself in an unchanged education system, falling back in this way into the configuration one-multiple, one-many which belongs to the masculine psychic world. Of course, it is not possible to have as many education systems as there are children at school, but passing from the one to the many – as is too often done today – does not allow for a departure from a monogendered culture in order to respect feminine subjectivity and values. Passing from a culture of the one to a culture of the many in fact jumps over a culture of the two, a culture which existed in the past, and is most fitting for women and for relationships in difference, as is shown through the examples of their language. Furthermore, if an education system cannot become appropriate to each subjectivity, it could transform itself to take into account the two worlds which really exist: the masculine world and the feminine world. Such a gesture is absolutely crucial to develop the subjectivity of both girls and boys.

In fact, if the education system is based only on the psychic necessities of masculine subjectivity, it does not favour a cultivation of this subjectivity. It merely confirms its tendencies which correspond to unconscious needs. The boy subsequently becomes more and more enclosed in his own universe, which he confuses with a real and single world. In his world, the masculine subject remains 'I', or the same as 'I', an 'I', or a 'he', who is constructing, appropriating, exchanging things, be they material or spiritual. Generally the masculine subject confronts only his own world and, when he enters into relation(s) with other(s), it is through things, material or spiritual, belonging to the same world. All the subjects are supposed to be sharing this world. The other, in this case, remains a same at the most basic level. And so, boys and men never discover what it means to relate with the other in difference. More generally, they never discover what intersubjectivity signifies. Now relations between subjects founded on a respect for mutual difference(s) are a crucial dimension for accomplishing humanity as such. Capable of so many and such great performances, man remains unable to make his humanity blossom because he lacks the means of gaining access to relations with the other in difference.

New Prospects in Education

If there is something wrong with our world today, it is because it is based only on masculine subjective requirements, which furthermore are in part unconscious and incomplete. For example, relating with the other in difference is needed to fulfil our humanity and to achieve happiness.

Thus the subjectivity of each boy requires a training for him to become able to relate in difference. It is necessary for the blossoming and the happiness of the boy himself, and also for the world in which he dwells and the other(s) with whom he meets. It is all the more necessary since we are entering into a time of multiculturalism. But the relational problems that multiculturalism raises are only a clear emergence of those that concern a universal and daily reality, and result from the difference between the sexes. This is the most basic and universal difference, and one that requires an unceasing weaving between nature and culture.

Boys need another cultivation of their subjectivity than the one which already exists. And this is even more true for girls, because our educational system does not correspond to their needs. Now the capability of girls for entering into communication, for horizontal relations in difference must be cultivated in order that they could pass from an almost natural and affective state to a civil and cultural state. If the boy has to learn how to consider and respect the 'you' and not only the 'I', the girl has to learn how to preserve the 'I' when relating with a 'you'. She also has to discover how to live difference not only as a natural link between man and woman, or mother and son or even girl, but also as a necessity for passing from nature to culture through the recognition of the transcendence of the other as other. In order to meet this other, the girl must learn how to acquire a certain objectivity even in love, without leaving her own subjective, affective and bodily belonging. It is the recognition of the transcendence of the other that can permit her to reach this objectivity, which does not amount to the preference for objects that we observe in the boys' world.

We have serious reasons for working towards changes in the status of sexual, or more exactly sexuate, identity and in communication between the sexes:

1. Such changes will allow us to make progress in human development, thanks to a better differentiation with respect to natural immediacy, both for women and for men, and thanks to a recognition of the other as other, as well as to relations to him, or her, that do not remain subjected to any sort of instinct – thus to domination, possession, or appropriation of the one by the other, even regarding sexual relations and procreation.

2. Change must also be realized towards a mutation in the way of speaking. The masculine subject has until now privileged, in language and in communication, speaking-of; but it is now necessary to cultivate speaking-with. This requires passing from a preference for mental or material objects to a preference for exchange between subjects.

3. Justice requires that we equally respect the characteristics or the merits of both sexes, and the evolution of our civilization needs us to move further in that direction. In an epoch in which the object itself vanishes in relational calculations, it seems essential to cultivate relations between subjects in order that we do not fall into the impasse of a blind nihilism and we escape the effects of the unlimited fragmentation and derealization of the subject. The qualities of feminine subjectivity can be of help in such a cultural evolution.

4. Unless we wish to remain cynical colonialists, because of globalization we are led to open ourselves to the recognition of other cultures. Thus we are forced to question the way in which the values of sameness, of identity, of property and of equality have dominated our logical tradition for centuries. We must also wonder about a conception of universality that is based on these paradigms, a conception whose partial, and thus normatively authoritarian, character is becoming quite clear.

I could suggest other changes that are needed, and show that sexual, or better sexuate, difference can become the principal vector, or at the very least a crucial dimension, for the elaboration of a new culture. A culture that could meet the aspirations and necessities of our times, provided it does not reduce men and women to mere objects of analysis instead of considering difference itself as the source of their relationship and their becoming.

May 2004

Note

1 This talk was given on the occasion of the exhibition of words and drawings of Italian children first at University College London in November 2003 and, second, during the seminar I held at the University of Nottingham in May 2004. I here reproduce the original answers of the samples in Italian with their English translation. As a part of this material was included in the exhibition, I am forced to quote some examples which already appear in the text 'Le partage de la parole' in *Le partage de la parole*, (Legenda, Special Lecture series 4; Oxford: European Humanities Research Centre, University of Oxford, 2001, pp. 1–23), translated into English by Gail Shwab as 'Towards a Sharing of Speech' in *Luce Irigaray: Key Writings* (London and New York: Continuum, 2004, pp. 77–94).

Chapter 19

The Return

Luce Irigaray

Why does Western culture have to start with Greece? Why does such a cut exist with respect to earlier traditions and other cultures? What is it to begin with the Greeks? Would it be an emergence of man as such, which also signifies an exile, a wandering, a growing away from home? Does the same go for all cultures? Does knowing necessarily mean an estrangement from oneself? Or does such a knowledge represent only a required historical passage? A kind of journey to come back home. A sort of sojourn abroad in order to appreciate returning to one's own country, one's own land – as Heidegger commented on some of Hölderlin's poems.

But the country, the land and even the house do not yet correspond to the self. Nevertheless, Western tradition keeps alive such a confusion, probably because its culture is mediatized by exteriority without a cultivation of the interiority of the self. And it is also a culture of uprooting from natural origin and belonging. Western culture corresponds to a culture of the outside, not of the inside. We make plans outside us in order to construct, to love, to know, and then we become, in some way, merely the consequence of the events which take place outside us. We are not that which gives measure to our culture, except indirectly as a result of a going outside ourselves, and of marks that we make or leave there.

About ourselves, we know almost nothing. And even when we imagine ourselves as constructing the world, it is as much this world which constructs us. Our projects with regard to the world are mostly a projection, and an evasion of ourselves, an escape from ourselves. Without a possible turning back to ourselves, in ourselves. In fact, a great part of history amounts to a succession of episodes of our rushing forward to build a world, including a world of knowledge, which little by little substitutes itself for us. A world in which historians will be in search of some traces, some 'skins', as testimonies of humanity's passage on earth.

Parallel to the estrangement from home, from oneself, we find, in Western culture, the theme of the return. It is not a pure coincidence that the text given as a reference to the earliest Greek culture tells us about both the departure of the hero who is going to war and his eventful journey in turning back home.

This double epic gives us an overall picture of our tradition, as do the motive put forward for waging war and the diverse episodes which prevent the hero from returning home. The first part of this prophetic account corresponds to the supposedly positive aspect of our culture, and the second part to its negative or reverse side. The first part talks about the emergence of a world of men amongst men, and the second part about the loneliness of the man who tries to return home. He finally succeeds because of his cunning character, but not without undergoing great trials that perhaps correspond to the stages of a passage from one era of the history to another.

The hero goes back home, but does he return to his self? I am not sure. Perhaps he comes back to the order of the hearth, of marriage, but not to the order of his self, to intimacy with his self. And if we hear many things about his relations with female figures outside the home, it is not the case with respect to his wife. We hear of him defeating his wife's suitors through his ruse and his skill with projectiles, which cause people to remember him. But the suitors seem to want the possession of the goods of the hero rather than love as such. In other cultures, we know a lot about amorous rituals, about the comparison of lovers to divine figures, and about the impact of love itself on the cosmic order. With this first epic of Greek culture, love is already becoming an institution bound to the πόλις, what we would call the State. And lovers already obey external public rules as much as, if not more than, their own affects. They are moving away from nature, from the body, from the economy of affects, and are becoming subjected to external laws.

Nevertheless, the hero still bears witness to self-affection. Ulysses is moved, he weeps, he worries . . . and these affects are expressed in Greek language by the middle-passive or middle voice, a morphologic form which expresses that he is affected in himself, with himself, outside of the economy of the pair of opposites: active–passive. This often happens with a certain loneliness, secretly and without an other sharing the affect. The journey of man is not yet deprived of self-affection, but this seems not to provide him with happiness and is lacking in reciprocity.

For What Western Man Feels Nostalgic?

The journey of Ulysses, his return home, happens before the construction of Western metaphysics, and announces it. After the end or accomplishment of metaphysics, the theme of the return is insistent again. I could cite Hölderlin and Nietzsche, for example, and comment on their feeling of nostalgia for an impossible return. Both of them have been removed from their own self by Western culture – by a Western culture firstly embodied in another thinker – and they cannot turn back to this self. As you know, their journey will end in a kind of madness, even though they are searching for a going back home in a different way. For Hölderlin, the matter is rather one of again finding familiarity or intimacy with a country, a landscape, a house, and also with friends or beloved. For Nietzsche, the matter is one of overcoming metaphysics through assuming an eternal return of the same, by bringing it together in a circle. The two are in search of an access to a beyond of metaphysics, but if they announce the necessity of exceeding metaphysics, they do not succeed in such a surpassing of their path, of their history, of their self. The inability to do that in part comes from the lack of a woman who could help them, above all in their self-affecting through love. They thus have both an intuition of the fact that the solution to their ill-being, to their failure in making their way, cannot be found in their cultural background or surroundings as they are, and that something or someone else has to arrive in order to go beyond such a horizon.

Some thinkers thus seek other values, shrouded or forgotten in our culture. But often their plan is one of integrating these values into our culture in order to improve it, without changing themselves. Once more, the question would be of going abroad in order to stay better at home – in one's own country, one's own culture, one's own home. Some also imagine that the solution to the nostalgia for a return might be a perpetual nomadism – an estrangement from home until one forgets what staying at home could be. In the era of globalization that is ours, we can observe two trends: that of the stay-at-homes who try to preserve at all costs their home, country or culture as they are, and that of the nomadic people who denigrate any home. Both of them disregard the relation with the other, which requires an ability to dwell with the possibility of opening oneself to the other, of leaving home to meet with the other but remaining able to return home, to oneself, within oneself in order to keep the two, the one and the other.

Such a going there and back to home, to the self, within the self, is lacking in our tradition, notably because man has searched for himself outside the self and not by making his way in his own self. And also because he searched for his becoming in objects, things, and their representations or mental reduplications. Man has searched for himself outside the self while intending to appropriate this outside, notably through representations. And this does not correspond to a cultivation of interiority, but to an exile in an external world that he intends to appropriate by means of a technique which reduplicates the real, of a logic through which he makes the world his own, the *logos*.

Why such a wish? And why has man imagined that the key to the happiness which has been lost, to the unaccomplished blossoming, could be found in his culture, his country, his home or language, and not in a maturity that is still to be reached? Why, above all, has man chosen a culture of performance, of know-how, of mastery, including through language, and not a culture of being-with, of speaking-with; that is, a culture of being in relation with the other? Why has man sacrificed a great part of himself to such a cultural orientation? Why has man immolated affectivity, desire and even life itself to a mental mastery? Why has man compared the evolution of Western consciousness to an inescapable calvary – as Hegel wrote in his *Phenomenology of Spirit*? Probably because man has wanted to give himself a proper identity without caring enough about differentiating himself from the relation with the first human with whom he shared life: his mother. He has intended to master the world before becoming conscious of the first world that he formed with her. They originally lived in the same horizon, without a clear separation between two worlds. It is by dwelling in the same world as her that he was born, has grown, has reached the surrounding environment, the external universe. Western man did not interpret such a sharing with, and lack of differentiation from, the mother. And neither the *logos* – a sort of generalized mental bobbin with respect to the world, to speak as Freud – nor the law of a natural, political or spiritual father might allow a passage from the first sensible immediacy of the relation with the mother to a level of consciousness which can transform it without abolishing it.

Western man has remained in some way confused with the maternal world, stuck to it, and no strategy of Western culture has been able to cultivate this first situation or experience. It stays, one could say, absolute and blind. A sort of maternal incest is generalized in Western culture – as is masculine homosexuality. And the taboos surrounding one and the other are all the more virulent since they are not found in the place where the question arises.

Thus what does it mean, the insistence on the theme of the return? In particular, what does the present turning back to Greek culture mean? And to what Greek culture are we turning? Are we in search of a completeness that we have lost? Or are we urged on by a want of something of which our cultural path has deprived us?

With regard to Greek culture, both are at stake, in my opinion. I think that we are trying to find the crossroads at which we have taken the wrong path. I will attempt to give some indications on this point, starting with the notable disappearance of some morphological forms or meanings which still exist in the first Greek culture. As examples, I will take the term ἕτερος, the verbal form called middle-passive or middle voice, and the evolution of the meaning of the word γενος, but also of the value of female or feminine genealogy, all these being accompanied by a loss of a sensible transcendental in the relations with nature and the other, especially the different other.

In the early stages of Greek culture, the word ἕτερος first of all expresses a relation between only two, two who are different and cannot merge into a one, as is the case in the relation with the mother, and also with God. While the word ἄλλος signifies the other in a group or a series, the word ἕτερος means the other of two: for example, the other hand, the other eye and also the other sex or gender. In Greek language, we find 'ἕτερο' as a prefix in many terms. There remain only a few such terms in our language; for example, heterodox, heterogeneous, heterosexual. And, in some of these words, the meaning of 'hetero' has already lost its reference to the number two, and now refers to several, many, not two.

It is fitting to add that the term ἕτερος is not the only allusion to the number two. We also find the nominal and verbal dual form. For example, we could say in English: 'You two are beautiful and you will make it in the cinema'; 'We two are nice and we will leave Paris to help people in difficulty'. In these sentences, the dual form could be used for the verb, and also for the subject and the predicative adjective. It could also be used when there is reciprocity: 'We two love one another'. The dual form does not exist in all cases nor all tenses, and it is employed above all in Attica; in other areas of Greece, the plural is used as well as, and even more than, the dual form.

With regard to the term γένος, I could note that originally this word refers as much to gender or sex as it does to generation, as well as to other meanings. What I would like to emphasize is the fact that the meaning 'generation' or 'genealogy' has gradually supplanted the meaning of 'gender' or 'sex' for which the dual form can be used. I will try to suggest an explanation for this as well as for the disappearance of the morphological verbal form: the middle-passive or middle voice.

The middle-passive or middle voice does not have the meaning of our reflexive, which presupposes a split of the subject, but marks a certain return of the action upon the subject. Thus, it can be partially reflexive – 'I wash my hands' – or reflexive in an indirect way: that is, the subject acts in its own interest – to itself, for itself, from itself. For example, to obtain something for oneself, to remove a danger from oneself. 'To marry' can be expressed by the middle voice (above all for a woman). To return in oneself to draw energy, inspiration, wisdom is also expressed by the middle voice. Sometimes this form can be used when the action's return is on the whole subject, but only if the body alone is concerned, or if it is a question of habits ('I take a swim'; 'To dress oneself'). The middle voice is also used to express reciprocity: 'They love each other'.

I would like to stress the fact that the middle-passive or middle voice is a form which conveys both activity and passivity, and requires an involvement that is not only mental. It can thus express a process of self-affection, and even of reciprocity, that neither simple active nor passive forms could convey. Now, in later cultures, the pair of opposites active–passive, and also the reflexive, will become substitutes for the middle voice. But, if they presuppose a split of subjectivity, which is the norm in our tradition, they do not permit self-affection nor reciprocity.

I will also question the simultaneous disappearance of these terms, meanings and morphological forms, and that of the original representation of the feminine lips, of the female or feminine genealogy, and of a transcendental feeling which could be linked to such an evolution.

Self-affection in the Masculine

The modalities of self-affection are not the same for man and woman, and nor are their lack or perversion the same.

For man, self-affecting is more linked with oneness, with the constitution of a world of his own, with the cultivation of this world until its idealization. As I am not a male subject, it is difficult for me to define what self-affection could be for a man. It would amount to substituting myself for him. I can only question a culture in the masculine. I note, then, that masculine subjectivity did not become differentiated enough from the maternal world. Thus the total relation that the male child has with his mother – the first other for him – has not been cultivated as such and, one could add, has not been submitted to a dialectic process. This has brought about several outcomes:

1 – It is through a division into body and mind, nature and culture, sensible and intelligible that masculine subjectivity has tried to emerge from an undifferentiated link with the first other.

2 – More generally, it is through a logic of pairs of opposites that masculine subjectivity seemingly separated off from its natural and affective origin, but such couplings became substitutes for difference between subjects belonging to the two sexes and, firstly, between the mother and the male child.

3 – Such a logic is thus ordered by genealogy, in particular in relation to certain of the couplings that are decisive for relational life: activity/ passivity, love/hatred, nearness/distance, but also male/female and even I/other(s); and these couplings will have an influence on self-affection and the possible reciprocity between people, especially between two people.

4 – This lack of differentiation from the maternal world prevents the definition of masculine subjectivity as a singular and, above all, a sexuate subjectivity.

5 – Hence the fact that the relations between subjects in our culture are reduced to relations amongst 'ones' or 'somebodies', who are neutralized and can be substituted the one for the other,

6 – And the fact that affect is imposed on the subject from the outside and that it is more a source of imbalance than of harmony, or of enriching becoming; it has thus to be reduced by a turning back to homeostasis.

7 – From this results the necessity of a closed mental world in order to protect the self from affects,

8 – And the absence of subjective difference, first of all of subjective sexuate difference; this has not been recognized and cultivated as such with regard to the mother, and, thus, difference has become in some way only quantitative and, for example, referred to God as the absolute other, the absolutely higher other.

9 – The lack of cultivation of sensible immediacy as an important dimension for the relational becoming of humanity.

The Western masculine subject has maintained an adhesion to the maternal world, which he never submitted to a dialectical process. Beyond the fact that this has paralysed his total becoming, notably his sensible and affective growth, it has perverted his perception of truth. The separation of intelligibility from sensibility does not solve the problem; rather, it denies or represses it. This repression results in a veiling in the perception of truth, which acts in every entering into presence. It is through a certain sleep or dream that man approaches the world. Pretending to unveil truth through his *logos*, by fabricating truth or the world itself by himself, he increases illusion instead of clarifying it. The world that man constructs in this way is a dream world, and such a dream sometimes takes a dramatic turn, as is the case today.

Furthermore, the world that man has built to supplant his adhesion to the maternal world, to assert himself against the mother, against the participation in her world, has become a screen, even a weapon, which intervenes between the masculine subject and himself, and prevents any man from turning back to himself, in himself. Man has fallen into his own cultural trap. He is not only sheltered but also enclosed by his *logos*, becoming a prisoner of his own productions. Even in his attempts to return, or turn around or reverse, he is trapped by substitutes of his unconscious beginnings to which he remains blind. Going back home is perhaps possible after many efforts, after suffering great hardships. Turning back to the self is no longer possible. Without freeing himself from his adhesion to the other, the first other, man cannot return to his self. For lack of cultivation of the sensible relation with his mother, that is, his first affects, man has cut himself off from experiencing his own self-affection.

The masculine culture as it is prevents man from turning back to himself. And even in his tradition, his country, his house, man is not 'at home'. The familiarity or intimacy that he feels is a web of habits or customs, and not a real nearness. Wanting to master the alternation between near and remote through his *logos*, notably by transforming spatial distance into temporality, man has lost the possibility of approaching – the things, the other(s), in particular the other of a different sex or gender. Familiarity has become for him the outcome of mastery, repetition, and even of confusion in worlds – unless it is mediatized by the other, in particular the feminine other. It does not result from a sharing of intimacy, not even with oneself. Self-affection has been confused with a dependence on the surrounding world, through which man believes he touches himself again. But the world which surrounds him is, in part, a substitute for a relation with the mother – a kind of placenta or of construction for mastering the maternal beginning of his life, employing an energy and a world common to the two. Culture, which intends to separate man from the maternal world, uses for its elaboration the relation with the mother herself.

In fact, the autonomy that man has gained is only apparent. Hence, the necessity for him of being and acting violently in order to enter into relations with the other: he tries to break the screen which divides him from everything and everyone. He attempts to demonstrate his competence, his know-how, while, or because, he is lacking in affective education, and even affective feeling, except at the quantitative level. What he feels is more or less intense but seems to be without nuances and singularities.

Not having worked out the first relation to the mother as an intersubjective relation, man merges with her in an energetic sharing, and merges with other men in a world made up of impersonal 'someones'. All men are supposed to share the same culture, the same values, and it is through such a uniformity that they should be affected from an outside – material or spiritual – without each being capable of affecting himself according to his own interiority. But without such an inner economy, affects have an immediate impact on energy; this increases and needs a release, or it spreads and gets lost because of fear, dread and lack of concentration. That which provokes affects is often something which bursts into the closed horizon that man considers his world. That which affects him, in an immediate way, is strange to the man's world, at least to his supposedly own world. And the masculine subject is all the more immediately affected since he has not elaborated in himself a cultivation of self-affection. Thus any affect troubles his usual economy – his homeostasis, as Freud wrote. And this explains why any disruption in his habits, all that which perturbs what is familiar to him – for example, the attraction or desire for the other or the coexistence with a foreigner – must end in a release, must become cancelled in one way or another. The surplus of energy produced by the relation with the other as different cannot be stored and cultivated through the internalization of self-affection. It must be dissipated or invested in things or actions which are part of the surrounding world.

Western man has at his disposal very few markers, very little information to make his way along in the relations with the other. Freud himself did not allude to a possible becoming with regard to sexual maturity, the so-called genitality. He spoke only about procreation, and about its necessity for the happiness of a marriage, the wife becoming able, in this way, to be a mother for her husband, and to give back to him his first lost relational world. Freud did not ask man to renounce his first relation with the mother or to sublimate it. On the contrary, he suggested that the wife has to substitute herself for the mother and become a mediation for the satisfaction of immediate male affects. The family will thus repeat on a small scale the cultural world based on the lack of differentiation between the subject and the maternal world. In any case, this constitutes the surroundings, including as other, which affect man without real self-affection internalized on his part.

In contrast to our culture, the relation with the mother has not been kept in the dark in all cultures, and it seems that the more it is eclipsed as natural origin and first sensible relation, the more it has influence on culture. This repressed dimension in our tradition has ultimately led to an overshadowing of another decisive natural dimension, that of sex or gender. The denial of the importance of the link with the mother has resulted in an emphasis on genealogy to the detriment of gender as sexuate identity. So the Greek word γενος increasingly came to express the vertical, and in some way hierarchical, genealogical dimension, and less and less the horizontal dimension of gender.

But emphasizing genealogy amounts to emphasizing natural reproduction and relations – a stress which is accompanied by many taboos in relation to nature – more than a relational cultivation of desire and love. A cultivation which asks us not to separate spirit from body, mind from affect. A cultivation which also requires each gender to care about its own self-affection, and to respect that of the other. Woman thus has not to substitute herself for the mother of man, but has to cultivate her self-affection as a means of turning back to herself, and helping man in the discovery of his own self-affection – outside or beyond any sensible immediacy in their relations, be it intensely close or possessive.

Self-affection in the Feminine

In contrast to man, woman is familiar with being two. A girl does not form a 'dyad' with the mother but a real duality. The similarity of their bodies and their psyches in their relational dimensions, amongst others with respect to generation, protects them from merging into a unique entity. The two of the mother–daughter couple nevertheless does not suffice in securing an autonomous self-affection. Of course, the two of the mother–daughter couple – which does not amount to the mother–son dyad – can protect the girl from projecting all she has, all she is, onto a masculine subject. But the two of the mother–daughter relation runs the risk of perpetuating an original given situation, which is not yet cultivated as a possibility of a return to one's own self. The adhesion to the maternal world is different from that of the boy, but it can exist as a continuation or a repetition of an original situation, including a situation of dependence with respect to the mother and a given context.

Thus to reassert the value of female or feminine genealogy is certainly useful, above all in allowing woman to relinquish her dependence on masculine genealogy. But going no further than genealogy could be a trap, an obstacle to the becoming of the subject. If dependence on masculine genealogy forces the girl or woman out of her own subjective becoming, going no further than female or feminine genealogy, in particular only in its natural dimension as is too often the case today, generally amounts to an adhesion to a first relation which prevents girls and women from becoming wholly autonomous and accomplishing their subjectivity.

The self-affection of feminine subjectivity cannot stop with the mother–daughter couple. But it has more to do with duality than the self-affection of masculine subjectivity. I suggested that the morphology of the two lips could be a privileged place for woman entering into a process of self-affection. Such a suggestion is supported by personal experience but also by a piece of cultural information. For example, in the archaeological gallery of Syracuse in Sicily, there are many statues of the goddess Kore. Of course, I have listened to the guide emphasizing the statues of gods, and presenting all of these Kore as 'simple women', perhaps only 'maid servants'. He did not know of the existence of the goddess Kore, even though her name was inscribed on the work. But the most interesting aspect was that these Kore do not have the same lips according to the century in which they were sculpted. The most ancient of them have closed lips, which touch one another and could be a good illustration of self-affection in the feminine. In later sculptures, the mouth is open and the lips no longer touch one another. And, finally, the mouth remains open and the lips are also distorted.

You know, I imagine, the story of Kore taken from her mother, the great goddess Demeter, by the god of the underworld. He raped her and kept her in the underworld – even changing her name – until her mother provoked a great famine on earth so that her daughter would be restored to her. You could understand, in this way, that the evolution of Kore's lips is linked to a change in self-affection, which leads her to become dependent on an external instrument, or an other as instrument, for self-affecting, as a boy or man is. You could also perceive here what I try to mean when I talk about the virginity of woman as a condition for autonomy. I allude to an ability to affect oneself through the lips touching one another without any external intervention or tool. It suffices that woman cares about gathering with herself, and remains concentrated on the affect which results from this touching, outside any other intervention or activity. It is interesting to experience what then happens, is felt, notably with respect to the two – that is the other and oneself – in a relationship. Such a gesture allows woman to come back to the self, within the self, and to respect the other, preserving a free space between the two.

How could we save this privileged place of self-affection in order to be able to return within ourselves, to be faithful to our self, and to cultivate our own becoming – a necessary condition for entering into a dual relation with the other which does not amount to a repetition of the first link with the mother? How can we reach a relation in two which does not reduce itself to a 'dyad' or a pair of opposites? This requires another culture to be elaborated. The cultivation of masculine subjectivity does not correspond to the same necessities, thus to the same values, as those of feminine subjectivity. Also, in the case of feminine subjectivity, a process of dialectization of sensible immediacy is necessary but in a different way from that which is needed by masculine subjectivity.

The feminine world is, by birth, more relational than the world of the boy, notably because of the privileged situation of the girl with respect to the mother, a same as the girl. This permits a duality of people from the very beginning, in particular through a relation to engendering different from that of the boy, of man. The girl knows what it means to beget, it is a familiar experience for her already, through intuition or feeling. Turning back to birth, or beyond, does not seem a dangerous abyss to cover, to veil, as is the case for a masculine subject. The problem for feminine subjectivity is how to escape from what is only a natural state, at the level of birth but also at the level of relations with the other(s) – be they the mother, the lover, or the child, for example. What a woman has to do is to maintain an irreducible difference between the other and herself, while preserving her natural origins or roots. This can happen by arranging and keeping a transcendental dimension between the other and herself, particularly the other who belongs to a different origin – the masculine other. The matter, for a woman, is one of interposing between the other and herself a negative that cannot be overcome. Thus the transcendence would not be immediately deferred to the absolute 'you' of a God – who, in fact, then substitutes himself for the mother, the first other – as is too often the case for man in our culture. The transcendental must unceasingly intervene between the other and myself – the 'you' and the 'I' – turning the sensible immediacy of the relation into a cultivation of affect which can save the irreducibility between the other and myself, the insuperable difference between the two – the 'you' and the 'I'.

Self-affection Needs To Be Two

A cultivation of self-affection by each one is what allows for the preservation and the becoming of attraction and desire between the two, by saving the difference between the two. It also permits an individual becoming thanks to a process of going back and forth between the self and the outside with regard to the self – another subject, object, or world.

A cultivation of self-affection seems to be lacking for us, Westerners, in particular for man. Perhaps some mystics and artists tried to approach it? But, even if they felt nostalgic for self-affection, most often they did not succeed in enjoying it. What could allow us to reach such a culture – beyond a cultivation of our own life, for example through a practice of breathing – is a cultivation of the relationship between two subjects, a two different from the dyad formed by the mother and the male child. A cultivation of desire and love between the two sexes and genders is needed, not, firstly, as a sexual relation, but as a relation between two differently sexuate identities, whose self-affections are different and needed as such. This 'two' can help man to leave a horizon built without a real differing from the mother's world – except through the neutralization of a 'someone', a so-called neuter or neutral subject. It can also help him to escape the prison of loneliness and the dependence on the other or external objects for self-affecting. Desire, in fact, affects an energy internal to the subject and appeals to another subject, to reciprocity with another subject. At least it should be so. Otherwise, it is not a question of desire, rather of instinct or drives. But only desire is really human.

Thus the relation between two is that which can help man, and also woman, to gain access to an autonomous and internalized self-affection. At the grammatical level, one could say: to return to the middle-passive or middle voice as a way of internalizing, the middle-passive and not the opposition between active and passive: to affect/to be affected, which is perhaps fitting to the parents–children relationship. This pair of opposites, which we have inherited from the first relation with the mother, has often been transferred between man and woman, with a reversal at the level of polarity: man becoming generally active with respect to woman, except, for example, in masochistic behaviour. But if the opposition active/passive becomes a substitute for the middle voice, replaces it, such an opposition prevents us from cultivating our affects towards their internalization and cultural becoming, amongst other things through reciprocity.

An anonymous world formed by 'someones' also leads us to the passivity of each one in relation to affects coming from the outside, and does not allow the economy of the middle voice, which requires us to pass from the outside to the inside of the self. A passage that only a relation between two permits, a relation that our tradition has deferred onto a unique God, whom humans would meet in another world.

Self-affection, expressed by the middle-passive or middle voice – and not an alternation between active and passive – is dependent on a relation in two: two who are different, even if they can form sometimes a whole, and who are not united by genealogy or hierarchy.

To Conclude

In Greek culture, we still find the existence of the middle-passive or the middle voice, of the verbal and nominal dual form, and of a pronoun – ἕτερος – which

expresses the relation in two or between two, two who are different, a difference that will later take on the value of subjection or opposition. The pronoun
ἕτερος does not have the same meaning as ἄλλος, which is closer to our word:
other. This ἄλλος – or other – in fact refers to any other and not to this other
with whom I am in relation as two. The word 'other' is suitable for a world of
'someones' but does not favour the relation with an other as different. It refers
to a neuter or neutral, or better a neutralized, other, a kind of abstract individual about whom we can speak, but whom we would meet only with difficulty
as a concrete and living other. It seems that we could communicate between
'someones', but we exchange only through a supposedly common world; and
this does not yet reach a communication between subjectivities.

Our nostalgia for a return, amongst other things to Greek culture, could arise
from a want of a return to our own self, within our own self, through self-affection. Cultivation of self-affection by woman as such seems to be the path which
could allow man to leave the maternal world to reach his own self-affection.

Self-affection is not secondary nor unnecessary. Self-affection – which once
more does not amount to a simple auto-eroticism – is as much necessary for
being human as is bread. Self-affection is the basis and the first condition of
human dignity. There is no culture, no democracy, without the preservation of
self-affection for each one.

Self-affection today needs a return to our own body, our own breath, a care
about our life for us not to become subjected to technologies, to money, to
power, to neutralization in a universal 'someone', to assimilation into an anonymous world, to the solitude of individualism.

Self-affection needs faithfulness to oneself, respect for the other in their singularity, reciprocity in desire and love – more generally, in humanity. We have
to rediscover and cultivate self-affection starting, at each time and in every situation, from two, two who respect their difference, in order to preserve the survival and the becoming of humanity, for each one and for all of us.

May 2005

Note

An earlier version of this text was presented for the first time on the occasion of the conference based on the writings of Luce Irigaray on Ancient Greek
thought that took place at Columbia University, New York City, in October
2004, and will be published in the proceedings of this conference, *Re-writing Difference: Luce Irigaray and 'the Greeks'*, ed. by Elena Tzelepis and Athena
Athanasiou (forthcoming SUNY Press).

Chapter 20

Listening, Thinking, Teaching

Luce Irigaray

Listening

Western tradition is founded on looking-at rather than on listening-to. In our tradition, listening is at the service of looking, especially with regard to teaching. From a certain moment of Greek culture, the master has taught the disciple that which he has already perceived; that is, that which he has already seen. All the world is, in a way, transformed in a gathering of objects that the master has to perceive – that is, to see – in an appropriate way, and to arrange into a parallel world thanks to his language, his linguistic logic, his logos. The discussions, the presumed dialogues, between master and disciple are based on the correct perception of the things or objects of the world and their correct arrangement in a whole. Thanks to his logos, the master constructs a kind of doubling, a kind of mental doubling, of the external reality. He grasps the external world and builds a sort of parallel world that he always keeps at hand.

Of course, the construction of this world always at hand is extremely difficult: the question is how to transform a multiple and various present reality into only one world always at hand. This requires the establishment of a pyramid of values linked together, in which the more permanent will supplant the more present, living and impermanent reality. The discussions or presumed dialogues between the master and the disciple thus develop based on the relevance of the designation or denomination of a thing of the world and its integration into the pyramid of values, but they both remain faithful to a way of relating together in which the two are subjected to a third world imposed on them and that is considered as the truth that they have to adopt in order to enter a cultural world.

Most of the time our way of teaching remains close to that of Socrates, with the difference that Socrates was constructing a new culture whereas we are obeying a tradition that already exists. The teacher thus transmits to the disciple the parallel constructed world that he, or she, has received in inheritance from their own teacher, and that they made their own world. This world is considered as the real and unique truth because it corresponds to the world at hand adopted by the teacher in our tradition.

Now this way of teaching is no longer appropriate to our times. It presupposes that only one world can amount to the universal truth, and it does not take into account that different worlds exist which do not envision the truth in the same way. There is no doubt, for example, that Socrates and Buddha do not share the same conception of the truth, and that it would be difficult to decide on the best truth in order to introduce their prospects into a unique pyramid. Their truths are different and we have to respect these differences if we want to be respectful of truth itself.

In our era, it becomes obvious that the truth is neither unique nor universal, and that we have to take into account various views and constructions of the world. How can we face up to this situation? In part by substituting listening-to for looking-at in any dialogue, at the very least by inverting the privilege of the one with respect to the other. Of course, the question then is not to simply listen to an abstract and presumed universal truth that we ought to share after our discussion, a truth that we could transform into universal mental images, but to listen to the way in which the other envisions and constructs their truth.

Little by little, this undoes our pyramid of values and elaborates another relation to truth in which the two worlds intertwine. The problem for us, as Westerners, is that it is no longer a question of mastery, but one in which we have now to let be done as well as to do, to let be as well as to be. We then imperceptibly enter another logic, another culture.

No doubt, the question is complex. For example, to listen to someone from another culture requires us to question the language used by each one. To pass from one language to another is the most important gesture for entering into multiculturalism. It also represents the most important resistance or difficulty we have to face in coexisting and sharing between cultures. This resistance and difficulty lie in our relation to language. The nationalism which is overcome with greatest difficulty is linguistic nationalism. We are moulded by language: it is not only a question of understanding each word. Words are endowed with another meaning in each language: more concrete or abstract, more sensible or mental, more subjective or objective, more relational or solipsistic, more in relation with an object or with another subject. When I seek the translation of a French word in the English dictionary, I am frequently surprised by the difference of meaning attributed by Anglophones to a similar term. Thus the question is not only one of listening to words, but also to the linguistic and cultural context in which they take place, to the world that they compose and construct.

To pass from one language to another requires a listening that is not only listening to words which supposedly convey a universal meaning. The matter is one of agreeing to be questioned by a different meaning, by a world whose sense remains invisible to us but which we agree to welcome, by which we agree to be questioned and touched when listening to it. Listening, then, does not amount to grasping something in order to integrate and order it into our own world, but to opening one's own world to something or someone external and strange to it. Listening-to is a way of opening ourselves to the other and of welcoming this other, its truth and its world as different from us, from ours.

Perhaps you are thinking that I am talking about a new subject to be taught: we ought today to teach students respect for other cultures. Of course, this is the case. But, more generally, I am talking about teaching itself. In a traditional education, the master expounds the truth and the disciple listens to his discourse. If we agree with the fact that the truth is not unique nor universal, the master also has to listen to the truth of the disciple. Of course, I am not alluding here to a mere psychological truth; for example, to some problem which could prevent the student from listening to and learning the ideal truth that I, as the teacher, have to teach him, or her. Rather, I am talking about a comprehensive truth which is proper to each one, and that we have to hear from one another.

The master and the disciple have to listen to one another to hear the human truth that they each convey. This preserves the singularity of each one, the two being in relation, and the horizontal relationship between their subjectivities.

Keeping being two in the relation between master and disciple also allows a community of students to be formed which respects the singularity of each one, instead of constituting a group of somebodies composed by their submission to a supposed common third already existing, or to the authority of the master functioning as a third term.

This also allows us to keep open the dimension of the present and the presence in teaching. Of course, the past experience of the teacher has to be respected, but it has to be put at the service of a present relation between master and student, which cannot amount to subjecting the present time and the entry into presence of the two to the past.

Such a gesture leads the teacher to question his or her own thought and to maintain it alive and loving. I could here borrow a word from Nietzsche affirming that such a gesture can protect teaching, and firstly each teacher, from resentment and revenge. In fact, resentment and revenge take the form of confining oneself to the past and of imposing this past on the other. Our way of teaching often involves a risk of resentment and revenge, resulting from our past submission to an authoritarian education. Once more, I do not refer to a mere psychological authority but to the imposition of a certain truth as being the only and universal truth that is to be learned. Of course, our way of subjecting the student to our own past education could also result from the fact that this education has transformed us into parrots or machines, because of a lack of listening to our own global being, and thus our becoming unable to be and do better. But I think that there anyway exists a resentment and revenge in our manner of teaching, that is a refusal to open ourselves, to welcome the youth of others, especially of our students, and so help them to make their own path towards the future. Too often we submit students to a past time in educating instead of awakening them to their present time and their task of preparing for a future proper to each one, sometimes for a future shared with the teacher in supplement. The teacher has to be the one who awakens younger people to the present and the future, and not the one who subdues and sometimes kills, in the name of education, the desires of students towards the present and the future, and their positive presentiments and plans.

The teacher has to avoid both the imposition of a past education and a demagogic nihilism which lets the student think, say and do anything and everything, without fulfilling the task of teaching, that is, of guiding, of helping the other to discover one's own path, to enter the space and time of his or her proper life and to accomplish it as a human being.

Teaching cannot amount to imposing on the other our knowledge, our competence, including through a paternalistic or maternalistic generosity. Teaching not only consists in speaking, but in being capable of remaining silent too, of withdrawing in order to let the other be, become and discover his or her path, his or her language.

Listening to the one whom we are teaching is also a means to educate them about the fact that the truth of each one crosses the path of the other, and that the matter then is both one of opening to the other, of listening to his or her truth, and of being faithful to one's own path, one's own truth. That is to say, of remaining able to return to ourselves without intending to become the other or to ask the other to become us. The problem is thus, at each crossroads, of encountering the other as other while remaining two.

In a way, the same could be said about the world. We have to meet the world, in particular the natural world, as other, to respect it instead of appropriating it into only one world: our world. Education ought to teach how to respect and contemplate the world, and not only how to grasp and master it, as has been too often the case in our Western culture.

Thinking

After listening to the other and to the world – and not only the world built by us – we have to return home, to return to ourselves, within ourselves. Teaching requires us to be, and not only to have knowledge. If the question were only one of communicating knowledge, a machine could substitute for the teacher. But a machine cannot be the substitute for a certain way of being, that the master has gained through his or her own training, his or her own experience of life, his or her own path.

In fact, the most important thing that a teacher has to pass on is a way of being more than a way of having, a way of being a someone and not a something. The Eastern masters taught me that transforming myself is the most important undertaking. To accomplish this task, we have to become able to be, to dwell, and not only to amass knowledge and techniques. The knowledge and techniques that do not work towards the transformation of our being risk harming us and the other(s), in particular our students. They contribute towards an exile of ourselves, that we transmit to the other(s) instead of being at the service of becoming ourselves, of accomplishing ourselves.

What is of use for this task is thinking. Thinking is not a luxurious activity reserved for a few people; thinking has to be an everyday task for each one. Thinking is the time of turning back to the self. Thinking is the time of building one's own home, in order to inhabit one's self, to dwell within the self.

Such a dwelling must unite in each one the past, the present and the future. Such a dwelling can exist only if we devote ourselves to building it at every moment. It is never built once and for all. And it is when we are building it that we can stay in ourselves. Thus dwelling is proper to each one. And it is because we are dwelling in ourselves that we can exchange with the other, with others.

Thinking is not a merely mental undertaking, nor a mere technical process. Thinking is, or ought to be, an activity of the whole being. In order to build a home in which to live, we have to use our body, our imagination and intelligence. Dwelling concerns the all that we are. Thought can coordinate, gather together, a thought that is not only abstract, logical and technical, but rather a living thought that the heart inspires and guides.

Thinking has to secure the return to home, the dwelling within oneself for reposing, for a becoming of one's own, for preparing future relations with the other, with the world.

Thinking must be the task of everyone. Thinking is especially the task of the teacher. The teacher has to build his or her own dwelling in order to help others to build their proper dwelling. The teacher has to teach the students how to dwell and how to find and keep a way of thinking that allows each one, but also present and future humanity, to dwell.

This implies that we question that which we too often consider as education. Teaching is generally understood as passing on – not to say instilling – knowledge, know-hows, techniques to students. Then teaching no longer has to do with humanity as such, and the teacher today becomes useless – as is the case for other workers. A machine can become a substitute for him or her. The teacher remains necessary only in so far as relations between humans in the name of thinking are concerned.

A few perils endanger thought in our times. The imperialism of the sciences and techniques, but also that of customs and habits, and of opinions or beliefs. And an arrogant criticism too which leads to a worse nihilism and sometimes amounts to personal psychic problems or cultural decay. And a wish to act merely for the sake of acting. I could add some other dangers resulting from our Western tradition: granting primacy to the mind and forgetting concrete and sensible experience; privileging appearance and visibility to the detriment of invisible reality; wanting to actively master without agreeing to passively receive, etc.

Thus one of the dangers of our times is acting merely for the sake of acting. Daring to act before thinking in part aims to surmount our Western logic and rules. Teaching then amounts to teaching acting. Then one could say that the relations between the teacher and the student are not really different from those between machines. Teacher and student could be replaced by robots, and teaching by a software programme to be inputted into the learning robot.

No doubt, acting merely for the sake of acting represents one of the present dangers for thinking, and more generally for humanity, through useless competitions with machines. To act merely for the sake of acting is also a slogan of totalitarian regimes which avoid thinking and prevent relations amongst people through thinking. To act merely for the sake of acting develops a culture of both competition and uniformity. Furthermore, some people consider acting merely for the sake of acting as creativity, while most of the time it only amounts to what

Freud called an acting-out; one could also say, the actualization of the unconscious input of a software programme.

The input of a software programme can today correspond to a sort of universal programme that it would be fitting for all of us to share. In this way, what thinking was in the past becomes a doctrinaire approach with a single path that, furthermore, intends to provide us with the real itself. In fact, in our times, a way of thinking could be imposed on us by means of techniques – amongst other things, the techniques of the media – that succeed in creating a global opinion or belief which our epoch would need for its survival. The exclusive privilege of the sciences can contribute to this, all the more so since they are now supported by technical methods and instruments which defy human experience. The sciences, techniques and globalization, amongst other things, are all gathered to prepare a global thinking, the imposition of a unique thought: a sort of totalitarianism without representation nor representative, but which is capable of abolishing humanity as such. Any thought, any way of thinking may obey a unique or doctrinaire approach. Thought is never under way once and for all. And a single impetus or impulse can never suffice in order that its programme could correctly develop.

Thinking always takes place between different paths. That is not to say that it spreads itself between this and that: some field or other, some thinker or other, some culture or other. Thinking requires that one remain faithful to one's own path. But this path needs a constant questioning, and questioning opens different possible ways. The problem is what path is to be taken in order to be faithful to one's own path.

Thinking demands faithfulness and opening, perseverance and initiative. Thinking is a journey, an internal journey, which has to take into account the past and the future, and to trace a path between the two. In the present, thought questions; it notably asks questions about the path. One of the modalities, one of the methods of questioning is to open oneself to the other. In our tradition, it is usual to consider dialogue as a relation between one person who is already capable of thinking and another person who is learning how to think, that is, between a master and a disciple or a student who have to agree on one and the same truth, valid for the two, and beyond them. Truth is then considered to be an objectivity external to the two, which has nothing to do with their relation and on which they have to come to an agreement after discussion.

In my opinion, a dialogue must be held between two different subjects who dwell in different worlds and do not share the same truth. In other words, the dialogue has not only to be held between two more or less competent subjects who have to come to an agreement about a third term, an object. A dialogue has to be held between an 'I' and a 'you' who are different and must remain different; then the exchange between them aims to light the way of each one and to prepare a possible coexistence between two worlds, two cultures, two truths, two places or spaces, two times.

As we are accustomed to transforming everything and everyone into representations, we immediately want to imagine who I am and who you are. But in this way we abolish the difference between I and you, and a dialogue cannot take place. If I can imagine who or what the other is, and transform them into representation, he or she no longer exists as other. The other is the one who escapes my way of imagining, and more generally that of Western culture. The other as other is the one who can question this culture without abolishing it. The other indicates the beyond of our culture without for all that annihilating it, notably through criticism.

The other is the one who can question us about our path. The other crosses our path and compels us to question our journey.

The other is the one who teaches us even when we are their teacher. For example, as they belong to another generation, the students challenge the teacher to discover a truth different from his or her own. And this is especially right today. Because of the imperialism of the sciences, because of the power of techniques, because of globalization, what we have to teach today is no longer what we have learned in past times. The subjects to be taught and also the methods of teaching are now different. The matter is no longer one of teaching how to reach a cultural horizon already existing. The matter is no longer one of teaching mere criticism. The matter is, rather, one of thinking what humanity could be as such, and what culture could be suitable for humanity. What we have to learn in our times is how to govern the world – as Nietzsche said. And this task does not amount to working out giant programmes, universally valid summaries, integrations of data into software packages that could be used on a global scale. All that is continually removing us from what we have to learn: what or who a human being essentially is.

In our times, we consider liberty to be the fact of living from day to day, quickly, outside of any responsibility. All that exhausts and destroys our humanity, which we then try to restore with social welfare, medical care, cultural pastimes and a supplement of morality. Education ought to escape the need for restoration. It must provide for the totality of being – and Being – and the capability of securing our proper becoming.

Another thing: thinking cannot content itself with going with or going against, an alternative which has ruled our Western history. This game of subjection and rejection is not sufficient for thinking and teaching thought. It falls to us to transform these games of for and against into another logic, a logic of coexistence in difference: a difference which cannot be quantitative, which cannot be reduced to some more or less, some for and against. A difference which is qualitative, irreducible, and must take into consideration the other as such and not only the things of our world, a state to which the other has too often been reduced.

The quantitative relation between material or spiritual things is then moved and it becomes a qualitative difference between persons. Through this transfer of difference from one place to another, we enter another era of thought. This requires us to freely give up a quantitative logic – based on the same, on equality-to, on identity-with, etc. – in order to have access to another logic.

Teaching

Western logic is today challenged in different ways: technology, globalization, the sciences, the outcomes of the works of Western thinkers and culture, etc.

These various elements could deprive us of any logic, of any moderation, of any reason if we do not quickly adopt another logic. To stop at criticism cannot be sufficient because this does not allow us to have access to another logic.

We have to relinquish a certain way of being moulded by our past logic in order to reach another way of Being. Such a passage asks of us both discipline and renunciation. We have to give up some perspectives in relation with the absolute, with the infinite, with the domination of the world and with reason itself. But this gesture is henceforth necessary to secure a future for humanity. Without such a gesture, criticism of our values risks ending in a worse nihilism, in the destruction of humanity itself, including through an attempt to impose on a global scale what subsists of our values: a kind of imperialistic economy and expertise which are not specific to humanity itself.

Of course, there exist other cultures which perhaps have greater resources to secure a future for humanity. It would be desirable that our Western cultures learn some truths from them, instead of seeking to surmount them with the risk of being surmounted themselves.

We have no alternative but to invent another logic. Even the predicative logic, on which Western thought and truth are based, can no longer meet the problems we are facing: the entry of women into discourse, the exchanges with other cultures, the outcomes of Western culture, that is, the influence of technology, the destruction of nature, the solipsism, indeed the annihilation, of the subject himself. We Westerners cannot impose our logic on all people, on all the peoples of the world. We rather have to listen to those who talk, think and act according to another logic than our own. All our more or less paternalistic or maternalistic gestures of integration are not equal to the sense that we have to discover and to elaborate for the present and the future: a sense that could be shared by all men and women of our planet. In fact, the most important thing we have to learn and teach is: how to communicate in difference without destroying our own values, without destroying the other or ourselves. Hence the necessity of building a home, a subjectivity, a being, to which we can return, and in which we can repose and restore ourselves in order to be able to leave our home, to open ourselves, to open our world to a global dimension, caring each time about the otherness of the other.

The consideration and the respect for the otherness of the other introduce us to another relation to transcendence. And this is a crucial step for reaching another logic and entering into multiculturalism. In our Western culture, transcendence is defined as a dimension outside us, beyond us, whether it is a question of things or of the other. Transcendence thus corresponds to an absolute, an ideal, a model beyond our reach and which imposes the law on us from on high, outside of our capability of estimating and experiencing its real value. Most of the time in our tradition, the master bases his or her authority on the relation that they have to such a transcendence, and their authority then becomes as unattainable as transcendence itself. Since the fall of the idols, this kind of authority no longer operates. But the fall of past idols as well as the lack of authority of the master can lead us to worse situations. I think, for example, of the exercise of a power lacking in any content on the part of the master but also on the part of the student, or even of the statement of our duties by a group of political, religious or academic people, who mistake an administrative task for establishing authority over others in the name of truth. All that is rather terrifying but fashionable today. And it is not a mere coincidence that it is now so often a question of totalitarianism. In fact, we are threatened by all sorts of totalitarianisms more subtle, imperceptible and destructive than those that we have already known. We are also put in danger by despair about a possible future for humanity. Now to envision and construct our future is the first and most basic gesture towards transcendence. A gesture which remains within our reach and asks courage and undertaking of us, but not blind faith in an unattainable ideal or absolute.

How could we thus replace the past ideal of transcendence and the conception of authority related to it? How could we release transcendence from the prison of entities in which it has been fixed by our past culture? From spiritual idols in which we no longer trust and which, furthermore, are not the same for all traditions and do not favour coexistence and peace between human beings.

To recognize and to respect the other as other can correspond to both a transcendence at work in the construction of a future on our scale and the transcendence which lies in someone or something which remains irreducible to us without being, for all that, beyond our reach, as the absolute of the ideal or God is. The other as other is, in a way, further beyond our reach than God himself because God has still been imagined starting from ourselves. God is made in our image. God is a subject, our subjectivity, but so perfect that no comparison between us is possible.

In some way, we can imagine God but we cannot imagine the other as other. And if the negative works on the attributes or the predicates of God in comparison with ourselves, the negative works on the subject itself when it is a question of the otherness of the other to which I am alluding – for example, the otherness which takes place between the sexuate identities.

We could say that God is our subjectivity in its pure or absolute state, while it is not the case for the other as such: the other is an other, that is, a different subject. With the other recognized as other, we enter another relation to transcendence. A transcendence whose elaboration and safeguarding are now incumbent upon us, as it has been incumbent upon the Greek philosophers to define the kind of transcendence that we have now to relinquish, to abandon.

Entering another relation to transcendence asks of us responsibility and effort. It is no longer a question of approaching an unattainable perfection, situated outside of our subjectivity, of our world, of which it nevertheless represents a model. The task is rather of transforming ourselves at every moment in order to respect and care about the subsistence and becoming of both myself and the other, that is, of two radically different subjects. The journey is now more internal and the other is no longer the one – the One – whom I have to become, even though I know that this Other is unattainable. On the contrary, the other is the one whom I must keep different from me. It is by maintaining the difference between our two subjectivities that I construct transcendence, mine and, as far as is possible, that of the other.

Such an elaboration cannot be only, or even above all, mental as it was for past transcendence. It happens through a transformation of our whole being. This implies the gathering of all that we are: body, breath, heart, word, mind, and their transformation into a more perfect humanity through a transmutation, a transfiguration of matter that, nevertheless, remains matter. A matter of another nature, less subjected to inertia, endowed with energetic capabilities which stay unknown when body and mind are kept separate and we do not enter into a relation with the other as other. Which provides us with new energetic resources.

Then authority can exist, an authority that results from our becoming human in a more accomplished way. An authority that imposes nothing if not a certain respect, attention and questioning. An authority that can awaken the other(s) to a beyond with respect to their present state and open a way to the future. An authority that calls the other to a transformation of himself or herself, to a becoming with the accomplishment of humanity in view. An authority that does not amount to the exercise of a power that is more or less repressive, but is teaching itself. Teaching has always to deal with becoming and with transcendence. The question is how we can teach a becoming towards transcendence that does not bring us again into our subjection to past idols. In other words: how can we teach the other to transcend himself or herself instead of submitting to the sorts of transcendence already existing?

This task seems to me appropriate to our times. It allows us to coexist in difference. It imposes on us a duty: to make transcendence exist beyond the fall of past idols. It teaches us how to respect difference amongst ourselves, instead of difference becoming a source of conflicts and wars, notably between transcendences or idols. It entrusts to us a becoming of humanity on our scale in an era in which we feel despair about the possibility for a future. It permits us to use the sciences, including social and psychological sciences, and also techniques in a manner which is not destructive for humanity.

In the seminars that I held at the University of Nottingham, I tried to teach in this way. I would like to thank this university again, in my name and in the name of all the participants in the seminars, for the hospitality offered on this occasion.

June 2006

Afterword

Michael Worton

University College London, United Kingdom

Luce Irigaray is rightly celebrated for her thoughtful unveilings of the gendered dimensions of social discourses, and she is undoubtedly one of the most signifi-cant – and most distinctive – voices of modern feminist thinking. However, it is important to recognize that her work and its implications go well beyond the boundaries of gender studies. She has written on fields ranging from art and architecture to education, to linguistics, to political theory, to theology, and her work is studied in schools, colleges and universities across the world, as well as increasingly shaping policy-making.

Underpinning all her work is a commitment to expose the prejudices that determine behaviours and prevent us from living more openly and more in dia-logue with others, with ourselves, and with what we do and say. Challenging and provocative, her work is a significant ethical intervention into debates about how we live today.

Irigaray is, above all, concerned with the relationship between philosophy, or thought, and collective and individual behaviour. In her work, she has con-sistently and forcefully argued that what we often call 'the Western tradition' is grounded in a desire to master the physical world. Nevertheless, this mastery – which is a quintessentially masculine drive and activity – seeks to construct a human, social world whose force and durability is derived from the fact that nature is harnessed and exploited in ways that ultimately, and determinedly, sever humankind from direct contact with the essence and the movements of the natural world. As Irigaray reminds us, this culture is one created by men and largely for men, and is one which continues to promote, as well as depend on, an androcentric world-vision that maintains a system of structuration and divisions as a result of male domination.

A striking feature of the Western tradition is that it is based on the logic, and the teleology, of identity and sameness. In this tradition, otherness gives rise to uncertainty, even to fear – as is seen particularly strongly in national anxieties in the West about immigration. This can lead only to ever deeper retrenchment into narrow, self-protective identities, whereas what we need to do is fully to recognize difference, complex and daunting as that can be. We then have to embrace otherness and finally – the most difficult step of all – be inhabited by otherness, and have all of our behaviour informed by dialogue with alterity, and even plural alterities.

The notion of dialogue is at the heart of Irigaray's thinking, and also of her practice. For instance, she chose the title *Dialogues* for a conference organized around her work in Leeds in 2001 – *International, Intercultural, Intergenerational Dialogues about the Work of Luce Irigaray*, and published the proceedings – in a special issue of *Paragraph* in 2002 – with dialogic interventions from her. The Irigarayan dialogue is on the one hand a new pedagogic form of Socratic dialogue; it is also more than a two-way interaction, calling out to others, and involving others, in an ongoing conversation towards discoveries.

For Irigaray, sexual difference is 'a reality which constrains us to pursue the becoming of consciousness, that leads to a new stage of the development of humanity. But without enacting this stage, the human as such does not exist' ('Questions', in Florinda Trani, 'From the same to the other', in *Dialogues*, p. 65). As she repeatedly makes clear, sexual difference is to be conceived in broad terms, because 'subjectivity is constituted differently by man and woman and [...] they live in two worlds foreign to one another' ('Questions', in Heidi Bostic, 'Reading and rethinking the subject in Luce Irigaray's recent work', in *Dialogues*, p. 30).

It is undoubtedly true that in modern times 'the relationship with alterity is, paradoxically, more and more foreign to our day-to-day behaviour' (Irigaray, 'Beyond All Judgement, You Are', in *Key Writings*, p. 66), as we struggle to negotiate a world that is increasingly complex. The Western tradition has taught the (male) subject the importance of having regard for truth and of respecting and dealing with his equals – by which he means those who share in the same world and the same identity as him. His cultural conditioning, however, can lead him so to privilege equality that he chooses to deny alterity as alterity, engaging in paternalistic processes of assimilation, with, as Irigaray reveals, serious consequences:

> While he may be overwhelmed by the problem of alterity, the strategy adopted by him will be to raise the other to the status of an equal and similar – a woman is as good as a man, a black is as good as a white – rather than to educate consciousness to perceive itself as limited, both on the level of sensibility and on the level of thinking. At worst, the masculine *I* will accept to descend, in his own eyes, a few levels in his established intellectual performances. Isn't a man feminine too? And isn't a white man also a little black?' (op. cit., p. 72; italics in original)

What is fascinating in Irigaray's work is the way in which she treats difference as a phenomenon, rather than simply as a problem. For her, difference is something that all human subjects need to analyse and creatively engage with, instead of seeking to marginalize it, deny it, or obliterate it. Respect for the difference(s) of the other is crucial in all exchange, whether this be linguistic or amorous. But it is important to move beyond that respect towards a new and more complex mode of living out identity. Identity is not about self-identity, or is only in part about self-identity – which, in any case, is itself seamed-through by difference. To use Irigaray's terms, identity must always be 'relational'. And 'relational' identity is always in a state of becoming. In an interview in 1996, she described her thinking in anthropological terms 'When I speak of relational identity, I designate that economy of relations to the self, to the world and to the other specific to woman or to man. This identity is structured between natural given and cultural construction' (Stephen Pluháček and Heidi Bostic, 'Thinking life as relation', in *Man and World*, 29, p. 353).

In her thinking, Irigaray steers a careful but creative course between essentialism and cultural relativism, aware of the dangers of each, but not wholly denying them. Indeed, one of the most engaging dimensions of her work is its openness and its *inclusiveness*. This does not mean any lack of rigour; on the contrary, she obliges us to scrutinize attentively every sentence and even every word, in a quest for meanings that will make sense of the world.

While there is rigour in her thinking, there is also poetry in her expression. In her writing, she uses voices from philosophy, sociology, linguistics, theology, history and so on, fusing these all into a single distinctive voice marked by what one might call 'a discursive diversity'. And, remarkably, the Irigarayan voice holds together, whilst also declaring its own referential and allusive complexity. In this, it is a linguistic enactment of the kind of diversity that is the focus of her thinking.

Irigaray does not like to repeat; rather, she seeks always to innovate, to invent – in the sense not so much of creating *ex nihilo* but of discovering, of coming upon new perspectives, of learning to listen with another ear and to speak in a new language, one which is always potentially within our standard discourses and grammatical structures.

An abiding concern for her is the fact that our inability satisfactorily to establish and maintain communication not only indicates a failure in social interactions, but leads to dysfunction both at the individual and at the collective levels:

> Since communication between us has not been put at the centre of our becoming human, we have become a little mad. For example we say that something is the very truth, but we do the opposite, divided in this way between saying and doing, perhaps because we do not produce a discourse of our own. We repeat, on the one hand, and we act, on the other. (Irigaray, 'Conclusions', in *Dialogues*, p. 207)

For Irigaray, dialogue or conversation must always be about discovery, a voyage into unknown territory whilst also being built on sacredness. This operates in terms of the relationship with the other, who can never be fully known, but who, for this very reason, is therefore a possible *you* and who, thanks to his or her irreducible and unappropriable difference, can ensure that they – or we – both can live again in and through duality and dialogue.

This also operates in our reconnecting with our own cultural traditions. Irigaray has written movingly about how she has for years 'navigated on the raft of [the] truths [and] dogmas' of the Roman Catholic tradition which is an important part of her cultural tradition, speaking of how she has been 'wounded by them' and thus 'distanced [herself] from them', but has returned to these 'truths and dogmas' in order to interrogate them, strengthened by her journey into the feminine, into *her* feminine. As she writes:

> I have therefore returned to my tradition in a more enlightened manner, more autonomous as a woman, and with a little Far Eastern culture which has given me some perspective on my own beliefs and taught me much about the figure of Jesus. I discovered him to be a master of energy. ('The Redemption of Women' in *Key Writings*, pp. 150–1)

In her relationship with the faith in which she was educated – and she is an example of how we can actually negotiate dialogically with that apparently oppressive tradition – she does not think to turn irrevocably away from it, or to destroy it, but rather to rediscover it as *transformed* – and transformed precisely by the difference that we ourselves as transformed beings can bring to it. In Irigaray's case, the differences that she brings include, she indicates, her own greater independence and selfness as a woman, and her encounters with Far Eastern traditions. However, there are also, I would argue, other forces at work in this reconnection. In her essay 'Fulfilling Our Humanity', for instance, Irigaray writes:

> Religious is the gesture which binds earth and sky, in us and outside of us. Which cultivates the terrestrial so that it does not harm the celestial and which venerates the celestial in such a way that it does not destroy the terrestrial. (*Key Writings*, p. 190)[1]

This poetic evocation of the nature of the religious phenomenon certainly has Eastern resonances in it. However, her expression also shows how Irigaray's work as a philosopher has been part of her ability to reconnect with faith issues, in that her discourse echoes that of Martin Heidegger in his 1951 lecture, 'Building, Dwelling, Thinking'.[2] The dialogue at stake here is not simply that of Luce Irigaray and Catholicism, but represents a network of interconnections and allusions that offer, simultaneously, individual and global perspectives.

In her recent work, Irigaray has insisted on the importance of the change of method as well as the change of attitude that is necessitated by the consideration of the other genuinely recognized as other. Her new dialectical method is not a singularly focused critique; rather, it seeks to displace established positions and to inscribe an irreducible difference as process and not only as state: as both the foundation and the driver of her thinking. Criticism can often be negative, but, in her interrogation of the constitution of subjectivity itself, Irigaray stresses the radical and the anti-negative nature of her critique: 'It affirms that no "I" can exist without a "you". This "you" can no longer be or remain an absolute "I", a God of my gender for example. It must be a subjectivity on my level, but radically different' ('Questions', in Trani, 'From the same to the other', in

Dialogues, p. 64).

One of the most exciting features of the last ten years of Irigaray's thinking, as is demonstrated by the essays in this book, is the way in which she simultaneously considers the individual and the social, the local and the global. An important development in this respect is the move in her thinking from a consideration of 'speaking [as] woman' to a broader focus on language as a site of difference and as a facilitator of creative dialogues through difference. She has recently argued powerfully for the importance of language and multi-linguistic communication, not only locally in families, but also in terms of creating truly universal and democratic systems: 'In all families, but above all in multicultural families, the question of language is decisive. [...] Speaking only in one language is not a good way for constructing a universal democratic culture' ('Introduction', in *Dialogues*, p. 2).

Irigaray reminds us that while subjectivity is different for men and for women, and while this difference is more complex than we usually think it is, it is important to recognize that subjectivity is not only a question of individuals: it needs also to be placed, problematized and thought on the social level, and – urgently today – in a global context. She seeks to contribute to the development of 'a new civic society in which democracy itself is recast' (see especially Irigaray, *Democracy Begins Between Two*).

For Irigaray, it is vital to locate the individual, sexually, politically and, indeed, emotionally in the global context, to accomplish a genuine progress towards the new vision of democracy that drives much of her current thinking. As she argues, 'cultivating the individual as global is necessary for humanity in order to resist globalization. And it is also necessary to pursue the becoming of humanity as humanity' ('Questions', in Bostic, 'Reading and rethinking the subject in Luce Irigaray's recent work', in *Dialogues*, p. 30).

Irigaray has done, and continues to do, much to challenge the intellectually restrictive binarism of the 'nature versus nurture' debate, demonstrating to us how these two views of social development interact with each other and can lead much more to dialogue with each other. As she shows both in general terms and in speaking of herself, it is crucial to recognize that each of us is culture-bearing and thereby contains the potential for significant (self-)transformation. Her challenge is to the Western tradition on both the general and the specific, personal level. This serves to remind us that to bear one single culture – or what one thinks of as a single culture – is inevitably to diminish one's capacity for transformation, and to condemn oneself to defensive conservativeness. Irigaray seeks also to encourage us to look beyond our subjectivities and beyond the conventional boundaries of our cultures in order to find new ways of thinking and a new civic language of citizenship.

Just as she shows that difference is neither bad nor good in itself, but has the potential to bring creativity to our own becoming and to social relations, so she exposes how diversity is not in itself either good or bad, but compels us to think beyond notions of selfness and subjectivity, which could be no more than articulations of retractive narcissism. It is Irigaray's positive approach to the challenges of globalization and of interdisciplinarity that makes her work so timely as well as so important. She proposes critical anatomizations of a wide variety of social practices. More meaningfully even, she offers new contextualizations, changing our horizons – our possibilities – and suggests creative ways of moving towards them.

Notes

1 Irigaray uses this same modified Heideggerian rhetoric in her reviewal and renewal of the figure of Antigone in her essay 'Civil Rights and Responsibilities for the Two Sexes', in *Key Writings*, pp. 202–13.

2 This appeared in German in 1954 as 'Bauen Wohnen Denken', in *Mensch und Raum, Das Darmstädter Gespräch 1951*.

Bibliographies for Chapters

Reborn from Silence and Touch – *Jessica Murray*

DeKoven, Marianne, *A Different Language: Gertrude Stein's Experimental Writing* (Madison, WI: The University of Wisconsin Press, 1983).

Hemmings, Jessica, 'The Voice of Cloth: Interior Dialogues and Exterior Skins', in *Sign and Taboo: Perspectives on the Poetic Fiction of Yvonne Vera,* ed. by Robert Muponde and Mandi Taruvinga, M (Harare: Weaver Press, 2002), pp. 57–62.

Irigaray, Luce, *An Ethics of Sexual Difference* trans. by Carolyn Burke and Gillian C. Gill (London and New York: Continuum, 2004).

> *Luce Irigaray: Key Writings,* ed. by Luce Irigaray (London and New York: Continuum, 2004).

> *Prières quotidiennes/Everyday Prayers,* bilingual edition with English version by Luce Irigaray and Timothy Mathews (Paris: Maisonneuve and Larose; Nottingham: University of Nottingham, 2004).

> *This Sex Which Is Not One,* trans. by Catherine Porter with Carolyn Burke (Ithaca, NY: Cornell University Press, 1985).

> *To Be Two* trans. from Italian by Monique M. Rhodes and Marco F. Cocito-Monoc (London and New Brunswick, NJ: The Athlone Press, 2000).

> *The Way of Love,* trans. by Heidi Bostic and Stephen Pluháček (London and New York: Continuum, 2002).

Ludicke, Penny, 'Writing from the Inside-out, Reading from the Outside-in: A Review of Yvonne Vera's "Nehanda" and "Without a Name" ', in *Contemporary African Fiction,* ed. by Derek Wright (Bayreuth: Bayreuth University Press, 1997), pp. 67–73.

Martin Shaw, Carolyn, 'Turning her back on the moon: virginity, sexuality and mothering in the works of Yvonne Vera', *Africa Today,* 51:2 (2004), 35–51.

Steiner, George, *Language and Silence: Essays on Language, Literature, and the Inhuman* (New York: Atheneum, 1977).

Suskin Ostriker, Alicia, *Stealing the Language: The Emergence of Women's Poetry in America* (Boston, MA: Beacon Press 1986).

Vera, Yvonne, *Nehanda* (Harare: Baobab Books, 1993).

> *The Stone Virgins* (Harare: Weaver Books, 2002).

Under the Tongue (Harare: Baobab Books, 1996).

Winter, Alexandra, 'Touching skin: demarcating the corporeal and conceptual' (AWSA conference proceedings, Institute for Women's Studies, Macquarie University, Sydney, Australia, 2001): <http://www.socsci.flinders.edu.au/wmst/awsa2001/pdf/papers/Winter.pdf> [accessed 12 May 2007].

Virginal Thresholds – *Christine Labuski*

Irigaray, Luce, *Elemental Passions*, trans. by Joanne Collie and Judith Still (New York: Routledge, 1992).

> *Luce Irigaray: Key Writings*, ed. by Luce Irigaray (London and New York: Continuum, 2004).

> *Sexes and Genealogies*, trans. by Gillian C. Gill (New York: Columbia University Press, 1987).

> *The Way of Love*, trans. by Heidi Bostic and Stephen Pluháček (London and New York: Continuum, 2002).

'The Power to Love Without Desiring to Possess' – *Sherah Wells*

Benson, Julietta, 'Varieties of "Dis-Belief": Antonia White and the Discourses of Faith and Scepticism', *Journal of Literature and Theology*, 7 (1993), 284–301.

Callil, Carmen, 'Introduction', in Antonia White, *Beyond the Glass* (London: Virago, 1979), pp. 4–7.

Freud, Sigmund, 'Femininity', in *New Introductory Lectures in Psychoanalysis*, ed. with trans. by James Strachey (Harmondsworth: Penguin, 1986), pp. 145–69.

Heather Ingman, *Women's Spirituality in the Twentieth-Century: An Exploration through Fiction* (New York : Peter Lang, 2004).

Irigaray, Luce, *Between East and West: From Singularity to Community*, trans. by Stephen Pluháček (New York: Columbia University Press, 2002).

> *I Love to You: Sketch for a Felicity Within History*, trans. by Alison Martin (New York and London: Routledge, 1996).

> *The Irigaray Reader*, ed. with introduction by Margaret Whitford (Oxford: Blackwell, 1991).

> *Luce Irigaray: Key Writings*, ed. by Luce Irigaray (London and New York: Continuum, 2004).

> *Prières quotidiennes/Everyday Prayers*, bilingual edition with English version by Luce Irigaray and Timothy Mathews (Paris: Maisonneuve and Larose; Nottingham: University of Nottingham, 2004).

> *This Sex Which Is Not One*, trans. by Catherine Porter with Carolyn Burke (Ithaca, NY: Cornell University Press, 1985).

> *To Be Two*, trans. by Monique Rhodes and Marco Cocito-Monoc (London and New York: The Athlone Press, 2000).

'Towards a Divine in the Feminine', in the proceedings of the conference *Women and the Divine*, University of Liverpool, June 2005, ed. by Gillian Howie (forthcoming).

'The Return', talk given during the seminar with Luce Irigaray, University of Nottingham, May 2005. This talk will be published in *Re-writing Difference: Luce Irigaray and "the Greeks"*, ed. by Elena Tzelepis and Athena Athanasiou (forthcoming SUNY Press), and also appears in this volume.

The Way of Love, trans. by Heidi Bostic and Stephen Pluháček (London and New York: Continuum, 2002).

King, Jeannette, *Women and the Word: Contemporary Women Novelists and the Bible* (Basingstoke: Macmillan, 2000).

Palmer, Paulina, 'Antonia White's *Frost in May*: A Lesbian Feminist Reading', in *Feminist Criticism: Theory and Practice*, ed. by Linda Hutcheon, Paul Perron and Susan Sellers (Toronto: University of Toronto Press, 1991), pp. 89–108.

Valentine, Kylie, *Psychoanalysis, Psychiatry, and Modernist Literature* (Basingstoke: Macmillan, 2003).

Warner, Marina, *Alone of All Her Sex: The Myth and Cult of the Virgin Mary* (London: Picador, 1985).

White, Antonia, *Antonia White: Diaries 1926–1957*, ed. by Susan Chitty (London: Viking, 1991).

As Once in May: The Early Autobiography of Antonia White and Other Writings, ed. by Susan Chitty (London: Virago, 1983).

Beyond the Glass (London: Virago, 1979).

Frost In May (London: Virago, 1979).

The Lost Traveller (London: Virago, 1979).

The Sugar House (London: Virago, 1979).

Music and the Voice of the Other – *Esther Zaplana*

Hirsh, Elizabeth and Gary A. Olson, 'Je-Luce Irigaray: A Meeting with Luce Irigaray', trans. by E. Hirsh and G. Brulotte (1996):
<http://www.cas.usf.edu/JAC/163/irigaray.html>

Irigaray, Luce, *An Ethics of Sexual Difference*, trans. by Carolyn Burke and Gillian C. Gill (London and New York: Continuum, 2004)

I Love to You: Sketch for a Felicity Within History, trans. by Alison Martin (New York and London: Routledge, 1996).

je, tu, nous: Toward a Culture of Difference, trans. by Alison Martin (New York and London: Routledge, 1993).

Luce Irigaray: Key Writings, ed. by Luce Irigaray (London and New York: Continuum, 2004).

Prières quotidiennes/Everyday Prayers, bilingual edition with English version by Luce Irigaray and Timothy Mathews (Paris: Maisonneuve and Larose; Nottingham: University of Nottingham, 2004).

Speculum: Of the Other Woman, trans. by Gillian C. Gill (Ithaca, NY: Cornell University Press, 1985).

This Sex Which Is Not One, trans. by Catherine Porter (Ithaca, NY: Cornell University Press, 1985).

The Way of Love, trans. by Heidi Bostic and Stephen Pluháček (London and New York: Continuum, 2002).

To Be Two, trans. by Monique M. Rhodes and Marco F. Cocito-Monoc (New York and London: Routledge and Athlone Press, 2001).

To Speak Is Never Neutral, trans. by Gail Schwab (New York and London: Continuum, 2000).

Whitford, Margaret, *Luce Irigaray. Philosophy in the Feminine* (London and New York: Routledge, 1991).

(ed.), *The Irigaray Reader* (Oxford: Blackwell Publishers, 1991).

'But What if the Object Started to Speak?' – *Lucy Bolton*

Francke, Lizzie, 'Jane Campion, dangerous liaisons', *Sight and Sound*, 13:11 (2003), 19.

Hudson, David, GreenCine: <http://www.greencine.com/static/primers/adult1.jsp> [accessed 1 September 2006].

Irigaray, Luce, *An Ethics of Sexual Difference*, trans. by Carolyn Burke and Gillian C. Gill (London and New York: Continuum, 2004).

Dialogues: Around her Work, ed. by Luce Irigaray, special issue of the journal *Paragraph*, 25:3 (Edinburgh: Edinburgh University Press, 2002).

je, tu, nous: Toward a Culture of Difference, trans. by Alison Martin (New York and London: Routledge, 1993).

Luce Irigaray: Key Writings, ed. by Luce Irigaray (London and New York: Continuum, 2004).

Sexes and Genealogies, trans. by Gillian C. Gill (New York: Columbia University Press, 1987).

Speculum: Of the Other Woman, trans. by Gillian C. Gill (Ithaca, NY: Cornell University Press, 1985).

This Sex Which Is Not One, trans. by Catherine Porter with Carolyn Burke (Ithaca, NY: Cornell University Press, 1985).

Kermode, Mark, 'Has porn entered mainstream cinema for good?', *Guardian*, 4 June 2006.

Mulvey, Laura, *Visual and Other Pleasures* (Hampshire and London: Macmillan, 1989).

'Visual pleasure and narrative cinema', *Screen*, 16:3 (1975), 6–18.

Sjogren, Brigit, *Into the Vortex: Female Voice and Paradox in Film* (Urbana and Chicago: University of Illinois Press, 2006).

Whitford, Margaret, *Luce Irigaray: Philosophy in the Feminine* (London and New York: Routledge, 1991).

Architectural Issues in Building Community through Luce Irigaray's Perspective on Being-Two – *Andrea Wheeler*

Blundell Jones, Peter, 'Özcül Postscript: The Gelsenkirchen School as Built', in *Architecture and Participation*, ed. by Peter Blundell Jones, Jeremy Till and Doina Petrescu (London and New York: Routledge, 2005), pp. 173–80.

Blundell Jones, Peter, Jeremy Till and Doina Petrescu, (eds), *Architecture and Participation* (London and New York: Routledge, 2005).

CABE, *Buildings and Spaces: Why Design Matters* (London: Commission for Architecture and the Built Environment, 2006).

Casey, Edward S., *The Fate of Place* (Berkley and Los Angeles: University of California Press, 1998).

DCMS, *Culture at the Heart of Regeneration* (London: Department of Culture, Media and Sport, 2004).

De Botton, Alain, *The Architecture of Happiness* (London: Hamish Hamilton Limited, 2006).

DMCS, *Better Public Buildings: A Proud Legacy for the Future* (London: Department of Media, Culture and Sport, 2000).

Egan, Sir John, *The Egan Review: Skills for Sustainable Communities* (London: RIBA Enterprises, 2004).

Empty Homes Agency, *A Manifesto on Empty Homes 2005* (London: The Empty Homes Agency, 2005).

Foltz, Bruce V. and Robert Frodeman, (eds), *Rethinking Nature: Essays in Environmental Philosophy* (Bloomington, IN: Indiana University Press, 2004).

Glazebrook, Trish, 'Heidegger and Ecofeminism', in *Feminist Interpretations of Martin Heidegger*, ed. by Nancy J. Holland and Patricia Huntington (Pennsylvania: Pennsylvania State University Press, 2001), pp. 221–51.

Ireland, David, *How to Rescue a House: Turn an Unloved Property into Your Dream Home* (London: Penguin, 2005).

Irigaray, Luce, *Being Two, How Many Eyes Have We?* (Rüsselsheim: Christel Gottert Verlag, 2000).

    Between East and West: From Singularity to Community, trans. by Stephen Pluháček (New York: Columbia University Press, 2002).

    Democracy Begins Between Two, trans. by Kirsteen Anderson (London: The Athlone Press, 2000).

    Dialogues: Around Her Work, editor and contributor, special issue of the journal *Paragraph*, 25:3 (Edinburgh: Edinburgh University Press, 2002).

    'From *The Forgetting of Air* to *To Be Two*', trans. by Heidi Bostic and Stephen Pluháček, in *Feminist Interpretations of Martin Heidegger*, ed. by Nancy J. Holland and Patricia Huntington (Pennsylvania: Pennsylvania State University Press, 2001), pp. 309–15.

    'How Can We Live Together in a Lasting Way', trans. by Alison Martin, Maria Bailey, and Luce Irigaray. A lecture given at the International Architectural Association of London, November 2000, published in *Key Writings* (New York and London: Continuum, 2004), pp. 123–32.

    I Love to You: Sketch for a Felicity Within History, trans. by Alison Martin (New York and London: Routledge, 1996).

    Luce Irigaray: Key Writings, ed. by Luce Irigaray (London and New York: Continuum, 2004).

Prières quotidiennes/Everyday Prayers, bilingual edition with English version by Luce Irigaray and Timothy Mathews (Paris: Maisonneuve and Larose; Nottingham: University of Nottingham, 2004).

The Age of Breath, trans. by Katja van de Rakt, Staci von Boeckman and Luce Irigaray (Rüsselsheim: Christel Göttert Verlag, 1999).

The Forgetting of Air: In Martin Heidegger, trans. by Mary Beth Mader (London: The Athlone Press, 1999).

The Way of Love, trans. by Heidi Bostic and Stephen Pluháček (London and New York: Continuum, 2002).

To Be Two, trans. by Monique M. Rhodes and Marco F. Cocito–Monoc (London and New York: The Athlone Press/Routledge, 2000).

ODPM, *The Sustainable Communities: Building for the Future* (London: Office of the Deputy Prime Minister, 2003).

Perez-Gomes, Alberto, *Built Upon Love: Architectural Longing After Ethics and Aesthetics* (Cambridge, MA: MIT Press, 2006).

RIBA, Sustainable Communities: Quality with Quantity (London: Royal Institute of British Architects, 2004).

Stefanovic, Ingrid Leman, 'Children and the Ethics of Place', in *Rethinking Nature: Essays in Environmental Philosophy*, ed. by Bruce V. Foltz and Robert Frodeman (Bloomington, IN: Indiana University Press, 2004), pp. 55–76.

Toadvine, Ted and Charles S. Brown, (eds), *Eco-Phenomenology: Back to the Earth Itself* (New York: State University of New York Press, 2003).

Wheeler, Andrea, 'Love in Architecture', in *Dialogues: Around Her Work*, ed. by Luce Irigaray, special issue of the journal *Paragraph*, 25:3 (Edinburgh: Edinburgh University Press, 2002), pp. 105–16.

'About being-two in an architectural perspective: interview with Luce Irigaray', *Journal of Romance Studies*, 4:2 (2004), 91–107.

Young, Iris Marion, 'House and Home: Feminist Variations on a Theme', in *Feminist Interpretations of Martin Heidegger*, ed. by Nancy J. Holland and Patricia Huntington (Pennsylvania: Pennsylvania State University Press, 2001), pp. 252–88.

Touching Hands, Cultivating Dwelling – *Helen A. Fielding*

Bernadec, Marie-Laure, *Louise Bourgeois* (Paris: Flammarion 1996).

Bourgeois, Louise, *Memory and Architecture* (Madrid: Mueseo Nacional Centro de Arte Reina Sofía 1999).

Brozan, Nadine, 'Chronicle', *The New York Times*, 3 October 1996: <http://query.nytimes.com/gst/fullpage.html?res=9F01E7DE153FF930A 35753C1A960958> [accessed 12 November, 2006].

Derrida, Jacques, '*Geschlecht* II: Heidegger's Hand', in *Deconstruction and Philosophy*, ed. by John Sallis (Chicago: University of Chicago Press, 1987), pp. 161–96.

Freud, Sigmund, 'The Uncanny', in *Sigmund Freud: Art and Literature*, ed. by Albert Dickson (Harmondsworth, UK: Penguin Books, 1985), pp. 339–76.

Heidegger, Martin, 'Building Dwelling Thinking', in *Poetry, Language, Thought*, trans. by Albert Hofstadter (New York: Harper & Row, 1971), pp. 145–61.

Introduction to Metaphysics, trans. by Gregory Fried and Richard Polt (New Haven: Yale University Press, 2000).

'Letter on Humanism', in *Pathmarks*, ed. by William McNeill (Cambridge: Cambridge University Press, 1998), pp. 239–76.

'The Origin of the Work of Art', in *Poetry, Language, Thought*, trans. by Albert Hofstadter (New York: Harper & Row, 1971), pp. 17–87.

'The Question Concerning Technology', in *The Question Concerning Technology and Other Essays*, trans. by William Lovitt (New York: Harper & Row, 1977), pp. 3–35.

What is Called Thinking? trans. by J. Glenn Gray (New York: Harper & Row, 1968).

Irigaray, Luce, 'Being Two, How Many Eyes Have We', in *Dialogues: Around Her Work*, ed. by Luce Irigaray, special issue of the journal *Paragraph*, 25:3 (Edinburgh: Edinburgh University Press, 2002), 143–51.

The Forgetting of Air: In Martin Heidegger, trans. by Mary Beth Mader (Austin: University of Texas Press, 1999).

'Importance du genre dans la constitution de la subjectivité et de l'intersubjectivité', in *Le partage de la parole* (Oxford: European Humanities Research Centre of the University of Oxford, 2001), pp. 24–42.

Luce Irigaray: Key Writings, ed. by Luce Irigaray (London and New York: Continuum, 2004).

Sexes and Genealogies, trans. by Gillian C. Gill (New York: Columbia University Press, 1993).

To Be Two, trans. by Monique M. Rhodes and Marco F. Cocito-Monoc (New York: Routledge, 2001).

The Way of Love, trans. by Heidi Bostic and Stephen Pluháček (London and New York: Continuum, 2002).

Nancy, Jean-Luc, *The Muses* (Stanford University Press, 1996).

Sultan, Terrie, 'Redefining the Terms of Engagement: The Art of Louise Bourgeois', in *Louise Bourgeois: The Locus of Memory, Works 1982–1993*, by Charlotta Kotik, *et al.* (New York: The Brooklyn Museum, 1994), pp. 28–50.

Wallach, Amei, 'To an artist, a tender image; to others, a grim reminder', *The New York Times*, 25 August 1997:
<http://query.nytimes.com/gst/fullpage.htm.?res=9F01E7DE153FF930A35753C1A960958> [accessed 12 November, 2006].

Swallowing Ice – *Christina Siggers Manson*

Irigaray, Luce, 'And the One Doesn't Stir Without the Other', trans. by Hélène Vivienne Wenzel, *Signs: Journal of Women in Culture and Society*, 7:1 (1981), 60–7.

An Ethics of Sexual Difference, trans. by Carolyn Burke and Gillian C. Gill (London and New York: Continuum, 2004).

Between East and West: From Singularity to Community, trans. by Stephen Pluháček (New York: Columbia University Press, 2002).

I Love to You: Sketch for a Felicity Within History, trans. by Alison Martin (New York and London: Routledge, 1996).

Luce Irigaray: Key Writings, ed. by Luce Irigaray (London and New York: Continuum, 2004).

Marine Lover: Of Friedrich Nietzsche, trans. by Gillian C. Gill (New York: Columbia University Press, 1991).

'The Return', talk given by Luce Irigaray during the week of the seminar for PhD students at the University of Nottingham in May 2005, in which I participated. This talk will be published in *Re-writing Difference: Luce Irigaray and 'the Greeks'*, ed. by Elena Tzelepis and Athena Athanasiou (forthcoming SUNY Press), and also appears in this volume.

Maraini, Dacia, *Colomba* (Milan: Rizzoli. 2004).

L'età del malessere (Turin: Einaudi, 1996).

Siggers Manson, Christina, 'In love with Cecchino: opening the door to violence in Dacia Maraini's *Colomba* and *Voci*', *Journal of Romance Studies*, 5:2 (2005), 89–100.

The Maternal Order Read through Luce Irigaray in the Work of Diamela Eltit
– *Mary Green*

Boyle, Catherine M., 'Touching the Air: The Cultural Force of Women in Chile', in *Viva: Women and Popular Protest in Latin America*, ed. by Sarah A. Radcliffe and Sallie Westwood (London: Routledge, 1993), pp. 156–72.

Craske, Nikki, *Women and Politics in Latin America* (Cambridge: Polity Press, 1999).

Eltit, Diamela, 'Consagradas', in *Salidas de madre*, with prologue by Alejandra Rojas (Santiago: Planeta/Biblioteca del Sur, 1996), pp. 97–104.

El cuarto mundo (Santiago: Planeta, 1988).

The Fourth World, trans. with introduction by Dick Gerdes (Lincoln, NE: University of Nebraska Press, 1995).

Garabano, Sandra and Guillermo García-Corales, 'Diamela Eltit', *Hispamérica*, 62 (1992), 65–75.

Grau, Olga, *et al.*, *Discurso, género y poder: discursos públicos. Chile 1978–1993* (Santiago: LOM/Arcis, [n.d.]).

Green, Mary, *Diamela Eltit: Reading the Mother* (Woodbridge, UK: Tamesis, 2007).

Irigaray, Luce, 'And the One Doesn't Stir Without the Other', trans. by Hélène Vivienne Wenzel, *Signs: Journal of Women in Culture and Society*, 7:1 (1981), 60–7.

An Ethics of Sexual Difference, trans. by Carolyn Burke and Gillian C. Gill (London: The Athlone Press, 1993).

The Irigaray Reader, ed. with introduction by Margaret Whitford (Oxford: Blackwell, 1991).

Luce Irigaray: Key Writings, ed. by Luce Irigaray (London and New York: Continuum, 2004).

Prières quotidiennes/Everyday Prayers, bilingual edition with English version by Luce Irigaray and Timothy Mathews (Paris: Maisonneuve and Larose; Nottingham: University of Nottingham, 2004).

Sexes and Genealogies, trans. by Gillian C. Gill (New York: Columbia University Press, 1993).

Speculum: Of the Other Woman, trans. by Gillian C. Gill (Ithaca, NY: Cornell University Press, 1985).

This Sex Which Is Not One, trans. by Catherine Porter (Ithaca, NY: Cornell University Press, 1985).

Munizaga, Giselle, *El discurso público de Pinochet: un análisis semiológico* (Santiago: CESOC/CENECA, 1988).

Pinochet Ugarte, Augusto, *Mensaje a la mujer chilena: texto del discurso* (Santiago: Editorial Nacional Gabriela Mistral, 1976).

Richard, Nelly, *Residuos y metáforas: ensayos de crítica cultural sobre el Chile de la Transición* (Santiago: Cuarto Propio, 1998).

'Revueltas femeninas y transgresiones de símbolos', *Revista de crítica cultural*, 21 (2000), 24–6.

Valdés, Teresa, *Las mujeres y la dictadura militar en Chile* (Santiago: FLACSO, 1987).

Feminist Generations – *Gillian Howie*

Adorno, Theodor, *Metaphysics: Concepts and Problems*, ed. by R. Tiedermann, trans. by E. Jephcott (Cambridge: Polity Press, 2000).

Alfonso, Rita and Jo Trigilio, 'Surfing the third wave: a dialogue between two waves of feminism', *Hypatia: a journal of feminist philosophy*, 12:3 (1997), 7–16.

Bailey, Cathryn, 'Making waves and drawing lines: the politics of defining the vicissitudes of feminism', *Hypatia: a journal of feminist philosophy*, 12:3 (1997), 17–28.

Cornell, Drucilla. *The Imaginary Domain: Abortion, Pornography and Sexual Harassment* (New York and London: Routledge, 1995).

Detloff, Madelyn, 'Mean spirits: the politics of contempt between feminist generations', *Hypatia: a journal of feminist philosophy*, 12:3 (1997), 76–99.

Dicker, Rory and Alison Piepmeier (eds), *Catching a Wave: Reclaiming Feminism for the 21st Century* (Boston: Northeaston University Press, 2003).

Felski, Rita, *Doing Time: Feminist Theory and Postmodern Culture* (New York and London: New York University Press, 2000).

Gillis, Stacy and Rebecca Munford, 'Genealogies and generations: the politics and praxis of third wave feminism', *Women's History Review*, 13:2 (2004), 165–78.

Gillis, Stacy, Gillian Howie and Rebecca Munford (eds), *Third Wave Feminism: A Critical Exploration*, 2nd edn (London: Palgrave, 2007; Westport: Greenwood Press, 2006).

Grosz, Elizabeth, 'A Note on Essentialism and Difference', *Feminist Knowledge: Critique and Construct*, ed. by Sneja Gunew (New York: Routledge; 1990), pp. 332–44.

Harding, Sandra, 'The instability of the analytical categories of feminist theory', *Signs: Journal of Women in Culture and Society*, 11:4 (1986), 645–64.

Heywood, Leslie L. (ed.), *The Women's Movement Today: The Encyclopaedia of Third Wave Feminism*, 2 vols (Westport: Greenwood Press, 2005).

Howie, Gillian, 'Interview with Luce Irigaray', in *Third Wave Feminism: A Critical Exploration*, ed. by Stacy Gillis, Gillian Howie and Rebecca Munford, 2nd edn (London: Palgrave, 2007; Westport: Greenwood Press, 2006).

Irigaray, Luce, 'The Fecundity of the Caress', in *Face to Face with Levinas*, ed. by Richard A. Cohen (Albany, NY: State University of New York Press, 1986), pp. 231–56.

  I Love to You: Sketch for a Felicity Within History, trans. by Alison Martin (New York and London: Routledge, 1996).

  The Irigaray Reader, ed. with introduction by Margaret Whitford (Oxford: Blackwell, 1991).

  je, tu, nous: Toward a Culture of Difference, trans. by Alison Martin (New York and London: Routledge, 1993).

  Speculum: Of the Other Woman, trans. by Gillian C. Gill (Ithaca, NY: Cornell University Press, 1985).

  This Sex Which Is Not One, trans. by Catherine Porter with Carolyn Burke (Ithaca, NY: Cornell University Press, 1985).

  The Way of Love, trans. by Heidi Bostic and Stephen Pluháček (London and New York: Continuum, 2002).

Kristeva, Julia, 'Women's Time', trans. by Alice Jardine and Harry Blake, in *Feminist Theory: A Critique of Ideology*, ed. by Nannerl Keohane, Michelle Rosaldo and Barbara Gelpi (Sussex: The Harvester Press, 1982), pp. 31–53.

Nietzsche, Friedrich, 'On the Uses and Disadvantages of History for Life', in *Untimely Meditations*, trans. by R. J. Hollingdale (Cambridge: Cambridge University Press, 1983), pp. 59–123.

Whitford, Margaret, *Luce Irigaray: Philosophy in the Feminine* (New York and London: Routledge, 1991).

Disinterring the Divine Law – Sabrina L. Hom

Hegel, G. W. F., *Phenomenology of Spirit*, trans. by A. V. Miller (Oxford: Oxford University Press, 1977).

Irigaray, Luce, *Democracy Begins Between Two*, trans. by Kirsteen Anderson (New York: Routledge, 2001).

  I Love to You: Sketch for a Felicity Within History, trans. by Alison Martin (New York and London: Routledge, 1996).

  Sexes and Genealogies, trans. by Gillian C. Gill (New York: Columbia University Press, 1993).

  Speculum: Of the Other Woman, trans. by Gillian C. Gill (Ithaca, NY: Cornell University Press, 1985).

  Thinking the Difference: For a Peaceful Revolution, trans. by Karin Montin (New York: Routledge, 1994).

Sophocles, *Antigone*, trans. by David Franklin and John Harrison (Cambridge: Cambridge University Press, 2003).

Writing the Body of Christ – *Emily A. Holmes*

Angela, of Foligno, *Complete Works*, trans. by Paul Lachance, O.F.M. (New York: Paulist Press, 1993).
  Il Libro della Beata Angela da Foligno, ed. by Ludger Their, O.F.M., and Abele Calufetti, O.F.M., (Grottaferrata, Rome: Editiones Collegii S. Bonaventurae ad Claras Aguas, 1985).
Babinsky, Ellen, 'Christological transformation in *The Mirror of Souls*, by Marguerite Porete', *Theology Today*, 60 (2003), 34–8.
Berry, Philippa, 'The Burning Glass: Paradoxes of Feminist Revelation in *Speculum'*, in *Engaging with Luce Irigaray*, ed. by Carolyn Burke, Naomi Schor and Margaret Whitford (New York: Columbia University Press, 1994), pp. 229–46.
Bynum, Carolyn Walker, *Fragmentation and Redemption: Essays on Gender and the Human Body in Medieval Religion* (New York: Zone Books, 1991).
  Holy Feast and Holy Fast: The Religious Significance of Food to Medieval Women (Berkeley, CA: University of California Press, 1987).
Cardinal, Marie, *Les Mots Pour Le Dire* (Paris: Grasset, 1975).
Chung, Hyun Kung, *Struggle to Be the Sun Again: Introducing Asian Women's Theology* (Maryknoll, NY: Orbis Books, 1990).
Cixous, Hélène and Catherine Clément, *La Jeune Née* (Paris: Union générale d'éditions, 1975).
Daly, Mary, *Beyond God the Father* (Boston: Beacon Press, 1973).
Delphy, Christine, 'The invention of French Feminism: an essential move', *Yale French Studies*, 87 (1995), 190–221
Farley, Wendy, *The Wounding and Healing of Desire: Weaving Heaven and Earth* (Louisville, KY: Westminster John Knox, 2005).
Grosz, Elizabeth, *Sexual Subversions: Three French Feminists* (Sydney: Allen and Unwin, 1989).
Grundmann, Herbert, *Religious Movements in the Middle Ages: The Historical Links between Heresy, the Mendicant Orders, and the Women's Religious Movement in the Twelfth and Thirteenth Century, with the Historical Foundations of German Mysticism* (Notre Dame, IN: University of Notre Dame Press, 1935; reprinted 1995).
Hadewijch, of Brabant, *Hadewijch: Brieven*, ed. by Jozef van Mierlo, S.J., 2 vols (Antwerp: Standaard, 1947).
  Hadewijch: The Complete Works, trans, by Mother Columba Hart, O.S.B. (New York: Paulist Press, 1980).
  Hadewijch: Mengeldichten, ed. by Jozef van Mierlo, S.J. (Antwerp: Standaard, 1952).
  Hadewijch: Strophische Gedichten, ed. by Jozef van Mierlo, S.J., 2 vols (Antwerp: Standaard, 1942).
  Hadewijch: Visionen, ed. by Jozef van Mierlo, S.J., 2 vols (Louvain: Vlaamsch Boekenhalle, 1924, 1925).
Hampson, Daphne, *Theology and Feminism* (Cambridge, MA: Blackwell, 1990).
Hollywood, Amy, *The Soul as Virgin Wife: Mechthild of Magdeburg, Marguerite Porete, and Meister Eckhart* (Notre Dame, IN.: University of Notre Dame, 1995).

Holmes, Emily A., 'Writing the Body of Christ: Hadewijch of Brabant, Angela of Foligno, and Marguerite Porete' (unpublished doctoral dissertation, Emory University, 2008).

Irigaray, Luce, *Ce sexe qui n'en est pas un* (Paris: Éditions de Minuit, 1977).

    Democracy Begins Between Two, trans. by Kirsteen Anderson (London: The Athlone Press, 2000).

    'Egales à qui?', *Critique*, 43:480 (1987), 420–37, translated as 'Equal to Whom?', by Robert L. Mazzola, in *The Essential Difference*, ed. by Naomi Schor and Elizabeth Weed (Bloomington, IN: Indiana University Press, 1994), pp. 63–81.

    Luce Irigaray: Key Writings, ed. by Luce Irigaray (London and New York: Continuum, 2004).

    Sexes and Genealogies, trans. by Gillian C. Gill (New York: Columbia University Press, 1993).

    Speculum: Of the Other Woman, trans. by Gillian C. Gill (Ithaca, NY: Cornell University Press, 1985).

    This Sex Which Is Not One, trans. by Catherine Porter with Carolyn Burke (Ithaca, NY: Cornell University Press, 1985).

Lorde, Audre, 'Poetry is Not a Luxury', in *Sister Outsider: Essays and Speeches* (Trumansburg, NY: Crossing Press, 1984), pp. 36–9.

Mazzoni, Cristina, *Saint Hysteria: Neurosis, Mysticism, and Gender in European Culture* (Ithaca, NY: Cornell University Press, 1996).

McFague, Sallie, *The Body of God: An Ecological Theology* (Minneapolis: Fortress Press, 1993).

McGinn, Bernard, *The Flowering of Mysticism: Men and Women in the New Mysticism (1200–1350)* (New York: Crossroad, 1998).

    'The Four Female Evangelists of the Thirteenth Century: The Invention of Authority', in *Deutsche Mystik im abendländischen Zusammenhang*, ed. by Walter Haug and Wolfram Schneider-Lastin (Tübingen: Niemeyer, 2000), pp. 175–94.

    (ed.), *Meister Eckhart and the Beguine Mystics: Hadewijch of Brabant, Mechthild of Magdeburg, and Marguerite Porete* (New York: Continuum, 1994).

Miller, Julie B., 'Eroticized violence in medieval women's mystical literature: a call for a feminist critique', *Journal of Feminist Studies in Religion*, 15:2 (1999), 25–49.

Newman, Barbara, 'The heretic saint: Guglielma of Bohemia, Milan, and Brunate', *Church History*, 74:1 (2005), 1–38.

Origen, *On First Principles*, Book IV.

Paulsell, Stephanie, *Honoring the Body: Meditations on a Christian Practice* (San Francisco: Jossey-Bass, 2002).

    'Writing as a Spiritual Discipline', in *The Scope of Our Art: The Vocation of the Theological Teacher*, ed. by L. Gregory Jones and Stephanie Paulsell (Grand Rapids, MI: Eerdmans, 2002), pp. 17–31.

Porete, Marguerite, *Corpus Christianorum: Continuatio Medievalis*, ed. by R. Guarnieri and Paul Verdeyen, vol. 69 (Turnholt, Belgium: Brepols, 1986).

    The Mirror of Simple Souls, trans. by Edmund Colledge, J. C. Marler and Judith Grant (Notre Dame, IN: University of Notre Dame Press, 1999).

Radford Ruether, Rosemary, *Sexism and God-Talk: Toward a Feminist Theology* (Boston, MA: Beacon Press, 1983).

Reineke, Martha J., ' "This is my body": reflections on abjection, anorexia, and medieval women mystics', *JAAR*, 58:2 (1990), 245–65.

Schleiermacher, Friedrich, *Christmas Eve; Dialogue on Incarnation*, trans. by Terrence N. Tice (Richmond: John Knox Press, 1967).

> *On Religion: Speeches to Its Cultured Despisers*, trans. by Richard Crouter (New York: Cambridge University Press, 1996).

Schüssler Fiorenza, Elisabeth, *In Memory of Her: A Feminist Theological Reconstruction of Christian Origins* (New York: Crossroad, 1983).

Teresa, of Avila, *Interior Castle*, trans. and ed. by E. Allison Peers (New York: Doubleday, 1989).

Vandenbroek, Paul, *Le jardin clos de l'âme: l'Imaginaire des religieuses dans les Pays-Bas du Sud, depuis le 13e siècle: Société des Expositions Palais des Beaux-Art de Bruxelles, 25 février-22 mai, 1994* (Bruxelles: Martial et Snoeck, 1994).

Vattimo, Gianni, *After Christianity*, trans. by Luca D'Isanto (New York: Columbia University Press, 2002).

> *Belief*, trans. by Luca D'Isanto and David Webb (Cambridge, UK: Blackwell, 1999).

Wessley, Stephen, 'The Thirteenth-Century Guglielmites: Salvation Through Women', in *Medieval Women*, ed. by Derek Baker (Oxford: Blackwell, 1978), pp. 289–303.

Whitford, Margaret, *Luce Irigaray: Philosophy in the Feminine* (New York and London: Routledge, 1991).

Sharing Air – *Roland J. De Vries*

Beattie, Tina, *God's Mother, Eve's Advocate* (London and New York: Continuum, 2002).

Deutscher, Penelope, *A Politics of Impossible Difference: The Later Work of Luce Irigaray* (Ithaca, NY: Cornell University Press, 2002).

Irigaray, Luce, *An Ethics of Sexual Difference*, trans. by Carolyn Burke and Gillian C. Gill (New York: Cornell University Press, 1993).

> *Between East and West: From Singularity to Community*, trans. by Stephen Pluháček (New York: Columbia University Press, 2002).

> *I Love to You: Sketch for a Felicity Within History*, trans. by Alison Martin (New York and London: Routledge, 1996).

> *Luce Irigaray: Key Writings*, ed. by Luce Irigaray (London and New York: Continuum, 2004).

> *Sexes and Genealogies*, trans. by Gillian C. Gill (New York: Columbia University Press, 1987).

> *To Be Two*, trans. by Monique M. Rhodes and Marco F. Cocito-Monoc (New York: Routledge, 2001).

> *The Way of Love*, trans. by Heidi Bostic and Stephen Pluháček (London and New York: Continuum, 2002).

Kierkegaard, Søren, *Works of Love*, ed. and trans. by Howard V. Hong and Edna H. Hong (Princeton: Princeton University Press, 1995).

Marshall, Bruce D., *Trinity and Truth* (Cambridge: Cambridge University Press, 2000).

The Holy Bible, New Revised Standard Version.

A Future Shaped by Love – *Eleanor Sanderson*

Chambers, Robert, *Whose Reality Counts? Putting the Last First* (London: Intermediate Technology Publications, 1997).

Cooke, Bill and Uma Kothari, 'The Case for Participation as Tyranny', in *Participation: The New Tyranny?*, ed. by Bill Cooke and Uma Kothari (London: Zed Books, 2001), pp. 1–16.

Escobar, Arturo, 'The Making and Unmaking of the Third World through Development', in *The Post Development Reader*, ed. by Maja Rahmena and Victoria Bawtree (London: Zed Books, 1997), pp. 85–102.

Esteva, Gustav, 'Development', in *The Development Dictionary: A Guide to Knowledge as Power*, ed. by Wolfgang Sachs (London: Zed Books, 1992), pp. 6–26.

Goebel, Alison, 'Process, perception and power: notes from "participatory" research in a Zimbabwean resettlement area', *Development and Change*, 29 (1998), 277–307.

Grimes, Seamus and Jamie Nubiola, 'Reconsidering the exclusion of metaphysics in human geography', *Acta Philosophica*, 6:2 (1997), 265–76.

Guijt, Irene and Meera Shah, 'General Introduction: Waking up to Power, Process and Conflict', in *The Myth of Community: Gender Issues in Participatory Development*, ed. by Irene Guijt and Meera Shah (London: Intermediate Technology Publications, 1998), pp. 1–23.

Irigaray, Luce, *Between East and West: From Singularity to Community*, trans. by Stephen Pluháček (New York: Columbia University Press, 2002).

    I Love to You: Sketch for a Felicity Within History, trans. by Alison Martin (New York and London: Routledge, 1996).

    Luce Irigaray: Key Writings, ed. by Luce Irigaray (London and New York: Continuum, 2004).

    Sexes and Genealogies, trans. by Gillian C. Gill (New York: Columbia University Press, 1993).

    Prières quotidiennes/Everyday Prayers, bilingual edition with English version by Luce Irigaray and Timothy Mathews (Paris: Maisonneuve and Larose; Nottingham: University of Nottingham, 2004).

    This Sex Which Is Not One, trans. by Catherine Porter with Carolyn Burke (Ithaca, NY: Cornell University Press, 1985).

    To Be Two, trans. by Monique Rhodes and Marco Cocito-Monoc (London and New York: The Athlone Press and Routledge, 2000).

    The Way of Love, trans. by Heidi Bostic and Stephen Pluháček (London and New York: Continuum, 2002).

Lennie, June, 'Deconstructing gendered power relations in participatory planning: towards an empowering feminist framework of participation and action', *Women's Studies International Forum*, 22:1 (1999), 97–112.

Mannion, Joe, and Eammon Brehony, 'Projects for the people or of the people: a look at villagers' participation in two villages in Tanzania', *Public Administration and Development*, 10 (1990), 165–79.

Martin, Alison, 'Introduction: Luce Irigaray and the culture of difference', *Theory, Culture & Society*, 20:3 (2003), 1–12.

Mosse, David, 'Authority, gender and knowledge: theoretical reflections on the practise of participatory rural appraisal', *Development and Change*, 25 (1994), 497–527.

Munck, Ronaldo, 'Deconstructing development discourse: of impasses, alternatives and politics', in *Critical Development Theory: Contributions to a New Paradigm*, ed. by Ronaldo Munck and Denis O'Hearn (London: Zed Books, 1999), pp. 196–211.

Nanda, Shrestha, 'On Becoming a Development Category', in *Power of Development*, ed. by Jonathan Crush (London: Routledge, 1995), pp. 266–77.

Nash, Catherine, 'Remapping the Body/Land: New Cartographies of Identity, Gender, and Landscape in Ireland', in *Writing Women and Space: Colonial and Postcolonial Geographies*, ed. by Alison Blunt and Gillian Rose (New York: Guildford Press, 1994), pp. 227–50.

Pain, Rachel, 'Social geography: on action-orientated research', *Progress in Human Geography*, 27:5 (2003), 649–57.

Rahnema, Maja, 'Towards Post-Development: Searching for Signposts, a New Language and New Paradigms', in *The Post-Development Reader*, ed. by Maja Rahnema and Victoria Bawtree (London: Zed Books, 1997), pp. 377–403.

Rist, Gilbert, *The History of Development: From Western Origins to Global Faith* (London: Zed Books, 1997).

Robinson, Jennifer, 'Feminism and the spaces of transformation', *Transaction for the Institute of British Geographers*, 25 (2000), 285–301.

Rose, Gillian, 'As if the Mirror Had Bled', in *Body Space*, ed. by N. Duncan (London and New York: Routledge, 1996), pp. 56–74.
    Feminism and Geography: The Limits of Geographical Knowledge (Cambridge: Polity Press, 1993).

Sanderson, Eleanor and Sara Kindon, 'Progress in participatory development: opening up the possibilities of knowledge through progressive participation', *Progress in Development Studies*, 4:2 (2004), 114–26.

Schrijvers, Joke, *The Violence of Development* (Amsterdam: International Books, 1993).

Schuurman, Frans, *Beyond the Impasse: New Directions in Development Theory* (London: Zed Books, 1993).

Slater, Terry, 'Encountering God: personal reflections on "geographer as pilgrim"', *Area*, 36:3 (2004), 245–53.

Tucker, Vincent, 'The Myth of Development: A Critique of a Eurocentric Discourse', in *Critical Development Theory: Contributions to a New Paradigm*, ed. by Ronaldo Munck and Denis O'Hearn (London: Zed Books, 1999), pp. 1–27.

Ver Beek, Kurt, 'Spirituality: a development taboo', *Development in Practice*, 10:1 (2000), 31–43.

Expression and Speaking-*with* in the Work of Luce Irigaray – *Donald A. Landes*

Derrida, Jacques, *On Touching-Jean-Luc Nancy*, trans. by Christine Irizarry, ed. by Werner.

Hamacher, *Meridian: Crossing Aesthetics* (Stanford: Stanford University Press, 2005).

Irigaray, Luce, *An Ethics of Sexual Difference*, trans. by Carolyn Burke and Gillian C. Gill (New York: Cornell University Press, 1993).

> *I Love to You: Sketch for a Felicity Within History*, trans. by Alison Martin (New York and London: Routledge, 1996).
>
> *Luce Irigaray: Key Writings*, ed. by Luce Irigaray (London and New York: Continuum, 2004).
>
> *Speculum: Of the Other Woman*, trans. by Gillian C. Gill (Ithaca, NY: Cornell University Press, 1985).
>
> *The Way of Love*, trans. by Heidi Bostic and Stephen Pluháček (London and New York: Continuum, 2002).

Merleau-Ponty, Maurice, *The Phenomenology of Perception*, trans. by Colin Smith, Routledge Classics (New York: Routledge, 2002).

> *The Visible and the Invisible*, trans. by Alphonso Lingus, ed. by Claude Lefort (Evanston, IL: Northwestern University Press, 2000 (1964)).

Nancy, Jean-Luc, *The Gravity of Thought*, trans. by François Raffoul and Gregory Recco, ed. by Hugh J. Silverman, Philosophy and Literary Theory (Amherst, NY: Humanity Books, 1998).

> *Le partage des voix* (Paris: Galilée, 1982).

On Rivers, Words and Becoming an Other – *Laine M. Harrington*

Bergren, Ann L. T., 'Helen's Good "Drug". Odyssey iv. 1–305', *Contemporary Literary Hermeneutics and Interpretation of Classical Texts*, ed. by Stephanus Kresic (Ottawa: University of Ottawa Press, 1981), pp. 200–14.

Clark, Gordon H., *The Johannine Logos* (New Jersey: Presbyterian and Reformed Publishing Company, 1972).

Hoffmann, E., 'Die Sprache u. d. archaische Logik', Heidelberger Abh. z. Philosophie u. ihrer Geschichte, 3 (1925), 77, in *Theological Dictionary of the New Testament*, ed. by Gerhard Kittel (Michigan: Wm. B. Eerdmans, 1967), pp. 69–136.

Irigaray, Luce, *Elemental Passions*, trans. by Joanne Collie and Judith Still (New York: Routledge, 1992).

> *Prières quotidiennes/Everyday Prayers*, bilingual edition, English version by Luce Irigaray with Timothy Mathews (Paris: Maisonneuve and Larose; Nottingham: University of Nottingham, 2004).

The Forgetting of Air: In Martin Heidegger, trans. by Mary Beth Mader (Austin: University of Texas Press, 1999).

I Love to You: Sketch for a Felicity Within History, trans. by Alison Martin (New York and London: Routledge, 1996).

je, tu, nous: Toward a Culture of Difference, trans. by Alison Martin (London and New York: Routledge, 1993).

Marine Lover: Of Friedrich Nietzsche, trans. by Gillian C. Gill (New York: Columbia University Press, 1991).

Speculum: Of the Other Woman, trans. by Gillian C. Gill (Ithaca, NY: Cornell University Press, 1985).

This Sex Which Is Not One, trans. by Catherine Porter with Carolyn Burke (Ithaca, NY: Cornell University Press, 1985).

To Be Two, trans. by Monique Rhodes and Marco Cocito-Monoc (New York: Routledge, 2001).

Jacobs, David C., (ed.), *The Presocratics after Heidegger* (Albany: State University of New York Press, 1999).

Kirk, G. S. (ed.), *Heraclitus: The Cosmic Fragments* (Cambridge: Cambridge University Press, 1954).

Kirk, G. S., Raven, J. E., and Schofield, M., *The Presocratic Philosophers: A Critical History with a Selection of Texts* (Cambridge: Cambridge University Press, 1983).

Kittel, Gerhard (ed.), *Theological Dictionary of the New Testament* (Michigan: Wm. B. Eerdmans, 1967).

Liddell, H. G. and Scott, S. (eds), *An Intermediate Greek-English Lexicon* (Oxford: Oxford University Press, 1995).

Osborne, Robin, 'The Polis and its Culture', in *Routledge History of Philosophy, Volume I: From the Beginning to Plato*, ed. by C. C. W. Taylor (London: Routledge, 1997), pp. 9–46.

Price, A. W., 'Plato: Ethics and Politics', in *Routledge History of Philosophy, Volume I: From the Beginning to Plato*, ed. by C. C. W. Taylor (London: Routledge, 1997), pp. 394–424.

Robinson, T. M. (trans.), *Fragments: A Text and Translation with a Commentary by T. M. Robinson* (Toronto: University of Toronto Press, 1987).

Schiappa, Edward, *Protagoras and Logos: A Study in Greek Philosophy and Rhetoric* (Columbia: University of South Carolina Press, 1991).

Masculine and Feminine Approaches to Nature – *Karen I. Burke*

De Beauvoir, Simone, *The Second Sex*, trans. by H. M. Parshley (New York: Vintage Books, 1989).

Hegel, Georg Wilhelm Friedrich, *Phenomenology of Spirit*, trans. by A. V. Miller (New York: Oxford University Press, 1977).

Philosophy of Nature, trans. by A. V. Miller (New York: Oxford University Press, 2004).

Philosophy of Right, trans. by T. M. Knox (New York: Oxford University Press, 1967).

Irigaray, Luce, *Between East and West: From Singularity to Community*, trans. by Stephen Pluháček (New York: Columbia University Press, 2002).

Democracy Begins Between Two, trans. by Kirsteen Anderson (London and New York: Continuum and Routledge, 2000).

I Love to You: Sketch of a Felicity Within History, trans. by Alison Martin (New York and London: Routledge, 1996).

je, tu, nous: Toward a Culture of Difference, trans. by Alison Martin (New York and London: Routledge, 1993).

Speculum: Of the Other Woman, trans. by Gillian C. Gill (Ithaca, NY: Cornell University Press, 1985).

Thinking the Difference: For a Peaceful Revolution, trans. by Karin Montin (New York: Routledge, 1994).

Sexes and Genealogies, trans. by Gillian C. Gill (New York: Columbia University Press, 1993).

Nietzsche, Friedrich, *The Use and Abuse of History*, trans. by Adrian Collins (New York: Bobbs-Merrill, 1957).

Afterword – *Michael Worton*

Heidegger, Martin, 'Building, Dwelling, Thinking', in *Poetry, Language, Thought*, trans. and introduction by Albert Hofstadter (New York: Harper and Row, 1971) pp. 145–61.

Irigaray, Luce, *Democracy Begins Between Two*, trans. by Kirsteen Anderson (London and New York: Continuum and Routledge, 2000).

Dialogues: Around Her Work, editor and contributor, special issue of the journal *Paragraph*, 25:3 (Edinburgh: Edinburgh University Press, 2002).

Luce Irigaray: Key Writings, ed. by Luce Irigaray (London and New York: Continuum 2004).

Pluháček, Stephen, and Heidi Bostic, 'Thinking Life as Relation: An Interview with Luce Irigaray', *Man and World*, 29 (1996), 343–60.

Notes on Contributors

Lucy Bolton has a Masters in Film Studies from the University of Westminster and is in her final year of PhD research at Queen Mary, University of London. Lucy's thesis concerns the representation of feminine consciousness on-screen, illuminated by the writings of Luce Irigaray. Lucy also teaches in the Film Department at Queen Mary.

Karen I. Burke was a doctoral candidate in Philosophy at Stony Brook University, where she specialized in Hegel's philosophy of nature and feminist theory. Karen earned a MA in Philosophy at Miami University in Ohio and a BA in English at the College of William and Mary in Virginia. She has been awarded an MPhil posthumously by Stony Brook University in December 2007. Karen was a founding member of the Luce Irigaray Circle and a valued member of the community of Irigaray scholars. Her translation of Luce Irigaray's 'Beyond totem and idol, the sexuate other' ('La transcendence de l'autre') will be published in *The Continental Philosophy Review*, 40:4 (December 2007), and her book review of Harry Frankfurt's *On Bullshit* was published in *Teaching Philosophy*, 30:2. She was the recipient of a Max Kade Foundation scholarship to study in Germany and was nominated by her department for the Stony Brook President's Teaching Award in 2007. Karen passed away on 26 September, 2007.

Roland J. De Vries is an ordained minister of the Presbyterian Church in Canada and a PhD Candidate in the Faculty of Religious Studies, McGill University. His research draws the writings of Luce Irigaray into dialogue with the writings of Søren Kierkegaard in the development of a theocentric ethics of sexual difference. Roland and his wife Rebecca live in Montreal with their children Tabea, Reuben and Esther.

Helen A. Fielding is Associate Professor in Philosophy and Women's Studies at the University of Western Ontario, Canada. Her research interests include phenomenology, feminist theory, embodiment and art. She draws upon the works of Luce Irigaray, Maurice Merleau-Ponty, Heidegger and Jean-Luc Nancy in her own publications. She is also a member of the International Merleau-Ponty Circle.

Mary Green is a Lecturer in Hispanic Studies, based in the Department of Modern Languages at Swansea University, UK. Her research interests include twentieth-century Chilean literature and cultural theory; feminist theory; and the representation of constructions of gender, sexuality and nationhood in Latin American literature and culture more broadly.

Laine M. Harrington received her PhD from the Graduate Theological Union, Berkeley, CA (2002). Her current publications include an essay in *Paragraph* (Edinburgh University Press, 2002) and 'La Boca' in *Women's Studies: An Interdisciplinary Journal* (Routledge, 2005). Laine Harrington has also assisted in re-reading the English version for introductions to several sections in *Luce Irigaray: Key Writings* (Continuum, 2004). She is a recent Postdoctoral Fellow and Visiting Scholar with the Beatrice M. Bain Research Group on Women and Gender at the University of California at Berkeley. Her research interests include the works of Luce Irigaray, issues in rhetoric, and the philosophy of religion. Laine Harrington has presented at a number of conferences, including: Histories of Theory (University of Western Ontario, Canada, 1998); the American Academy of Religion Annual Meeting (Orlando, FL, 1998); International, Intercultural, Intergenerational Dialogues about and with Luce Irigaray (University of Leeds, 2001); Luce Irigaray and 'the Greeks': Genealogies of Re-writing (Columbia University, 2004); Women and the Divine (University of Liverpool, 2005); and In All the World We are Always Only Two: Towards a Culture of Intersubjectivity (University of Nottingham, 2006).

Emily A. Holmes is a doctoral candidate in theological studies in the Graduate Division of Religion at Emory University in Atlanta, Georgia (USA). Her dissertation, 'Writing the Body of Christ: Hadewijch of Antwerp, Angela of Foligno, and Marguerite Porete', examines the role of the incarnation in the writings of medieval women mystics through the insights of French feminist theory. Currently, she teaches part-time at Rhodes College in Memphis, Tennessee.

Sabrina L. Hom is a Lecturer in Women's Studies at the McGill Centre for Research and Teaching on Women at McGill University in Montreal. She is a doctoral candidate in Philosophy at Stony Brook University and holds a Graduate Certificate in Women's Studies and an MA in Philosophy from the same institution. She is a co-founder, with Mary C. Rawlinson and Serene Khader, of The Luce Irigaray Circle, a group fostering work on and inspired by Luce Irigaray through annual conferences and publications. Sabrina is currently completing a dissertation on the relation between subjectivity and women's work in the family in G. W. F. Hegel and Luce Irigaray. Her research interests include ethics, social theory, feminist theory, domestic work, and women's relations to death.

Gillian Howie is Senior Lecturer in Philosophy at the University of Liverpool, UK. She is author of *Deleuze and Spinoza: Aura of Expressionism* (2002), editor of *Critical Quarterly's* special issue on higher education, 'Universities of the UK: Drowning by Numbers' (2005) and *Women: A Cultural Review's* special issue 'Gender and Philosophy' (2003), co-editor of *Gender, Teaching and Research in Higher Education* (2001), *Third Wave Feminism: A Critical Exploration* (2007) and *Menstruation: A Cultural History*. She is currently writing *Fugitive Ethics: Feminism and Dialectical Materialism* (Palgrave, 2009).

Christine Labuski will receive her PhD in Social Anthropology from the University of Texas at Austin in May of 2008. Her dissertation, 'It Hurts Down

There: An Ethnographic Exploration of a Genital Pain Syndrome', analyses the impacts of US culture's discomfort with the female sexual body on women living with chronic unexplained vulvar pain. Her interests include feminist theory, sexuality, and critical anthropology of the body. This is her first book chapter.

Donald A. Landes is a PhD candidate in philosophy at the State University of New York at Stony Brook where he is working on a dissertation on the paradoxical logic of expression under the co-directorship of Professors Edward S. Casey and Hugh J. Silverman. Since having completed a Masters in Philosophy from Dalhousie University in Halifax, Nova Scotia, Canada in 2002, Landes has presented numerous papers at national and international conferences and has published on the work of Maurice Merleau-Ponty, Jean-Luc Nancy, Jacques Derrida, and now Luce Irigaray. He is also the assistant editor for the book series *Continental Philosophy* and is working towards publishing a number of translations.

Jessica Murray did her undergraduate degree and an MPhil at the University of Stellenbosch in South Africa. A Commonwealth Scholarship then enabled her to do a PhD at the University of York's Centre for Women's Studies. She received her PhD in November 2007. The title of her thesis is 'Trauma and Testimony in the Work of Antjie Krog and Yvonne Vera'. Jessica Murray participated in the seminar held by Luce Irigaray for researchers doing their PhD on her work at the University of Nottingham in May 2005.

Reverend Dr Eleanor Sanderson has a background in Geography from Bristol University, England, and Development Studies from Victoria University of Wellington, where she also completed her doctorate from which this work is drawn. She currently serves as a priest in the Anglican Church at the Wellington Cathedral of St Paul, New Zealand. Her research interests include the intersections of social science and theology, and the exploration of participatory research methodologies. She is part of the Social Theory Spatial Praxis Research Cluster at the School of Earth Sciences at Victoria University of Wellington.

Christina Siggers Manson was awarded her PhD in Italian literature in July 2007 at the University of Kent, UK, after gaining a First Class Honours Degree in German and Italian. Her doctoral thesis is entitled 'Donna in guerra, uomi in crisi: familial roles and patriarchal legacies in Dacia Maraini and Natalia Ginzburg'. Her research interests also include comparative literature and gender studies. She teaches part-time in the Italian department at Kent and has worked for Intute since March 2005 as Subject Reviewer for Italian and German Studies.

Sherah Wells is currently completing her PhD thesis with a submission date of summer 2008. The title of her thesis is 'Antonia White and Emily Holmes Coleman: Psychosis, Catholicism, and French Feminist Theory'. She has written a chapter on the correspondence between Antonia White and Emily Holmes Coleman, published by Rodopi, forthcoming 2008.

Andrea Wheeler completed her doctorate at the University of Nottingham, Department of the Built Environment, in 2005. Her thesis is entitled '. . . With Place Love Begins: The Philosophy of Luce Irigaray and the Issue of Dwelling'.

She took part in the seminar for students doing their PhD on her work held by Luce Irigaray at the University of Nottingham in May 2004. She has also assisted Luce Irigaray in the presentation of her exhibition of the words and drawings of Italian Children, 'Chi Sono Io? Chi Sei Tu?' [Who am I? Who are You?], at University College London in November 2003 and at the University of Nottingham, May 2004. In January 2007 she was awarded a prestigious three year ESRC/RCUK Interdisciplinary Early Career Research Fellowship to explore the role of schools design in building sustainable communities. The project is shared between Schools of Architecture and Education of the University of Nottingham.

Michael Worton is Vice-Provost and Fielden Professor of French Language and Literature at UCL (University College London). He was chair of the HEFCE/ AHRC Expert Group on Research Metrics, and is a member of the HERA/ European Science Foundation Steering Committee, 'Building a European Index for the Humanities', a member of UUK/SCOP/HEFCE Measuring and Recording Student Achievement Steering Group, and of the Advisory Board, Clore Leadership Foundation. He is also a Director and Trustee of The Council for Assisting Refugee Academics (CARA). From 1998–2006, he was a member of the AHRB/AHRC Council, chairing first the Museums and Galleries Committee and then the Knowledge and Evaluation Committee. Broadly speaking, his research focuses on twentieth- and twenty-first-century literature and on aspects of critical theory.

Esther Zaplana is near completion of a PhD on contemporary musical performance and female vocality at the International Centre for Music Studies, University of Newcastle, United Kingdom. She is currently teaching in the Department of Languages, Faculty of Arts at the Universidad de Castilla-La Mancha, Spain, and has also taught in the Department of Modern Languages in the University of Northumbria, United Kingdom. Her research interests include cultural, feminist and theoretical approaches to aesthetic questions in musical performance, with particular emphasis on the work of Luce Irigaray and French feminism, as well as the relationship between the visual and the auditory and self-representations of women. She has published on the cultural meaning of music and gender, and Spanish and English feminists' narratives.

Bibliography of Luce Irigaray

Le langage des déments, in series *Approaches to Semiotics*, 24 (The Hague and Paris: Mouton, 1973).

Speculum. De l'autre femme (Paris: Editions de Minuit, 1974); Eng. trans. by Gillian C. Gill as *Speculum: Of the Other Woman* (Ithaca, New York: Cornell University Press, 1985).

Ce sexe qui n'en est pas un (Paris: Editions de Minuit, 1977); Eng. trans. by Catherine Porter with Carolyn Burke as *This Sex Which Is Not One* (Ithaca, New York: Cornell University Press, 1985).

Et l'une ne bouge pas sans autre (Paris: Editions de Minuit, 1979); Eng. trans. by Helene Wenzel as *And the One Doesn't Stir without the Other*, in *Signs, French Feminist Theory*, 7.1, 1981, pp. 56–59.

Amante marine. De Friedrich Nietzsche (Paris: Editions de Minuit, 1980); Eng. trans. by Gillian C. Gill as *Marine Lover: Of Friedrich Nietzsche* (New York: Columbia University Press, 1991).

Le corps-à-corps avec la mère, (Montréal: Editions de la Pleine Lune, 1981); the chapter with the same name is also taken again in *Sexes et parentés*; Eng. trans. as *Sexes and Genealogies*.

Passions élémentaires (Paris: Editions de Minuit, 1982); Eng. trans. by Joanne Collie and Judith Still as *Elemental Passions* (London–New York: Continuum–Routledge, 1992).

La croyance même (Paris: Editions Galilée, 1983); also taken again in *Sexes et parentés*; Eng. trans. as *Sexes and Genealogies*.

L'oubli de l'air. Chez Martin Heidegger (Paris: Editions de Minuit, 1983); Eng. trans. by Mary Beth Mader as *The Forgetting of Air: In Martin Heidegger* (Austin–London: University of Texas Press–Continuum, 1999).

Éthique de la différence sexuelle (Paris: Editions de Minuit, 1984); Eng. trans. by Carolyn Burke and Gillian C. Gill as *An Ethics of Sexual Difference* (Ithaca, New York–London: Cornell University Press–Continuum, 1993).

Parler n'est jamais neutre (Paris: Editions de Minuit, 1985); Eng. trans. by Gail Schwab as *To Speak is Never Neutral* (London–New York: Continuum, 2002).

Divine women (Sydney: Local Consumption, 1986); Eng. trans. by Stephen

Muecke from 'Femmes divines'; also taken again in *Sexes et parentés;* Eng. trans. as *Sexes and Genealogies.*

Zur Geschlechterdifferenz: Interviews und Vorträge (Wien: Wiener Frauenverlag, 1987).

Sexes et parentés (Paris: Editions de Minuit, 1987); Eng. trans. by Gillian C. Gill as *Sexes and Genealogies* (New York: Columbia University Press, 1993).

Le sexe linguistique, editor and contributor; other contributors: J.-J. Goux, E. Koskas, M. Mauxion, M. Mizzau, L. Muraro, H. Rouch and P. Violi; Journal *Langages,* 85 (Paris: Larousse, 1987).

Il divino concepito da noi, editor and contributor; other contributors: M. Bolli, G. Careri, S. Crippa, R. P. Droit, E. Franco, J.-J. Goux, L. Marin, R. Mortley, A.-C. Mulder, L. Muraro, D. Van Speybroek; Journal *Inchiesta,* n.° 85–86 (Bari: Dedalo, 1989), pp. 1–100.

The Irigaray Reader, ed. Margaret Whitford (Oxford–Cambridge: Basil Blackwell, 1991).

Le temps de la différence. Pour une révolution pacifique (Paris: Libraire Générale française, Livre de poche, 1989); Eng. trans by Karin Montin as *Thinking the Difference: For a Peaceful Revolution* (London–New York: Continuum–Routledge, 1994).

Sexes et genres à travers les langues, Éléments de communication sexuée, editor and contributor; other contributors: R. Bers, C. Cacciari, M. Calkins, M. Dempster, P. Ecimovic, P. Galison, M. V. Parmeggiani, K. Stephenson, A. Sulcas, K. Swenson, R. Tyninski and P. Violi (Paris: Grasset, 1990); Eng. trans by Gail Schwab and Katherine Stephenson as *Sexes and Genders Through Languages: Elements of Sexual Communication,* (not yet published).

Je, tu, nous. Pour une culture de la différence (Paris: Grasset, 1990); Eng. trans. by Alison Martin as *Je, tu, nous: Towards a Culture of Difference* (London–New York: Routledge, 1993).

J'aime à toi. Esquisse d'une félicité dans l'Histoire (Paris: Grasset, 1992); Eng. trans. by Alison Martin as *I Love to You: Sketch for a Felicity Within History* (New York–London: Routledge, 1996).

Genres culturels et interculturels, editor and contributor; other contributors: M.-T. Beigner, J.-L. Bouguereau, E. Brinkmann to Broxten, A. Bucaille-Euler, E. Casamitjana, S. Crippa, C. Fleig-Hamm, B. Menger, G. Schwab, K. Stephenson and M. Surridge *Langages,* 111 (Paris: Larousse, 1993).

Könsskillnadens etik och andra texter, collection of texts with an Introduction; Swed. trans. Christina Angelfors (Stockholm: Brutus Östlings bokförlag, 1994).

La democrazia comincia a due (Torino: Bollati-Boringhieri, 1994); Eng. trans. from the Italian by Kirsteen Anderson as *Democracy Begins between Two* (London–New York: Continuum, 2000).

Le souffle des femmes, editor and contributor; other contributors: M. Bolli, R. Braidotti, I. Guinée, R. Hablé, C. Heyward, Marie, C Mortagne, A.-C. Mulder, L. Muraro, M. T. Porcile Santiso, F. Ramond, M.-A. Roy, S. Vegetti Finzi, A. Vincenot, M. Yourcenar, M. de Zanger and A. Zarri (Paris: ACGF, 1996).

Être Deux (Paris: Grasset, 1997); Eng. trans. by Monique M. Rhodes and Marco F. Cocito-Monoc from the Italian *Essere Due* (Torino: Bollati Boringhieri, 1994) as *To be Two,* (London–New York: Athlone–Routledge, 2001).

Progetto di formazione alla cittadinanza per ragazze e ragazzi, per donne e uomini, research report presented to regional authorities of the Emilie Romagne Region on May 27, 1997 (unpublished, but available from the Commission for parity of the Emilie Romagne Region or from Luce Irigaray).

Le temps du souffle (Rüsselsheim: Christel Göttert Verlag, 1999); Eng. trans. by Katja van de Rakt, Staci von Boeckman and Luce Irigaray as *The Age of the Breath* (includes also the German and Italian versions of the text).

Chi sono io? Chi sei tu? La chiave per una convivenza universale (Casalmaggiore: Biblioteca di Casalmaggiore, 1999).

Entre Orient et Occident. De la singularité à la communauté (Paris: Grasset, 1999); Eng. trans. by Stephen Pluháček as *Between East and West: From Singularity to Community* (New York: Columbia University Press, 2001).

À deux, nous avons combien d'yeux? (Rüsselsheim: Christel Göttert Verlag, 2000); Eng. trans. by Luce Irigaray, Catherine Busson and Jim Mooney as *Being Two, How Many Eyes Have We?* (includes also the German and Italian versions of the text).

Why different?: A Culture of Two Subjects, Interviews with Luce Irigaray by P. Azzolini, H. Bellei, R. Bofiglioli, H. Bostic and S. Pluháček, O. Brun, M. Bungaro, O. Delacour and M. Storti, I. Dominijani, R. P. Droit, F. Iannucci, L. Lilli , M. Marty, M. A. Masino, B. Miorelli, R. Rossanda, P. de Sagazan, C. Valentini, E. Weber; edited by Luce Irigaray and Sylvère Lotringer (New York: Semiotext(e), 2000); Eng. trans. by Camille Collins, Peter Carravetta, Ben Meyers, Heidi Bostic and Stephen Pluháček from the French or Italian.

Le partage de la parole, Legenda, Special Lecture series 4 (Oxford: European Humanities Research Centre, University of Oxford, 2001).

The Way of Love (London–New York: Continuum, 2002); Eng. trans. by Heidi Bostic and Stephen Pluháček from the French *La Voie de l'amour*.

Dialogues: Around Her Work, editor and contributor, special issue of the journal *Paragraph*, 25, number 3 (Edinburgh: Edinburgh University Press, November 2002); a collection of essays on Irigaray's work by an intergenerational and international range of contributors: C. Bainbridge, H. Bostic, M. J. García Oramas, L. Harrington, M. Joy, K. Kukkola, A.-C. Mulder, S. Pluháček, H. Robinson, J. Still, F. Trani, L. Watkins and A. Wheeler; each paper is followed by questions from L. Irigaray.

Luce Irigaray: Key Writings, ed. Luce Irigaray (London–New York: Continuum 2004).

Everyday Prayers. Prières quotidiennes, bilingual edition (University of Nottingham and Paris: Maisonneuve & Larose, 2004).

Oltre i propri confini (Milano: Baldini Castoldi Dalai, 2007).

Sharing the World (London–New York: Continuum, 2008).

Luce Irigaray: Teaching (London–New York: Continuum, 2008).

Conversations with S. Pluháček and H. Bostic, J. Still, M. Stone, A. Wheeler, G. Howie, M. R. Miles and L. M. Harrington, H. A. Fielding, E. Grosz, M. Worton, B. H. Midttun (London–New York: Continuum 2008).

Articles

'Le dernier visage de Pascal', Journal *Revue Nouvelle* (Bruxelles, 1957).

'Inconscient freudien et structures formelles de la poésie', Journal *Revue philosophique de Louvain*, 61 (Louvain: Editions de l'Institut supérieur de philosophie, 1963), pp. 435–66.

'Un modèle d'analyse structurale de la poésie: A propos d'un ouvrage de Levin', Journal *Logique et analyse*, 27 (Louvain–Paris: Editions Nauwelaerts, 1964), pp. 168–78.

'Transformation négative et organisation des classes lexicales', avec J. Dubois et P. Marcie, Journal *Cahiers de lexicologie*, 7.2 (Paris: Didier–Larousse, 1965), pp. 3–32.

'Approche expérimentale des problèmes intéressant la production de la phrase noyau et ses constituants immédiats', avec J. Dubois, *Linguistique française, Le verbe et la phrase*, Journal *Langages*, 3 (Paris: Didier–Larousse, 1966), pp. 90–125.

'L'inconscio premeditato', Journal *Sigma*, 9 (Torino: Silva, 1968), pp. 23–34.

'La psychanalyse comme pratique de l'énonciation', Journal *Le langage et l'homme* (Bruxelles: Institut Libre Marie Harps, 1969), pp. 3–8.

'Où et comment habiter ?', Journal *Cahiers du Grif*, 24, March 1983.

'Une lacune natale', *Le Nouveau Commerce*, 62–63, 1985, pp. 39–47; Eng. trans. by Margaret Whitford as 'A Natal Lacuna', *Women's Art Magazine*, 58, May–June 1994, pp. 11–13.

'Égales à qui ?', Journal *Critique*, 43 (Paris: Edition de Minuit, 1987) pp. 420–37; Eng. trans. by Robert L. Mazzola as 'Equal to Whom?', *The Essential Difference*, edited by Naomi Schor and Elizabeth Weed (Bloomington–Indianapolis: Indiana University Press, 1994), pp. 63–81.

'Sujet de la science, sujet sexué ?', *Sens et place des connaissances dans la société* (Paris: Editions du CNRS, 1987), pp. 95–121.

'L'ordre sexuel du discours', *Le sexe linguistique*, Journal *Langages*, 85, 1987, pp. 81–123.

'Questions à Emmanuel Lévinas, Sur la divinité de l'amour', Journal *Critique*, 522 (Paris: Editions de Minuit, 1990), pp. 911–20; Eng. trans. by Margaret Whitford as 'Questions to Emmanuel Levinas', *The Irigaray Reader* (Oxford: Blackwell, 1991), pp. 178–89.

'Comment nous parler dans l'horizon du Socialisme?', *L'idée du socialisme a-t-elle un avenir?*, eds. J. Bidet and J. Texier (Paris: Puf, 1992), pp. 227–236; Eng. trans. by Joanne Collie and Judith Still in *Luce Irigaray: Key Writings*, pp. 214–23.

'Une culture à deux sujets', *Apport européen et contribution française à l'égalité des chances entre les filles et les garçons* (Paris: Ministère de l'Éducation nationale et de la culture, 1993), pp. 145–54; Eng. trans. by Kirsteen Anderson in *Democracy Begins Between Two*, pp. 142–55.

'Un horizon futur pour l'art ?', *Compara(i)son: An International Journal of Comparative Literature*, Bern, January 1993, pp. 107–16; Eng. trans. by Jennifer Wong and Luce Irigaray in *Luce Irigaray: Key Writings*, pp. 103–11.

'Transcendants l'un à l'autre', *Homme et femme, l'insaisissable différence*, ed. Xavier Lacroix (Paris: Editions du Cerf, 1993), pp. 101–20.

'Importance du genre dans la constitution de la subjectivité et de l'intersubjectivité', *Genres culturels et interculturels*, Journal *Langages*, 111, 1993, pp. 12–23.

'Le lotte delle donne: Dall'uguaglianza alla differenza', Encyclopedie *Europa 1700–1992, Il ventesimosecolo* (Milano: Elekta, 1993), pp. 345–56.

'Ecce mulier?', bilingual French-English publication *Nietzsche and the Feminine*, ed. Peter Burgard (University Press of Virginia, 1994), pp. 316–31.

'La voie du féminin', bilingual French-Dutch Catalogue for the exhibition *Le jardin clos de l'âme* (Bruxelles: Palais des Beaux Arts, 1994), pp. 138–64.

'L'identitié femme: Biologie ou conditionnement social ?', *Femmes: moitié de la terre, moitié du pouvoir*, ed. Gisèle Halimi (Paris: Gallimard, 1994), pp. 101–108; Eng. trans. by Kirsteen Anderson in *Democracy Begins Between Two*, pp. 30–9.

'Verso una filosofia dell'intersoggettività', Journal *Segni e compresione*, 22, Lecce, May 1994, pp. 29–33.

'Homme, femme: les deux "autres"', Journal *Turbulences*, 1, October, 1994, pp. 106–13.

'La question de l'autre', *De l'égalité des sexes* (Paris: CNDP, 1995), pp. 39–47; Eng. trans. by Kirsteen Anderson in *Democracy Begins Between Two*, pp. 121–41.

'La diferencia sexual come fondamento de la democrazia', Journal *Duoda*, 8 (Barcelona: University of Barcelona, 1995), pp. 121–34.

'Pour une convivialité laïque sur le territoire de l'Union Européenne', *Citoyenneté européenne et culture*, Journal *Les Cahiers du symbolisme* (Mons: University of Mons, 1995) pp. 197–205.

'Femmes et hommes, une identité relationnelle différente', *La place des femmes, Les enjeux de l'identité et de l'égalité au regard des sciences sociales*, ed. Ephesia (Paris: La Découverte, 1995), pp. 137–142.

'La famille commence à deux', Journal *Panoramiques*, ed. G. Neyrand (Arlea-Corlet, 1996), pp. 107–12; Eng. trans. by Stephen Pluháček in *Between East and West*, pp. 105–119.

'La rédemption des femmes', *Le souffle des femmes*, ed. Luce Irigaray (Paris: ACGF, 1996), pp. 183–208; Eng. trans. by Jennifer Wong, Jennifer Zillich with Luce Irigaray in *Luce Irigaray: Key Writings*, pp. 150–64.

'Scrivo per dividere l'invisibile con l'altro', *Scrivere, vivere, vedere*, ed. Francesca Pasini (Milano: La Tartaruga, 1997) pp. 35–8.

'Sostituire il desiderio per l'altro al bisogno di droghe', Journal *Animazione Sociale* (Torino: Abele, 25, February 2000), pp. 12–20, reprinted in *Senza il bacio del Principe* (Modena: Ceis, 2002), pp. 5–25.

'Comment habiter durablement ensemble?', a lecture at the International Architectural Association of London, November 2000, translated from the French by Alison Martin, Maria Bailey and Luce Irigaray, as 'How Can We Live Together in a Lasting Way?' in *Luce Irigaray: Key Writings*, pp. 123–33.

'Da *L'Oblio dell'aria* a *Amo a te* e *Essere due*', Introduction to *L'Oblio dell'aria* (Torino: Bollati-Boringhieri, 1994); Eng. trans. (from French) by Heidi Bostic and Stephen Pluháček as 'From *The Forgetting of Air* to *To Be Two*',

Feminist interpretations of Martin Heidegger, edited by Nancy Holland and Patricia Huntington, University Park (Pennsylvania: The Pennsylvania State University Press, 2001), pp. 309–15.

'Why Cultivate Difference?', *Dialogues: Around Her Work*, Special issue of the journal *Paragraph*, 25, number 3 (Edinburgh: Edinburgh University Press, November 2002), pp. 79–90.

'Being Two, How Many Eyes Have We?', *Dialogues: Around Her Work*, special issue of the journal *Paragraph*, 25, number 3 (Edinburgh: Edinburgh University Press, November 2002), pp. 143–51.

'La transcendance de l'autre', *Autour de l'idolâtrie, Figures actuelles de pouvoir et de domination*, Publication of l'Ecole des sciences philosophiques et religieuses (Bruxelles: University of St Louis, 2003), pp. 43–55; Eng. trans. by Karen Burke, Journal *Continental Philosophy*, forthcoming.

'What Other are We Talking About', *Legacy of Levinas*, Special issue of Journal *Yale French Studies*, 104, ed. Tom Trezise, 2004, pp. 67–81.

'Animal Compassion', *Animal Philosophy*, eds. Matthew Calarco and Peter Atterton (London–New York: Continuum, 2004), pp. 195–201.

'Entering a Space and a Time in the Feminine', in Catalogue of the exhibition *La dona, metamorfosi de la modernita*, ed. Gladys Fabre, Fundation Joan Miró, Barcelona, November 26, 2004–February 2, 2005, pp. 353–55.

'The Path Towards the Other', *Beckett after Beckett*, eds. Stan Gontarski and Anthony Uhlmann (University Press of Florida, 2006), pp. 39–51.

'How to make feminine self-affection appear', in Catalogue of the exhibition *Two or Three or Something: Maria Lassnig and Liz Larner*, February 4–May 7, 2006 (Graz: Kunsthaus Graz am Landesmuseum Joanneum, 2006), pp. 36–67.

'La démocratie ne peut se passer d'une culture de la différence', *Libido : Sexes, genres et dominations*, Journal *Illusio*, octobre 2007, pp. 17–28.

'The Ecstacy of the Between Us', *Intermedialities*, eds. Hank Oosterling and Krysztof Ziarek, Lefington Books, forthcoming, pp. 21–32.

'Between Myth and History: The Tragedy of Antigone', to be published by the Oxford Press in the proceedings of the conference *Interrogating Antigone*, Dublin, 6–7 October 2006.

'Towards a Divine in the Feminine', in *Women and the Divine*, (ed. Gillian Howie), proceedings of the conference which took place at the University of Liverpool, 9–11 June 2005; Palgrave Macmillan, forthcoming.

'Why is There the Other Rather Than Nothing?', Eng. trans. by Kathleen Hulley and Donald A. Londes in collaboration with Luce Irigaray from the French 'Pourquoi y a-t-il de l'autre et non pas plutôt rien?', to be published by Suny Press, New York, in the proceedings of the conference organised by the Irigaray's circle of the University of Stony Brook, 23–24 September 2006.

Index